Crisis, Trauma, and Disaster

4 Kay 4 Ever

—L.L.B.

For my wife Meredith and children, Corrina, Anelie, and Eliza.

—S.V.F.

Crisis, Trauma, and Disaster

A Clinician's Guide

Linda Lutisha Black
University of Northern Colorado

Stephen V. Flynn
Plymouth State University

Foreword by Allen J. Ottens

Los Angeles | London | New Delhi
Singapore | Washington DC | Melbourne

FOR INFORMATION:

SAGE Publications, Inc.
2455 Teller Road
Thousand Oaks, California 91320
E-mail: order@sagepub.com

SAGE Publications Ltd.
1 Oliver's Yard
55 City Road
London, EC1Y 1SP
United Kingdom

SAGE Publications India Pvt. Ltd.
B 1/I 1 Mohan Cooperative Industrial Area
Mathura Road, New Delhi 110 044
India

SAGE Publications Asia-Pacific Pte. Ltd.
18 Cross Street #10-10/11/12
China Square Central
Singapore 048423

Printed in the United States of America

ISBN: 978-1-4833-6903-7

This book is printed on acid-free paper.

 SUSTAINABLE FORESTRY INITIATIVE — Certified Sourcing — www.sfiprogram.org — SFI-00756

Acquisitions Editor: Abbie Rickard
Editorial Assistant: Elizabeth Cruz
Production Editor: Vishwajeet Mehra
Copy Editor: Tammy Giesmann
Typesetter: Hurix Digital
Proofreader: Jeff Bryant
Indexer: Joan Shapiro
Cover Designer: Candice Harman
Marketing Manager: Zina Craft

20 21 22 23 24 10 9 8 7 6 5 4 3 2 1

• Contents •

Chapter 3 • Caring for Those Affected by Crisis 73

• Foreword •

Allen J. Ottens, PhD
Professor Emeritus
Northern Illinois University

While I was putting these words to paper, the announcement came over the local news that the automobile assembly plant near where I live would soon eliminate an entire shift of workers. I morosely considered the consequences for the soon-to-be unemployed workers, the crises facing the financially strapped families, and the rippling impact on the larger community. Add one more to the expanding list of crises and disaster sweeping through society: devastating natural calamities (fires, floods) fueled by climate change, an epidemic of narcotic addictions (and fatal overdoses), and growing animosity directed toward racial, ethnic, and religious minorities, just to name three.

If there is any silver lining in that dire picture, it might be that "crisis may be viewed in various ways, but most definitions emphasize that it can be a turning point in a person's life" (Yeager & Roberts, 2015, p. 13). But helping distressed individuals and families to plot courses to arrive at those turning points (e.g., retraining, relocating, rethinking, rededicating, renewing) requires a cadre of helping professionals (psychologists, counselors, social workers, psychiatric nurses) who have the training and skills to intervene effectively. *Crisis, Trauma, and Disaster* by Linda Lutisha Black and Stephen V. Flynn can now be added to the arsenal of training materials to equip these professionals. Moreover, one of the features that makes *Crisis, Trauma, and Disaster* an important addition is its sweeping coverage of knowledge, skills, and techniques designed to mitigate the impact of crisis and trauma that are applicable for students-in-training as well as seasoned clinicians.

The authors impart a full spectrum of perspectives from various theoretical approaches, sharing *knowledge* and insights from generations of leaders in the crisis intervention field. Coverage extends from understanding in what ways deleterious events affect physiological functioning to how crises are experienced across the lifespan. The authors address intervention *skills* needed to implement change across affective, behavioral, and cognitive dimensions with individual clients, as well as the skill of advocacy, whereby the clinician works toward environmental changes on behalf of a particular client or class of clients. *Techniques* receiving focus include steps for applying psychological first aid as well as selecting and administering the Mental Status Exam (MSE) and a variety of triage assessment instruments.

Besides the expected heavy emphases on knowledge, skills, and techniques, the authors should be commended for taking a firm stance on the importance of clinicians being self-aware of their assumptions, intentions, and self-talk. Constant self-examination is a must for the crisis worker as well as supervision as needed to address *blind spots* and to provide feedback. The person of the helping professional is the primary tool in crisis intervention and success in this endeavor requires that the professional exhibit certain essential characteristics (Ottens, Pender, & Nyhof, 2009). Black and Flynn present stimulus questions and exercises geared to help the reader to concretize, synthesize, and personalize the chapter material. Finally, the reader will find a rich and up-to-date compendium of resources for further information, referral sources, and related texts.

With the seemingly ever-increasing prevalence of acute crisis events (e.g., violence, catastrophic illnesses, community disaster), *Crisis, Trauma, and Disaster* helps equip practitioners with the knowledge, skills, techniques, and resources to assess clients' needs, develop a plan of action, and strengthen their capacity to cope. *Crisis, Trauma, and Disaster* should rightly find its place on the bookshelves of those who provide crisis intervention services.

References

Ottens, A., Pender, D., & Nyhof, D. (2009). Essential personhood: A review of the counselor characteristics needed for effective crisis intervention work. *International Journal of Emergency Mental Health, 11*(1), 43–52.

Yeager, K. R., & Roberts, A. R. (2009). Bridging the past and present to the future of crisis intervention and crisis management. In K. R. Yeager & A. R. Roberts (Eds.), *Crisis intervention handbook: Assessment, treatment, and research* (4th ed.), (pp. 3–35). New York: Oxford University Press.

• Preface •

Purpose of the Textbook

This text provides a developmental overview of the history, theories, skills, and context of crisis, trauma, and disaster counseling. The previous two decades have witnessed tremendous growth in crisis, trauma, and disaster research and counseling across many countries and many disciplines. Interests now center on how to link the various theories and models with specific interventions, assessments, and skills. Due to the tumultuous nature of crisis, trauma, and disaster events, most early, mid, and late career professionals want to experience a snapshot of what takes place during these experiences, what entities are involved, and what is expected of them.

This text serves multiple audiences. Set in the context of counselor development and reflective practice, it provides introductory material as well in-depth, detailed synopsis of the practice of crisis, trauma, and disaster counseling. Concepts are illustrated within the running text and at the end of the chapter with specific skills geared toward early-, mid-, and late-career professionals. To help organize three distinct yet interrelated fields, the entire textbook is organized around theory and skills. Specifically, beginning with Chapter 2, we present the historical foundations, theories, and models of crisis, followed by Chapter 3, which describes the knowledge, skills awareness, techniques, and resources used in crisis counseling. We utilize a format of foundational knowledge followed by application of skill in subsequent chapters. For example, Chapters 4 and 5 address trauma and Chapters 6 and 7, disaster. Chapter 8 discusses counselor wellness, and we conclude with an examination of emerging trends—Chapter 9. Throughout the textbook, we highlight the most important, useful, and pragmatic aspects of crisis, trauma, and disaster counseling including end of chapter extended learning exercises and helpful resources. We believe beginning crisis, trauma, and disaster counselors will find useful techniques and examples and the experienced practitioners will find useful summaries of the latest empirically based theories and interventions.

Audience of the Textbook

The primary audience for this textbook is graduate students in the behavioral sciences learning about crisis, trauma, and disaster counseling for the first time. In addition, mid- and late-career professionals who have experience with crisis, trauma, and disaster counseling should find this book useful to support their understanding of relevant interventions, models, and theories. Professors and seasoned practitioners will hopefully see this textbook as including state-of-the-art theories, interventions, and ideas. Professionals from related, fields of nursing, law enforcement, psychiatry, and education will understand the roles and responsibilities of graduate-educated clinicians. Given the norm of interdisciplinary crisis or disaster response teams, it is important to have clear distinction and understanding of one's role in the event of a crisis or disaster. Finally, we see this book as core reading in graduate-level professional and school counseling, social work, marriage and family therapy, and psychology crisis and trauma courses.

Textbook Features

The text opens with an introduction to crisis, trauma, and disaster counseling and describes how they relate to clinician self-awareness, reflective practice, professional development, and the spectrum of these events. Chapter 2 presents the historical and theoretical foundations of crisis counseling. Chapter 3 showcases the knowledge, skills awareness, techniques, and resources necessary for crisis counseling. The format of a foundations chapter preceding the skills chapter continues for trauma (Chapters 4 and 5) and disaster (Chapters 6 and 7). Chapter 8 focuses on clinician wellness and the prevention of burnout, and Chapter 9 reviews emerging trends. Unique features of this text include the focus on the clinician's level of professional development, developmentally graduated case studies, and the *Counselor's Toolkit*. Each chapter provides *Extended Learning Exercises* and *Helpful Resources*.

Pedagogical Aids

Crisis, Trauma, and Disaster: A Clinician's Guide is presented in a logical sequential manner, grounded in professional development that aids readability and supports student readiness. Structurally, each chapter begins with an overview and objectives section and ends with a summary section. Educators can direct student's attention to the chapter learning exercises, case studies and encourage further student learning with the suggested web links and readings. Lastly, throughout the textbook we provide clear, detailed, and contextually relevant examples of a variety of crisis, trauma, and disaster experiences and interventions. Incorporating these examples into student learning can greatly enhance and contextualize the student's understanding of the material.

• Acknowledgments •

This textbook and our process have benefited tremendously many individuals and their contributions. We begin by thanking our SAGE Acquisitions Editor, Abbie Rickard, for her coordination, encouragement, and support throughout the project. We also thank the entire SAGE staff for their encouragement of the field of crisis, trauma, and disaster counseling.

The author(s) and SAGE would like to thank the following for their feedback during development:

Reviewer	Affiliation
Rejoice A. Addae	Arkansas State University–Jonesboro
Karisse A. Callender	Marquette University
Robert M. Cox	Pfeiffer University–Charlotte
Amanda B. Faulk	Richmond Community College
Sherrie Foster	Tennessee Tech University
Darren H. Iwamoto	Chaminade University of Honolulu
Lia Willis Jennings	Columbia College
Wendy Killam	Stephen F. Austin State University
Rose Marie Lichtenfels	Northern Arizona University–Yuma Branch
Kristina A. Peterson	Roosevelt University
Michael Roadhouse	Spalding University
Michelle L. Williams	Paradise Valley Community College

Linda Lutisha Black, EdD:

Writing is rarely a solo endeavor. So, too, was it with this project. I was sustained and supported by a strong circle of family and friends, professional colleagues who read and gave feedback on multiple drafts, students, and Harper and Olive, our two goofy labs. Special thanks go to the Kay, for all she did and is about to do! To the Pelicans, who did not complain too loudly when I missed social events to write, and in particular Bill Caldwell, who greeted me every day, 'How's the book going?' Oorah! buddy and "Semper Fi."

Stephen V. Flynn, PhD:

I would like to acknowledge a number of individuals who were important in helping me with the writing of this textbook. None of this would have been possible without my supportive spouse, Meredith. She has supported me through every struggle, success, and provided helpful feedback on my initial chapter drafts.

I am eternally grateful to my children Corrina, Anelie, and Eliza for providing a tremendous amount of inspiration and motivation to complete the first edition of this textbook.

I would like to thank my mother, Joyce, for her unconditional support during this project and in all aspects of my life.

A very special thanks to my sisters Janet and Suzie for their unconditional love and support.

I would like to thank the following graduate assistants for their contributions to this textbook, including Ryan Aquilina, Desmond Stern, Tynisha Ingerson, and Casey McCabe.

• About the Authors •

Linda Lutisha Black, EdD, is a professor of counselor education at the University of Northern Colorado. In her 19 years at UNC, Linda has served as Associate Provost & Graduate Dean and AVP for Research and Sponsored Programs. As a licensed professional counselor, she has 28 years of clinical mental health experience and is a member of the Colorado Crisis Education and Response Network. Linda and Kay live on the high plains of Colorado with Harper and Olive and a host of great friends.

Stephen V. Flynn, PhD, LPC, LMFT-S, NCC, ACS, is an associate professor of counselor education and is a research fellow in the Center of Research and Innovation at Plymouth State University, Plymouth, New Hampshire. He teaches clinical, research, and writing courses for the Counselor Education, Marriage and Family Therapy, and Educational Leadership graduate programs at Plymouth State University. He is a licensed professional counselor (CO), licensed marriage and family therapist (CO, NH), national certified counselor, approved clinical supervisor, American Association of Marriage and Family Therapy (AAMFT) Clinical Fellow, and an AAMFT Approved supervisor. He has taught graduate crisis counseling courses, and he has provided crisis intervention training to diverse groups such as school personnel. He has conducted crisis, trauma, and disaster-based counseling with survivors and families recovering from numerous clinical issues. Stephen enjoys spending time with his family and is an outdoor enthusiast.

Sara Miller McCune founded SAGE Publishing in 1965 to support the dissemination of usable knowledge and educate a global community. SAGE publishes more than 1000 journals and over 800 new books each year, spanning a wide range of subject areas. Our growing selection of library products includes archives, data, case studies and video. SAGE remains majority owned by our founder and after her lifetime will become owned by a charitable trust that secures the company's continued independence.

Los Angeles | London | New Delhi | Singapore | Washington DC | Melbourne

The Context of Caring

We live in a dynamic and unpredictable world where change is ever present. Some changes are intentional, growth producing, and within one's control, while others, particularly those associated with exposure to a crisis, trauma, or disaster, are arbitrary, injurious, and beyond one's control. Crisis or traumatic events are, by definition, unpredictable and threatening; they disorder and devastate lives. They challenge our perceptions, coping skills, and resources—we are in unfamiliar territory. Many respond to these challenges by seeking and hopefully returning to previous routines despite the ever-evolving backdrop of possibility, transformation, and disruption. Those unable to access previous ways of coping may find themselves in episodic crises or traumatized by their exposure.

Crises, trauma, and disaster (CTD) events range from the personal—death of a loved one, to the communal—Flint water crisis, to the societal—terrorist attacks. They may occur simultaneously and vary in meaning, scope, intensity, frequency, and duration. How one responds to a CTD event varies from the deeply personal to shared concerns within or among a group to the more customary or universal. In sum, CTD responses are contextual, personal, and intersect deeply with individual and group contexts, cultures, and ways of being. Because of your skill and training as a clinician, you will be called upon to provide specialized treatment. With that said, it is important for you to understand not all exposed to CTDs seek or receive acute services or ongoing treatment.

It is impossible to determine the percentage of individuals who might benefit from CTD counseling, yet a report from the Substance Abuse and Mental Health Services Administration (SAMHSA) provides some insight. The authors note that in 2014, approximately 45% of United States (US) citizens, with a diagnosable mental condition, sought professional treatment (Center for Behavioral Health Statistics and Quality, 2015). This means *more than half* of those identified as eligible for professional treatment did not seek it. Therefore, it is quite likely that fewer than half of individuals affected by a CTD will seek professional treatment; others will opt for help from natural or lay helpers; and a substantial number will seek not treatment due to personal and or cultural reasons, proximity to care, stigma, or confidence in counseling. Given the extent and gravity of these events, it is important to remember that although 70% to 80% of the U.S. population will experience at least one traumatic event in their lifetime and 7% to 9% will develop PTSD, most will never seek counseling or therapeutic services. This book focuses on the theoretical foundations and skills related to crisis, trauma, and disaster counseling within the context of counselor's professional development. We hope you find it a useful resource throughout your career.

Learning Objectives

After reading this chapter and participating in the reflective exercises provided, you will be able to

1. Differentiate helping professionals from natural helpers

2. Distinguish important issues related to the development and training of helping professionals

3. Understand key aspects to reflective practice and self-awareness

4. Compare key techniques at each stage of your development

5. Understand and discuss the spectrum of crisis, trauma, and disaster

Organization of the Text

From the moment we conceived this book, we designed it with you, the reader, in mind. We have three goals: (a) to present the historical contexts, theories, models, and skills necessary to conduct effective CTD counseling; (b) to support your learning relative to a continuum of professional development, regardless of your level of experience; and (c) to provide strategies for self-care and wellness. Because students take their CTD counseling course at different points in their education, we begin by briefly revisiting and reinforcing content you have previously studied. We discuss different types of helpers, components of your professional education and development, and the importance of self-awareness and reflective practice. In-text examples and end of chapter exercises focused on CTDs help you apply your learning.

Beginning with Chapter 2, we deepen and extend your learning by first presenting a chapter on the historical context, theoretical foundations, and treatment models of crisis, followed by Chapter 3, which details specific skills and dispositions for crisis counseling at each stage of your professional development; Chapters 4 and 5 focus on trauma and its treatment and Chapters 6 and 7 on disaster. Chapters 3, 5, and 7 provide a ready reference—the *Counselor's Toolkit,* which details specific knowledge, skill(s), awareness, techniques, and resources used in CTD counseling for individuals, groups, and communities at each stage of your professional development. Chapter 8 provides you strategies for self-care and wellness and the text concludes with emergent trends in Chapter 9. Each chapter begins with learning objectives to guide your reading and terminates with case examples and resources for applied practice. Throughout the text, we use the term *clinician* to describe all professional helpers, to be inclusive and to aid the readability of the text. When global references to gender are made, we intentionally use the term *they*, rather than the binary terms he and she, despite the traditional conventions of grammar.

Many Kinds of Helpers

Help and support come in many forms. Those dealing with crisis, trauma, or disaster may seek help with safety, medical issues, food or housing needs, transportation, resources, vocation, spiritual or religious support, or longer-term planning. In the immediate aftermath of a CTD event, individuals turn to those in closest proximity, some of whom may be natural helpers. Natural helpers are friends, loved ones, religious or spiritual laypersons, or members of support groups. These helpers are often known to and trusted by the individual(s) in distress. Natural helpers are sympathetic listeners who offer encouragement, instrumental support like childcare or transportation or hope, and a connection to informal social networks with limited support and resources. In contrast, professional helpers are typically not known to those seeking assistance. Professional helpers provide structured support, professional services, and have greater access to resources. Graduate-level training allows clinicians to systematically identify and respond to the unique and common needs of those exposed to crisis, trauma, or disaster and is why you are reading this book!

Educating Clinicians

Your advanced education focuses on theories, skills, and assessments and occurs in classrooms, counseling laboratories, and field placements over your professional lifespan. But this is only one form of education. You may also have had training at the baccalaureate and associate levels, which may or may not have involved applied or supervised practice or resulted in a certification or credential. Generally, CTD Clinicians seek post-degree professional development, certifications, and self-study specific to CTD counseling like Red Cross certification, nonviolent crisis intervention training, Eye Movement Desensitization and Reprocessing [EMDR], and trauma informed care. Although formal education is critical, so too is your personhood, personal awareness, and ways of being. In the sections that follow, we describe the perspective—clinician as instrument; context—accreditation standards and educational programs; and processes—self-awareness, reflective practice, supervision, and professional development that provide the foundation of your CTD education.

Perspective—Clinician as Therapeutic Instrument

For well over 50 years, clinicians have been called to learn about *who* they are as a person and how their personhood influences or impacts clients. Morey Appell writing in 1963 said,

> The most significant resource a counselor brings to a helping relationship is himself. It is difficult to understand how a counselor unaware of his own emotional needs, of his expectations of himself well as others, of his rights and privileges in relationships, can be sensitive enough to such factors in his counselee. (p. 146)

The professional expectation for personal awareness and accountability is not new! Contemporary authors like Gerald Corey agree and highlight the interconnectedness of the person and the professional. Corey (2013) noted, "one of the most important instruments counselors have to work with is themselves" and that the "person and professional are intertwined facets that cannot be separated in reality" (p. 18). Unlike almost any other profession, your professional training *and* personhood matter. Their importance is evidenced by their inclusion in accreditation standards, graduate curricula, expectations of reflective practice, and professional development. With respect to CTD counseling, clinicians aid their clients and themselves when they are aware of and address their personal histories of crisis or trauma, burnout, and personal and professional wellness. We address these elements in the sections that follow. Matters related to burnout and wellness are presented in Chapter 8.

Context—Accreditation Standards and Educational Programs

Accreditation

Many graduate programs are accredited by national organizations like the Council for Accreditation of Counseling and Related Educational Programs (CACREP), the American Psychological Association (APA), or the Council on Social Work Education (CSWE). Accrediting organizations are populated with members from the professions they govern. These organizations establish operating standards focused on the institution, faculty, curriculum, and program support; conduct periodic formal reviews to determine the extent to which the standards are met; and publicize their findings. Accredited programs engage a continuous review process to meet and maintain standards set by the profession. In many states, a graduate degree, from an accredited program, is necessary to achieve licensure for professional practice. The goal of accreditation is to ensure that education, provided by institutions of higher education, meets acceptable levels of quality (U.S. Department of Education, 2016) and our client needs for ethical and quality treatment. Accreditation standards or requirements focused on CTD counseling are relatively recent and reflect the growing body of research, theory, and knowledge in this subspecialty. We encourage you to review the CTD standards in your graduate program.

Educational Programs

Students in graduate counseling, psychology, or social work programs typically complete a minimum of two years of study and supervised practice. Likely, you have completed courses on counseling theories; core counseling skills for individual, groups, and families; assessment and treatment planning; case management; cultural competence; advocacy; and supervised practice. Within the last decade, accrediting bodies (CACREP, APA, CSWE) and university faculty have determined clinicians need additional and specialized education related to crisis, trauma-informed counseling, and client advocacy within an ethical and social justice framework. Thus, many graduate programs have at least one academic course dedicated to CTD counseling as well as expectations that clinicians will work with clients experiencing crisis, trauma, or disaster during their field placements.

Advanced CTD education provides you specialized knowledge and skills focused on individual, family, or community treatment and services. Students use conceptual and procedural knowledge (deJong & Ferguson-Hessler, 1996) to address a variety of client needs, to promote stability, to improve coping, and to aid the client's return to adaptive functioning. Adaptive functioning is described as the necessary cognitive and social skills, comprehension, and communication required to navigate environmental demands. In sum, clinicians are educated to support the health, recovery, and well-being of those experiencing acute or chronic crisis, trauma, or disaster. Advanced education is the hallmark of a professionally trained clinician and includes the ability to engage in a reflective practice and continuous personal and professional development. Three elements—advanced education, reflective practice, and continued personal and professional development—form the pillars of your professional practice. These pillars are highlighted throughout professional codes of ethics, standards of practice, and distinguish clinicians from other helpers.

Processes—Self-Awareness, Reflective Practice, and Professional Development

Self-Awareness

Awareness of self emerges around 18 months of age (Stern, 1985), yet researchers struggle to identify how it develops over the remainder of the life span. Self-awareness is conscious knowledge of one's existence, feelings, thoughts, motives, desires, and ways of being separate from others and the environment. Duval and Wicklund (1972) conceptualized self-awareness as an active process in which one evaluates and compares their current behavior to their internal standards and values. This process simultaneously engages introspection and meta-cognition. Perhaps you've experienced increased self-awareness during your practicum or internship supervision. How aware were you of your actions, thoughts, and feelings? As you focused on yourself, did you feel momentarily separate from your environment and others? It's incredible that human beings can think, act, and experience while thinking *about* what they are thinking, doing, and experiencing *while* they are thinking, acting, and experiencing. Active self-awareness aids clinician's reflective practice, combats burnout, and helps clinicians empathize with clients who feel overwhelmed, anxious, or hypervigilant after exposure to a crisis, trauma, or disaster.

There are two types of self-awareness—public and private (Lewis & Brooks-Gunn, 1978). Public self-awareness recognizes that each of us is perceived and evaluated by others *and* that those perceptions and evaluations matter. What we perceive others think about us is believed to stimulate socially acceptable behavior and adherence to social norms. For example, consider your response to peers' feedback in practicum, internship, or a team meeting. In what manner, if any, did you modify your behavior or beliefs about yourself considering their feedback or perceptions? Alternatively, private self-awareness, commonly described as conscious knowledge, is the perception or recognition of one's emotions, thoughts, motives, desires, and ways of being. Private self-awareness is not self-understanding or insight; it is simple recognition. Again, consider your internal feelings, thoughts, experiences, and self-talk related to your appraisal of your performance in practicum or internship or in your present clinical work. What do you say to yourself about your performance?

Time for an example; consider the student clinician who has experienced intimate partner sexual violence. Their self-talk centers on self-blame, self-recrimination, and fear of others' judgement. The student clinician is privately aware of their trauma, unsure how or if it might impact their work with similarly traumatized clients, is anxious and fearful about peer feedback or criticism in practicum, and terrified their story will come out in class. During post-session feedback, the student clinician responds to peers with anger, agitation, and tears. The student clinician ruminates on self-statements like: "Who are they to judge me?" "I *am not* scared of my client." "The rape does not affect me, anymore." "Feedback is stupid." With their supervisor, the student clinician is distant, disengaged, and at times tearful. The supervisor invites the student clinician to describe their experience and expectations of peer feedback and supervision. The student clinician does not respond. The supervisor gently asks if they think some type of support, like personal counseling outside of the training setting, may help. Without responding, the student clinician abruptly terminates the supervision session and resigns from the program. The research of Cavanaugh, Wiese-Batista, Lachal, Baubet, and Moro (2015) sheds light on our student's reactions. They found therapists, with an individual or family history of trauma, used more defense mechanisms with clients in therapy, had more confused feelings, and exhibited stronger countertransference emotions and reactions than those without this history. This example illustrates how public and private self-awareness may function and demonstrates these are necessary, but not sufficient components of your training and supervision.

Self-Awareness and the CTD Clinician

Self-awareness is not to be confused with self-concept, self-efficacy, or self-esteem as these terms imply a combination of analysis, insight, and understanding in addition to recognition. Authors studying the role of self-awareness and emotional intelligence (Mayer & Salovey, 1997; Sternberg, 1990; Goleman, 1995) distinguish it from general intelligence. Mayer and Salovey identified five categories of emotional intelligence: knowing one's emotions or private self-awareness; managing one's emotions; motivation; recognizing emotions in others; and managing relationships. The abilities contained in these five categories are at the heart of any therapeutic relationship, particularly CTD counseling.

Nonconscious processing, implicit versus explicit awareness of clients (Fosshage, 2005; Schore & Schore, 2008), clinicians' perceptions of self vis-a-vis their clients, and professional roles (Sue et al., 2007) have been examined to understand how clinicians make sense of themselves, clients, and counseling. Other researchers studied the role self-awareness plays in acquisition of theoretical orientations (Guiffrida, 2005; Hanna, 1994; Wong-Wylie, 2007), culturally competent counseling (Collins & Arthur, 2010; Roysircar, 2004; Ho, 1995), as well as the management of transference and countertransference in the counseling relationship (Williams, Judge, Hill, & Hoffman, 1997; Cashdan, 1988; Grayer & Sax, 1986). Pearlman and Saakvitne (1995) suggest clinicians, who exclusively treat clients traumatized by incest, develop a specific form of countertransference not related to clinical interactions or clients. This form of countertransference presents as a broad negative attitude toward counseling and life in general. Adams and Riggs (2008) examined vicarious trauma in relation to the history of trauma, experience level, trauma-specific training, and defense style in a sample of 129 graduate clinicians. They found over half their participants indicated a self-sacrificing defense style, a known risk factor for vicarious trauma. Trauma symptoms—anxious arousal, intrusive experiences, defensive avoidance, disassociation—were significantly associated with the defense style and moderated clinician's personal trauma history and experience level. Research findings detail that clinicians attempt to block out unwanted thoughts and feelings through conscious suppression or unconscious repression. Whether such attempts are successful or not, they are controversial. Despite the controversy, credible research findings will improve clinicians' education and the importance of self-awareness, which in turn, should improve clinical outcomes for clients.

Clinicians, who provide CTD counseling, are repeatedly subjected to horrific and often tragic descriptions of client experiences. The cumulative impact of clients' traumatic stories can foster feelings of doubt, anxiety, and professional inadequacy and negatively influence how clinicians view themselves, their clients, and the world. Wilson and Dunn (2004) believed that research psychologists had "artfully dodged" (p. 494) investigations of self-knowledge, opting to avoid questions about the nature of unconsciousness, limits of consciousness, or an individual's desire to avoid the anxiety that accompanies self-knowledge. Given the intensity and impact of CTD counseling, we wondered if this statement may also be true of clinicians and, perhaps, their faculty or supervisors. Do we avoid self-knowledge to lessen our stress related to client's CTD experiences? As you progress through your education related to CTD counseling, we encourage you to use supervision and reflective practice to examine and address how you respond to CTD clients concerns and how you are impacted by them.

Reflective Practice

Clinician self-awareness is a critical competency for clinicians and supervisors (Rosin, 2015; Collins, Arthur, & Wong-Wylie, 2010) and is "closely associated" (Rosin, 2015, p. 89) with reflective practice. Wong-Wylie (2010) stated reflective practice is a primary method for *how* counselors advance their self-awareness, clinical skills, and professional development (Skovholt & Rønnestad, 1995). Simply put, reflective practice is an intentional, step-wise process which allows you, the clinician, to learn from your experiences by making the implicit explicit and by associating thoughts related to an event with the outcome of the event. Let's say you feel unsettled after a session with traumatized client. You wonder if their story triggered your uneasy feelings. You attempt to identify when the discomfort emerged and recall the verbal exchanges between yourself and the client. By examining, rather than ignoring or avoiding your experience with the client, you may reveal the interactions that triggered your distress.

"Know thyself" is an Ancient Greek aphorism or saying. In 1997, Meier and Davis noted the importance of clinicians *knowing themselves* when they wrote "In no other profession does the personality and behavior of the professional make such difference as it does in counseling. Beginning counselors need to work at increasing their self-awareness as well as their knowledge of counseling procedures" (p. 61). We contend that knowing *that* you need to work at increasing your self-awareness is different from knowing *what* works on or *how* you might increase it. Knowing you may be negatively impacted by providing CTD counseling is only the first step. Reflective practice is a method that turns that first step in to your professional journey.

Reflective practice is predicated on reflective thinking, thinking that is active, purposeful, methodical, and "impels inquiry" (Dewey, 1933, p. 7). Reflective thinking is sequential and persistent; it is neither random nor haphazard. According to Dewey, reflective thinking begins when one is in state of doubt, hesitation, or is perplexed. To resolve this state, one intentionally seeks to "puzzle out the entanglement" by "turning a subject over in the mind and giving it serious consecutive consideration" (p. 3). Recall the example of the student clinician who was traumatized by intimate partner sexual violence. If the student clinician takes a moment to think reflectively about their peers' feedback, they could suspend judgment about themselves and their peers and seek support from their supervisor. Over time and with repeated practice, the student clinician can embrace ambiguity, employ skepticism, and engage personal and professional humility. Their self-talk changes from recriminations and blame to statements like: "At times I *am* scared. I don't know what they want from me." "I bet everyone else is scared too." "When I am confused by feedback I can talk to my supervisor." In sum, reflective thinking challenges one's cognitive certainty, reductionistic thinking, habitual responding, and desire for simplistic answers. Slowing down and engaging formal reflective thinking frees the clinician to consider alternative explanations, acknowledge the pain associated with clients' crises or trauma, and support emotional self-regulation.

Donald Schön (1983) described two modes of reflective practice in education: *reflection-in-action* and *reflection-on-action*. Wong-Wylie (2007), Pedro (2005), Osterman (1990) and Knott and Scragg, (2016) contextualized Schön's work for mental health professionals. Reflection-in-action is thinking about something while you are doing it, then making in-the-moment improvements to the situation. This type of reflection integrates your tacit and implicit patterns with your spontaneous and intuitive actions. For example, a CTD clinician assessing a person in crisis recognizes the depths of their pain. In the middle of the assessment, in the moment, the clinician asks the individual to focus their breathing and directs them to center their thoughts in the here and now. Alternatively, reflection-on-action is more akin to the earlier description of Dewey's reflective thinking as it occurs *after* the event or interaction. This type of reflection involves an evaluation of what occurred, what could have been different, and what could be done differently in the future. Purposeful engagement with a supervisor allows you to explore your thoughts, actions, and reactions to traumatized clients is an example of reflection-on-action. For example, let's say you feel tense and on the verge of tears each time a child client describes being beaten by their parent. You examine your in-session behaviors and thoughts with your supervisor and realize three things: Almost every time the child begins to describe being beaten you shift the conversation to something more positive, you fantasize about rescuing or adopting this child, and you feel overwhelmed and uncertain about what to do next. Reflection-on action allows you to examine and correct your productive and nonproductive therapeutic behaviors and to identify needed education or support.

Although Schön's work (1983; 1987) faced criticism (Edwards & Thomas, 2010; Court, 1988, Finlay, 2008; Munby, 1989) reflective practice is "considered to be the *sine qua non* [essential condition] of professional development" (Edwards & Thomas, 2010, p. 403) and professional training. Finlay (2008), writing about teacher education, provides an additional cautionary note,

some consensus has been achieved amid the profusion of definitions. In general, reflective practice is understood as the process of **learning through and from experience** towards gaining **new insights** of self-and/ or practice (Boud, Keogh, & Walker, 1985; Boyd & Fales, 1983; Jarvis, 1992). This often involves **examining assumptions** of everyday practice. It also tends to involve the individual practitioner in being **self-aware** and **critically evaluating** their own responses to practice situations. The point is to recapture practice experiences and mull them over critically to gain new understandings and so improve future practice. This is understood as part of the process of **life-long learning**. Beyond these broad areas of agreement, however, contention and difficulty reign. There is debate about the extent to which practitioners should focus on themselves as individuals rather than the larger social context. There are questions about how, when, where and why reflection should take place. For busy professionals short on time, reflective practice is all too easily applied in bland, mechanical, unthinking ways. Would-be practitioners may also find it testing to stand back from painful experiences and seek to be analytical about them. (p. 1) (Emphasis original)

We respectfully disagree with Finlay's and others' statements that professionals should focus on the larger social context, are too busy, and may be challenged to engage in reflective practice. Intentional actions taken to improving one's professional practices serves the client as well as the clinician. Effective clinicians take the time to consider themselves and their practice through increased self-awareness, personal reflection, and formal supervision (Orchowski, Evangelista, & Probst, 2010; Ward & House, 1998). Do you want to be treated by a physician who is too busy to reflect on their interactions with their patients? How else is one to gain perspective on their therapeutic stance or counseling practice?

Researchers in counseling, psychology, and social work note the benefits reflective practice (Furr & Carroll, 2003; Knott & Scragg, 2016). Numerous authors have expanded on Schön's original concepts (Wong-Wylie, 2007; Collins, Arthur, & Wong-Wiley, 2010) within the field of counseling (Rosin, 2015). Schön's model focuses on practitioners' professional experiences; in contrast, Wong-Wylie (2007) focused on the personhood of the clinician and coined the term *reflection-on-self-in/on action*. Reflection-on-self-in/on action "emphasizes salient personal experiences" (p. 60) believed to augment clinicians' *personal practical knowledge* (Connelly & Clandinin, 1988) and fosters increased self-awareness and professional growth. Engaging Wong-Wylie's mode of reflection requires you to develop personal capacity for cognitive and emotional maturity (Kitchener, 1986) through clinical supervision or direct instruction, to possess enhanced emotional intelligence (Goleman, 1995) and to engage critical reflectivity (Kondrat, 1999). Critical reflectivity is a deeper level of understanding of yourself, your assumptions, and their interaction with social structures. For example, using the reflection of self in-/on action process, our practicum student who experienced intimate partner sexual violence, could ask, "Why do I feel responsible for what happened to me?" "How am I different from my client who was raped?" "What would happen if I told my supervisor I was terrified of practicum?" These reflections challenge the social constructs of rape myth, self-blame, and desire for perfection.

Developing personal capacities and learning the process of reflective practice occurs in varying degrees. Hopefully you will encounter or have encountered these processes during numerous classes, specifically practicum or internship. Reflective practice is an intentional and systematic process learned during clinical supervision and developed and incorporated into one's practice over time. In her exploratory research, Wong-Wylie (2007) identified conditions, presented in Table 1.1, that facilitate or hinder reflective practice for doctoral students in counselor education.

Wong-Wylie's findings should be viewed with caution due to the exploratory, point-in-time nature of the study. She and others (Rosin, 2015; Kramer, 2000; Collins, Arthur, & Wong-Wylie, 2010; Guiffrida, 2005) illuminate a long standing and often unspoken concern in counselor, psychology, and social work

TABLE 1.1 ● Conditions Facilitating or Hindering Reflective Practice in Doctoral Level Counselor Education

Facilitating	Hindering
Experiencing a trusting relationship	Experiencing mistrust/unsafe relationship
Opening up to fellow students	Interacting with nonreflective fellow students
Engaging in reflective tasks	Receiving unsupportive/jarring feedback
Having self-trust/risking	Facing a systemic barrier
Interacting with supportive academic personnel	Interacting with unsupportive academic personnel

education—challenging the *inner and outer* worlds of the clinician (Kramer, 2000). Overtly challenging students in this manner is fraught with ethical, boundary, and gatekeeping concerns as well as great opportunities (Jungers & Gregoire, 2013; Reamer, 2013). With respect to CTD education, graduate clinicians would be challenged to engage in reflection related to their personal histories of crisis or trauma, strategic processing of their therapeutic interactions, and may be encouraged or required to attend counseling, external to their program, to address previous crisis situations or traumatic exposure. This type of education requires intentional changes and modifications in graduate programs (Tobin, Willow, Bastow, & Ratkowski, 2009). Are you willing to disclose and process your personal assumptions and history with crisis and trauma? Regrettably, not all graduate programs specifically educate clinicians about reflective practice or supervise in a manner that enhances clinicians' critical reflection leaving us to speculate when or *if* novice and experienced professionals gain these critical experiences.

Clinical Supervision

Clinical supervision is/was a separate component of your practicum or internship experience. Through evaluation, supervision is designed to improve your performance on behalf of your clients. Bernard and Goodyear (2009) define clinical supervision as a hierarchical, evaluative relationship designed to enhance professional functioning, clinical skills, and the clinician's understanding, performance, dispositions, and interventions with clients. Their definition does not explicitly address the personal functioning of the supervisee, yet, as we stated earlier, clinical training, by its very nature involves the intimate intertwining of the personal and the professional (Corey, 2013). Therefore, because supervisory feedback is supportive and corrective in nature, the supervisory relationship can feel simultaneously tough and tender. Therefore, it is not surprising researchers have found some graduate clinicians experience disputes, disappointment, or unmet needs during supervision (Gray, Ladany, Walker, & Ancis, 2001; Ladany, Hill, Corbett, & Nutt, 1996; Dupre, Echterling, Meixner, Anderson, & Kielty, 2014). We assert that supervisors, at all levels of the profession, have a responsibility to clearly articulate the foci, purpose, goals, and processes of supervision, specifically elements that address the personhood of the clinician, including the nature and extent of personal disclosures. With respect to the supervision of clinicians providing CTD counseling, we believe supervisors must possess a combination of experience, professional development, and advanced certifications in trauma-informed treatment and disaster responding. The combination of supervisor's CTD education and experience allows the supervisor to more critically examine the treatment approaches and experiences of CTD clinicians, including the precursors of burnout.

Rønnestad and Skovholt (2013) identified five supervisory principles to structure, organize, and describe the relational nature of supervision to trainees. The first principle encourages supervisors to "lay the ground work" (p. 178) and ensure appropriate field placements and supervision. For CTD clinicians, this means having the opportunity to provide supervised services to clients exposed to crisis and traumatic events. The second principle asks the supervisor to establish a supervisory alliance—a safe environment for learning with clear expectations and specific learning goals. Supervisors recognize and discuss that supervision can be an intense and emotional experience. Graduate clinicians may be uncertain about expected levels of self-disclosure, ethical and cultural responsibilities, and issues of power, communication, and interpersonal boundaries. This is particularly important for supervision of CTD cases because personal and professional reactions to traumatized clients are intertwined with the clinician's history. The third principle recommends supervisors create a reflective culture in supervision. Rønnestad and Skovholt state reflection is "a prerequisite for successful cycling through the phases characterizing optimal professional development" (p. 184). Specific to CTD counseling, your supervisor might pose a series of content-based or reflective questions: "What information do you need to learn about suicide assessments, treatment and referral?" "What thoughts and emotions come up for you as you think about working with a client who is actively suicidal? Homicidal?" "What are your strengths and vulnerabilities related to working with person actively considering suicide or homicide?" "What is a positive treatment outcome for a traumatized person?" Recall our example of the student clinician who experienced intimate partner sexual violence; their supervisor, who does not know of the student's history, might ask the student to reflect how their life experiences are similar and dissimilar to those of their client. Assuming the supervisory relationship is structured, authentic, and transparent a broadly focused question, not focused on the student's traumatic experience, provides an open and less threatening environment. For our now anxious student, this opportunity potentially promotes trust and provides a platform of increased self-awareness and reflection. To extend your learning a set of reflective questions adapted and expanded from the works of Johns (2004; 2006) are presented in Table 1.2. You can use these on your own or in supervision, with your supervisor's permission. We encourage you to create your own list.

TABLE 1.2 ● Sample Reflective Questions for Clinical Supervisors and Supervisees

Questions	Area of Focus
What was my experience?	Description of the experience
What essential factors contributed to this experience? (identifying a cause)	
What are the significant background factors to this experience? (Context)	
What are the key processes (for reflection) in this experience?	
What was I trying to achieve?	Reflection
What are the assumptions I hold about the client?	
Why did I intervene as I did? Or why did I choose not to intervene?	
What were the consequences of my actions for myself? The client/family? The people with whom I work?	
What do believe the client was feeling?	
What evidence demonstrates how the client felt?	
What was I feeling?	
Have I had these feelings before? If so, under what conditions? How did I feel about this experience when it was happening?	
How do I feel about this experience now?	
What internal factors influenced my decision making/action?	Influencing factors
What external factors influenced my decision making/action?	
Under what circumstances have I made similar decisions/actions?	
What is/are the consequences for the client, for me?	
What sources of knowledge did/should have influenced my decision making?	
What role, if any, did personal identities play in the decision/action?	
What other choices/options did I have?	Choices
What are the consequences (positive/negative) of those choices?	
What role could the client have played in the decision/action?	
What, if anything, would I do differently?	
How do I feel now about this experience?	Learning
How do my feelings and thoughts about this experience influence my feelings or thoughts about previous experiences? About future practices?	
How has this experience changed my perceptions of myself, my practice, or my view of my client?	
What have I learned about myself?	
What do I need from my supervisor?	Resources
What would I like my supervisor to tell me?	
What do I would I like to hear from peers?	
What additional learning might benefit my understanding or perspectives?	

We believe these questions provide a basis for reflective conversations or dialogues with your peers and supervisors. Researchers are exploring reflective dialogues in supervision (Borders et al., 2014; Hill, Crowe, & Gonsalvez, 2015; McLean & Whalley, 2004). Their initial findings hold the promise of improving clinical supervision. The fourth supervision principle calls supervisors to "be attuned" (Rønnestad & Skovholt, 2013, p. 186) to the level of challenge faced by the supervisees, particularly the nature and number of clients served as well as the severity and intensity of client concerns. Clinicians treating those affected by CTDs have particular needs in supervision-interpersonal support, instruction in trauma-informed care, risk management, vicarious trauma, cultural conflicts, and emergency procedures. An attuned supervisor demonstrates empathy and understanding for your experiences *while* holding you accountable for your performance. As noted earlier, some supervisees experienced supervision as unsupportive and unhelpful. These experiences may be exacerbated by stressful interactions with CTD clients making it critical for you, the supervisee, to speak up. The fifth and final supervision principle focuses on accurate and timely evaluation of the supervisee. Timely, formative evaluative feedback provides the foundation for self-awareness and reflective practice, supports growth in your CTD skills and treatment, and aids your professional development.

Professional Development Process

Like other professionals, clinicians are believed to progress through a series of professional development stages or sequences. The concept of development, according to Lerner, (1986) implies change over time that occurs in a systemic or somewhat predictable manner. Historically, scholars (Hogan, 1964; Hill, Charles, & Reed, 1981; Loganbill, Hardy, & Delworth, 1982; Stoltenberg, McNeill, & Delworth, 1998) conceptualized professional development through the lens of a stage theory. They believed development was discontinuous, occurred in discrete stages, and was segmented into stage specific tasks. In the developmental model, clinicians remain at a stage of development until most of the identified tasks are completed. In contrast, Rønnestad and Skovholt (2013) assert professional development is more continuous, occurs in phases rather than stages, and is iterative and recursive. As you gain conceptual and procedural knowledge, increase your personal and professional understanding and reasoning, and continue to integrate your personal and professional selves, the process of change continues. For Rønnestad and Skovholt, each phase has generally agreed upon tasks which are continually learned and relearned in a recursive manner and over time results in growth and change. Assuming you remain engaged, utilize skilled supervision, and practice purposeful self-reflection, you should experience improvements in your knowledge, skills, and abilities during your formal education and throughout your career.

Throughout this text, we rely on Rønnestad and Skovholt's (2013) professional development framework of therapists and counselors, which depicts five phases—novice student, advanced student, novice professional, experienced professional, and senior professional. We briefly introduce the novice student phase as a reference point and focus, in greater detail, on the next three phases: advanced students, novice professional, and experienced professional. Although novice students may find the content in this text helpful, we believe those with advanced education and supervision are more likely to direct the treatment of individuals facing crisis, trauma, or disaster.

Novice Students

Graduate students or clinicians vary in age, life experiences, and personal and employment histories. Variation in students' background and identities provides great richness to the training environment. Generally, novice students are a more homogenous group comprised of white females 24 to 30 years old. Thus, the developmental tasks, influences, and phases described in this model are not expected to fully represent all students' experiences or world views. For example, a 40-year-old Latinx male will most likely demonstrate performance anxiety differently than a 24-year-old white female. What is important is that both students, and all students, have opportunities to be understood and to identify, contextualize, and address their needs in a manner befitting their learning styles and cultural backgrounds within the framework of the program's standards. Novice students spend most of their first two years in academic classrooms learning the foundations of their profession, and sometime during their second year, encounter their first lab- or field-based practicum or extended internship. This is often a time of great excitement and emotional intensity as students negotiate the acquisition-application-validation model of learning (Rønnestad & Skovholt, 2013). The model works like this: You acquire or learn an abundance of information in a variety of contexts. This knowledge draws on theories and research; direct and indirect client feedback; modeling and feedback from professional elders; personal life experience; peers' and colleagues' experiences; and your social cultural environment. As you apply this knowledge in all facets of your life and experience positive results, your knowledge and beliefs are validated even when they conflict with previous personally held beliefs or experiences. Ideas not validated or those yielding negative results gradually lose their influence and are typically discarded.

This is a stimulating and perplexing phase, fraught with anxiety, self-doubt, and insecurity related to academic and professional performance. Students, like you, spend much of the first year to year and a half evaluating the match between personal expectations of the graduate program and the program's expectations of you. This evaluation is most often demonstrated by conflict between your desire for professional autonomy and your needs for appropriate dependency on your faculty and supervisors. Table 1.3 presents a summary of the critical elements of the novice student phase.

Novice students report a vibrant and dynamic time marked by the demands of acquiring extensive theoretical, conceptual, and procedural knowledge; maintaining a sense of openness to new ideas and approaches; managing intense and often unpredictable emotions; and negotiating the challenges of learning *while* doing. With respect to CTD counseling, the feelings and expectations of the novice student may be exacerbated by their personal history, the acuity, magnitude, and

TABLE 1.3 ● **Novice Graduate Student Phase**

Description	Development Crises	Emotional/Cognitive Experiences	Developmental Tasks	Sources of Influence
First 1 to 2 years of graduate study *primarily engaged in academic study *nature and quality of experiences depend on students' culture and demographics	Students question their: *intellectual and emotional appropriateness for the profession *capacity for graduate study *degree of fit with demands of professional versus lay helping *desire to foreclose on one theory or practice to reduce confusion and feelings of being overwhelmed	*increased performance anxiety, intensity, psychologizing, self-doubt; fluctuating motivation; *overwhelmed/ confused by the amount and diversity of information/ knowledge *possible foreclosure on more complex methods and models—opts for specific, less complex, unambiguous inventions/theories *fluctuating feelings: stress, anger, happiness, fear, excitement, disappointment	*acquire extensive conceptual and procedural knowledge of the field *recognize and anxiety/fear as a part of the learning process *explore ways conceptually organize the complexity *maintain openness to various theories and approaches *manage confusion *define and clarify professional role of student *manage experience of vulnerability in supervision including degree of disclosure and need for honest feedback *use pragmatic, less complex approaches to develop mastery *initial role adoption	*in-class discussion of theories and research, feedback from clients, feedback from professional elders, modeling personal-peers, faculty, family

Adapted from Rønnestad and Skovholt (2013)

tragic nature of CTD clients' concerns and the sheer volume of new knowledge specific to CTD diagnosis and treatment. Self-awareness, reflective practice, and supervision support your progression to the advanced student phase.

Advanced Student

The Advanced Student phase builds on the challenges, successes, and experiences of the previous phase. In this phase, you begin to reconcile your performance with academic and professional expectations set by you, your clinical supervisors, and your graduate program. You may vacillate between feeling overconfident and feeling overwhelmed, leading researchers to dub this phase of counselor development *Confusion* (Loganbill, Hardy, & Delworth, 1982) or *Conditional Autonomy* (Skovholt & Rønnestad, 1995). At times, you may experience increased confidence in your skills particularly after positive client and supervisory experiences. Alternatively, you may experience feelings of doubt and uncertainty related to your perception of your mastery of counseling skills and belief that your peers have met or will meet the training standards before you do. The central task in this phase is to function at a professional level while remaining a student who is open to learning and not knowing. With respect to CTD counseling, the uncertainty and role ambiguity of this phase might result in heightened anxiety and cognitive confusion. This is uncomfortable and normal. Crisis, trauma, and disaster counseling requires advanced knowledge and skill; because you are eager to work independently, yet are still learning, you behave cautiously and conventionally with your clients. The supervisory relationship takes center stage as you attempt to process and balance supervisors' confirmatory feedback with their negative feedback. Table 1.4 presents a summary of the critical elements of the Advanced Student phase.

Advanced students value quality supervision. The opportunity to see multiple clients with diverse concerns provides you a range of experiences, increases the opportunities for positive outcomes, and reduces your self-imposed expectations to be perfect.

Novice Professional

The Novice Professional phase described by Rønnestad and Skovholt (2013) is a highly intense and engaging period, lasting from two to five years post-graduation. It is further segmented into three subphases—confirmation, disillusionment, and exploration. Clinicians in the *Confirmation* subphase have a multitude of decisions to make about employment, types of clients, and development of a clinical specialty. Novice professionals feel free from professors or supervisors, value networking and continuing education, and are excited to start their therapeutic careers. Some novice professionals experience a sense of loneliness and isolation due to the loss of their peer group and identity as a student. Clinicians in the second subphase, *Disillusionment*, may feel dismayed or discouraged. They are disenchanted with their professional performance, graduate education, and profession. They realize clients do not improve as much or as quickly as expected or hoped; acknowledge current theories or techniques are insufficient; experience unfulfilling supervisory relationships; and recognize psychotherapy is a complex and multifaceted processes. Table 1.5 presents a summary of the critical elements of the Novice Professional phase.

The third and final subphase, *Exploration*, is best described as a rebirth or revival of professional interest. Clinicians move away from the stagnation of the *Disillusionment* subphase into a more active and dynamic time where they question professional beliefs and prior education, develop congruence between personal and professional selves, and experience increased creativity, stimulation, and personal reflection. The desire to learn is reawakened as clinicians evaluate the meaning and relevance of their work. Many novice professionals seek to distinguish themselves by developing expertise in an area by seeking additional education, experiences, and supervision. In this phase, CTD counselors may engage in advanced professional development like EMDR or Red Cross Crisis and Disaster training or join local emergency response networks.

TABLE 1.4 ● Advanced Student Phase

Description	Development Crises	Emotional/Cognitive Experiences	Developmental Tasks	Sources of Influence
2nd year of formal study to the end of graduate study	Students are	*eager to work independently yet still risk being adverse	*learn and understand the complexities of conceptual and procedural knowledge required by the educational institution	*those identified in earlier phase continue
*Involved in a field placement	*aware of their personal issues and less productive ways of being	*increasing expectations to "do things right" while still feeling uncertain about skill level	*sufficient mastery of therapeutic and assessment skills as assessed by supervisors	*evaluation of self is based on comparison with assumed competence of more experienced clinicians, skill level of other interns, skill level of beginning practicum students
*independent practice with supervision	*experiencing independence/dependence conflict	*in the early part of this phase behavior is cautious and conservative	* continue to maintain openness to various theories and approaches at a meta level	*peer and client feedback become more important sources of feedback
*has completed most academic coursework	*more critical of others as student gains independence and autonomy-process of professional individuation	*professional self at times is fragile	*modify perfectionistic or unrealistic images of psychotherapy and the role of the clinician	*measures of success are more nuanced and extend beyond whether or not the client returns for next session
	*traversing feelings of vulnerability and agency	*more refined use of modeling	*manage perplexity that originates from viewing counseling as increasingly complex	
	*negotiating the supervisory relationship	*increased ability to assess, accept, or reject suggested interventions/processes		
		*more critical of educational program, professors, and assumed experts		
		* oscillating feelings of competence and incompetence		
		*improved understanding of the professional role sympathy ≠ counseling		
		*persistent exploration of knowledge		

Adapted from Rønnestad and Skovholt (2013)

TABLE 1.5 ● Novice Professional Phase

Description	Development Crises	Emotional/Cognitive Experiences	Developmental Tasks	Sources of Influence
First 2 to 5 years of professional practice	This phase is divided into three subphases: *Confirmation *Disillusionment *Exploration *Each phase is navigated though increased experiences with clients; *Supervision is less focused on skill acquisition and development and more focused on treatment planning, client feedback, and client outcomes *apply rule guided learning *recognize situations in a holistic manner *distinguish important from unimportant material	*Confirmation* *pride *sense of freedom *excitement *intensified association with the profession *desire for formal continuing education/certifications *Disillusionment* *recognition that one approach does not work for all clients *isolation—fewer peers *dismay that not all clients improve as much as expected *turmoil with others during collaboration *disheartened as one's training or abilities seem insufficient for clients *continued consideration of theoretical orientation(s) *Exploration* *creative *developing congruence between personal and professional selves *increased self-reflection *self-directed attention toward personal and theoretical issues *reduction of imitative modeling *learning renaissance	*develop professional identification and commitment *complete transformation from states of dependency to independence expected of a professional *address disillusionment and disappointment with graduate education, professional performance, and profession that may surface postgraduation *continue to explore and define professional role *continue role adoption	*feedback from clients, feedback from professional elders, modeling personal-peers, faculty, family *these sources while still present have less influence *increased reliance on self *anchored conceptual structures—integration of personal ways of knowing and worldview with professional self *Introspection

Adapted from Rønnestad and Skovholt (2013)

Experienced Professional

Experienced professionals have a minimum of six years or more of professional experience and have mastered the developmental tasks of the novice professional phase. Typically, experienced professionals have experience in a variety of settings— inpatient, outpatient, private practice, or community and agencies with a wide range of clients who have a diverse set of concerns. Clinicians in this phase embody a more well-defined professional self-concept, that is, they know who they are as a clinician, professional, and person. Experienced professionals have moved beyond the simplistic or unidimensional view of themselves and now enjoy a rich and multidimensional understanding of themselves. The match between clinician's self-concept and characteristics of their work setting is critical. The degree of congruence between these two factors bolsters clinicians' desires to be helpful clients and is associated sense of competence. This phase is often when one extends their expertise or specialty techniques like the Advanced Training Certificate Program offered by the International Society for Trauma Stress Studies (ISTSS) and may include supervision to other clinicians. Clinicians providing CTD counseling may experience burnout due to a mismatch or dissatisfaction between their self-concept and the work setting. This mismatch may lead to a waning interest or apathy in helping clients. It is important to note that not all clinicians progress to this phase despite having many years of experience. Some do not progress because they have not mastered the tasks of earlier phases while others do not progress because they were not able to manage the expectations of more complex conceptual or advanced procedural knowledge, display a distant or detached interpersonal style with clients, or because they remain confused when encountering the complexities of psychotherapy. Interestingly, clinicians who develop into Experienced Professionals seem to develop a natural style of psychotherapy, which fuels feelings of competence and professional humility. Table 1.6 presents a summary of the critical elements of the Experienced Professional phase.

Ethical Expectations of CTD Counselors

Rønnestad and Skovholt (2013) note optimal professional development involves integration of the counselor's personal self with her or his coherent professional self as evidenced by increasing consistency between the professional's personality and theoretical or conceptual beliefs. Understandably, graduate students and many early career professionals work to gain a coherent understanding of general counseling, let alone the specialized knowledge required to provide CTD treatment. This integration takes time and dedication; with work and supervision, you can get there! Regardless of your phase of development, clinicians are expected to maintain professional role and responsibilities. This means you practice within the scope of your training, abide by your respective professional society's code of ethics (ACA, 2014; APA 2010; NASW, 2008), and practice in a culturally competent and socially just manner (Ratts, Singh, Nassar-McMillan, Butler, & McCullough, 2015; APA, 2002). Specifically, you are to protect client welfare through the application of mandatory and aspirational ethics (ACA, 2014; APA, 2010; NASW, 2008), engagement in a culturally responsive and ethical decision-making model(s), and the understanding that each client or family or community has a particular culture and individual variations within that culture. You must be aware of your privilege, power, and status

TABLE 1.6 ● Experienced Professional Phase				
Description	**Development Crises**	**Emotional/Cognitive Experiences**	**Developmental Tasks**	**Sources of Influence**
6+ years in the profession	*continue to find meaning in therapeutic work appropriateness for the profession	*satisfaction with colleagues, professional autonomy, self-concept, and perception of work role *more willing to share information about personal life and its relationship to therapy *increased use of disclosure *interaction between personal life and professional practice influences clinicians' perceptions of self and their development *more comfortable confronting clients *see power in the therapeutic residing in the client rather than the clinician *more flexible with approaches and techniques *better regulation of interaction with clients-appropriate therapeutic distance	*maintain a sense of professional growth and resiliency *avoid burnout *continue to integrate personal and professional self coherently * seek extensive and varied experiences with clients	feedback from clients, feedback from professional elders, modeling personal-peers, faculty, family *influence is now experienced in the role of supervisor, mentor, instructor *continuing learning in diverse fields other than counseling, marriage and family therapy, psychology, or social work

Adapted from Rønnestad and Skovholt (2013)

and of the intersectionality of those statuses with the lives of your clients and the multiple contexts in which they live. Intersectionality describes the interconnected social categorizations such as race, class, sexual orientation, genders, religion, and socio-economic status as they apply to an individual or group. These categorizations create overlapping and interdependent systems of discrimination or disadvantage.

The Counselor's Toolkit

In the chapters that follow, we present a counselor's toolkit for caring for those experiencing crisis, trauma, or disaster. Each toolkit provides multiple tools to address individuals, groups, or communities that are affected by crisis, trauma, or disaster. Specific tools include essential knowledge, skills, awareness, techniques,

and resources for individuals, groups, and communities at each level of professional development.

- Knowledge—the foundational information and understandings clinicians
  possess

- Skills—specific abilities or proficiencies in counseling

- Awareness—perceptions of self, clients, situations, and environments

- Techniques—intentional combinations of counseling skills with identifiable
  processes or procedures resulting in specific outcomes

- Resources—access, relationships, means, connections, services, supplies that
  may be brought to bear in service of clients and communities

Spectrum of Crisis, Trauma, and Disaster

Oftentimes clients and, for that matter, clinicians and researchers, use the terms
crisis, trauma, and disaster interchangeably. The conflation or overlapping of
these terms is understandable for those we serve, yet clinicians require more pre-
cise language. Yeager and Roberts's (2003) framework for differentiating stress,
acute stress, disorder, and crisis provides a useful model for consideration. In
their discussion, they identify three potential measures of the impact of crisis
producing events; *spatial dimension, subjective time clock, and perceived reoccurrence.* Spatial dimension describes the proximity or distance between the client
and the crisis event or relationship to the victim of an event. The closer the
individual or group is to the event or the person who experienced the event,
the greater the magnitude of impact. The subjective time clock is a measure of
the intensity and the duration of the exposure to sensory experiences—sight,
sound, smell, touch, and hearing; the more intense and prolonged the exposure, the greater the impact. Finally, perceived recurrence describes a subjective
state of the individual's expectation or anticipation that the crisis will reoccur. Perceived recurrence contributes to an active crisis state for the survivor
(Young, 1995, as cited in Yeager & Roberts, 2003). Using these three concepts
we offer you, the following conceptual framework (Figure 1.1) and caveats. The
image below presents three braided ropes representing the spectrum of crisis,
trauma, and disaster. The image of the braided rope illustrates the interconnectedness of the three in experiences in which individuals experience increasing levels distress and dislocation. Crisis events are represented at the left of the
diagram and describe their proximity (near) or direct (to) the event, the degree
of exposure (brief to moderate), and perception of event reoccurrence (low).
Traumatic events, positioned in the center represent very close proximity or
direct experience of the traumatic event, with moderate to prolonged exposure
affecting multiple senses. These individuals perceive a moderate to high risk
of a trauma or traumas reoccurring. Disaster events, represented on the right

FIGURE 1.1 ● **Spectrum of Crisis, Trauma, and Disaster**

Crisis | Trauma | Disaster

Close personal/direct proximity brief to moderate exposure

Low perceived recurrence

Very close personal/direct proximity moderate/repeated/prolonged engaging multiple senses

moderate to high perceived recurrence

Personal/direct proximity prolonged/severe exposure engaging multiple senses

high perceived recurrence

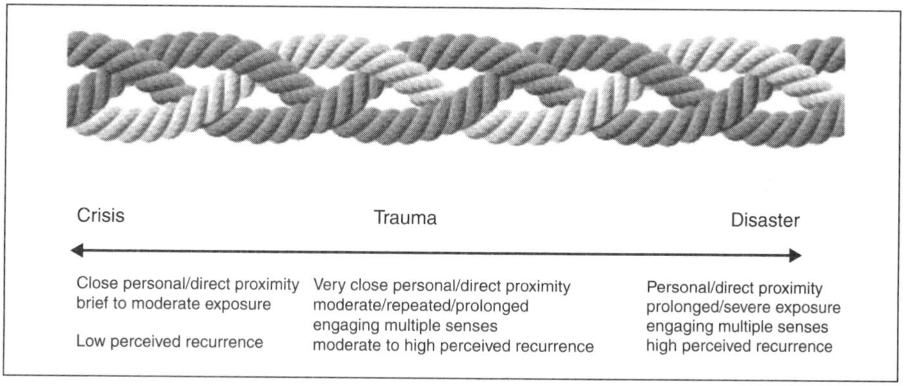

© Can Stock Photo / piai

side of the spectrum describe direct and personal proximity to the disaster event with prolonged and severe exposure affecting multiple senses and status (housing, vocation, transportation). These individuals perceive a high likelihood that a disaster will reoccur.

The double-headed arrow and image of a braided rope exemplifies our belief that experiences of crisis, trauma, and disaster are not a linear process; rather, they are dynamic, interconnected, multiply influenced, and multi-directional. For example, one can experience a disaster event that becomes a crisis and which is experienced traumatically. This framework is neither meant to represent *hard and fast truths* nor will it represent all clients' experiences. It is offered as one method for you to organize and categorize voluminous amounts of information about which hundreds of texts have been written.

Summary

The context in which clinicians learn and develop professional skills and dispositions and the foundational elements of self-awareness, reflective practice, clinical supervision, and professional development intersect in the life of the clinician and their clients. Clinical education of counselors, psychologists, and social workers takes place during phases of professional development and is the lens through which CTD counseling is viewed. The spectrum of crises, traumas, and disaster delineates unique and common elements of these client experiences or events and sets the framework for the remainder of the text.

Extended Learning Exercises

Exercise 1

The questions below are provided for you to consider on your own or in small groups. The groupings reflect the major sections of the preceding chapter and are designed to promote a process of dialogue and thought rather than a singular answer.

Experience

What are my experiences of crisis, trauma, or disaster?

What are my assumptions about people experiencing crisis, trauma, or disaster?

Under what conditions would I seek counseling or therapy?

What assistance or services might benefit me?

How might my personal experiences aid or impede my work with clients?

How do I discern sympathy from empathy?

Self-Awareness

How do I describe myself to others?

How would my partner, spouse, or family members describe me?

Why do I want to become a clinician?

What do I like about psychotherapy?

What do I dislike about psychotherapy?

What are my strengths as a clinician?

What are my vulnerabilities as a clinician?

Reflective Practice

What do I want to achieve in psychotherapy or counseling?

What do I want the client to achieve in psychotherapy or counseling?

What do I do in counseling that facilitates client change?

What do I do in counseling that impedes client change?

What skills or ways of being do I want to change about how I conduct counseling?

What skills or ways of being do I want to enhance about how I conduct counseling?

Who can assist me in making improvements to my practice?

Supervision

What do I believe is the purpose of supervision?

How much safety do I experience in supervision?

How honest am I with my supervisor?

How much do I trust the feedback from my supervisor?

To what degree is supervision helpful?

To what degree can I ask my supervisor for what I need?

Professional Development

How well do I reflect the advanced graduate student, novice professional, or experienced professional phase?

How are my experiences similar? How are they different?

What experiences, education, or feedback do I need to continue to progress?

What areas of expertise within crisis, trauma, or disaster counseling would I like to develop?

Exercise 2

The Spectrum of Crisis, Trauma, and Disaster

Consider the spectrum of crisis, trauma, and disaster presented in Chapter 1. Next, ask yourself two questions: (1) What are the primary differences between these constructs? and (2) What are the primary similarities between these three constructs? As you reflect on the similarities and differences, we invite you to list the distinguishing factors, boundaries, and intersections of crisis, trauma, and disaster, identify the pros and cons of each factor and intersection, and describe the potential client impact of each pro or con.

Additional Resources

Helpful Links

American Psychological Association: https://www.apa.org/ed/accreditation

Council for Accreditation of Counseling and Related Educational Programs: http://www.cacrep.org/

Council on Social Work Education: http://www.cswe.org/accreditation.aspx

EMDR Institute Inc: http://www.emdr.com/distance-learning/

International Society for Traumatic Stress Society: http://www.istss.org/education-research/online-learning/advanced-training-certificate-program.aspx

Office of Program Consultation and Accreditation: http://www.apa.org/ed/accreditation/

Substance Abuse and Mental Health Services Administration (SAMHSA): http://www.samhsa.gov/

Training Standards: professional counselors at www.cacrep.org; psychologist at www.apa.org; and social workers at www.cswe.org/getattachment/Accreditation/Accreditation-Process/2015-EPAS/2015EPAS_Web_FINAL.pdf.aspx

Vista Continuing Education: http://www.vistaceus.com/Default.aspx

History and Theoretical Foundations of Crisis and Crisis Counseling

Most humans are confronted by crisis at some point in their existence and, as a result, experience powerful emotions, cognitions, distress, and dislocation. The universal and historic nature of crisis led individuals and societies to create and promote cultural narratives of crisis (Campbell, 1970). These powerful stories, passed from generation to generation, provide a contextual frame of reference for the world around us and communicate the meaning of language, norms, and beliefs. In a typical account, one unexpectedly encounters a dangerous or threatening event that warrants a larger-than-life decision at a critical moment. Enduring stress and hardship, the protagonist confronts danger, is transformed, and returns to a triumphant or renewed state. Echterling, Presbury, and McKee (2005) note the term crisis originates from early 17th century Greek word *krisis* and refers to a judgment or a decision point. Historic narratives like the *Odyssey* or Joan of Arc's victory at the Siege of Orleans and more recent ones like Nelson Mandela, Cesar Chavez and Delores Huerta represent the complexities and extent of crisis events—a decision (or evaluation) made at a critical junction that results in transformation. Cultural crisis narratives almost always end on a positive or aspirational note allowing others to learn what it takes to overcome a crisis. Hopefully, most of your clients will never face crises of similar magnitudes, yet lessons about the overwhelming nature of crisis, the restorative power of relationships, perseverance, and recovery are individually and collectively instructive. In this chapter, we define crisis counseling within a mental health context; discuss the history and theoretical foundation of crisis and crisis counseling; distinguish the types, categories, and nature of crises; identify models of crisis counseling; and distinguish the unique and common elements of crisis events.

Learning Objectives

After reading this chapter and completing the reflective exercises, you will be able to

1. Define crisis in a mental health context
2. Contextualize the history and theoretical foundations of crisis counseling
3. Articulate and understand the relationships between and among the types, categories, and nature of crises
4. Describe crises how affects individuals; and groups and subsystems
5. Distinguish acute and chronic crisis events
6. Discuss and apply the various approaches/models of crisis counseling

Crisis Counseling Within a Mental Health Context

Most clinicians will respond to a client's crisis during their career. A common definition of crisis counseling promotes shared understanding, consistent terminology, and more effective treatments and accurate research. However, many behavioral health professional societies distinguish their profession and membership by laying claim to greater expertise, a specific approach or intervention or service despite their clients receiving similar services from a variety of professionals. While pride in one's profession is admirable, unnecessary competition fragments clinical knowledge and services, limits quality research, results in a proliferation of terms and definitions, and most importantly, is tone deaf and irrelevant to clients.

With respect to crisis counseling we also see different definitions. For example, the American Counseling Association (ACA) defines individual crisis counseling as a discrete intervention with

> limited goals to ensure safety and promote overall stability. The goal is to provide emotional support and concrete feedback/assistance for the individual. Crisis counseling helps problem-solve and assists individuals in obtaining available resources. . . . [C]risis counseling can range from 15 minutes to 2 hours, whereas the frequency of 1:1 crisis counseling with the same person ranges from 1 to 3 times. (2010)

The American Psychological Association defines crisis counseling as "immediate drop-in, phone-in, or on-site professional counseling provided following a trauma or sudden stressful event, often for emergency situations or in the aftermath of a disaster" (APA Dictionary, 2018). And social workers seem to focus on crisis intervention rather than counseling. Some social workers provide clients support as part of a crisis intervention team (CIT) in hospitals and or schools and support to clients in acute phase of a crisis. Many professional publications and social work websites identify Robert's Seven-Stage Crisis Intervention Model

(Roberts, 2005) as the preferred model of intervention. Thus, despite desires to distinguish ourselves by profession, paraphrasing Maya Angelou, "We are more alike my friends, than we are unalike" (Angelou, 1994, p. 224).

Another area of likeness in crisis counseling is Levers's (2012) definition. She describes crisis counseling as

> short-term interventions focused on assisting disaster survivors in understanding their current situation and reactions, mitigating additional stress, assisting those individuals in reviewing their options, promoting the use or development of additional coping strategies, providing emotional support, and encouraging linkage with other agencies that can assist survivors in recovering to their pre-disaster level of functioning. (p. 467)

We view Lever's definition as a bridge across the professional divides and note minor differences in intervention are apparent when one knows the clinician's professional lens. For example, when confronted with crisis events, you, an emerging clinician may utilize a model of intervention designed for individual and developmentally oriented crises (The ACT Model of Crisis; Roberts, 2005) while a marriage and family therapist may use a systemic approach (Hill, 1949; McCubbin & Patterson, 1983). A social worker may view the crisis as stemming from contextual and environmental factors and consequently use a developmental and ecologically based model (Developmental-Ecological Model of Crisis; Boss, 2002) while a psychologist may view the crisis from a psychophysiological perspective and utilize the Bioecological Model of Crisis (Hoffman & Kruczek, 2011). Regardless of professional differences in definitions and treatment foci, most clinicians define crisis as an unexpected negative event, perceived intensely as a threat that briefly destabilizes and overwhelms one's previous coping resulting in feelings of anxiety and vulnerability. Thus, all points of view have value when they contribute to positive outcomes for our clients and, after all, isn't that the point of professional help! Exercise 1, at the end of the chapter, is provided to contextualize your learning about professional standards.

The History and Theories of Crisis Counseling

History

The history of contemporary crisis counseling and intervention is associated with a variety of societal issues emerging over the last two centuries. While an exhaustive list of historical antecedents is beyond the scope of this book, it would undoubtedly reach back well before written history. Significant historical events central to understanding crisis counseling and intervention are presented. As you read, we call your attention to the difference between current conceptualizations of crisis and historic ones.

The history of contemporary crisis counseling and intervention in the United States begins with the protection of those with suicidal ideation. In 1906, Harry Marsh Warren, a minister in New York City, founded the first organized volunteer service dedicated to preventing suicide (Colt, 2006), the *Save-A-Life League*. Warren was contacted by a New York City hotel manager at the request of a distraught young woman. She was distressed after a break up and was contemplating suicide. The hotel manager was unable to reach Warren and the young woman was found near death the next morning. This event, as well as his knowledge of a young man who recently committed suicide after other ministers declined to see him, moved Warren to action. He rallied his parishioners from the pulpit saying, "I wish that all who believe death is the only solution for their problems would give me the chance to prove them wrong" (Barlow, 1933, p. 20, as cited in Miller & Gould, 2013). Warren's interventions were active and engaged. He placed newspapers ads in New York City papers asking those considering suicide to contact him directly and visited the homes and hospital rooms of those with suicidal ideation or where a suicide was attempted. Warren established a group of volunteers who responded to distressed individuals in the League's central office. Miller and Gould recount Warren's statement in 1921 in *The New York Times*, "The Save-A-Life League has received thousands of letters from different parts of the world telling of sorrows beyond human endurance and begging for all possible help. Quantities of inspirational literature, which the league publishes, have been sent out. At the headquarters hundreds and thousands have come either for personal help or in behalf of others" (p. 13). James and Gilliland (2017) note the National Save-a-Life League established the first crisis phone line in further demonstrating those in need could benefit from support from someone, outside their family. Warren's advocacy and actions are credited with saving at least 1,000 lives (Miller & Gould, 2013).

The second seminal event occurred in 1942 in Boston. The Cocoanut Grove nightclub was one of Boston's most popular venues. A series of unfortunate events contributed to the horrific fire and destruction that occurred on November 28, 1942. The Club's interior, a labyrinth of bars, lounges, and dining rooms, was decorated with highly flammable materials like palm fronds and heavy draperies. Additionally, the club's owner was believed to have locked and concealed exits to prevent patrons from skipping out on their tabs. The origin of the fire was undetermined, but the death toll, 492 souls, was catastrophic. Given the magnitude of the fire, death, and destruction, the need for crisis counseling and intervention to aid victims, their families, first responders, and the Boston community was obvious.

In response to the Cocoanut Grove disaster, Dr. Erich Lindemann (1944) described normal grief reaction upon which his colleague, Gerald Caplan, devised a theory of crisis. Not all crises receive the attention they deserve. For example, the Cocoanut Grove fire is often heralded as the event most associated with the development of modern crisis theories, yet our third historical event, the Rhythm Club fire, was as consequential for those involved. In 1940, two years *before* the Cocoanut Grove tragedy, a devastating fire occurred at the Rhythm Club in Natchez, Mississippi. Despite the deaths of 209 African Americans (Ward & Butler, 2008), there was no outcry for support for the 17 survivors, their families, or first responders, and no researchers or theorists studied the event. The only support came from the $5,000 in donations to the Red Cross raised by local residents. As a counselor, it is critical you remain attuned to issues of social justice and injustice as our collective history is replete with tragic examples like this.

Three grassroots movements also contribute to the history of contemporary crisis counseling and intervention: Alcoholics Anonymous (AA), Vietnam veterans, and the Women's Movement of the 1970s. These groups addressed acute and chronic crises and resulting emotional, psychological, financial, vocational, and relational needs of those directly and indirectly suffering from alcoholism or alcohol dependence, the effects of the Vietnam War, or domestic violence, rape, or child abuse. Movements like these emerge when a critical mass of those affected informally comes together because no formal acknowledgment or systems exist. The sociopolitical influences of Vietnam veterans and Women's Movement are explored in greater depth in Chapter 4.

Specific to alcohol abuse, Mothers Against Drunk Driving (MADD) was formed in 1980 by Candance Lightner after the death of her daughter Cari. Lightner wanted to address the needs of families who lost a loved one at the hands of a drunk driver. Through their support groups, MADD members shared their grief and anger and sought to influence legislation through grassroots public advocacy. Most importantly, MADD partnered with Alcoholics Anonymous (AA) to address the need for formal recognition and treatment of alcoholism. While a review of AA is beyond the scope of this chapter, it is important to note the collaboration between AA chapters and veteran's groups in establishment of free storefront clinics for Vietnam veterans and veteran specific AA meetings. In essence, Candance Lightner transformed an acute traumatic crisis into assistance and support for those experiencing the chronic crises of alcoholism.

Theories

The pioneering work of Lindemann (1944) and later Gerald Caplan (1961; 1964) provide a firm theoretic foundation for crisis and crisis counseling. Building on their work, subsequent scholars and clinicians drew upon related psycho- and sociological theories to deepen and advance the knowledge base. As a result, theories and practices related to crisis were developed demonstrating that the previous focus on psychodynamic perspectives was insufficient. We agree with James and Gilliland (2017) who advise that the right blend of developmental, sociological, psychosomatic, ecological, and situational factors be considered as anyone can fall prey to brief pathological symptoms related to a crisis.

Theories presented in this section reflect the framework of expanded crisis theory (James & Gilliland, 2017) and draw on contributions from psychoanalysis, adaptational, and interpersonal, chaos, and systems theories. We extend this framework and include a discussion of transactional theories of appraisal and coping. The theories are presented in the approximate chronological order they contributed to our understanding of crisis theory.

Psychodynamic Theory

In Victorian times, grief was associated with the physical pain of a *broken heart*. Freud and others considered grief from a psychodynamic framework. Grief was believed to cause distress as survivors *let go* of their attachment to the deceased to move beyond their anguish (Neimeyer, 2001) and return to a new normal.

Lindemann (1944) and later others (Bowlby, 1980; Kübler-Ross, 1969, 1975; Parkes, 2006) examined the nature and pattern of responses to grief, expected (uncomplicated) and unexpected (complicated or pathological), as well as the processes: stages, phases, and course. A note of caution: you may be familiar with Kübler-Ross's stages of grief, which are commonly believed to describe how one grieves. For the past three decades, a growing number of scholars (Attig, 1991; Parkes, 2013; Stroebe, Schut, & Boerner, 2017) have challenged the accuracy and appropriateness of Kübler-Ross's stage model of grief noting (a) grieving and bereavement are a recursive, not linear process; (b) the absence of empirical support (Parkes, 2013) for the model; (c) the universal view of grieving ignores cultural or subcultural influences and practices; and (d) potential harm to clients (Silver & Wortman, 2007). Silver and Wortman's criticism serve as a warning to clinicians that their clients, whose grieving process fails to conform to Kübler-Ross's model, may feel their manner of grieving is wrong. The perception they are not grieving the right way leaves these individuals further isolated, criticized, and diminished by their supportive network and health care professionals. We note this challenge to Kübler-Ross's model as an example of how historic and current conceptualizations of a concept differ. Returning to Lindemann, he identified five symptoms of grief and related tasks experienced by mourners. Symptoms ranged from somatic/physical distress, preoccupation with the deceased, guilt, and hostility, to loss of routine. To achieve symptom relief, mourners were to free themselves from their attachment to the deceased, adjust to life without the deceased, and establish new relationships. For Lindemann, much like Freud and Bowlby, the process of letting go and forming new attachments allowed the mourner to focus on the future and to complete the grieving process.

Gerald Caplan (1964) and his colleagues expanded Lindemann's concepts of grief and bereavement and incorporated his experiences with post–World War II Israeli immigrants to devise his theory of crisis intervention. Caplan described a crisis as an upset in the steady state, aggravated by an abrupt and disruptive event, that overwhelms customary problem-solving strategies. Individuals in crisis seek a return to precrisis function and a sense of balance or homeostasis. He identified the subjective nature of crisis, namely that it was the individuals' emotional reaction to the problem that makes it a *crisis*, rather than the problem itself. An example may be helpful. During a suicide assessment you, the clinician, unexpectedly feel stressed, scared, and anxious. Despite your training and previous experiences with clients' suicidal ideation, you are unsure what to do next and feel incompetent. You have a colleague join the session and the suicidal client is voluntarily admitted to the hospital. In post-session supervision, you are in crisis. You feel anxious, confused, and wonder out loud why an issue you've handled numerous times—suicidal ideation—now has you panicking. For the next week, you feel depressed, can't sleep, and are irritable. Clearly, your previous coping skills are insufficient and, according to crisis theory, your appraisal of a previously experienced event (client's suicidal ideation) is different than before, (more about appraisal later in the chapter).

Like responses to other events, crisis responding follows a general pattern. Roberts and Ottens (2005) credit Caplan as the first clinician to "describe and document the four stages of a crisis reaction" (p. 332). The first stage—increasing stress or anxiety associated with the crisis event—is followed closely by the second stage—daily disturbances functioning resulting from the unresolved crisis. Because the crisis remains unresolved, individuals' stress and anxiety escalate, and they go "into a depression or mental collapse or may partially resolve the crisis by using new coping methods" (p. 332). Caplan's contributions to crisis theory highlight the subjective nature of crises. According to the theory, the subjective definition arises out of a perceived imbalance between the difficult event and the individual's available resources. Caplan argued physical or psychological threats engage the individual's coping or problem-solving skills with the goal of restoring balance. This imbalance is experienced as disequilibrium causing distress because individuals continually seek balance but have yet to achieve it.

Psychoanalytic Theory

We distinguish psychodynamic from psychoanalytic theories, as the former focuses on inter- rather than intrapsychic process. As noted above, a psychodynamic view of grief involved the individual *letting go* of the attachment/interpersonal relationship to the deceased. A psychoanalytic view of grief, at its essence, focuses on client's understanding of their postcrisis disequilibrium by accessing and processing their unconscious thoughts and past emotional experiences—a decidedly intraindividual experience. Further, psychoanalytic theorists posit that early childhood fixations, once explored, explain an individual's response to events. Vulnerability to specific stressors is believed to be associated with factors such as ego organization, fixation, unconscious drive, and coping mechanisms (Fine, 1973). From this theoretical perspective, relief comes when the client recognizes and modifies ineffective defensive patterns through active engagement in suggestion, abreaction, clarification, and dynamic interpretation (Glick & Meyerson, 1981). Due to the dynamic nature of a crisis, clients are believed to be in a more regressed state signaling increased attention to and management of transference and countertransference issues.

Adaptational Theory

In her 1981 article, Schlossberg described adult adaptation to transitions and acknowledged the connection between her proposed model and Lindemann's 1965 study on Cocoanut Grove survivors. Schlossberg intentionally rejects the term *crisis* due to the "negative connotations" (p. 6), opting for the term *transitions*. For her and others, (Parkes, 1971) transitions represented a more fluid process in which gains as well as losses are experienced and events—both dramatic and those less observable—result in "psychological growth" or "deterioration" (Moos & Tsu, 1976, p. 13; as cited in Schlossberg).

Adaptational theories applied to crisis counseling suggest that clients sustain the experience of a crisis through nonproductive behaviors, negative thoughts, denial, and rationalization. Adaptation results when the client engages in a series of thoughts, behaviors, and emotions to offset the experiences of crisis and reestablish a sense of balance or homeostasis. Specifically, adaptation is evidenced when clients demonstrate a good enough balance between the experience of crisis, available interpersonal and tangible resources, and reduced feelings of anxiety. Thus, nonproductive behaviors replace adaptive ones. Schlossberg notes three factors believed to aid one's adaptation to transition. The first describes characteristics of the transition—gains/losses, positive/negative affect, source/event, duration, timing, and degree of stress. The second examines the pre- and post-transition support and environment. Individual demographics, values, and prior experience with similar type of transition complete the third factor. Schlossberg cautions these factors are not equally weighted for individuals, that is, some matter more than others. Consider the example of Pat who just found out he was immediately laid off from his job. His company sent him to you for counseling. Applying adaptational theories, you understand his transition (crisis) may be mitigated when he is able to acknowledge his family's financial stability—they own their home and his wife has a substantial and steady income. With counseling, Pat can reconcile and reframe being laid off as an opportunity to seek a management position—which he has desired—and feeling more in control, he can be encouraged to seek the support of his spouse. These adaptations should engender a return to pretransition functioning.

Interpersonal Theory

Interpersonal theory has its roots in Rogers's person-centered humanistic theory (1959). Fundamentally, persons experiencing a crisis experience incongruence and diminished positive regard and self-worth. Interpersonal theory applied to crisis counseling assumes individuals cannot sustain a personal state of crisis if they believe in themselves and others. This belief is an antecedent to the necessary confidence that helps them work toward a sense of self-actualization, build community with others, and eventually return to equilibrium. Clinicians utilizing this theoretical approach understand the importance of sharing, unconditional positive regard, accurate empathy, clients' locus of control, personal agency, and problem exploration and interpersonal support. This therapeutic approach enhances clients' self-esteem and self-confidence.

Chaos Theory

Chaos theory has been used to describe everything from the order of the universe, weather patterns, and problems in mathematics. Basically, chaos theory states there is order in chaos and from this chaos an open and ever-changing system of self-organization emerges. This theory is predicated on evolution, where order comes from chaos under the conditions of spontaneity, creativity, and cooperation. With respect to crisis counseling, clients in crisis experience a host of intense emotions: fear, dislocation, anxiety, and disruption. Clinicians aid clients in viewing the order or adaptive patterns that emerge from the chaos of the crisis event. Clinicians encourage and support clients' experimentation with trial and error. Through trial and error, clients attempt to instill order and acknowledge the relevance of false starts. Because clients continue to experiment, they come to recognize dead ends and learn to follow a course of action despite the outcome.

Clients actively engage to make personal sense of and cope with a crisis. The disorganization yields organization and, in the case of crisis intervention, recovery.

Whether in counseling or on their own, individuals use a process of trial and error to reestablish a sense of equilibrium and, eventually, homoeostasis. Achieving a sense of homeostasis does not mean the individual is necessarily in a better position than they were prior to the crisis. It means they are less overwhelmed by their circumstances. Individuals constantly strive for a sense of homeostasis or balance, whatever that means to them personally, culturally, and environmentally. It reminds us of the adage, "It is better to dance with the devil you know than one you don't know."

Family Systems Theory

In the 1960s, Bowen (1978) applied systems thinking to families and developed family systems theory. The family is considered an emotional unit. Clinicians utilizing this perspective address clients' concerns in the context of their families and include interpersonal and intrapersonal functioning. The client's interrelationships, interdependence, interactions, roles, group norms, communication, and contextual factors between and among individuals in the client's life, the crisis event(s), and the return to equilibrium are the focus of therapy. In sum, counselors explore what happens in the client, their system, and the interactions between and among relationships during and after the crisis.

A systemically oriented crisis counselor may reflect on questions such as "Who is most likely to support or criticize the client?" "How do these reactions impact relationships?" "How do members of the client's system view crises?" and "What resources, if any, might the members of the system provide or withhold?" Remember, one's system is culturally and relationally viewed from the client's perspective. This means that *family* may include individuals who are not biologically related yet are deeply connected to the client. In this context, relationships may not conform to expected hierarchies of the dominant group and the offer or provision of resources is context dependent. Skilled clinicians encourage clients to identify individuals who comprise their system, to define the nature of those relationships and any cultural and personal values potentially influencing the system. The encouragement comes without pathologizing or judging the client and their culture.

Transactional Theory

Stress, or mental or emotional strain, was described by Hans Selye (1956) as a physiologically based pattern of responding. Selye viewed stress as a defense mechanism comprised of three successive stages—alarm, resistance, and exhaustion. Prolonged and severe stress impacts one's adaption and health. He introduced the General Adaptation to Stress (GAS) model in which stress coping occurs in the alarm and resistance stages. Stress in the first two stages may be experienced positively or negatively, depending on one's cognitive interpretation of their symptoms and experience. Thus, when one encounters a threat, the *alarm* response signals the sympathetic nervous system, increasing adrenaline, respiration, and heart rate in preparation to confront or avoid the threat. The resistance response engenders the fight or flight response in reaction to the stressor in an attempt to regain homeostasis. The exhaustion stage occurs when the individual is unable to cope with the distress.

Lazarus (1966) viewed stress and coping as a dynamic process. He extended Selye's work beyond a physiological framework to a transactional theory of stress and coping. Transactions take place between the individual their systems—affective, cognitive, psychological, and the environment. One's evaluation or appraisal of these interactions determines whether they are experienced as stressful and in what manner the individual will respond or cope. Mechanic (1978) identified personal and contextual factors—capacities, skills, abilities, limitation, resources, and norms likely to influence one's view of a stressor has harmful.

Lazarus and Folkman (1984) noted three forms of appraisal: primary, secondary, and reappraisal. Primary appraisal involves evaluating the nature of the event and then determining whether the stressor is a threat. In *secondary appraisal*, one evaluates their resources—mental, physical, financial—available to confront the perceived threat. The final form, *reappraisal*, involves continual evaluation of the nature of the threat and available resources. Lazarus and Folkman noted individuals respond or cope with stress through emotion- or problem-focused coping. Emotion-focused coping is utilized by individuals who have appraised the stressful event and do not believe they can respond effectively. Experiencing a lack of control, the individual may dismiss or attempt to avoid the stress or engage in denial or magical thinking. Problem-focused coping is utilized by individuals who have appraised a stressful event and believe they have the resources to manage or address the stressor by engaging in analyzing, planning, and executing a response.

A person in crisis deems the situation as a threat and believes they have insufficient resources to cope. Similarly, Bard and Ellison (1974) defined a crisis as a subjective reaction to a stressful life experience. This reaction paired with an individual's inability to cope effectively equals a crisis. These internal experiences, particularly those that are severe and prolonged, may result in trauma and impair an individual's coping. The structure of a crisis event includes the perception of threat, an inability to reduce the impact of the event, increased fear or confusion, excessive discomfort, and disequilibrium followed by a "rapid transition to an active state of crisis" (Dass-Brailsford, 2007, p. 94). The speed at which one resolves a crisis and its impact can dictate whether a crisis evolves into a trauma.

The Process of Coping and Adaptation

The term coping is often used interchangeably with the term adaptation, creating confusion. Jackson-Cherry and Erford (2010) describe coping behavior as, "All actions taken in an effort to manage stress, regardless of whether they are successful..." (p. 12). An individual in crisis utilizes coping behaviors to assess the event or environment, the risk of harm or injury, and responses or reactions to minimize harm or injury. For example, a child bullied by another scans their environment to assess or anticipate where they may encounter the bully—school lunchroom or restroom. Anticipating verbal or physical altercations, the child evaluates potential harm and gauges the degree of risk associated. Potential responses to limit harm might include limiting or avoiding eye contact, running away, fighting back, or submitting to the bully's demands. Additional responses include post-event strategies such as keeping the altercation a secret, telling only their peers, or informing school authorities or their parents. These behaviors, cognitions, and actions are ways the child copes with being bullied.

At their core, coping behaviors reduce emotional arousal (Jackson-Cherry & Erford, 2010). Effective coping behaviors are directly connected to events the individual wishes to manage. Ineffective coping behaviors may appear random, impulsive, and disconnected to the present event. For example, a client is fearful of speaking in public. Despite the requirements of their job, they actively avoid any situation where they may be asked to speak in front of others. They are considering leaving a job they love. As their counselor, you help them practice positive and encouraging self-talk (effective coping) during intense bouts of fear and self-doubt rather than resigning their job. The strategies identified represent control-based coping mechanisms. The client seeks to *control* their sense of fear and self-doubt when speaking publicly which may include an overwhelming desire to fight (refusing to speak), flight (avoiding settings where are expected to speak publicly), or freeze (being physically unable to speak). As their counselor, you encourage your client to engage in emotion- and problem-focused coping responses. Emotion- and problem-focused coping, described earlier, are clear and concise action-oriented behaviors used in the social environment. For example, you ask the client to practice their speech in front of you or supportive friends to successively gain feelings of control. Or you could suggest they practice deep focused breathing prior to their practice, utilize self-talk, visualization, or mental imagery to set a positive tone.

In contrast, adaptation is an outcome or result of stress or crisis and describes the degree to which one's functioning has *changed*, because of the event, over an extended period. When a personal crisis is maintained through cognitive distortions, maladaptive behaviors, and poor defense mechanisms, the overarching treatment goal is to reduce the client's dependence on maladaptive behaviors and install more adaptive ones. Theoretically, once adaptive behaviors are identified and employed, the crisis should be reduced or eliminated. Consider a client who suffered from physical abuse at the hands of an intimate partner. They come to you for counseling and state, despite being deeply in love with their current partner, they are afraid to engage in handholding, kissing, and cuddling. The client believes this will lead to the end of the relationship. The presence of a trusting and safe partner, who communicates clearly and manages expectations of physical closeness, should encourage the client to address their feelings of vulnerability or threat and build trust in the relationship. Therapeutic activities may include positive self-talk, risk taking, and open exchange of personal and environmental needs. This new ability to trust represents a positive adaptation to different relational circumstances.

Crises create stress and impel a response/reaction to restore psychological and physical safety (Baum, 1990). Puleo and McGlothlin (2010) note, "All actions taken in an effort to manage stress, regardless of whether they are successful or not, are referred to as coping" (p. 12). Coping with a crisis involves thinking and behaving in a way that calculates the occurrence of an event and its propensity for harm. Coping strategies are not viewed as adaptive or maladaptive; instead they are evaluated against the specific purpose for which they were selected. That is, did the coping strategy reduce, increase, or have no effect on the crisis? While coping is considered an intentional behavior designed to relieve stress, resiliency is considered an innate nondeliberate behavior.

The ability of a person to cope or adapt when confronted with adversity (e.g., crisis) or other significant sources of stress is defined as resiliency (Puleo & McGlothlin, 2010). As an outcome of stress and crisis, resilience is considered to be a protective factor. Resilient individuals are believed to be protected by various innate factors such as attribution, response, cognitive styles, and problem-solving skills (Boss, 2002; Puleo & McGlothlin, 2010). Exercise 2 at the end of the chapter will help you apply and contextualize your understanding.

Classifying Crisis and Crisis Events

The breadth and depth of crisis, trauma, and disaster information can overwhelm readers. To address this concern, we created a classification system to order the types, categories, and nature of these events. We present a broad description of three classes of crisis followed by a discussion of distinguishing elements in each class. For example, *Types of Crisis* describes the origins of crises initiated by humans, nature, or technology. To provide context, each type of crisis is further distinguished in *Categories*—developmental, situational, existential, psychiatric, traumatic, and ecosystemic. *Nature,* the last class, describes the level at which impact crisis events occur—individual, group, and community crises—and distinguishes acute from chronic states. A similar classification scheme is presented in Chapter 4—Trauma, and Chapter 6—Disaster. We organized the information in this manner to provide structure and clarity to these concepts and we hope you find it useful.

Human-Initiated Crises

Human-initiated crises result from intentional and unintentional human activity impacting individuals, groups, and communities and occur on a smaller scale (intimate partner violence, microaggressions) or larger scale (terrorism, the Holocaust). In stories retold by Holocaust survivors, Dorsey (1968) identified characteristics of human-initiated traumas: life-endangering situations like chronic starvation, physical maltreatment, and fear of total annihilation; degradation to the point of dehumanization; recurrent terror episodes; assaults on one's identity resulting in changes of self-image; and a prolonged "living-dead existence "with no way to escape it (Dorsey, 1968, p. 64). These conditions often led to what Dorsey (1968) termed as the "Muselman" stage, a devastating physical and psychological condition where one has lost the will to live after enduring horrific and relentless depravation of the concentration camps. The term "Muselman" seems to have originated from the crouched, prayer-like stance individuals in this condition exhibited. The posture was likened to that of Muslim in prayer. Common reactions to human-initiated crisis events included emotional detachment, regression, identification with the aggressor, and numbness to life represented by a *living dead* or *walking dead* existence. Lifton (1968) studied those who survived the bombing of Hiroshima and found similar reactions. He noted, however, that while many of the reactions to this event were like Holocaust survivors, the difference was the *total unpreparedness* of the Japanese survivors (p. 171). In both studies, survivors recounted vivid and accurate memories of the event, sometimes decades later (Dorsey, 1968; Lifton, 1968), and feeling of "death in life" (Lifton, 1968, p. 173).

In war, some military personnel experience what Solomon, Laror, and McFarlane (1996) called a "combat stress reaction" (p. 106). Those affected attempted to distance themselves from their thoughts and others hoping to block intrusive memories and anxiety related to fear of death, guilt, loneliness, and loss of self-control. Distancing sometimes manifested in impulsive behaviors (aggression) and somatic complaints (fatigue, sleeplessness). War takes a significant toll on veterans, civilians, and the environment. Civilians in war-torn areas, such as Iraq and Rwanda, face a long-term threat to survival (Dyregov, 2003), an antecedent to PTSD. In a study of 317 children, researchers investigated the well-being and mental health consequences of residing in a war zone. Dyregov (2003) discovered many children and adolescents had come to see fear as a normal part of daily life. The youngest participants articulated their fear, understood the violence put them in great danger, and resulted in destruction and death. The common threads of constant fear and the knowledge that "we can all die" (Dyregov, 2003, p. 114) was present in all age groups.

Nature-Initiated Crises

Nature-initiated crises are defined as "biologic, climate-related, or geophysical" (Leaning & Guha-Sapir, 2013, p. 1836) events occurring separate from human activity. Hurricanes, earthquakes, tornadoes, volcanic eruptions, and wildfires are but a few of these natural-occurring and devastating events. The number of incidences of nature-initiated crises is increasing exponentially. There were three times as many nature-initiated crises from 2000 to 2009 as there were in the 1980s (p. 1836). Following a nature-initiated crisis there is an immediate need for medical, food, and housing services. Although temporary, many events result in longstanding impairments in health for the affected populations (Leaning & Guha-Sapir, 2013). The response to nature-initiated crises can lead to social injustice and differential responding. For example, Willison, Singer, Creary, and Greer (2019) found

the federal government responded on a larger scale and much more quickly across measures of federal money and staffing to Hurricanes Harvey and Irma in Texas and Florida, compared with Hurricane Maria in Puerto Rico. The variation in the responses was not commensurate with storm severity and need after landfall in the case of Puerto Rico compared with Texas and Florida. (p. 1)

Response inequities cause increased mortality and complicates individual and community recovery.

Technology-Initiated Crises

Technology-initiated crises describe a failure of a technological structure or human error in operating technology. Like nature-initiated crises, most technology-initiated crises involve human mismanagement and may also be categorized as human-initiated crises in that there is an *identifiable cause* attributable to a person or persons. Thus, as in human-initiated crises, the psychological impact on individuals and communities from technology-initiated crisis may be more detrimental (Goldsteen & Schorr, 1982).

The number and severity of technology-initiated crises are on the rise as technology becomes more complex, integrated, automated, and ever present. As of 2019, machine learning and artificial intelligence permit software programs to make decisions based on algorithms derived from big data embedded in software and applications. This means there may no longer be an identifiable cause attributable to a person, rendering technology-initiated crisis like nature-initiated crisis in that there is no one to blame. Technology-initiated crises most often occur at the communal or societal level—the 2008 U. S. financial crisis, Chernobyl nuclear meltdown, or Deepwater Horizon oil spill. Individually experienced technology-initiated crisis may take the form of identity theft or hectoring by internet bots—a form of automated cyberbullying.

Categories of Crises

The categorical depiction of crises began with Brammer (1985) and was extended by Cavaiola and Colford (2006, 2011) and James and Gilliland (2017). Using applied crisis theory, these authors identified six categories of crisis: developmental, situational, existential, psychiatric, traumatic, and ecosystemic. While these descriptive categories focus on the individual, it is clear the impact of the crisis may be equally experienced by groups and communities.

Developmental Crises

For infants and children, developmental crises occur within the milestones of human growth when a significant transformation or change occurs yielding atypical response (James & Gilliland, 2017). Puberty is a milestone indicative of significant physiological, psychological, and social changes in adolescence marked by increasing independence and autonomy from caregivers. While most progress through this development phase with minor disruptions, others experience disruptions that can last a lifetime. The hallmarks of developmental crises in adolescence include the constant redefining of self and seeking a sense of mastery of interpersonal, social, and academic skills and, depending on one's culture, a gradual acquisition of autonomy and independence. Developmental crises of adulthood tend to be centered on emerging and maintaining intimate relationships, adjustments to aging, raising children (negotiating adolescence and eventual emancipation), choosing not to have children, retirement, and caretaking of one's parents or siblings, which involves familial role confusion, financial strain, and adjustment.

Infancy and Childhood

Developmental tasks associated with infancy include bringing hands and toys to mouth, visually following conversations, imitation of sounds, turning head and eyes toward sound, calming down while being rocked, and sleeping regularly for three to four hours at a time. According to the National Research Council (2000), early childhood is an acute period for brain expansion. Between birth and two years of age, the human brain more than triples in size, attaining 75% of its adult size by age two. The initial phases of neural development consist largely of primitive cells journeying to and forming particular sections of the brain. Recent research revealed that infants store memories as young as two months of age, within the limbic system of the brain (Markese, 2007). These memories are stored as somatosensory experiences. Thus, early distressing and traumatizing experiences, in infancy and toddlerhood, are stored in the brain as sensory experiences, even if the child cannot verbalize what has taken place (Green, Pouget, & Bavelier 2010; Markese, 2007). At birth, infants are reliant on their caregivers to meet their basic needs and to protect them from external stressors. Caregivers regulate the infant's sleep and eating cycles. Through countless interactions with caregivers, infants begin to control these cycles themselves. When caregivers repeatedly fail to protect infants from stressors or fail to support self-soothing behaviors, the infant's development and sense of security are impaired. Infants cannot yet communicate verbally and express their distress through behavior.

Emotional regulation is a process that begins in infancy with instinctive responses to distress (crying) and pleasure (eye contact, smiling). According to Ford (2009a), the purpose of emotional regulation is to utilize biological sources of information to screen and preserve the integrity of internal bodily conditions either automatically or self-reflectively. When an infant has repeated success in coping with mild, transitory incidents of fear, self-regulation is improved. Infants who endure a crisis and are traumatized may demonstrate increased distress, fussiness, and irregular sleeping and eating routines (Lieberman & Knorr, 2007). If the crisis or abuse continues, intensifies, or prevents new learning, unanticipated situations create an insecure basis for understanding and invoke fear and anxiety.

Newborns have multiple self-regulation systems—sucking, swallowing, breathing, thermoregulating, and vocalizing (Doussard-Roosevelt, Porges, Scanlon, Alemi, & Scanlon, 1997; Ford, 2009b). These innate processes depend on the brainstem and its functions to provide feedback along the vagus nerve bundle to biological organs. The vagus nerve is the longest of the 12 cranial nerves and monitors a range of crucial functions, communicating movement and sensory impulses to organs allowing one's body to adjust to a fluctuating environment. Self-regulation processes are the foundation for more multifaceted self-regulatory tasks that precede self-regulation in toddlerhood. Infancy is a period defined by low levels of responsiveness; this is partly due to limited stress hormone release and dormant hypothalamus pituitary adrenal axis reactivity (Andersen, 2003).

Consistent with the development of early dopamine chemical messenger systems, newborns continuously explore their environment (Rogeness & McClure, 1996). Environmental exploration, along with facilitative caregiver relationships described by Bowlby as goal-directed partnerships, are vital to the enhancement of self-regulation in infancy. Bowlby stated humans work throughout their life to acquire the ability to purposively adjust bodily, affective, and mental processes to have conscious control of self-regulation (Bowlby, 1992). Between six and twelve months of life, evolving neural pathways from the prefrontal cortex (PFC) to the amygdala and hippocampus provide the ability to discriminate unfamiliar and familiar things. Due to this phenomenon, fear of the unfamiliar will occur (Kagan, 2001). Infants develop the ability to discriminate through countless encounters. Infant self-regulation improves as they achieve regular success in handling mild, fleeting episodes of fear.

Developmental tasks associated with toddlerhood include managing emotions, delaying gratification, cooperating with others, acquiring new skills, and actively communicating. During the second and third year of life, continued rapid growth in the brain (Andersen, 2003) helps to organize consciousness of self and others as well as recognition of self as distinct with particular goals, emotions, and expectations (Adolphs, 2002). Once this process is complete, synaptogenesis and myelination begin (Nelson & Bosquet, 2000). Myelin is a fatty substance produced by glial cells that forms a sheath (myelination) around a nerve. The sheath allows more efficient movement of nerve impulses. Synaptogenesis is the process by which the speed of communication between brain cells and myelination increases. The speed of synaptic connections is highest in the first years of life. The toddler's processing speed is largely dependent on the quality of stimulation to which children are exposed. Positive child rearing experiences have been associated with increased synaptic connections, whereas traumatic early experiences have been associated with decreased synaptic pruning (Siegel, 1999).

Experiences shape the brain and alter neural networks throughout one's life, but never as much as in early childhood and adolescence. Although adjustments to neural pathways are possible throughout the lifespan, it is difficult to change personality after early childhood and challenging to change behavior, thinking, and emotion patterns after adolescence. With parental modeling and guidance, toddlers learn to experience and express emotions, recognize caregivers' emotional states, and learn emotional regulation. If development is interrupted during the first two to three years of life by significant traumatic events or compromised caregiving, the brain becomes organized around stress and reactivity. For example, frequent abuse and neglect in toddlerhood can lead to states of extreme emotional anguish and impairment in the ability to express or control these feelings and contingent behaviors (Cicchetti, Ackerman, & Izard, 1995). Ford (2009a) describes individuals who have encountered frequent early life traumatic experiences as developing a *survival brain*. The survival brain seeks to anticipate, prevent, or protect against the damage caused by potential or actual dangers, driven and reinforced by a search to identify threats, and attempts to mobilize and conserve bodily resources in the service of this vigilance and defensive adjustments to maintain bodily functioning (Ford, 2009a). Thus, psychosocial impairments involved in complex traumatic stress disorders can be traced back to early life alterations in neural network development involving a shift, due to environmental adversity, from a learning brain to a survival brain. The shift causes lasting changes in key brain functions, neural/neurochemical activity, and key brain structures.

Attachment in Childhood

A preoccupation with survival is fundamentally incompatible with a child's development of dependable emotional bonds with caregivers. Indeed, most complex occurrences of psychological trauma tend to involve interactions with those closest to the child. Traumas that occur during a transitional period are likely to result in lasting changes in personality and self. Instead, experiencing a nurturing and engaging caregiver and appropriate environmental structure, the child subjected to crises or trauma learns to focus on survival and threat rather than on trust and learning. Nurturing bonds and the sense of security they provide advance the capacity for relational attachment. A secure attachment provides comfort and nurturance to the developing child and is necessary for the development of self-awareness (Bowlby, 1982).

Attachment is a relationship of interacting, affection, long-lasting emotional connection, and physical closeness (Thompson, 1998). Infants are born with attachment-promoting behaviors such as smiling, crying, and clinging. These behaviors elicit a response in the caregiver to comfort, protect, and feed the infant. Repeated and predictable positive interactions between infants and caregivers provide the infant security, predictability, a sense of identity, as well as an internal working model of relationships. Insecure attachment patterns emerge when the primary caregiver responses show a lack of predictability or when responses are harsh, punitive, or abusive (Ainsworth, Blehar, Waters, & Wall, 1978). Research demonstrates that the parental relationship plays a central role in the generational transmission of working models of attachment (Cohn, Silver, Cowan, Cowan, & Pearson, 1992). Repeated experiences with caregivers who have fractious relationships and provide inconsistent or abusive care may result in an internal working model that views relationships as unsafe and hurtful. If one's internal working model frames relationships as unpredictable and unsafe, when in crisis, the individual may resist or be mistrustful of help and support.

Individuals move through various phases of attachment (Bowlby, 1982). The initial phase lasts from birth through the first eight weeks of life. This period is recognized as an orientation phase when the infant is relatively indiscriminate in terms of the target of his or her attachment behaviors. The second phase occurs between the 8th and 12th week and involves an orientation phase and signaling toward one (or more) differentiated figure(s). The infant is beginning to show preference for one or more specific caregivers. The third phase has the infant or toddler seeking close physical proximity to the primary care giver by crawling or walking and verbal or nonverbal signals. This phase occurs from the 12th week to 18 months. The fourth phase of attachment begins at about 18 months and continues through adulthood. This phase is characterized by the formation of goal-corrected partnership where the toddler tests the limits of proximity and safety. The main goal of these phases is to draw the caregiver in to close proximity for safety and security. As the child moves through the phases of attachment, the behaviors become increasingly discriminating in favor of the primary caregiver (Ainsworth, 1964).

Attachment Styles

Children who experience a loving, playful, consistent, and engaging caregiver develop a secure attachment pattern (Sroufe, 2000). Securely attached children cope with stress by using age-appropriate coping skills, are connected to their peer relationships, explore their environment, and demonstrate a balance of internalizing and externalizing behaviors. Children repeatedly exposed to inconsistent caregivers have limited or ineffective coping skills and are more isolated and at risk for developing one of several insecure attachment styles—dismissive/avoidant, anxious/ambivalent, disorganized/disoriented, or reactive (Ainsworth et al., 1978; American Psychiatric Association, 2013; Main & Solomon, 1986).

Dismissive/Avoidant

The dismissive/avoidant attachment style results from neglectful, absent, or unpredictable caregivers or environments and is marked by detached caregiving behaviors. The child with a dismissive/avoidant style of attachment rarely displays emotion, engages others in distant or detached manner, and may be viewed as hyper-independent. These children learn to avoid hurt and fear by dealing with events and emotions themselves, rather than depending on an unpredictable caregiver.

Anxious/Ambivalent

An anxious/ambivalent attachment style is rooted in inconsistent caregiver–infant attunement. The infant is confused by caregivers' behaviors that unpredictably oscillate between nurturing, attuned, and responsive to intrusive, insensitive, or unavailable. Understandably, these children feel confused, insecure, and suspicious of their caregivers yet cling to them to survive. Children with an anxious/ambivalent style behave unpredictably in relationships, have difficulty trusting others (Ainsworth et al., 1978), and remain wary in strange situations, even with the caregiver present. They respond to caregivers' departures and reunions with aggression/anger or helplessness/passivity, attempting to maintain a connection to the caregiver by varying their interpersonal responses—crying/fussing versus resignation/helplessness. These children reflect the relational inconsistencies experienced with their primary caregiver (Ainsworth et al., 1978).

Disorganized/Disoriented/Reactive

A disorganized/disoriented attachment style is often, but not exclusively, associated with grossly neglectful and abusive caregivers or environments. Children experience little to no caregiving, poor interpersonal boundaries, role-confusion, and pervasive errors in communication (Main & Solomon, 1986). Children with a disorganized/

disoriented attachment style demonstrate unique behavior in the playroom such as: rocking, freezing, and active dissociation. As the child matures, they have profound difficulties establishing intimate, enduring relationships, seem devoid of empathy, and experience low self-esteem, anxiety, and poor boundaries. Some children with a disorganized/disoriented attachment style are later diagnosed with reactive attachment disorder. The *Diagnostic and Statistical Manual of Mental Disorders, Fifth Edition (DSM—5)* characterizes reactive attachment disorder as "a pattern of markedly disturbed and developmentally inappropriate attachment behaviors, in which a child rarely or minimally turns preferentially to an attachment figure for comfort, support, protection, and nurturance" (American Psychiatric Association, 2013, p. 266). Reactive attachment disorder is hypothesized to emerge from pathogenic caregiving during infancy, child abuse or neglect, and frequent changes in primary caregiver. Distinctive behaviors associated with the disorder are extreme and sociopathic behavior, an inability to attach in relationships, and lack of conscience and empathy. Researchers and clinicians are not clear why some children develop this disorder and others do not; more research is needed to improve diagnosis and treatment.

Mikulincer and Shaver (2012) note one's attachment style and associated coping skills learned in infancy and childhood continue into adulthood. Those with secure attachment styles trust and depend on others and expect to be loved and valued by their partners. Those with insecure attachment styles are, in varying degrees, distrustful of relationships, mistrust others, and avoid interpersonal dependency. According to Fraley and Waller (1998), the way one responds to an unresponsive caregiver can be defined in two dimensions of anxiety and avoidance. The anxious response is characterized by proximity-seeking behaviors—clinging, pursuit, or anger to provoke a response from the other person. The avoidance response is characterized by deactivation of attachment behaviors—limited eye contact, indifference—to avoid or limit emotional contact and suppress one's emotional needs. The fearful-avoidant strategy is a combination of the two previous responses and is characterized by an individual seeking contact and then rejecting the contact when it is offered (Palmer & Lee, 2008). It is not difficult to imagine how one's attachment style influences a response to a crisis or the offer of assistance after a crisis.

Childhood Trauma

Hirsch (2004) found a wide range in the development of PTSD across children who have experienced childhood maltreatment, were medically ill, or disaster survivors. For very young children, trauma-reexperiencing symptoms often manifest in repetitive play that is devoid of fun or creativity and that may resemble the content or emotions of the traumatic event. If the child is mobile, they may physically avoid reminders of the traumatic event. Alternatively, if the child is not yet mobile, they may avoid eye contact or, in the case of abuse or neglect, noticeably may be distraught by the presence of the abusive caregiver. These avoidance symptoms manifest in terms of the child's developmental capacity.

A diagnosis of PTSD in young children is made using the same three criteria that are used to diagnose PTSD in adults: reexperiencing, avoidance, and hyperarousal (Coates & Gaensbauer, 2009; Levendosky, Huth-Bocks, Semel, & Shapiro, 2002).

To further elaborate, Lenore Terr (1991) described two types of trauma among children. Type I refers to child victims who had experienced a single traumatic event. Type II trauma refers to child victims who experienced multiple traumatic events such as ongoing incest or child abuse. Research demonstrates that most children who experienced a single traumatic event had detailed memories of the event but did not experience dissociation or memory loss. In contrast, child survivors experiencing multiple or repetitive incest and child sexual abuse trauma exhibited dissociative processes, recurring trance-like states, depression, suicidal ideation and suicide attempts, sleep disturbances, and, to a lesser degree, self-mutilation and PTSD (Ford, 2014).

Neurodevelopment and Plasticity

From a neurodevelopmental perspective, the human body reacts to extremely stressful situations by the brain's activation of the HPA system flooding the central nervous system with neurotransmitters, such as cortisol and norepinephrine. The HPS activation causes some individuals to experience a fight or flight response to the stressful situation (Kalat, 2013). Neuropeptides are small protein messengers that neurotransmitters use to communicate. Neuropeptide Y (NPY) is abundant and widespread in the human brain and has been evidenced as providing protection and mediating resilience (Enman, Sabban, McGonigle, & Van Bockstaele, 2015) during extreme stress. Studies attribute superior performance, positive feelings of self-confidence, and lower psychological stress during interrogation simulations in soldiers with the increased presence of NPY (Morgan et al., 2000; Morgan et al., 2001; Morgan et al., 2002).

The manifestation of emotions involves striatal (putamen, caudate, nucleus accumbens) brain regions that are stimulated by input or afferents from the cortex and selectively alter sensory perception via the thalamus. The hypothalamus, a small region of the brain, modulates bodily states by producing the production of neuropeptides while engaging the autonomic nervous system (Heim & Nemeroff, 2001). The limbic system governs emotions, attention and memories, and arousal as well as conscious responses based on the emotional significance of perceptual and memory retention data (Milad et al., 2007). It organizes responses based on the general context, including previous experiences and current situations (Bremner, 2008; Ford, 2009a).

Neural plasticity also known as neuroplasticity, brain plasticity, and cortical plasticity, is a developmental process over the lifespan. Plasticity refers to the capacity of the central nervous system (CNS) to alter its existing cortical structures (anatomy, organization) and functions (physiological mechanisms or processes) in response to experience, learning, training, or injury (Ballantyne, Spilkin, Hesselink, & Trauner, 2008; Hubel & Wiesel, 1970; Kolb, Gibb, & Robinson, 2003). In sum, brain structure and function are use dependent.

Researchers typically "map" brain structures and functions to indicate which region of the brain responds to what stimuli resulting in a particular understanding or representation (Buonomano & Merzenich, 1998). When an individual obtains new skills and information, the experience changes the neural "maps" (Wall, Xu, & Wang, 2002). The explication of these cognitive and motor activities and their consequential synaptic pathways have been entitled *brain fitness*. Brain fitness must be intellectually stimulating and physically appropriate to bring about maximal benefits to the aging brain (Colcombe et al., 2006). Actively engaging in physical, motor, or intellectual exercises and multisensory stimulation is believed to prevent functional decline and preserve cognitive functions. Brain fitness creates structural and functional changes like neural reorganizations of the brain including the development of new neurons (neurogenesis) and glial cells (gliogenesis), creates new and strengthens existing synaptic connections (synaptogenesis), and creates new blood vessels (Buonomano & Merzenich, 1998; Cotman & Berchtold, 2002; Dong & Greenough, 2004; Ming & Song, 2005; Voelcker-Rehage & Willimczik, 2006; Ponti, Peretto, & Bonfanti, 2008). Consequently, activity-dependent neural plasticity is induced by extensive and brief-intensive practice (Ziemann, Iliać, Pauli, Meintzschel, & Ruge, 2004) and expands the size of adult gray matter in the posterior and lateral parietal sites (Draganski et al., 2006).

Adolescent Development and Crises

Adolescence, a socially constructed phase of development occurs between the ages of 13 and 19 and is characterized by the ability for abstract thought (Piaget, 1952). Developmental tasks of adolescence are many and varied. The transition from childhood into adolescence signals puberty, sexual maturation and attraction, independence from caregivers, maturing peer relationship, differentiation of morals, values and personal ethics, social role adoption, and career exploration (Havighurst, 1949). Developmental crises are a normal part of development and occur across the lifespan. For example, identity crises are common in adolescents (Kidwell, Dunham, Bacho, Pastorino, & Portes, 1995). However, normal aspects of development—acknowledging one's sexual orientation—can cause distress, confusion, impulsivity, and impaired coping. The crisis may be due to the intake of new stimuli that cannot or has yet to be incorporated into an individual's reality because of developmental constraints. This distress continues until it is reconciled. During adolescents, the prefrontal cortex continues to develop and refine executive functioning, allowing for improved coordination and management of thinking and behavior (Choudhury, Blakemore, & Charman, 2006). Age-appropriate interpersonal experiences during this developmental period solidify personality and identity formation influencing adulthood (Smith & Handler, 2007).

Kanel (2012) identified typical adolescent situations that can evolve into crises for some individuals. For example, adolescents simultaneously seek and test the extent or boundaries of their independence, their environment, and caregivers' nurturance. Appropriate testing by teens and congruent caregivers' responses reinforce attachment and promote individuation and self-efficacy. Inappropriate testing and incongruent or destructive caregiver responses may lead teens into dangerous, risky, or novel behaviors involving violence, illegal drugs, or illicit sex. Adolescents' capacity to negotiate their autonomy and independence is in large part dependent on their reaction to family/caregiver structure, feedback, and temperament.

Regarding adolescent brain development, Giedd et al. (1999) noted the brain continues to increase in total volume until 14 years of age. According to Lenroot and Giedd (2006), a longitudinal magnetic resonance imaging (MRI) result demonstrates that human brain frontal and parietal grey matter volume peaks at about 14 years of age before deteriorating. The decrease in frontal and parietal grey matter volume is probably due to synaptic loss during adolescence. Many speculate the brain develops in response to experience and pertinent environmental needs—the "use it or lose it theory." Synaptic pruning is a process by which redundant synapses overproduced in the early years of life are eliminated. In comparison to general development of structures in the infant or child brain, the adolescent brain is more specific. Indeed, neuro-developments are taking place in specific regions like the limbic system and prefrontal cortex (PFC). The limbic system is responsible for pleasure seeking and reward processing, emotional responses, and sleep regulation. The PFC manages the area responsible for executive functions like decision making, organization, impulse control, and planning (Blakemore & Robbins, 2012). Connected with these important changes are personality traits, including high novelty seeking and low harm avoidance (Cloninger, Sigvarsson, & Bohman, 1988; Wills, Vaccaro, & McNamara, 1994). Maturation occurs in all areas of the adolescent's life and simultaneously promotes individuation and independence, which, in turn, increases the risk of harm, crises, and, for some, psychological disorders. Results of the National Comorbidity Survey Replication study of over 9,000 participants identified 14 years of age as the most common age for onset of a variety of mood, eating, and substance abuse disorders as well as psychosis and schizophrenia (Kessler et al., 2005). Important neuronal developments continue into adolescence and despite encountering crises, the adolescent brain has significant neural plasticity and high ability to change (Spear, 2013).

Adolescents in crises often encounter disturbed peer and family relationships, isolation, self-recrimination, and impaired academic performance not experienced in childhood. The calamitous flood at Buffalo Creek in 1972 illustrates this differential responding. On the night of February 26th, the coal slurry impound dam #3, located on a hillside, burst, flooding 16 coal-mining towns of Logan County, West Virginia. The consequences were catastrophic; 125 individuals killed, 1,121 injured, and over 4,000 individuals lost their homes (Stern, 1972). Two years after the Buffalo Creek Disaster, adolescents affected by the disaster were found to have higher levels of distress than younger children (Green et al., 1991). A major factor contributing to this tragedy was a loss of community as well as a belief in duplicity on the part of the mining company whose carelessness led to the disaster.

Adolescents traumatized by a crisis or traumatic event feel isolated and alone when peers are unable or unwilling to offer support. The presence of physical injuries may exacerbate their fragile self-concept and impair their fit with a peer group. Psychological injuries may result in confusion, withdrawal and isolation, antisocial behavior, suicidal ideation, academic failure, alcohol and drug abuse, sleep disturbance, depression, legal problems, and a host of physical complaints (Ford, Hartman, Hawke, & Chapman, 2008; Gordon, Farberow, & Maida, 1999; Halpern & Tramontin, 2007). Neural plasticity aids the adolescent's coping with change and crises and is bolstered by more mature cognitive, language, and decision-making skills.

Adulthood and Older Age

In the latter stages of human development, individuals continue physical maturation, adopting adult roles, relationships, and responsibilities and have capacity for empathy and intimacy. The adult brain maintains its plasticity as one encounters their career, marriage, children, financial responsibilities, and, toward the end of this stage, the effects of aging. Recent research findings on the adult brain indicate they continue to change and develop in response to external stimuli (Sowell et al., 2004; Lenroot et al., 2007). Attachment in adults also continues and is based on the internal working models established in childhood. Adult attachment is defined as "the bond that exists between individuals who are emotionally connected to one another and who have primary significance in each other's lives" (Palmer & Lee, 2008, p. 163). Biologically, humans are driven to find and preserve intimate relationships with a select few.

Older adults face continual transitions as they age, some of which may invoke a crisis. Loss of one's intimate partner and status changes in vocation, health, and physical abilities (mobility, hearing, vision) impact one's sense of self, independence, and quality of life. Long-term care and end of life issues frequently involve adult children and family caregivers, particularly when the older adult's cognitive functioning is impaired.

Age Related Decline and Neural Plasticity

Gradual age-related decline in neural-behavioral functionality significantly influences adults 65 and older (Yan, Thomas, Stelmach, & Thomas, 2000). This includes a decline in cognitive, motor, social, psychological, and physical domains. In addition, some older adults experience increased anxiety, failing memory and waning attention, sluggish processing speeds, a decrease in motor control and learning capabilities, and greater behavioral unpredictability. The consequence of these changes can be neurodegenerative disorders like mild cognitive impairment (MCI), Alzheimer's disease (AD), and dementia as well as impacts to physical mobility and hearing. Changes in functionality challenge the quality of life, often require support and resources, and may be, as noted earlier, experienced as a crisis in and of itself. For a moment, consider how older individuals, with age-related declines might respond to crisis events. They may be confused because of impaired hearing and slower to react and process events. What seems like cognitive impairment is actually hearing loss. Clinicians, working with older adults in crisis, must ensure clear unambiguous communication/directives are delivered while facing clients. Active engagement, cognitive challenges, and physical activities stimulate neural plasticity, support physical fitness, and contribute to overall well-being.

Situational Crises

Both situational and developmental crisis events have a significant impact on individuals and society. Situational crisis arises out of unusual, unexpected, or unpredicted events like sexual violence, suicide, or an accident. Situational crises are "random, sudden, shocking, intense, and often catastrophic" (James & Gilliland, 2013; p. 17) impacting the individual, a system, or community. Recent situational crisis events include the human-initiated events like mass shootings at Stoneman Douglas High School or Tree of Life Synagogue and natural ones like the 2018 California wildfires or the 2019 floods in Nebraska.

Existential Crises

Existential crises are a turning point when one questions or considers their life's purpose and meaning, values, and responsibilities (James & Gilliland, 2013). For adolescents, existential crisis may be associated with identity development as they strive to understand who they are relative to their family and what they are *supposed* to be. Older adults may experience existential crises at transition points like marriage, vocational changes (new careers or retirement), and age-related changes in health and status. At its core, an existential crisis signals the individual that their way of being in the world no longer works. Faced with this dilemma, individuals experience anxiety and, for some, despair as they consider their beliefs and assumptions about freedom and responsibility, limitations and mortality, feelings of isolation, and life's meaning. This category of crisis can be challenging to identify since there are few, if any, outward signs of the experience; however, many individuals describe tumultuous or confusing inner experiences, such as depression, apathy, general dissatisfaction, lack of mental acuity, lethargy, and inability to focus and accomplish tasks (Cavaiola & Colford, 2006).

Psychiatric

While not everyone who meets the diagnostic criteria for a diagnosis within the DSM–5 of the American Psychiatric Association experiences a crisis, several psychiatric disorders may result in sense of crisis for those who suffer as well as their support system. A psychiatric crisis may be a component or a symptom of the disorder, particularly personality or anxiety disorders, and interferes with one's ability to effectively cope with a crisis. For example, an individual diagnosed with generalized anxiety disorder may feel a sense of fear when asked to leave their apartment during a fire. Their anxiety, fright/fear response, and hesitation to evacuate escalate the risk of harm to them and others. Similarly, an individual experiencing a dissociative fugue wanders away with no explanation or intention causing a crisis for family members who are terrified. Once the fugue remits, the individual and their family will deal with different categories of crisis, individual and situational.

Traumatic

A traumatic crisis is caused by a sudden, unanticipated, and intense event. The acute emotional shock and temporary feeling of being overwhelming may lead some to appraisal the event as life threatening. Traumatic crisis events impel those experiencing crisis to immediately rely on habitual coping strategies as opposed to depending on coping strategies specific to the crisis event. Traumatic crisis events include nature- and human-initiated crises.

Ecosystemic Crises

An ecosystemic crisis originates from natural- or human-caused events. Akin to a disaster, an ecosystemic crisis negatively affects individuals within groups and communities (James & Gilliland, 2013) rather than a single individual. Earthquakes, epidemics, financial meltdowns, and terrorist attacks are examples of this type of crisis that requires advanced preparation, planning and communication, and resource management plans.

Nature of Crises

James and Gilliland (2017) offer a comprehensive array of crisis definitions in two categories: individual and systemic. Individual crises occur when one perceives an incident as unbearable and believes they possess insufficient resources and coping strategies to respond. Without support or assistance, the crisis may lead to emotional dysregulation, impaired cognition, ruptures in relationships, and behavioral acting out. In contrast, a systemic crisis occurs when response systems (medical, social, or governmental) cannot contain or control an event, and services, rather than individuals, are overwhelmed. The crisis event causes organizations, ecosystems, and societies to react, psychologically and physically, and may result in environmental or interpersonal volatility. In sum, the two categories provide helping professionals a vantage point and conceptual framework for the crisis event. Individual crisis definitions promote the experience of the individual while in crisis, whereas the systemic crisis definitions delineate a contextual experience based on interdependence and multiple crisis-oriented forces moving simultaneously.

Individual Crises

Grieving

Grief or bereavement affects every person at some point of their lives. Whether it be a parent or caregiver, a child, a partner, or another loved one, someone important to us will die and we experience their loss. For many, grief is expected to be a short-term experience as codified in many companies' two- to three-day bereavement leave benefits. However, intensity and length of grief not only varies from person to person, but from incident to incident and culture to culture. No two occurrences or reactions are the same. The American Psychiatric Association (2013) describes typical grieving as an "intense yearning or longing for the deceased, intense sorrow and emotional pain, and preoccupation with the deceased or the circumstances of the death" (p. 194). However, when symptoms persist for at least 12 months for adults or six months for children, grief is considered pathological and may result in a diagnosis of Persistent Complex Bereavement Disorder (p. 789). Grieving, not categorized in the *DSM*, may be associated with a loss of status—employment, divorce, homelessness; changes in functionality (age-related decline in mobility, independence, and sexual functioning); or longing for an earlier time. These experiences may be as disruptive as diagnosable disorders.

Suicide

Suicide or self-directed violence includes acts of fatal and nonfatal suicide attempts and is distinguished from nonsuicidal intentional self-harm—cutting or self-mutilation (Meyer et al., 2010). Suicide is the tenth leading cause of death among Americans (Centers for Disease Control and Prevention [CDC], 2012). In 2011, someone in the United States committed suicide every 13.3 minutes. According to the same report, women were more likely to have suicidal thoughts or ideations and men were more likely to die by suicide due to the lethality of their means. Evidence suggests that as we age our suicide risk increases. The highest suicide rate was among people ages 45 to 64, followed by those 85 and older. According to the Center for Disease Control and Prevention (2017) suicide rates were highest for American Indian/Alaska natives, non-Hispanic males and females, followed by White, non-Hispanic males and females. Lesbian, gay, bisexual, and transgendered youth are almost three times more likely to contemplate suicide and five times as likely to attempt suicide than their heterosexual peers.

Substance Abuse

Substances are divided into 10 classes, including caffeine, tobacco, alcohol, cannabis, inhalants, hallucinogens, opioids, sedatives, stimulants, and other substances. These substances trigger the reward system, which is directly implicated in the strengthening of memories and behaviors (American Psychiatric Association, 2013). Substance use becomes abuse when it is chronic and unremitting and leads to a chemical addiction characterized by the development of tolerance and withdrawal (American Psychiatric Association, 2013). It is important to note that substance abuse and misuse impacts more than the individual. Abuse and misuse often occur within the context of a family or community and affects the quality and nature of interpersonal relationships, employability, financial resources, housing, crime, and interpersonal violence.

Diagnosis of Chronic or Terminal Illness

The diagnosis of a chronic terminal illness impacts individuals and families on many levels. How one responds to the diagnosis depends largely on their access to resources (Ziebland & Kokanovic, 2012) and premorbid functioning. The disease or illness alters the course of individual's lives and roles (Papadopoulos, 1995), relationships, employability, spirituality/religious beliefs, and finances. Family systems change as partners or children become caretakers or family members take on unfamiliar responsibilities or respond to situations for which they are unprepared. Individuals diagnosed with a chronic or terminal illness confront issues of mortality, organizing their affairs and uncertainty, and grieve the loss of normalcy, autonomy, and their future. Crisis originates from one's perceptions about their change in status and subsequent adjustment to those changes.

Disability or Injury

Accidents that result in partial or permanent disability or injury are like traumatic crises because many occur suddenly and create a significant emotional shock to the individual. Examples of injury-inducing incidents include traffic accidents, work injuries, and physical assaults, among others (Koren, Arnon, & Klein, 1999). Injuries can result in disabilities like traumatic brain injuries, psychological disorders such as PTSD, paraplegia, blindness, loss of hearing, or other physical disabilities (Diedericks, 2014). Because of the sudden nature of many of these incidents, a long-term traumatic response may be elicited irrespective of the severity of the injury (Koren, Arnon, & Klein, 1999). Injuries and permanent disabilities impact family systems as roles may change to incorporate new expectations for family members as the person injured heals, or if permanent role changes are necessary. There may also be loss of income, legal involvement, or lack of access to adequate medical care that can result in a crisis for many individuals and families involved in accidents (Diedericks, 2014).

Group or Subsystem and Community Crises

Family Crisis

There are many ways in which families experience crisis including child or sibling abuse, intimate partner violence, neglect, or violence originating outside the family, financial hardships, homelessness, and immigration status. Wolf and Pillemer (1989) defined abuse as the infliction of physical pain or injury, or physical coercion (p. 18) through physical, sexual, and emotional violence. They include psychological/emotional abuse—anguish, name-calling, shaming, and humiliation—in their definition of family violence. Wolf and Pillemer (1989) also identified two types of neglect: *active neglect* or the refusal or failure to fulfill a caretaking obligation and *passive neglect* or the unintentional failure to fulfill a caretaking obligation because of "inadequate knowledge, laziness, infirmity or disputing the value of prescribed services" (p. 18). These neglect and abuse occur in all types of families to all kinds of individuals at any stage of life.

Elder abuse is similar in scope and type to that faced by infants, children, and adults. It ranges from the psychological, physical, sexual—and extends to violations of rights and material abuse—exploiting an aging person for material gain (Lau & Kosberg, 1979, as cited in Wolf & Pillemer, 1989). The additional types of abuse are indicative of vulnerable adults with adult rights but perhaps diminished capacity in some area of life. State by state, definitions of elder abuse vary. Some states define elder abuse only when there is an active abuser while others characterize elder abuse as an aging person not being able to meet their own needs and there is no intervention to assist them (Wolf & Pillemer, 1989). As a person ages into older adulthood, their vulnerability to abuse rises due to increased frailty and vulnerability and decreased ability to carry out everyday tasks. Elders often depend on others to meet their basic needs to rise (Wolf & Pillemer, 1989). In American culture, older adults are not valued as evidenced by the way we relegate them to out-of-home facilities versus in-home care and the lack of adequate community programming that meets their needs and interests. The isolation and devaluation contribute to a loss of meaning (Newell, 1961, as cited in Wolf & Pillemer, 1989) and potential existential crises.

Aggression

Siann (1985) defined aggression as "involving an intent to inflict hurt or appear superior to others" (as cited in Loue, 2001, p. 1). Violence, on the other hand, was defined by Gelles and Straus (1979) as "an act carried out with the intention or perceived intention of physically hurting another person" (as cited in Loue, 2001, p. 1). This not only includes physical violence but also sexual assault. Also prominent in intimate partner violence is emotional abuse, such as intense criticism,

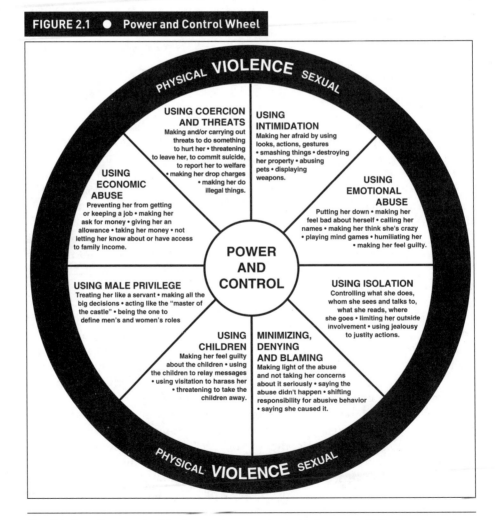

FIGURE 2.1 ● Power and Control Wheel

Note: This figure illustrates the eight elements of power and control in the context of intimate partner violence.
Source: National Center on Domestic and Sexual Violence, 2014.

harassment, control, or withholding of basic needs (Karakurt, Smith, & Whiting, 2014). Intimate partner violence has less to do with the need of a person to inflict physical violence on their partner, and more about the need for power and control. Figure 2.1 presents the Power and Control Wheel that is used commonly to educate both survivors and perpetrators of intimate partner violence.

Divorce

According to the American Psychological Association (APA; 2014), 40% to 50% of marriages end in divorce. The impact of the divorce process extends well beyond the dissolution of a marriage, particularly if there are children involved (Blaisure & Saposnek, 2008). The process and aftermath of divorce often result in crises that stem from adjustment to living without a partner or without one parent. Family functioning is more difficult when there is conflict and blaming between the partners or spouses. Other common stressors associated with divorce can include loss of custody, emotional support, economic hardship, decline in parental control, changes in family roles, and changes in identity (Amato, 2000, p. 1271). Like other crises, it is important for clinicians to note, experiencing the same event does not equal experiencing it in the same way. Some members of the family, including partners, children, or grandparents, may feel relief while others experience mourning, loss, anger, and frustration.

Teen Pregnancy

Teen parents, particularly teen mothers, are highly stigmatized in the United States (Smith-Battle, Lorenz, & Leander, 2013). The stigma originates from religious and gendered expectations of young women to be pure, virtuous, and virginal prior to marriage in contrast to young men who are expected have sexual conquests and to sow their wild oats as a rite of passage. These differential expectations extend to teen mothers' decisions regarding the pregnancy. Should she marry the father, raise the child alone or with family, consider adoption, or abortion, and to what degree, if any, should she consider the father's perspective? Cultural or religious stigma and the resulting shame create significant barriers for teen mothers and fathers and accelerate role transition, delays of post-secondary education or desired vocation, encourages premature marriage or coupling and may put the infant at risk. Teen moms are stereotyped as unmotivated, irresponsible, neglectful (Lewis, Scarborough, Rose, & Quirkin, 2007; Usdansky, 2009), and sexually promiscuous. As a result, depression and other psychological disorders are common among teen mothers (Reid & Meadows-Oliver, 2007, as cited in Smith-Battle, Lorenz, & Leander, 2013). Many adolescent fathers experience psychological distress whether they were active in co-parenting, absent from parenting, or if the pregnancy was terminated. In a study of 2,522 young men (Buchanan & Robbins, 1990) first surveyed as seventh grade students, 15% were involved in a nonmarital adolescent pregnancy. At age 21, they reported shortened educational experiences, greater rates of divorce and job dissatisfaction, and lower income. Unexpected teen pregnancy is often viewed as a crisis because its unplanned nature creates disequilibrium in both family systems and alters the lives of all involved. Families must consider how to inform others of the pregnancy and decide whether to continue or terminate the pregnancy. If the pregnancy is continued to term, matters of kinship care or adoption need to be addressed as well as anxieties about the future (American Academy of Child and Adolescent Psychiatry, 2012).

Hate Crimes

A hate crime is "a crime in which a victim is targeted because of the victim's real or perceived group membership, which can be defined by race, religion, sexual orientation, gender, gender identity, ethnicity/nationality, disability, political affiliation, and so on" (Stotzer, 2007, as cited in Cheng, Ickes, & Kenworthy, 2013, p. 761). There are three types of hate crimes—crimes against people involving intimidation, simple assault, aggravated assault, and murder (Cheng, Ickes, & Kenworthy, 2013); crimes against property like vandalism, arson, larceny/theft, burglary, and robbery; and crimes against society like the *Pulse* nightclub shooting or terrorist attacks (Federal Bureau of Investigation, 2014). Hate crimes impact the victim's mental health and result in anxiety, depression, or PTSD and decreased self-worth. Consistent with many historically marginalized populations, those victimized by hate crimes experience disempowerment and believe the world is no longer safe (Hein & Scharer, 2012).

Relocation

Families or individuals relocate for new employment, foreclosure, disruption, death, divorce, military assignment, or retirement. Relocation can create crisis for individuals and families due to the loss of a support network (Sluzki, 1992) or unfamiliarity of the new location. People who relocate may experience grief, isolation, uncertainty, loneliness, and difficulty adjusting to their new location or setting. For adolescents, the crisis may be magnified because of the loss of security and belonging to their previous peer group. For couples, relocation is a source of stress because one partner must find employment, child care, community resources, or a new educational program due to their partner's relocation. Relocation can also result in initial isolation requiring couples to lean on each other for support in new and unexpected ways to meet needs that were previously met by others.

Financial Instability, Poverty, and Unemployment

During the U.S. economic crisis of 2008, the suicide rate accelerated by 3% to 8% (Reeves et al., 2012). This pattern continued throughout other countries also affected by the financial crisis, such as England and Wales (Kinderman, 2014). Financial instability is associated with sharp rises in foreclosures (Cagney, Browning, Iveniuk, & English, 2014). This group of researchers identified the need for crisis support among people and communities who experience high rates of financial instability, poverty, or unemployment. Foreclosure and community financial crisis are not just limited to the individuals and families they affect; it can also result in lower-density communities, degradation of available housing due to lack of maintenance, and a decrease in community investment among remaining residents (Cagney et al., 2014).

Community Crises

Community crises or socially generated crises are not easily defined (Enander, Lajskjö, & Tedfeldt, 2010) and change the very fabric of a community. Examples of community crises include large-scale events like the Flint Water crisis or personal data breaches and smaller scale events like a crime spree in a small community or high-profile hostage situation. Community crises are defined as any event that affects an identified community, results in loss of status for the community, evokes mistrust of authorities, or a sense of shame for the community. While there is a gradual return to normalcy after a community crisis event, conflicts may keep occurring, sometimes for generations.

Acute and Chronic Crises

Clinicians can offer short-term interventions to help individuals in crisis and are not expected to conduct long-term psychotherapy. Thus, as a crisis counselor, you are likely to find yourself coordinating ongoing care and services for those who may require longer-term care. Crisis care and coordination begin with assessment and evaluation of how and where clients experience disequilibrium and the suppleness of their functioning across all domains. Through an effective assessment, crisis counselors determine the acuity, chronicity, duration, and severity of the crisis, extent of the client's immobilization, resources available, lethality, and likely success of specific interventions (Kanel, 2012).

Crises vary in type, intensity, and severity. Clinicians respond to clients' acute crises by conducting one of several standard assessments such as a suicide checklist, mini-mental status exam, or triage assessment followed by application of appropriate and available resources designed to help the individual in need. The assessment helps you determine the level of need and needed resources. Consider the following example: Pat, mentioned earlier in the chapter, was informed this morning that he and others were laid off from their jobs. Pat has worked at the same firm as an accountant for 15 years. He walks into your counseling center, despondent and tearful, and tells the receptionist, "I don't want to live anymore. I am an embarrassment to my wife and kids. I want my boss to die. I need some help." The clinician conducts a clinical assessment or interview, reviews Pat's completed suicide or homicide checklist, and responds to his devastation and embarrassment over the loss of his job and fears of the future. Pat reports he is embarrassed to tell his wife and children. After about 30 minutes, the clinician and Pat normalize his grief and shock, explore how he has handled previous crises, and discuss future-oriented options like calling his wife to discuss the layoff. Although upset and tearful, Pat expresses a future orientation in his marketable skills, the generous separation package from his company, and his knowledge, deep down, that his wife will be supportive—she always has been. Pat is working his way back to state of precrisis equilibrium, or close to it, and can vocalize how he might utilize his previous ways of coping.

Chronic crises are approached differently. Individuals experiencing chronic crises benefit from reviewing their current coping skills, accessing community and familial resources, and support from the clinician. Chronic crises may include health or persistent mental health issues, child neglect, and the effects of poverty. Those experiencing chronic crises can be urged or supported to recall times when they successfully negotiated the crisis, returned to a sense empowerment, and saw themselves as capable rather than overwhelmed. Crisis counseling is not intended to provide long-term, in-depth psychotherapy, thus it is important to refer individuals with long-term, life histories of crisis to a helping or support professional with experience and resources to assist on an ongoing basis.

Models of Crisis Counseling

Common Crisis Concepts and Stages

We begin this section with an exploration of several universally understood concepts related to crisis counseling. As noted in Chapter 1, Yeager and Roberts (2003) and Young (1995) identified constructs related to the personal impact of a crisis situation, specifically, spatial dimensions or proximity to the crisis event, sense of a subjective time clock, and the perception the event will reoccur. Along with this information we add the common stages of a crisis.

Common stages and progression of crisis events begin with the precrisis status including personal demographics and ways of being. Next, an event occurs resulting in psychological disruption or disequilibrium and perception of threat. Threat appraisal and attempts at coping follow. Threats that are considered manageable with current resources support the individual's return to a state of equilibrium. When threats are considered overwhelming and beyond the individual's resources and coping skills, a crisis state emerges distressing the individual. In the sections that follow, we present crisis intervention and response models, ordered chronologically, utilized in crisis counseling. As you review each model, consider the progression, changes, and refinement of concepts and intervention strategies.

The Equilibrium Model of Crisis Counseling, Intervention, and Management

Erich Lindemann (1944) and Gerald Caplan (1964) were the architects of the equilibrium model. Lindemann's theory argued crisis intervention should be utilized when one experiences loss. Gerald Caplan expanded on Lindemann's theory with the premise that one's current state becomes impaired when they experience a crisis and cannot utilize adequate or traditional coping mechanisms to restore a sense of psychological equilibrium. If one's state of disequilibrium goes unaddressed and normal coping skills remain insufficient or inaccessible, then one falls into a state of temporary psychological distress (Wang, Chen, Yebing, Liu, & Miao, 2010). The equilibrium/disequilibrium paradigm attends to individuals whose normal coping strategies fail during the midst and in aftermath of a crisis. The model addresses disturbed equilibrium, brief therapy, clients working through the grief, and restoration of equilibrium (Brown, Shiang, & Bongar, 2003).

Empirical evidence supports the use of the equilibrium model in a cross-cultural setting. Wang, Chen, Yebing, Liu, and Miao (2010) evaluated the equilibrium model's effectiveness with Chinese families admitted to a hospital setting on an emergency basis. The authors sought participants whose family members were admitted to an ER, received some level of treatment, and died within 24 hours due to the gravity and extent of their wounds or presenting problem. Research participants were administered the Symptom Checklist–90 (SCL-90) Questionnaire three days after the death of their family member and were randomly assigned to either the intervention or control group. Participants receiving the intervention were given a four-step intervention that included self-introduction, expression of feelings, information to prevent negative feelings, and creation of effective support to increase coping capacity through appropriate training. Participants in the control group received no intervention. One month later, participates were again administered the SCL-90. The findings indicate that while both groups showed positive change, results for participants receiving the intervention reported fewer physical ailments and a greater reduction in the symptoms of depression, anxiety, and phobic anxiety as measured by the SCL-90.

The equilibrium model is focused on *psychological homeostasis* (Brown et al., 2003). As mentioned previously, crisis disrupts one's typical functioning or homeostasis as traditional coping mechanisms fail. Clinicians assess the client's current functioning and employ crisis counseling to contextualize events and aid the client's return to their precrisis functioning. It is important to note that a psychological crisis may last for four to six weeks, thus, it is imperative to assess and address signs of disequilibrium during each interaction before issues develop into more persistent concerns.

Gerald Caplan described the basics of crisis intervention in his landmark book, *Principles of Preventive Psychiatry* (1964). Effective interventions like conflict management and social skill instruction promote a positive-growth orientation and reduce factors known to contribute to psychological impairment. Caplan described a four-stage model of crisis reaction: first, tension is created and associated with the crisis event. Next, the client is unable to handle the degree tension and feels powerless to manage the crisis. Third, coping mechanisms fail and the client enters a state of despair, leading the client to seek different and usually less effective coping strategies. Caplan's interventions address the importance of identifying and employing alternative coping mechanisms until the client returns to a state of equilibrium. Zhang and Lester (2008) found clients who did not develop sufficient coping skills early in treatment were at increased risk for suicidal ideation, suicidal attempts, and psychological illnesses. Zhang et al.'s findings confirm the significance of using the appropriate assessments and interventions at the onset of a crisis to aid the client's return to the precrisis state; time is of the essence! Generally, research indicates that providing some form of crisis counseling after a crisis or trauma, aids one's return to equilibrium. The equilibrium model will not prevent posttraumatic stress disorder or any other diagnosable condition; rather the techniques are designed to contextualize events and support the individual's functioning. Following the establishment of their model, Lindemann and Caplan went on to collaborate on other crisis-oriented projects such as the Wellesley Project. Members of the Wellesley

Project (Caplan, 1964) focused on assisting individuals through a traumatic experience, specifically women who lost an infant or delivered a differently abled child. Women in this group received preventative psychiatry, which entailed early mental health consultation and support. Clinicians sought to lower participants' emotional distress to a nonacute level through coping strategies, appropriate referrals, physical exercise, and attendance of consultation groups.

The ABC-X Model of Crisis Counseling, Intervention, and Management

Reuben Hill (1949, 1958) applied crisis theory to families. The ABC-X Model of Crisis came into fruition because of Hill's research on families experiencing separation and reunion during World War II. The main thrust of Hill's ABC-X Model of Crisis focuses on the precrisis variables in families. The ABC-X model implies an interaction between (A) the crisis provoking stressful event(s) and (B) the family's resources and (C) the meanings/perceptions the family attaches to (A). The crisis (X) represents an acute state of disequilibrium and immobilization of the family system (Boss & Sheppard, 1988) and is an outcome of the interaction of ABC. The double ABC-X model of crisis counseling, intervention, and management expanded on Hill's 1958 model and was based on the longitudinal work of McCubbin and Patterson (1983). McCubbin and Patterson worked with families of Vietnam servicemen designated as missing in action or held as prisoners of war. McCubbin and Patterson added five considerations to predict and explain family's recovery in the post crisis/stress phase: additional life stressors and strains; psychological, intrafamilial, and social resources; changes in the family's definition; family-based coping strategies; and a range of possible outcomes.

The double ABC-X model displays the double A as the provoking stressor plus the buildup of other stressors, changes occurring unrelated to the event, and any consequences of attempts to cope. The family experiences greater intensity and the crisis seems more severe. The double B describes utilization of resources available to the family at the time of the crisis, tangible and intangible resources, plus resources external to the family system designed to address the severity of the crisis. The double C describes family members' perceptions and meaning assigned to the original provoking stressor, accumulated stressors, resources, and how best to restore stability to the family. Perceptions are influenced by religious beliefs, family and cultural values, and how the situation may have been framed or reframed. Finally, McCubbin and Patterson's Double X occurs later than the original X factor and includes the concept of adaptation. Adaptation is an outcome variable involving positive changes in functioning and perception and the degree to which long-term change occurred in response to the demands of the crisis event. It is important to note that adaptation is context dependent and what appears to be success for one family will differ from what looks like success in another family. Patterson (1988) noted the goal of the double ABC-X model was to explain the differentiation in postcrisis responding among families.

Psychosocial Transition Model of Crisis Counseling, Intervention, and Management

Parkes (1971) coined the phrase *psychosocial transition model of crisis counseling*, drawing on the works of Alfred Adler's Individual Psychology Theory (1956), Salvador Minuchin's Structural Family Theory (1974) and Erik Erikson's Psychosocial Development Theory (1997) as she developed the Psychosocial Transition model. The Psychosocial Transition model for crisis counseling asks clinicians to collaborate with clients to assess internal and external difficulties influencing the current crisis, aid them in choosing alternatives to current behaviors and attitudes, and encourage use of environmental resources. The focus of this model is on the client and their social system. Crisis counseling outcomes are limited when clients fail to modify social situations and do not accept or understand the dynamics of their relationships or the impact on adaptation. This model is most effective after the acute phase of the crisis. The psychosocial transition model assumes internal and external factors produce psychological and social disturbances that accompany the crisis. The concepts of psychosocial transition and posttraumatic growth are consistent with existential theory. Confronted with one's mortality, clients reevaluate and redefine life goals and priorities to emerge with a greater investment in and appreciation of life. The greater the magnitude of the threat posed by the stressor, the greater the opportunity for growth.

The psychosocial transition model has been examined by researchers. Studies involving parental adjustment to childhood diabetes (Lowes, Gregory, & Lyne, 2005), mental health, and coping mechanisms during war time (Carballo et. al, 2004) and post-traumatic growth in breast cancer survivors (Cohen & Numa, 2011) demonstrate initial efficacy of the model. Findings indicate the category, timing, and amount of social assistance provided those in crisis influenced the positive or negative outcomes of the event (Almedom, 2005).

A crisis counselor using this model assesses and addresses clients' emotions and cognitions and resources and interpersonal support. According to the model, these factors can be problematic for a client to overcome and interfere with postcrisis event stability. Interventions associated with this model are grounded in cognitive theories and target modifying behaviors, attitudes, and environmental systems. Consider your client, Shamika, with whom you are working. Shamika and her family's home was consumed by fire. She seems stuck and believes she is doomed. Shamika is immobilized and distraught. She asks you why "do things like this only happened to me?" To challenge her irrational beliefs, you may inquire, "The fire was due to a lightning strike from a severe thunderstorm, and two of your neighbors' homes burned as well. How do you explain that this only happened to you?" Later, you may work with Shamika to adjust her language and thinking patterns by replacing *musts*, *oughts*, and *shoulds* with more personally accountable language like *choose*, *desire*, and *opt to*. Helping Shamika create a sense of personal agency with internal and external language should result in a change in her assumptions, beliefs, and ultimately, her behavior.

Psychological First Aid Model of Crisis Counseling, Intervention, and Management

The term psychological first aid (PFA) was first used by Raphael (1977) to describe the issues that emerged from an Australian railway disaster (as cited in James & Gilliland, 2017). The PFA model is akin to Maslow's (1943) theory of human motivation and prepotent needs. A prepotent need is one that has the greatest influence on our behavior. For example, those affected by the 2017 mass shooting in Las Vegas sought first to flee to safety, before seeking medical care, nourishment, psychological support, loving, or belonging. Need fulfillment is hierarchical. While numerous authors criticize Maslow's theory for its ethnocentrism and failure to distinguish the social and intellectual needs of those reared in individually oriented societies from those reared in collective-oriented societies, in times of crisis, the basic human need to be safe and secure take primacy. Like Maslow, the PFA model focuses the clinician's assessment on a similar hierarchy, beginning with physiological and safety needs, progressing to belonging, self-esteem, and self-actualization. Thus, the criticisms Maslow faced may also extend to the PFA model. We urge counselors to avoid a *one size fits all* approach to responding to client crises.

Ruzek et al. (2007) reported that PFA was created as the initial component of a comprehensive crisis response model aimed at alleviating the negative effects of post-trauma distress. Steps in the model include (a) contact and engagement through crisis team debriefing and assessment of the situation; (b) safety and comfort associated with empathy; (c) stabilization by meeting basic needs; information gathering like personal contact information; (d) practical assistance—providing a phone or a blanket; (e) connection with social supports; (f) coping instruction like deep breathing or positive self-talk, and linkage with nonemergent collaborative services. PFA provides empathy and support, resources, information, and education to those experiencing a crisis based on their most immediate needs.

Prior to traditional counseling, probing, or reexperiencing of a traumatic event, survivors must meet their basic needs. For example, PFA was the intervention of choice used by first responders in New York on 9/11 (Jackson-Cherry & Erford, 2010), and James and Gilliland (2013), in the immediate aftermath of Hurricane Katrina (James & Gilliland, 2013), reported, "Many counselors, social workers, and psychologists helped meet basic support needs of food, shelter, clothing, and other survival needs . . . before they ever did any counseling." (p. 19). Thus, PFA is best suited for individuals and groups surviving a traumatic event, terrorism, or mass disaster (Everly, Phillips, Kane, & Feldman, 2006).

The ACT Intervention Model for Acute Crisis and Trauma Treatment

Albert Robert's (2002) ACT Model of Crisis Counseling is a three-stage model emphasizing assessment of the presenting problem, connecting clients to support systems, and helping those in crisis work through the distress and emotional pain. This sequential intervention model integrates assessment and triage protocols with Robert's seven-stage crisis intervention model and was one of the first to address clinician self-care to avoid the negative effects of compassion fatigue and vicarious trauma. Self-care and counselor wellness are explored in greater detail in Chapter 8.

The acronym ACT stands for Assessment, Crisis Intervention, and Trauma Treatment. The *Assessment* component incorporates the psychiatric and psychological triage assessment and associated protocols. The clinician asks a series of questions or statements to determine the psychological and medical needs of the individual. Questions such as: Are you injured or hurt? Show me. Are you bleeding? Where and for how long? Please, tell me your name. Tell me where you are. Answers to these and other questions allow you to make time-sensitive decisions and involve other first responders. In this phase, client's concerns are triaged based on pre-agreed upon protocols. This assumes the clinician is aware of and has had training in those protocols. Hint: this means you are involved in your community. After the Assessment phase the clinician moves to the provision of *Crisis Intervention Strategies* including short-term (3–4) contacts to stabilize the client and connecting them with an appropriate support group, community relief groups, social services, and critical incident debriefing (Mitchell & Everly, 1993). The Crisis Intervention stage introduces Robert's Seven-Stage model (Roberts, 1996). *Trauma Treatment* is the final stage and incorporates interventions aimed at treating traumatic stress reactions, sequelae, and PTSD. This includes trauma interventions, trauma-informed treatment plans, recovery strategies, and the Ten Step Acute Trauma and Stress Management Protocol (Lerner & Shelton, 2001). In the ten steps, the clinician assesses for danger/lethality; determines the presence of physical and perceptual injuries; evaluates client responsiveness; addresses medical needs; observes and identifies presence of traumatic stress; introduces and connects the clinician; supports client telling of the trauma story for stabilization; listens actively; normalizes, validates, and educates; and encourages a present orientation and provides referrals. As with other models, the ACT model may not fit for all persons or in all settings the individual in context matters and the skilled counselor maintains a socially just mindset that emphasizes people over processes or models.

Cognitive Model of Crisis Counseling, Intervention, and Management

While Albert Ellis's Rational Emotive Behavior Therapy (REBT) and Aaron T. Beck's Cognitive Therapy (CT) are the foundation for the cognitive approach to counseling, neither specifically addressed crisis-situations. Roberts and Ottens (2005) are credited with the first cognitive model of crisis counseling, intervention, and management detailed in their 2005 article, "The Seven-Stage Crisis Intervention Model Road Map to Goal Attainment, Problem Solving, and Crisis Resolution." Robert's Seven-Stage Crisis Intervention Model (R-SSCIM) integrates brief cognitive therapy and crisis responding. The seven stages are: plan and conduct a thorough biopsychosocial and lethality/imminent danger assessment; make psychological contact and rapidly establish the collaborative relationship; identify the major problems, including crisis precipitants; encourage exploration of

feelings and emotions; generate and explore alternatives and new coping strategies; restore functioning through implementation of an action plan; and plan
follow-up sessions.

Interventions utilized within Robert's Seven Stage Crisis Intervention Model
are organized around the seven stages. Within the first stage, *Psychosocial and
Lethality Assessment*, clinicians conduct a biopsychosocial assessment; assess client's environmental supports and stressors; address medical needs and medications; assess current use of drugs and alcohol; explore client's internal and external
coping methods and resources, suicidal thoughts, and lethality; ascertain whether
the client has initiated a suicide attempt; and inquire about client potential for
self-harm. In the second stage, *Rapidly Establish Rapport*, the clinician establishes
an efficient and time-sensitive therapeutic alliance through culturally responsive
respect, acceptance, nonjudgmental attitudes, nonverbal behaviors such as eye
contact, physical proximity, clinical flexibility, and a positive attitude to instill
hope, reinforce treatment gains, and encourage resiliency. *Identify the Major Problems or Crisis Precipitants* is the third stage in which the clinician explores clients'
precipitating event(s) and prioritizes problems. The fourth stage, *Dealing With Feelings and Emotions* has the clinician encourage the client to verbalize their feelings
and stories related to their crisis. Clinicians use counseling skills such as active
listening, paraphrasing, reflections, and probing questions and may challenge
some elements to help reveal unfounded assumptions and errors in thinking. In
the fifth stage, *Generate and Explore Alternatives*, the clinician and client explore
alternative behaviors, thoughts, and feelings that worked for them in other crises.
In stage six, *Implement an Action Plan*, client and clinician devise a treatment plan
with action steps. Working together toward a positive outcome supports the client return to a sense of equilibrium. Lastly, stage seven, *Follow-Up*, describes how
clinicians practice continuity of care by following up with the client to monitor
the resolution of the crisis and assess the client's postcrisis functioning. Typically,
postcrisis assessments occur at least one month after your last session and include
an evaluation of the client's cognitions related to the crisis' precipitating event.
Questions like: In what manner, if any, are their thoughts managed? Do they
perseverate on the crisis? Do they occasionally think about the crisis? Additional
components evaluation examines the client's overall functioning, progress, need
for additional referrals, and coordination of treatment. If the client is engaged
with another clinician, ethical standards require coordination of care with the
current clinician being mindful of anniversary dates marking the event, deaths,
and other significant losses.

The Developmental-Ecological Model of Crisis Counseling, Intervention, and Management

Barbara and Thomas Collins provided a new perspective on crisis events
through their developmental-ecological model of crisis counseling. Their book,
Crisis and Trauma: Developmental-Ecological Model (2005) described crises from
developmental and environmental standpoints. The Collinsess considered the
developmental phase, age, and level of cognition of the individual in crisis as well

as the impact of the community surrounding those in crisis. According to Zubenko and Capozzoli (2002), the developmental-ecological practitioner observes the interrelationships between the client and the world around them. Appropriate and inappropriate developmental interactions are witnessed over time and the changes are considered when making crisis-related decisions (Volling, 2005). The model is grounded on the work of Bronfenbrenner's Ecological Systems Theory, Erikson's Life-Stage Virtues, and Piaget's Developmental Stages (Guiffrida & Douthit, 2007). The developmental-ecological model of crisis counseling does not offer a specific set of techniques; instead, this model promotes a strength-based perspective grounded in developmental theory. According to Anderson and Mohr (2003) the model ". . . underscores the importance of recognizing that a child's development is affected by the context in which development occurs . . . that can either enhance or impede their development of competencies relating to a specific stage" (p. 58). Clinicians are encouraged to look past the individual to the environmental context of their lives (Murray & Hudson-Barr, 2006) and promote a more socially just model of service that considers the person, their development, and their development in the context of their environment. Although this model is emerging, there is evidence to suggest this theory of crisis counseling may be helpful to those who experience emotional disturbance that disrupts a developmental stage (Anderson & Mohr, 2003). Guiffrida and Douthit (2007) stated this model may be useful in response to natural disaster, domestic violence, terrorism, accidental disasters, death, school crisis, health crisis, child abuse and neglect, and sexual assault.

The Contextual-Ecological Model of Crisis Counseling, Intervention, and Management

Rick Myer and Holly Moore (2006) developed the contextual-ecological model (also called crisis in context theory [CCT]). Crisis in Context Theory presented a formula to gauge the impact of a crisis on the individual and system surrounding the individual. The CCT model is also grounded in Bronfenbrenner's Ecological Systems Theory, theorizing that individuals develop in relation to both proximal and distal environmental influences. Additionally, CCT is influenced, to a degree, by Kurt Lewin's Field Theory, which asserts that behavior is a function of person and environment. Given that this theory is relatively new, there is little to no empirical support for its application. The professional literature does indicate contextual factors affect crisis situations, specifically that social support decreases depressive symptomology following a flood (Tyler, 2000); high postcrisis stress levels and loss of economic standing are highly correlated with social support (Sattler, et al. 2002); familiar surroundings preserve family cohesion and a sense of community post-disaster (Galante & Foa, 1986); and women, viewed as the main emotional support for a family, become particularly overwhelmed during a crisis and the family adapting to this change (Shumaker & Brownell, 1984).

Although Myer and Moore (2006) do not offer specific CCT interventions, they do promote several premises: (a) The effect of a crisis is consistent with the proximity to the crisis event; (b) reactions are particular to their systems, relationships, and individuals; (c) interactions of primary and secondary relationships influence recovery; and (d) the magnitude of change as well as the previous element are affected by time. The first premise asks you to discover the layers within a crisis. Essentially, the more a client discloses about their experience as it relates to a crisis, the better they will cope with the after effects. As the client elaborates on the macro and micro aspects of their experience, they begin to recall more details, achieve higher self-confidence, develop a more robust support system, and explore the deeper meaning attributed to their crisis. The second premise describes the reciprocal effect of the crisis on others and the degree of change triggered by the event. Recognizing interactions among primary and secondary relationships is essential to conceptualizing and effectively aiding those who have experienced a crisis. Primary relationships are defined as those which no intervening component mediates the relational connection like intimate partners or family members. Secondary relationships are indirect in nature and are mediated by indirect components of the crisis. The third premise addresses the degree of change triggered by the event and the degree to which a client and his or her systems modify their long- and short-term goals. The final premise of this model describes the discovery of the time factor. In general, as time passes, a crisis event has less impact and individuals and their systems are more likely to return to a state of equilibrium. This model brings attention to anniversary dates and holidays that may trigger a reexperiencing of the crisis and ask clinicians to thoughtfully explore the client's meaning of the experience, negative or positive. An example may be helpful. Joe is a 45-year-old Caucasian male living in southeast South Dakota. He owns several businesses and is a long-time resident. A nonmandatory evacuation order is issued for the Missouri River flooding, which passes through Joe's hometown. Joe and his family are torn between the decision to stay and protect their business or leave the area to be safe. Joe feels very anxious and is indecisive. He feels short-tempered and yells at his family about little things. Joe's family avoids him even though they need to prepare for the impending flood. Teri, Joe's wife, has been tearful; Max and Emma, their children, are now quiet and withdrawn. The more Max and Emma withdraw the more Joe yells to get their attention. Many of Joe's neighbors already evacuated. The flood comes; Joe and his family did not evacuate. Two of Joe's three businesses are incapacitated, and the family home is uninhabitable due to standing floodwaters. Joe is anxious and annoyed because he has not been able to run the day-to-day operations of his remaining business and cannot repair the other two. Orders go unfilled and Joe is sure his customers will go elsewhere. Teri's employer, located in a neighboring community, is not impacted by the flood, is supportive, and allows her to use sick time for days she's missed. Teri is relieved and focuses on caring for the kids and Joe. A clinician applying the CCT model to Joe's experience would examine the various factors involved in his crisis. Joe, Teri, Max, and Emma were in direct proximity to the flood. Joe experiences his family's withdrawal as abandonment, is worried sick about his business, and is tearful and tense. Teri is silent most of the time and Max and Emma just look scared. This flood and its aftermath have been going on for one week and are anticipated to continue for at least two months. The clinician's assessment indicates a significant crisis impact, from the perspective of CCT. Therefore, immediate services, including psychosocial support, communication, short-term resources—housing and food—are needed to assist Joe and his family.

Unique and Common Elements Among Crisis, Trauma, and Disaster

Personal crises, such as suicide, homicide, and severe physical injury, and natural disaster, such as typhoons, earthquakes, and hurricanes, are terrifying and potentially traumatizing. Individuals have perceptions of the precipitating concerns and the crisis event based on their personal, cultural, and psychological histories. These perceptions play a major role in how the crisis affects individuals and their recovery. According to James and Gilliland (2017), the client's subjective interpretation of an event as a crisis and the clinician's understanding of the client's meaning significantly affect the client's experiences and recovery from a crisis. On an individual level, the consequence of a crisis can range from psychological trauma to intrapersonal resilience. Erikson (1976) provided the following definition of individual trauma, "By individual trauma I mean a blow to the psyche that breaks through one's defenses so suddenly and with such brutal force that one cannot react to it effectively" (pp. 153–154). While the construct of resilience is not the opposite of trauma, it provides an alternative to the experience of individual traumatization. Walsh defined resilience as "the capacity to rebound from adversity, strengthened and more resourceful. It is an active process of endurance, self-righting, and growth in response to crisis and challenge . . . the ability to withstand and rebound from disruptive life challenges" (Walsh, 2007; p. 4).

Perceptual Influences

Crisis counselors work to understand the felt meaning clients ascribe to crisis events. According to Kanel (2012), one's perception of the precipitating event and inability to cope with the subjective stress from the situation are key to understanding their psychological state following a crisis. For example, consider the child who witnesses repeated acts of interpersonal violence like fistfights at school, gang or gun violence, sexual battery of sex workers. This child is likely to have a very different perception of and sensitization toward aggressive acts when compared to another child who rarely witnesses interpersonal violence in their immediate environment of home, school, or neighborhood.

Proximity of Events

Crisis counselors consider clients' proximity to the crisis event. Considering the crisis event in the context of the client's day-to-day life is essential in understanding the impact of the event. For example, while many witnessed and mourned the devastation wrought by Hurricane Katrina, to the residents of New Orleans, particularly those in the Lower Ninth Ward, the horrors were beyond measure. Eighty-six percent (86%) of the 1,170 deaths in Louisiana attributed to Katrina occurred in Orleans and St. Bernard Parishes. Those who died were more likely to die at home, be elderly, black, and male (Markwell & Ratard, 2014). Loss of life, livelihood, homes, community, belongings, and relocation to the convention center and Superdome disproportionally affected New Orleans most vulnerable residents. The direct proximity, intensity, and duration of these residents resulted in profound differences in experiences, attributions, coping trajectories, and restoration of health and well-being.

Individual, Group, and Communities Constructed Meanings of Crisis

Following a crisis, the individuals, groups, and communities involved in the event will eventually start a *meaning making process* (Saul, 2014). These meaning-making efforts typically involve the dissemination of information regarding the crisis and its impact through various mediums; word of mouth, social networks, broadcast television, local print outlets, and social media platforms. The sharing, interpretation, and contextualization of information as well as personal narratives provide the foundation for the creation of a *new normal*. The new normal provides a context for understanding the postcrisis environment and, often, focuses on the community or societal adaptations made because of the crisis. Crisis counselors work with individuals, groups, and communities to create functional adaptations following a crisis event.

While the authentic socially constructed meaning within any group of people should be honored, at times the crisis counselor must help crisis survivors to construct a meaning that will limit subsequent crises. For example, if a survivor of school bullying punches their bully, school officials may expel the bullied student for fighting rather than understanding the lack of school-based support for bullied children. Helping individuals and their systems understand the context and meaning of the crisis event does not excuse the survivor's behavior but explains why crises may occur without appropriate interventions and resources.

Crisis counselors cannot rid clients of all subjective distress. The task of the clinician is to help clients contextualize their perceptions of precipitating events and encourage coping behaviors. Without discomfort, clients are often not as motivated to change. The crisis counselor works with clients' disequilibrium and vulnerability to promote cognitive, emotional, and behavioral change. Clients with adequate ego strength and no history of mental illness can often psychologically work through a crisis without ongoing counseling or medication. Others may require medication, therapy, or a combination of the two to support them through the initial crisis. Understanding when the situation calls for more resources in addition to therapy is a vital skill for crisis workers.

Individual Appraisal and Coping Methods/Behaviors

According to Pearlin and Schooler (1978), any effort taken to deal with stress may be considered coping. Thus, coping is a process and requires cognitive and behavioral activities. Cognitively, people under stress appraise what is happening and assess any potential for harm. They also evaluate the consequences of possible response actions. According to Lazarus (1966), appraisals occur before coping mechanisms are employed. Following the appraisal, there are three types of coping responses that may be used, including direct actions like removing oneself from a dangerous environment, managing mental imagery, and regulation of emotions. When a person is unable to use coping behaviors and is faced with an overwhelming stressor they experience a subjective state of crisis.'

Subjective distress, such as anxiety or grief, overwhelms the individual, preventing them from coping or functioning in a variety of areas. When such individuals realize they can no longer function at work, home, in social situations, or emotionally, many seek counseling. In the postacute phase of a crisis, clinicians help clients identify and employ coping strategies. Caplan's (1964) seven characteristics of effective coping behavior include (a) actively exploring reality and searching for information; (b) freely expressing both positive and negative feelings and tolerating frustration; (c) actively invoking help from others; (d) breaking problems down into manageable bits and working through them one at a time; (e) awareness of fatigue and pacing coping efforts while maintaining functioning; (f) mastering feelings where possible, being flexible and willing to change; and (g) trusting in oneself and others and having a basic optimism about the outcome. These coping behaviors guide the clinician in creatively constructing a treatment plan that changes cognitions, lowers subjective distress, and increases functioning.

The Physiology of Anxiety

Anxiety increases in times of stress. Individuals in crisis experience shock, disbelief, distress, or panic. In certain circumstances, anxiety has the power to generate energy and increase coping abilities. For example, when a child is in danger, their parent rushes in to rescue them, or when a natural disaster occurs and individuals tune out extraneous stimuli to focus on rescuing others, despite threats to themselves. Anxiety has a curvilinear relationship in that too much overwhelms and immobilizes people while too little leaves them in a state of apathy or with undirected and disintegrative energy (Janosik, 1986).

Following a traumatic event or witnessing a traumatic event, the central nervous system (CNS) begins to develop neurochemical pathways and physiological adaptations to respond to the situation. Areas of the brain that involve memory, such as the amygdala and hippocampus, have increased reactivity to stimuli following acute situations (Yehuda, 2002). Individuals are also believed to experience changes in hippocampal functioning and memory processing, which suggests a possible reason for the postcrisis frequent reexperiencing of the event. Individuals diagnosed with posttraumatic stress disorder (PTSD) can demonstrate increased levels of norepinephrine, a chemical or neurotransmitter released from the locus coeruleus, a structure located in the brain stem. Researchers believe increased levels of norepinephrine are responsible for the fight, flight, or freeze response commonly witnessed in PTSD survivors. The increased levels of CNS norepinephrine have the secondary effect of increased reactivity of the alpha 2 adrenergic receptors, which are associated with increased heart rate, blood pressure, and anxiety responding. Increased levels of norepinephrine, coupled with increased sensitivity of the adrenergic binding sites, promote worsening of the anxiety symptoms common in PTSD and anxiety disorders. Researchers and training programs have recently begun to incorporate a more holistic view of crisis and trauma responding, one which includes bio-psycho-physio-social aspects of individuals.

Physiologically speaking, anxiety disorders such as generalized anxiety disorder, panic disorder, and PTSD are characterized by a CNS imbalance between two distinct neurotransmitters: serotonin and norepinephrine. Serotonin, which is responsible for mood regulation in the brain, is found to be normal to slightly diminished in persons diagnosed with anxiety disorders. The serotonin center of the brain is located within the upper brain stem in the form of two organelles: the dorsal and rostral raphe nuclei. An organelle is a specialized component or subunit of a cell with a particular function. The raphe nuclei release serotonin for mood regulation as well as other bodily functions such as gastrointestinal regulation, skeletal muscle tone, platelet function, and temperature regulation. Located just near the rostral raphe nuclei is the norepinephrine center of the brain, the locus coeruleus. Norepinephrine released from this structure increases anxiety, tremors, focus, and blood pressure. When an increase in norepinephrine is overlaid with normal to decreased serotonin function, crisis survivors present with symptoms attributable to extreme anxiety or more significant pathology (Charney, Woods, Goodman, & Heninger, 1987). Clients may present with nervousness, agitation, sleep disturbances, hypervigilance, and heightened memory and thought processing. Secondarily, they may also complain of somatic symptoms of anxiety, such as tachycardia; high blood pressure; rapid, shallow breathing; and tremors.

Perceptions Regarding Precipitating Events

Precipitating events are triggers that set the stage for the crisis event and associated responding. For individuals and communities, precipitating events may be interpreted as both a threat and an opportunity (Echterling, Presbury, & McKee, 2005; Kanel, 2012) but rarely does this interpretation occur in the immediate throes of a crisis! According to Kanel (2012), identification of the precipitating event and the meaning attributed to it by the client are important elements associated with recovery. Herman, (1997) and Kanel (2012) suggest clients benefit from describing the precipitating event(s) contributing to the crisis, the meaning of the event(s), painful feelings related to the crisis, and other losses or changes related to the crisis and the postcrisis aftermath, like occupational, academic, behavioral, and social challenges.

Summary

Crisis events, no matter their origin, intensity, severity, or duration, have the potential to effect long-term changes in the lives of people who experience them. Additionally, no matter what their impact on an individual, crisis events are rarely isolated to a single person; it is important to remember that a crisis event can affect a whole family, community, or society. This chapter presented the history, theories, categories, and models of crisis and crisis intervention. Special attention was paid to human development, neuropsychological functioning, and a systemic view of crisis.

Extended Learning Exercises

Exercise 1: ACA and APA Chartered Divisions

Directions: Review the chartered divisions within the American Counseling Association (ACA) and the American Psychological Association (APA). Write down the names of two divisions within ACA and two additional divisions from APA that are likely to have an emphasis in crisis counseling. Type out the four chartered divisions and, beneath every name, brainstorm the different ways they will assist you in becoming a more effective crisis counselor. Next, review what you brainstormed and indicate the divisions that produced the most interest. Do a web-based search for the ACA/APA divisions that were most salient and review their websites. Find out member benefits, name of the professional journal associated with the division, when and where the next division meeting will be, and determine the requirements for becoming a member.

Exercise 2: Youth and Family Trauma Professional Organizations

Directions: Locate the websites for the Child Trauma Academy, Learning Center for Child and Adolescent Trauma, National Center for PTSD, and Penn Center for Youth and Family Trauma Response and Recovery. Within each website, you will find resources for helping youth, parents, and individuals suffering from trauma and PTSD. As you are reviewing, consider which professional organization has the most rigorous set of resources and pay attention to the unique aspects of each organization.

Exercise 3: Unique and Common Elements of Crisis Counseling

Directions: Review the roots, tenets, and history of each model of crisis counseling. Consider how each model is similar and different. As you are reflecting on these factors, write down the elements of each model that you find interesting, exciting, and inspiring and consider which model seems to be more in line with your interests and inspiration. Next, begin creating a list of crisis counseling tenets, from various models, that you find meaningful and add something unique to your emerging model.

Additional Resources

Helpful Links

Alameda County Behavioral Health Care Services: http://www.acbhcs.org/providers/QA/docs/2013/TR_Suicide-Homicide_Risk_Assesment.pdf

American Academy of Experts in Traumatic Stress: https://www.aaets.org/index.htm

The Federal Emergency Management Agency: https://www.fema.gov/

Mothers Against Drunk Driving: http://www.madd.org/

The National Domestic Violence Hotline: http://www.thehotline.org/

National Suicide Prevention Lifeline: http://suicidepreventionlifeline.org/

West Virginia Division of Culture and History, Buffalo Creek Disaster: http://www.wvculture.org/history/buffcreek/bctitle.html

Helpful Books

Acute Traumatic Stress Management: Addressing Emergent Psychological Needs During Traumatic Events. (2001). Mark Lerner & Ray Shelton.

Crisis Intervention Strategies, 8th Edition (2017). Richard K. James & Burl E. Gilliland.

Crisis Intervention Handbook: Assessment, Treatment, and Research, 3rd Edition (2005). Albert R. Roberts.

Crisis Assessment, Intervention, and Prevention, 2nd Edition (2017). Lisa Jackson-Cherry & Bradley Erford

The Complete Guide to Crisis & Trauma Counseling: What to Do and Say When It Matters Most! (2011). H. Norman Wright

Healing the Fragmented Selves of Trauma Survivors (2017). Janina Fisher

3

Caring for Those Affected by Crisis

Humans help each other. Sometimes help stems from care and compassion or altruism or one's personal, religious, or spiritual beliefs. Researchers in the helping professions have investigated what leads a person to help another, particularly under risky conditions, and what, if any, intrinsic value humans derive from the interaction. A substantial amount of research seems to point to altruism (Wispé, 1972). Altruism takes many forms—an act disguised as self-interest, referred to as the exchange fiction hypothesis (Holmes, Miller, & Lerner, 2002); a dynamic expression of altruism and self-interest (Flynn & Black, 2011); a strategic cost/benefit decision based on analysis and reciprocity (Fehr & Henrich, 2003); an intentional act to enhance one's reputation—competitive altruism (Hardy & Van Vugt, 2006); a product of natural selection (Darwin, 1859); genetic predisposition (de Waal, 1996); and or a decision based on human morality (Echterling, Presbury, & McKee, 2005).

Anthropologists theorize that the higher one's frequency of altruistic acts the higher their level of *fitness* (Sober, 1993). Fitness is the strength and amount of an individual's genes transferred to the next generation. Genes with greater fitness become more common through the process of natural selection. Thus, helping others is a survival mechanism!

Have you ever wondered why, when others are in distress, most offer to help? From a neural developmental perspective, oxytocin, a hormone, associated with love, altruism, and social altruism (Carter, 1998; Marsh et al., 2015), is also associated with the desire and motivation to help others. Neurologically, helping behaviors are reinforced through recognition and positive outcomes leading to a cycle of helping and positive reinforcement. Specifically, during and immediately after a helping behavior is engaged in, oxytocin is secreted through the posterior lobe of the pituitary gland. This release of oxytocin delivers positive reinforcement for the helping behavior. The overall increasing levels of oxytocin within the brain will cause an increase in the desire to help further (i.e., cycle). It feels good to help another out of harms' way and to maintain or restore community.

Although theories identifying the motivation to help others are prevalent, there is scant information regarding the particular knowledge, skills, awareness, techniques, and resources clinicians need to assist those experiencing crises. In this chapter, you are presented a toolkit, described in Chapter 1, designed to inform your treatment of individuals, groups, or communities suffering from crises. To paraphrase Apple cofounder Steve Jobs (Goodell, 2011), we have faith in you because you are smart, and given the tools you will do wonderful things.

Learning Objectives

After reading the chapter and engaging the case vignettes and reflective exercises provided, you will

- Be familiar with the knowledge, skills, awareness, techniques, and resources essential for individual, group, and community crisis counseling and interventions
- Understand the knowledge, skills, awareness, techniques, and resources essential at your level of professional development
- Understand the role of informal and formal crisis assessments
- Understand assessment methods, case conceptualization, and evaluation of individuals, groups, and communities in crisis
- Be able to devise a comprehensive treatment plan
- Consider a variety of techniques to clinical vignettes

Knowledge, Skill(s), Awareness, Techniques, and Resources

The essential knowledge, skills, awareness, techniques, and resources described below are essential for crisis counseling and are assumed to be progressive and continuous. Each domain builds on the one that precedes it both in terms of the type of client served—individual, group, community, and level of professional development described in Chapter 1. We expect that many of the skills and techniques will be familiar to you. We include them in the Toolkit to contextualize their application to crisis counseling. Due to the complex and ever-evolving nature of knowledge, skills, awareness, techniques, and resources, the descriptions are not intended to be comprehensive or exhaustive.

Knowledge

Clinicians, across the professional lifespan, acquire knowledge and possess varying degrees of competency in the numerous content areas of counseling. Caring for those in crisis requires a deeper understanding and application of knowledge, particularly human motivation and hierarchy of needs, developmental processes, intersections of crisis, and cultural, triage, and psychological first aid (World Health Organization [WHO], 2011). Advanced knowledge provides the foundation for understanding and assessing clients' needs and processes during and after a crisis, the clinician's role and responsibilities, and the potential personal impacts—burnout.

Human Motivation and Hierarchy of Needs

In Chapter 2, Maslow's (1943) theory of human motivation was discussed. Maslow argued that individuals seek to meet their prepotent needs or needs that have the greatest influence on one's actions. Everyone has prepotent needs and they vary among individuals, groups, and communities. For example, food insecurity over an extended period leads to severe hunger pangs, distress, sickness, and in some cases, death. Profound hunger motivates one to search for and secure food above all else. Food, in any form, momentarily satisfies the need, reduces distress, and improves one's sense of equilibrium. Humans seek to meet basic physiological, safety, and relational needs in a hierarchical fashion, and satisfying one need does not necessarily mean one is no longer striving or struggling.

Individuals experiencing crisis, trauma, or disaster (CTD) may seek safety, while others seek sustenance or shelter. As a clinician caring for those in crisis, you will encounter and assess individuals struggling to survive, searching relentlessly for basic need fulfillment and equilibrium. It is critical you understand clients may seek to meet their needs in ways that may be unfamiliar to you. An accurate assessment of clients' needs, strengths, resources, and abilities is paramount in the early stages of crisis counseling. Maslow focused on the individual, yet survival and need fulfillment take place in a social context. Human motivation and hierarchical need fulfillment for groups or communities has received much less attention in the professional literature. Group or community behavior is more than an amplification or sum of individual ways of being and is influenced by, within, and across group interactions, competition, and communication. Social psychologist Pamela Rutledge (2011) highlighted the limitations in Maslow's theory in the digital age. She stated, "None of these needs—starting with basic survival on up—are possible without social connection and collaboration" (p. 6). Rutledge noted that in complex and interconnected societies, connection and collaboration are prerequisites for physical and emotional survival. One need only to reflect on the use of social media (Facebook and Twitter) during tragic events such as the 2016 Pulse Nightclub in Orlando or the police shootings in Dallas during a peaceful protest of Black Lives Matter. Rutledge rejects the notion of hierarchy and reconceptualizes Maslow's model placing connection and collaboration at the center of our dynamic and interactive socio-cultural context. We believe Rutledge's conceptualization of human needs is right on in the digital age *and* has application for

FIGURE 3.1 ● **Maslow Reconceptualized**

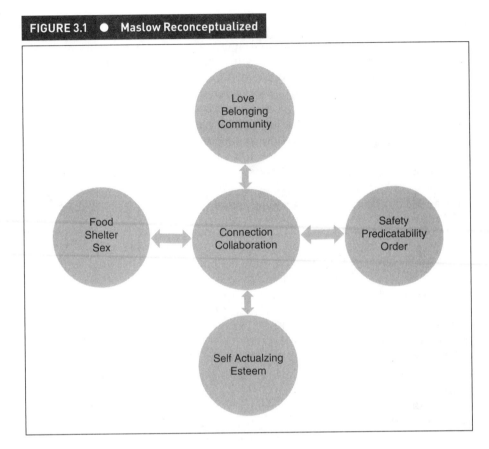

CTD counseling. For example, a motor vehicle accident occurs and there is fire and life-threatening injuries. It is not uncommon for witnesses to run toward the accident to rescue crash victims. The witnesses-turned-rescuers ignored the first two levels of Maslow's hierarchy—physical integrity and safety—to collaborate with others in service of their human connection with the crash victims. Social connection and collaboration restore one's faith in humanity. Figure 3.1 is our representation of Rutledge's concepts.

In times of crisis individuals, groups and communities seek safety, security, control, and agency. Clinicians, serving those affected by crisis, draw on their understanding of group theory and social psychology to empower individuals within and across groups and communities. Clear communication and empowerment promote social connections and collaboration, aid management of the immediate environment, and restore equilibrium. Groups and communities in crisis use formal and informal leaders and organizations (e.g., Red Cross, local mental health and social service agencies) to provide structure or service and reduce uncertainly and chaos. Interactions with groups and communities, prior to a crisis, provide you, the clinician, the foundation and knowledge for adaptive individual, group, and community responding.

Developmental Considerations

Knowledge of developmental considerations is critical for clinicians' understanding of the social, emotional, cognitive, spiritual, physical, language capacities, and resources of individuals, groups, and communities. James and Gilliland (2017) describe this as an imperative stating, "Many crises have their bases in developmental stages that humans pass through, developmental theory must play a part in the crisis intervention" (p. 18). Table 3.1 presents significant developmental considerations from multiple theorists (Piaget, 1952; Erikson, 1959; Fowler, 1995; Labouuie-Vief, 2006; Levinson, 1978; Levinson & Levinson, 1996; Vaillant, 2002; and Agronin, 2014). Due to the variety and conflicting nature of theories, we synthesized the information, reduced the number of conflicts, and urge you, the reader, to investigate these theories more fully.

Although a clinicians' understanding of individual development is critical to the skilled provision of crisis counseling services, it is important to remember that most individuals live within the context of a family. Families, like small social groups, are governed by a hierarchy, norms, roles, history, and progress through stages. The stages distinguish different family structures, roles, context, and norms, all of which are influenced by demographics and culture of the family. Families come in many forms and configurations and we, the authors, contest long-held notions of a family life cycle (Mattessich & Hill, 1987). As an artifact of their times, these theories represent mono-cultural, gender-based views of what it means to be a family. Clinicians, responding to those affected by crisis, are most effective when they understand the structure, norms, and roles within family groups from the socio-cultural perspectives of family members to determine the appropriateness and enhance the impact of their interventions.

Intersection of Crisis and Culture

Clinicians, by virtue of their training, have been exposed to multicultural counseling concepts and processes. Yet, most would agree their formal education was insufficient given the realities they face as an intern or professional. Not only do crisis-counseling situations demand attention to multicultural issues, but because crises are acute and tumultuous, clinicians take great care not to act in privileged or uninformed ways.

When crisis strikes, individuals and groups may look for someone or some group to scapegoat. Attributing the disruption, injuries, threat, and emotional upheaval to another reduces feelings of helplessness and vulnerability, provides a *target* for accountability, and is ineffective and inhumane. Individuals with perceived identities similar to the perpetrators may, by association, become targets of threats, oppression, or violence. Stop for a moment and consider the experiences of Muslim Americans following 9/11 or Latinx citizens during the 2019 "migrant crisis." According to Crandall, Eshleman, and O'Brien (2002) prejudice is "a negative evaluation of a group or an individual on the basis of group membership" (p. 359). Prejudice, oppression, and threat create a sense of daily fear and terror for affected groups and are believed to contribute to the intergenerational effects of historical trauma (Chapter 4). Clinicians address their biases, privilege,

TABLE 3.1 ● Developmental Consideration in Crisis Counseling

Developmental Level	Social/Emotional	Cognitive	Physical	Spiritual	Interpersonal Relationships
Infants and toddlers	**Infants:** look to primary caregiver for consistent, predictable, & reliable environment **Toddlers:** become more mobile; constant exploration of environment; engages in trial and error learning	understands via senses & actions and interactions; in the infant phase most behavior is reflexive	rapid growth & development of all systems & senses; gains in weight & height; increasing control over mobility & intentional actions; walks, skips, jumps; development dependent on good nutrition	unknown	dependent on primary caregivers; little to no separation between self and others; toddlers engage in parallel play
Early Childhood	play is central to growth; increased interactions with peers and teachers; initiates independent activities; tests limits set by parents	understands through language and mental images; acquires information	continued physical growth, less rapid; more mastery over physical movements & balance; good nutrition matters	fantasy and reality often confused; basic religious or spirituality ideas usually transmitted by parents and/or society and imitated by child	primary relationships are with adult caregivers, play is more relational due to group interaction; beginning demonstration of empathy
Middle Childhood	begins to develop a sense of self; seeks the approval of others; peers become more important	understands through logical thinking & categorization; acquires & begins to apply information	Pre-puberty; rapid growth of skeletal & muscular systems in preparation for puberty	world is viewed in more logical ways; accept the stories told to them by their faith/spiritual communities and are understood in a literal manner; some individuals remain in this stage through adulthood	development of & preference for same gender groups; increase in empathy; desire to please significant adults; loyalty and belonging matter

Adolescence	develops a sense of self; seeks independence; learns adult roles; desires to fit in while being seen as unique	understands through hypothetical thinking & scientific reasoning; applies information	onset of puberty; emergence of secondary sex characteristics; increase hormone production; development of reproductive systems	social & peer groups have greater influence and individuals usually adopt some form of all-encompassing belief system & may struggle to accept different systems of belief; authority is usually placed in individuals or groups that represent one's beliefs. Most individuals remain at this stage	increased association and influence of peers; may experience 'first love'; sense of self as a sexual being with cross- or same gender attractions; self-conscious
Young Adulthood	desires to be viewed as a unique individual; idealistic; seeks independence; risk taking behavior peaks	thoughts are flexible & adaptive; engages in exploration of adult roles; information in service of achievement; peak of creativity	physical functioning, reproductive organs and metabolism are at peak performance	most remain in the previous phase, but some critically examine their beliefs & become disillusioned with their former faith	strong sense of identity with peers; less sense of identity with family; capacity and desire for intimate relationships
Middle Adulthood	shares self more intimately with others; explores longer-term commitments non-family members; seeks commitment and security in relationships; career consolidation	thoughts are flexible & adaptive; information in service of achievement	physical functioning remains stable throughout the early part of this phase; mid- to late phase metabolism begins to slow resulting in some weakening of muscular system & decline sexual activity/performance	previous phase continues	seeks intimate, longer lasting personal relationship; develops smaller, more intimate group of friends, which may be a proxy for extended family

(Continued)

TABLE 3.1 (Continued)

Developmental Level	Social/Emotional	Cognitive	Physical	Spiritual	Interpersonal Relationships
Later Adulthood	settles in to life's routine; women may experience increased assertiveness; desires to give back to others/society; career consolidation	cognitions focus on responsibility	metabolism continues to slow; onset of menopause in women; drop in hormone production; for some onset of age-related vision concerns and impact of lifestyle choices (smoking, drugs, overeating)	realize the limits of logic & start to accept life's paradoxes; see life's mystery and often return to sacred stories and symbols free of formal teachings	re-establish relationship with partner as children leave home; fluctuations in the quality and intensity of friendships; may become simultaneous caregiver of parents and grandchildren
Older Adulthood	contemplates personal accomplishments; reflects/evaluates degree of success in life; seeks meaningful intergenerational relationships	cognitions focus on issues of personal concern for the greater good	decline in performance of most systems (vision, hearing, cognition, cardio-vascular, mobility, balance); harder to keep warm	few individuals reach this level of development; focus on service to others; experience few worries or doubts	loss of relationships due to death or declining health; seek relationships that recognize vitality and ability of older adults; desire companionship

and assumptions to prevent harming clients from historically marginalized groups and enhance their cultural responsiveness through personal wellness activities like meditation, mindfulness, physical exercise, and health diet.

Triage

Triage is a rapid and systematic set of techniques used to assess the severity of clients' presenting concerns and determine a direction for helping. They can be applied to individual, group, or community settings and involve communication and collaboration with others. A working knowledge of triage helps you understand the relationship between clients' needs, their disequilibrium, and available resources. At its core, triage is about identifying and acting on priorities. Whether you are responding to an individual's crisis—suicidal ideation, divorce, death—or responding to a site with mass injuries, the following four principles guide your work: (a) practice within the *scope of your training* (American Counseling Association [ACA], 2014; American Psychological Association [APA], 2010; National Association of Social Workers [NASW], 2008). Clinicians responding to crisis first ensure there are no life-endangering injuries. Whether you are assessing an individual for homicidal ideation or responding to a school shooting, physical safety and integrity are paramount. (b) Develop and maintain an up-to-date *referral network* of services and providers in your area. After the initial assessment, clients need to secure resources or services including referrals for temporary housing, food bank, or emergency medical or psychiatric care. Accessing known professional service providers instills hope and confidence in those affected by crisis. (c) A heightened *environmental and situational awareness and focus* helps the clinician and those they serve establish and maintain a safe-enough environment for initial crisis intervention to take place. Crisis events are unpredictable, tumultuous, and potentially threatening; clinician's improve their awareness and focus during a crisis by minimizing distractions like cell phones, attending to matters in a logical, sequential manner, and regulating their emotional responses.

Groups and Communities

Clinicians work with individual crises like suicidal ideation, sexual violence, grief, and bereavement, and some clinicians choose to serve as first responders to a crisis event. In group crises, effective triage is paramount. Group crisis events involve mass injuries or casualties and may unfold from the effects of one of the three types of crises presented in Chapter 1. Typically, there is a coordinating or organizing agency or group that provides structure to the crisis response. For example, in the immediate aftermath of a group crisis event like the 2017 Las Vegas mass shooting, it may be difficult, if not impossible, to locate EMTs or medical first responders. Thus, nonmedical first responders should be aware of systems developed for triaging large groups of people. Smith (2012) developed a system for organizing individuals based on the severity of their injury. In this system clinicians coordinate with other first responders and utilize a metaphorical traffic light to color code the injury based on level of severity. In this model, red designates the most critical victims with a life-threatening injury; yellow identifies those with critical but not life-threatening injuries; and green signals those designated with minor injuries not requiring immediate medical care. Blue is reserved for those mortally wounded for whom death is expected. After physical injuries are triaged, clinicians triage individuals with psychological and emotional needs. Priority is given to those with impairments in mental status—orientation, registration, attention, and recall; followed by those experiencing intense psychological disruption—disassociation, agitation, or who appear inconsolable. The next section on psychological first aid guides you through the intervention and short-term stabilization process.

Psychological First Aid

Psychological first aid (PFA) is a technique comprised of eight steps that was developed in 2006 by staff at the National Center for Post-Traumatic Stress Disorder and external researchers. PFA is applied in the immediate aftermath of crisis or disaster to mitigate initial distress, stabilize those exposed, increase opportunities for adaptive functioning, and reduce the occurrence of posttraumatic stress disorder. Using a combination of assessment and goal-directed care and referrals, clinicians meaningfully engage with those in crisis to compassionately acknowledge their concerns, reestablish a sense of homeostasis, and provide support and practical assistance, along with brief psycho education and social connection.

In this initial step, clinicians introduce themselves to the individual in crisis and ask for permission to engage. You recall cross-cultural considerations and professional humility throughout the process of engagement. You focus on nonintrusive interactions, support, and encouragement.

Next, you provide immediate, physical, and emotional safety and comfort as is appropriate to clients' culture. You are mindful of culturally influenced interpersonal interactions such as physical proximity and contact; cross-gendered verbal and physical interactions; and degrees of eye contact and use of silence. Individuals who feel respected and cared for begin to engage with you by sharing their personal contact information and discussing their needs. The quality of the clinician/client engagement foreshadows the process of stabilization.

In the immediate aftermath, individuals exposed to crisis events seek balance. In the PFA model, clinicians are encouraged to *look*, *listen* and *link* to aid stabilization. *Look* refers to the process of continued assessment and evaluation of safety and the individuals' needs. Those utilizing PFA are urged to engage in active and empathic listening and to respond with encouragement and support. At this step and in this model, it is unlikely the clinician would process the traumatic event with the individual. Similar to the criticism of psychological debriefing, expecting or encouraging a cathartic discharge in the immediate aftermath of an event is counterproductive, disruptive, and may lead to harm. The final element in stabilization is to create a *link* between the individual and needed services or providers. Referral for service helps the individual focus on something outside of them and may motivate them to take an action in service of their recovery.

The goal of this stage is to assess the needs of the individual. You engage in a flexible and intentional manner, assess and rank the concerns of the person in crisis, and consider your assessment and available resources. Specific referrals are offered; additional contacts or meetings may be necessary. At this point, the person in crisis should be less emotionally or psychologically escalated, have a plan in hand, and demonstrate sufficient mental status and executive functioning.

Practical concerns permeate all aspects of psychological first aid; however, in this stage, they are deliberately explored. The goal is to create an environment that promotes problem solving for the individual regarding current and anticipated problems. This step involves more than provision of referrals; clinicians discuss individuals' needs and options related to concerns and the timing and provision of resources. This discussion allows the person in crisis to experience a sense of agency and control. At the point of referral, you identify the most immediate needs; discuss potential providers including their availability, location, and transportation needs; develop an action plan including dates by which contact will be made; and determine what if any further support is needed. Occasionally, the acceptance of assistance from one agency may exclude the individual from being offered other services, and they may have exceeded their eligibility for aid. It is important for you to at least mention and perhaps document the importance of understanding all the conditions under which relief aid is given.

Social support can provide a sense of wellness and is paramount to stabilization and eventually recovery. Family members, community, and friends are the cornerstone of social support, and a goal is connecting clients to these various resources and particularly primary support persons. You may offer to contact supportive persons, but if the individual is reluctant for you to do so, you support their decision and seek alternative contacts.

Clinicians provide those in crisis information on the common reactions to stress, traumatic experiences, and loss. Focused psychoeducation about crisis and stress responding informs individuals and provides direct instruction on effective coping strategies such as self-talk, deep breathing, and talking with friends. Also, because you are familiar with stages of physical, emotional, cognitive, and social development, you can use this information to help families understand the impact a crisis can have on their expectations and coping. Coping with highly negative emotions, such as anger, shame, and guilt, is key to assisting a return to stabilization and eventually recovery. Empathizing with natural reactions to a crisis supports stabilization by normalizing or contextualizing the individual's experiences, aids the recall of previously successful behaviors, and fuels the recovery process. For example, some individuals report sleep disturbances after a crisis like trouble getting to sleep, frequent awakenings, remaining on alert all night, and worrying excessively about their life post-crisis. Utilizing psychoeducation, you would discuss the tenets of sleep hygiene like sleep routines, sleep journals, and reduced caffeine intake at least six to seven hours before bedtime.

The last step in this process asks you to link the person in crisis to local longer-term services to address their identified needs and to provide continuity of care. Most crisis clinicians do not provide post crisis care. Psychological First Aid is an efficient and effective interaction to temporarily stabilize individuals in crisis. As such, clinicians are more directive and goal oriented in their interactions with clients.

Skills

Individual

As noted earlier, in this text, skills describe specific abilities or proficiencies in counseling. Most clinicians learn a set of core skills in their graduate counseling, psychology, or social work programs. Novice graduate students are taught and practice core skills in the classroom prior to or as a part of practicum. Many of the core skills training programs developed and researched in the late 20th century (Carkhuff, 1969; Ivey, 1971) were modeled after Carl Rogers's client-centered approach (Rogers, 1951, 1957). The counseling literature has endorsed using various empirically validated classification systems to assess counseling skills, dispositions, and behaviors (Hamlet & Burnes, 2013; Swank, Lambie, & Witta, 2012); counseling skills, phases of a counseling session, and aspects of the counseling relationship (Flynn & Hays, 2015); attending and multicultural skills (Larson et al., 1992; Ponterotto & Potere, 2003); counselor effectiveness (Eriksen & McAuliffe, 2003; Horvath & Greenberg, 1989); cross-cultural counseling competencies (Kocarek, Talbot, Batka, & Anderson, 2001; Sodowsky, Taffe, Gutkin, & Wise, 1994); trainee verbal response to clientele (Porter, 1943); and facilitative conditions (Truax & Carkhuff, 1967).

Although the counseling, psychology, and social work professionals have created various methods for both understanding and assessing counseling skills and techniques, until recently, there were few publications dedicated to the explication of a comprehensive set of skills focused on crisis counseling. For example, James and Gilliland (2017) describe the application of core counseling skills as they relate to crisis counseling. Myer and James (2005) describe nine strategies deemed essential to crisis counseling intervention. These include creating awareness, allowing catharsis, providing support, promoting expansion, emphasizing focus, providing guidance, promoting mobilization, implementing order, and providing protection. As you read the nine strategies, what skills came to mind? What skills might you use to create awareness in a person experiencing a crisis? Myer and James's (2005) strategies require core and advanced counseling skills focused on the clients' experience and perceptions of the crisis event. In the sections below, we expand on the works of several scholars (Cormier, Nurius, & Osborn, 2009; Flynn & Hays, 2015; Ivey, Ivey, & Zalaquett, 2010; James & Gilliland, 2017; Young, 2013) and apply these skills to crisis counseling.

Observation

The clinician observes and conveys awareness of difference of the status or behaviors in client speech patterns, grooming, posture, build, gait, hesitation, stammer, and other nonverbal behavior. Due to the nature of crisis counseling, sometimes clinicians will be meeting clients for the first time while they are in the throes of a crisis. In this case, change of status is irrelevant due to the lack of prior history. Clinicians assess speech, behavior, or patterns that seem inconsistent with a person in crisis and filter their observations through a multicultural lens that acknowledges the intersections of culture, crisis, and individual ways of being.

Clarification

This is a *go-to* skill. Clarification focuses your client's attention on precision in speech and meaning. Utilizing this skill, the clinician asks the client to elaborate on vague, ambiguous, or implied statements. Clarifications are usually expressed as a question such as "Are you saying this…?" or "Do you mean…?" Clarifications can also take the form of statements that imply a question like, "*They* are always talking about you?" In crisis counseling, the use of clarification is tempered by the client's psychological state (e.g., numb, overwhelmed, or agitated) as it may be experienced as intrusive or provocative. This as a *go-to* skill because, used skillfully, you and your client create a shared pool of understanding.

Open-Ended Questioning

Questioning strategies that encourage clients' exploration and disclosure rather than a discreet answer are referred to as open-ended questions. This type of inquiry support clients' examination of assumptions as well as the who, what, how, when, where, could, would, and should of crisis events. Additionally, an open-ended questioning strategy supports the individual in crisis as they disclose their immediate reactions and worries related to the crisis event. In acute crisis responding, like PFA, open-ended questions should be used sparingly to prevent premature emotional processing of distressing content prior to the establishment of psychological safety.

Closed-Ended Questioning

This type of question is direct and used to illicit information like demographic information or assessment of needs. Clients' responses are dichotomous (yes/no, good/bad, right/wrong) or brief in nature. This type of questioning is often used in the initial stages of assessment to focus and engage individuals in crisis.

Challenging

This skill allows you to appropriately address discrepancies, conflicts, and mixed messages that emerge from the client's feelings, thoughts, and actions. You use this process gently but directly to engage and clarify inconsistent statements from the person in crisis. Precision and care are urged when employing this skill. Because persons in crisis often exhibit escalated emotions or behaviors they may misinterpret your intent and experience your challenge as inappropriate blaming, argumentativeness, or cruelness.

Encouragers

Encouraging phrases or gestures provide support and time for the person in crisis. Nonverbal minimal encouragers, like a nod of acknowledgment or an invitational gesture, prompt clients to continue at their own pace. Verbal responses are typically monosyllabic or a short phrase: "Oh?" "So?" "Then?" or repetition of key words used by the individual. With respect to crisis counseling, the timing of encourages is critical; too much encouragement can feel invasive to those in crisis, too little can feel mechanistic.

Reflection of Feeling, Content, and Meaning

With this core set of skills, you state succinctly the feeling, content, or meaning of the problem expressed either tacitly or implicitly by the client. Content reflections involve integration and clarification of facts or statements—typically used in the early or acute phases of crisis counseling. Reflections of feeling focus on the emotional valence—tone or intensity and expressed or perceived feelings—terrified or angry. Reflection of feelings is a powerful way to demonstrate empathy and engagement, but much like an encourager, the timing and depth of the reflection must be congruent with the client's presentation to avoid therapeutic misunderstandings or client harm. Meaning reflections are statements from you to the client that offer a meaning or reason for the client's experience and are grounded in advance accurate empathy. Reflections of meaning are most appropriate in the mid to later stages of crisis counseling when clients have a great sense of homeostasis. Reflections of meaning are a more advanced skill and akin to what Reik (1948) described as listening with your "third ear." Using your "third ear," you listen for deeper layers of meaning in the client's story then respond with a synthesis of their latent or unspoken felt experience. Reflections of meaning advance the individual's understanding and may result in what Teyber and McClure (1994) referred to as a corrective "emotional experience" (p. 30). After a corrective emotional experience, Teyber and McClure indicate the client may feel safer and experience deep or painful feelings more fully and resolve "ambivalence and make important personal decisions" (p. 30) and felt experience.

Cutoff

To maintain an emotional focus with a client, you may utilize the skill of therapeutic interrupting or cutting off the client's expression when they persist in storytelling or superficial dialogue. This technique should be used with an ample amount of empathy and judiciously, particularly with those in crisis, as it may be misinterpreted as rudeness or a lack of caring or concern.

Paraphrasing

This skill is often used in conjunction with reflections of content, feeling, and meaning as you rephrase the client's actual words and expressions, paying selective attention to the content contained in the individual's story. A well-paraphrased response translates or presents the individual's key ideas in a summative and hopefully clearer form. In crisis counseling, when clients are overwhelmed by emotion and thoughts, a clinician can choose to pair the skill of paraphrasing with clarification to help ground the client who may be emotionally or cognitively overloaded.

Directives

Your ability to provide a clear and compassionate direct suggestion to individuals in crisis may be one of the most valuable skills in a counselor's toolkit. Directives may take the form of "I suggest...", or "I urge you to..." followed by the activity to be taken by the person in crisis. Additional directives may include contacting a family member or friend or connecting with community resources. This contrasts with how you might use directives in traditional counseling during a role-play or empty chair exercise. The goal of a directive in a crisis setting is to urge the individual to engage in services or options while preserving and respecting their right to choose. We caution you that misapplication of this skill can turn into advice giving, which is inappropriate and restricts and impedes client freedom.

Groups and Communities

In a group setting, clinicians utilize and enhance the skills designed for individuals. As an effective clinician, you remain keenly aware that interpersonal dynamics, needs, roles, and communication styles multiply exponentially as each person joins the group. As the professional, you are responsible for facilitating the group's communication. A student of the first author likened the group leader's role in a crisis group to that of an air traffic controller at O'Hare Airport during a snowstorm; a demanding task indeed! While it is beyond the scope of this text to provide a full review of group process, we believe it is important to identify the knowledge and skills required for therapeutic interactions with groups in crisis.

Groups serving those affected by crisis typically have a primary focus—bereavement, substance abuse, grief, divorce—to create a community of individuals with broadly similar experiences. Crisis, by its very nature is disturbing and dislocating, thus sharing ones' stories with those similarly affected provides a foundation for empathy and understanding that may be absent in other relationships. Crisis groups usually have a closed membership to facilitate trust and community building, are time limited, and a balance of support, psychoeducation, and interpersonal process. Remember the focus of a crisis group is on aiding members' return to adaptive functioning, not long-term affective, cognitive, or behavioral change. The focused and short-term nature of group crisis counseling does not mean that clients exit therapy or supportive services; in fact some clinicians use short-term crisis group counseling as an adjunct to individual or support group therapy.

Leading a group for those affected by crisis requires your full attention, focus, and awareness of your personal triggers, particularly those rooted in crisis or trauma. Due to the nature of crisis, the content and interactions of group members is usually emotional and intense. The skilled clinician understands their personal leadership style and effective group leadership while demonstrating confidence and constancy and empathy. Members of crisis groups may exhibit heightened sensitivity, heightened or restricted emotionality, or hypervigilance. In these states, they may project or ascribe emotions onto the leader or other group members. These types of interaction are common, should be worked through, and are the work of the group! Clinicians, who lead groups for those affected by crisis, must expand their knowledge base beyond the basics of group leadership to ensure that within the group process individuals and boundaries are protected and affect is regulated (Yalom, 1995). As noted earlier, crisis groups, by definition, can be highly evocative and emotional. The skilled group leader protects group members from the pressure to disclose emotional contagion and enmeshment with other members while balancing the best interest of all group members with the therapeutic work to be done.

Group counseling, for those affected by crisis, has both benefits and limitations. Individuals affected by crisis can gain support and understanding, access new resources, and form bonds with others with similar experiences. This provides the opportunity to have their experiences of and reactions to their particular crisis normalized and contextualized by other group members. This contextualization reframes one's perspective, highlights effective and less effective coping strategies, models support and understanding for others, which in turn supports a return to equilibrium. At times, crisis group counseling is contraindicated due to the recency, nature, or intensity of the client's crisis, their prior psychological functioning, or willingness to commit. Clients may resist group counseling because it is inconsistent with their personal or cultural norms or mores—one does not expose family problems to strangers—or because they fear being judged or seen as incompetent.

Responding to communities experiencing crisis involves a combination of individual and group skills. Most often, clinicians work within a community response structure focusing on systems of care. You may engage this work through organizations such as the Red Cross, local mental or behavioral health agencies, and nonprofits, and be asked to provide individual or group services. For example, in Colorado, clinicians may be involved in a state level network like Colorado Crisis Education and Response Network (CoCERN), a multi-agency, inclusive, organized, collaborative network for behavioral health crisis/disaster response. In a community crisis or disaster, CoCERN members are mobilized to support and provide services to the requesting agency, survivors, responders, responders' families, and the public. Services range from mental health to victim assistance, to spiritual or pastoral care. We encourage you to explore similar networks in your location by exploring your state's emergency preparedness websites.

Awareness

As noted in Chapter 1, self-awareness is critical to the provision of services to clients and those experiencing a crisis. Though not a specific technique, clinicians improve their self- and other-awareness by purposefully engaging in reflective practice. Examining your understandings, motives, and actions leads simultaneously to a sense of freedom and accountability. Through the techniques of immediacy, advanced accurate empathy, and confrontation, you invite clients to examine and evaluate their response to and behaviors related to the present crisis. Further, as the process of increasing awareness grows, you ask clients to examine and evaluate their beliefs, thoughts, and actions related to the crisis. Increased awareness should enable the client to put the crisis event in context and reframe the experience consistent with who they are.

Techniques intentionally combine counseling skills with processes or procedures designed to result in a specific, positive outcome. Crisis clinicians select from a variety of techniques based on their assessment of client needs at specific points in the crisis counseling process. It is important to note that while the techniques described below are also utilized in traditional counseling, in crisis counseling, the desire outcome is a product or outcome, not a process. By this, we mean techniques in crisis counseling are designed to aid the clients' return to stabilization (a product) rather than to process clients' experiences. Crisis counseling is more directive and time sensitive than most forms of traditional counseling.

Providing Support

Clinicians may be the primary or immediate helper for those affected by crisis. Providing support means offering normalization and empathy related to their crisis experience. An individual in crisis will likely have a cascade of diverse and complex experiences and feelings evoked by the crisis event. These reactions may range from a state of intense fear to self-introspection to feeling or being *crazy*. When intervening in a crisis, it is common for an individual or group in crisis to be dependent on the clinician for a short time. We remind you that this may be necessary for a brief period and it is your ethical duties to maintain clear professional and culturally relevant boundaries that empower those recovering from crisis to experience self-sufficiency.

Providing Protection

Clinicians are intentional about protecting clients from engaging in danger- ous, hurtful, and destructive behaviors and thoughts. Clinicians engage the skills of open- and closed-ended questions, clarification, challenging, and directives to actively assess and support clients at risk of harm to self or others. In the acute phase of a crisis and if clients present as with an identifiable and credible threat to them- selves or others, you may need to secure short-term interventions like hospitaliza- tion to assess and stabilize the client.

Providing Guidance

Crises are chaotic and often clients need specific direction and guidance to regain some semblance of order and decision making to their experiences. Guidance from the clinician often comes in the form of clear direction, options, and suggestions, which will lead the client to resources they did not previously have or require.

Immediacy

This technique combines the skills of observation, encouragers, paraphras- ing, reflection of content, and feeling within the counseling relationship to rec- ognize the here and now at a particular moment in the therapeutic interaction. Immediacy is immediate and intentional, never impulsive. As the clinician, your intention is to momentarily suspend the therapeutic exchange to accentuate the clients' feelings, assumptions, or interpersonal behaviors or reactions with you which may be influencing the individual's current functioning. For example, if the person in crisis is repeatedly dismissive or disdainful of your attempts to assist them, and assuming no intercultural misunderstandings on your part, you can use immediacy to say something like "I am experiencing tension between us when I try to help you. You seem to want me to stop. I am confused; I wonder if you are too?" In the process of immediacy, you describe your perceptions related to the interaction, provide specific details, state your interpersonal experience, and inquire as to the client's experience. As you discuss your experiences, you make note of patterns and themes in the client/clinician relationship. As with other techniques, the focus remains on the client and their experiences. Your use of immediacy should remain limited, or as the kids say, "It's not always about you!"

Catharsis

Catharsis has its roots in psychoanalysis and psychoanalytic theory. Freud postulated those with hysteria could only be cured through talking and emotionally reexperiencing feelings related to the traumatic incident. While the term catharsis has a historic context in psychotherapy, clinicians provide clients the opportunity to vent their feelings and thoughts with the intention of and focus on their relationship to the crisis event. Encouragers, paraphrasing, directives, reflection of feeling, and meaning support this technique. Clinicians typically employ this strategy when the client has a difficult time getting in touch with their feelings. While it is difficult to predict what will lead the client to experience a cathartic reaction, additional techniques may motivate and support clients' processing.

Interpretation

As a technique, interpretation aids the clinician in identifying and articulating alternate explanations for clients' behaviors, patterns, goals, wishes, and feelings. Interpretations arise out of the skills of clarification, challenging, paraphrasing, reflection of feelings, and meaning that are suggested or implied by the client's communication. Clinicians use hunches to make implied client messages more explicit.

Focusing

At times, individuals like Joe, the hypothetical client in Chapter 2, feel flooded with anxiety. The skills of observation, clarifying, close-ended questioning, and paraphrasing are intentionally used to focus the person in crisis on the more manageable aspects of the crisis event. For example, with respect to Joe's concern for his family, you might ask, "What is one step you can take to finding shelter this evening?" As you discuss his response, you can encourage him write down specific steps to achieve this manageable goal and one or two alternatives.

Creating Awareness

Awareness is a capstone feature for many forms of therapy; however, as it pertains to crisis intervention, awareness has a specific purpose. Awareness can be activated for a person in crisis through the skills of observation, reflection of content, feeling and meaning, encouragers, and clarification. Following a crisis, survivors may be confused, may minimize, or be in denial about what transpired. While it would be impossible to bring every aspect of an experience into consciousness, you work with those in crisis to mobilize essential information, feelings, thoughts, and behaviors based on your assessment of their needs.

Silence

This is one of the most powerful techniques to use with clients in crisis. The skills of observation, minimal encouragement, and reflection provide the foundation for pauses or periods of silence. Silence, as a technique allows you to reduce your level of activity, slows down the pace of the session pace, gives clients time to think and reflect. It creates space for them to take responsibility for their needs. Using silence supports the clients' capacity to focus and regulate their emotions.

Expanding the Client's View

You want to be selective and deliberate about initiating activities that expand the perspectives of the person experiencing a crisis. Many individuals in crisis are overly focused on certain aspects of the crisis situation and experience a form of tunnel vision. Clinicians use the skills of clarification, challenge, and paraphrasing to expand the clients' viewpoint and present alternative explanations or multiple perspectives related to the client's concerns. Alternative explanations encourage clients to reconsider and reframe crises into something more manageable.

Reframing

This technique builds on expanding the client's perspectives. Open-ended questioning, clarification, challenging, and paraphrasing are essential to success- ful execution of this technique. As the clinician, you intentionally encourage your client to see their concerns, feelings, or behaviors from different perspectives to explore and challenge the client's underlying assumptions and meanings.

Normalizing

The intention of this technique is like that of reframing in that the individual in crisis is provided a broader context for considering their concerns. Clinicians' use the skills of observation, clarification, reflection, content, feeling, and mean- ing to note the unique and common elements of the present crisis. Clinicians must take care not to dismiss or minimize the experiences of the person in crisis. The goal is to present the crisis within a broad context demonstrating that others have experienced and recovered from similar, but not exact concerns. Normalizing clinician responses often start with phrases like, "It is normal to…," "Most people would…," or "In circumstances like this, you might…"

Emphasizing What's Manageable

Clinicians empathize with the client about the overwhelming and unmanage- able aspects of the crisis event while simultaneously emphasizing aspects of the event that are within their control, like contacting family members, making a short list of steps to secure housing, or safety. Skills utilized in technique include observation, encouragers, and directives.

Summarizing

Clients in the initial stages of a crisis often have difficulty recapping the essen- tial elements of their experiences and may communicate in a somewhat disorganized manner. The technique of summarizing allows the clinician to tie together multiple elements of the client's message, identify themes or patterns, and provide feedback and focus. Summarizing can be used to cut off a client's disorganized discourse. Skills that support this technique include clarifying, close-ended questions, and paraphrasing.

Implementing Order

Clients in the throes of a crisis often feel disorganized and confused. Part of your role as a clinician is to appropriate aid for the client to organize, prioritize, and coordinate specific events in a linear and step-wise manner while insuring the client's freedom and self-sufficiency. By clarifying the client's needs, asking closed-ended questions, and offering directives, you intentionally act to help the client structure and organize their needs in a hierarchical and behaviorally specific manner.

Promoting Mobilization

While many clients may want to take a particular action, at times the external resources are not in place to support them. This technique asks the clinician to help the client organize their internal resources and to assist with the mobilization of external resources. The crisis clinician provides encouragement and support to clients who are ready to act and augment client's interest with realistic plans of action. The following counseling skills are helpful in promoting mobilization: observation, directives, closed-ended questioning, and open-ended questioning. The essence of this aspect of crisis counseling is to marshal client internal resources, while encouraging the use of external support systems to help them cope and problem solve.

Care Coordination

Individuals experiencing a crisis often interact with multiple agencies and care providers. It can be consuming. This technique helps the clinician organize client care activities with stakeholders helps facilitate the delivery of helpful services. Providing care coordination requires you to be are aware of local resources, health providers, and transportation options.

Psychoeducation

After the acute phase of the crisis, you may find the opportunity to provide psychoeducation to those affected by crisis. This service supports increased awareness, clarification, and the achievement of goals. Through this process, the client learns to adopt pragmatic behaviors and generalize the learning to their life. This technique involves several therapeutic and instructional skills such as provision of information, observation, clarification, and open-ended questioning.

Advocacy

This technique, while not a direct service to the client, is an expectation of all clinicians. While listed as a technique, advocacy is more of a service-focused welfare of individuals and groups. Clinicians seek to eliminate oppression, obstacles, and hindrances that prevent access, progress, and development of services for those in need. With respect to various types of crises, clinicians may begin with questions as "What does our community do to support those experiencing domestic violence?" "How can we work to improve mental health and preventive services in high schools to address school violence?" Table 3.2 presents an overview of the knowledge, skills, awareness, techniques, and resources needed utilized by developmental level and client type.

TABLE 3.2 ● **Knowledge, Skills, Awareness, Techniques, and Resources for Crisis Counseling by Client Type and Level of Professional Development**

	Knowledge	Skills	Awareness	Techniques	Resources
		Advanced Graduate Students and Novice Professionals			
Individuals	Hierarchy of human needs (Maslow) Developmental processes Cultural context and individual differences Triage Equilibrium/ disequilibrium Crisis counseling/ intervention models: Psychological First Aid (WHO, 2011); Roberts's 7 Stage Model (2015); Myer and Moore (2006)	Informal assessment: basic needs Informed decision making related to triage Data gathering Management of personal emotion Compassion Empathic listening Compassion and hope Observation Closed, and open-ended questioning Reflection of content, feeling & meaning Restatement, summary, clarification of client statements Personalizing clients' feelings to promote their ownership, Collaborative owning statements	Various ways in which people will respond Sympathy vs empathy Personal need to rescue clients Multicultural competencies: 4 core Multicultural attributes Culturally bound assumptions Emic and etic models of helping Locus of control	Immediacy Interpretation Focusing Creating awareness Silence Expanding the clients view Reframing Normalizing Emphasizing what's manageable Summarizing Implementing order Psychoeducation Promoting mobilization Care coordination Providing support Providing protection	Local information on services, health and safety, social, housing, counseling, financial, food, religious/ spiritual supports Referral list of pro bono providers Personal support/ debriefing for the clinician

(Continued)

TABLE 3.2 (Continued)

	Knowledge	Skills		Awareness	Techniques	Resources
			Advanced Graduate Students and Novice Professionals			
			Disowned statements, conveying understanding Positive reinforcement, Limit setting Facilitative listening		Providing guidance Advocacy Triage	
Groups	Stages of a group Purpose of the group Group process Group roles Group leadership/co-leaders Ethical decision making	Active listening Modeling Linking member's content and feelings Initiating and facilitating communication Blocking Summarizing	Self-awareness Intersectionality Allow member self-identification Protect clients Protect boundaries Guard against universality Cross-cultural communication	Scanning-eye contact (as is culturally appropriate) with each member Set a support and goal-oriented tone Modeling desired behavior Ice-breakers, initial activities designed to promote member to member sharing Round Robin: each member shares their perspective or may pass		

Communities	History of previous crisis events, particularly natural and human caused events Local health and safety organizations Community emergency communication/disaster plan			Dyads and triads-promotes more focused conversation Linking or bridging-members comments to each to demonstrate mutuality	Referral list First responders list
Experienced Professionals*					
Individuals	All those listed above and How crisis events can result in a trauma response Specialized focus on special populations (children, older adults, police, educational settings)	All those listed above and Reflective listening for meaning and intent Appropriate self-disclosure	Personal and professional humility Anxiety no longer impacts performance Looks inward for guidance Engages in reflective practice and professional development	Interpretation Advanced accurate empathy deepens clients' experience via metaphor stories, analogies Empathic confrontation	Local information on services, health and safety, social, housing, counseling, financial, food, religious/spiritual supports Personal support/debriefing for the clinician

(Continued)

TABLE 3.2 (Continued)

	Knowledge	Skills	Awareness	Techniques	Resources
	Experienced Professionals*				
	Learn supervision Advanced training in trauma informed methods Partnerships with local psychiatrists, psychiatric treatment centers and continuum of care Therapeutic patience-inventions timed for maximum impact/learning Cognitive complexity Relativistic thinking	Role model for advanced graduate students and novice professionals		Provide support and debriefing for clinicians	
Groups	Addressing complex & layered group dynamics Facilitating complexity and conflict in groups Using conversations rather than directives to effectively facilitate Understanding your style & patterns in group facilitation Reflective practice: how you relate to groups and personal triggers				

	Managing disruptive members' behaviors Facilitating emergent agendas and change Using Fishbowls and other experiential tools Promoting group's self-directed learning				
Communities	Leadership and command structure of crisis responders Regional resources History of previous crisis events, particularly natural and human caused events Local health and safety organizations Community emergency communication/disaster plan	Advanced practice Supervision Leadership Organization Advocacy Networking	Public health and safety Communication plans Public Affairs including medical needs, food and housing announcements Recognition of underserved communities Non-human (animals and wildlife) and environmental concerns Immediate, short- and longer-term planning	Panel discussion Community listening sessions/forums Engaging regional or national service organizations (short term)	State and local referral list; Pro bono services Serve on local and state crisis and disaster response teams

Assessment and Case Conceptualization

Individuals continually assess each other in informal ways. We notice who notices us; we listen to the intonation of a friend's speech and try to determine if the group of teens in the car next to us is just having a good time or looking for trouble. As clinicians, we are in the business of assessing our clients, our reactions, our environments, and our outcomes. For example, when a client mentions wanting to "hurt their neighbor," most clinicians would assess the client's tone and intensity of voice, facial expression, prior history of statements, or actions. We ask about the historical relationship with this neighbor and consider this comment in the context with what they know about the client's prior behaviors. You will use a variety of informal and formal assessments with clients in crisis and each assessment will be informed by your knowledge and history with the client, their presentation of concerns, and resources available.

Hood and Johnson (2007) report that the first counseling centers in America were referred to as counseling and testing centers due to their focus on assessment. Various labels describe the assessment process: assessment, appraisal, testing, evaluation, and measurement. While there is some overlap in these terms, each word is unique in its meaning. Walsh and Betz (1995) defined psychological assessment as a process of understanding and helping people cope with problems. In this process, tests are used to collect meaningful information about the person and their environment. Others define psychological assessment as "any systematic method of obtaining information from tests and other sources, used to draw inferences about characteristics of people, objects, or programs" (National Council on Measurement in Education [NCME], 1999, p.17). Appraisal, like evaluation, implies going beyond measurement to provide interpretations and statements regarding human attributes and behaviors assessed. The process of assessing or estimating attributes is used interchangeably with evaluation. Testing refers to paper and pencil or computerized instruments believed to consistently measure a given sample of behavior across a particular population. Lastly, measurement has been defined as a general process of determining the dimension of an attribute or trait.

According to James and Gilliland (2017), there are five areas that crisis clinicians focus on during assessment—severity; mobility in the areas of affect, cognition, and behavior; resources available to the client, like coping mechanisms; and level of lethality and ability to defuse a situation and return to a state of equilibrium. A primary concern of assessment is disturbed equilibrium. Specifically, clinicians continually assess client's affect for evidence of numbness, fear, or confusion; behavior, which may be agitated or detached; and cognition, which may present as disorientation or disordered thinking. Assessment of these domains allows the clinician to triage concerns, determine the impact of the crisis incident, and offer needed resources.

Unlike traditional forms of counseling, a crisis assessment almost always involves immediate changes or contrasts in the client's functioning. You may ask the client, "Do you typically feel this overwhelmed by other people?" "How do you determine what you do next?" or "What have you done in the past to feel less anxious?" Assessment in counseling specialty areas often involves a scheduled appointment where the client completes an instrument; crisis assessments are often conducted on-scene through observation and verbal interactions to evaluate heightened emotions, cognitive confusion, and behavioral disorientation. Clinicians responding to a crisis often have no history with and are unaware of the individual's baseline functioning. Additionally, the clinician interacts with individuals who are reacting to events that appear beyond their capacity to manage. Common phrases to determine one's baseline function include, "To what extent are your emotions related to the (crisis) event?" or "In the past, what do you do when things are out of control?" A complete assessment involves the person in crisis, their family, friends, coworkers, or loved ones to gain other perspectives on the individual's precrisis modes of functioning.

Differentiating Formal and Informal Assessment

Evaluations or assessments of persons in crisis can be completed in several settings through a variety of means. Standardized interviews, paper and pencil or computerized tests, and protocol-based observations are typically categorized as *formal assessments*. The *formality* is evidenced in the construction of the assessment tool, its administration, and the training of the practitioner. It's a lot like quality control! Formal and for that matter informal assessments begin with the desire to *know* something. Researchers, scholars, and clinicians assess individuals to observe, explain, classify, predict, or plan. In counseling, psychology, and social work, formal assessments are analogous to the physical exam in medicine.

Most formal assessments are subjected to a rigorous instrument development process. This process begins with researchers creating test items designed to capture the essence of a phenomena. Researchers use the professional literature, documented observations, and case histories to formulate clear and concise items or activities designed to measure the variables of interest, like mood, perceptions, or abilities. Next, these items and activities are grouped into a formal assessment survey then subjected to further scrutiny through repeated administrations to members of an identified group or population. Respondent's assessments are scored and statistically analyzed to establish the psychometric properties, including validity or degrees to which the assessment measures what it says it measures, and reliability or the degree to which the instrument or activity produced consistent and stable results over time with the same or similar population. Formal assessments involving standardized instruments are administered, scored, and interpreted utilizing uniform procedures (Drummond & Jones, 2010). Standard procedures reduce variability and errors.

Formal Assessments

A full review of formal assessments is beyond the scope and purpose of this text; we identified and present what we consider to be the two most useful tools for your toolkit.

Mental Status Exams

These assessments provide client's data on their mental status, crisis severity, and suicidality.

Triage Assessments

The Mental Status Exam (MSE) and the Mini-Mental Status Exam (MMSE) are drawn from the previous work of Folstein and are standard observational procedures in most crisis and acute psychiatric practices. Folstein and his colleagues (Folstein, Folstein, & McHugh, 1975) devised a series of questions or an informal assessment to evaluate the cognitive functioning in patients who presented with some form of impairment. Throughout the 5- to 10-minute assessment, the clinician asks the client to repeat certain prompts (names or terms), follow simple commands, and demonstrate their orientation to person, place, and time. The MSE is a structured assessment that evaluates the mental state of the crisis survivor and reviews the major systems of psychiatric functioning (Davis, King, & Schultz, 2005). Specifically, the interviewer observes and assesses the client's thoughts, appearance, behavior/psychomotor activity, speech, actions, mood, and perception. Most MSE interviews involve similar questions and tasks. The clinician continuously assesses and documents the client's verbal and nonverbal behavior. Your observations as well as the client's responses are included in a mental status examination report. The individual writing the report presents a tentative conclusion.

The triage assessment system (TAS) for crisis intervention was developed by Myer, Williams, Ottens, and Schmidt, (1992). It is a model for understanding clients' reactions during a crisis from three domains: affective, behavioral and cognitive. Simultaneous assessment of all three domains was and is considered critical to support a return to homeostasis and avoid intervention failure or worsening of the client's condition. According to Myer and colleagues, "The TAS guides clinicians in the identification of the complex interaction among the three domains and helps prevent protracted mental health concerns." (p. 960). By formally assessing the crisis severity the clinician is informed as to how to triage your client's needs and concerns.

James and Gilliland (2017) recommend the Triage Assessment Form (TAF; Myer, 2001; Myer, Williams, Ottens, & Schmidt, 1992), Triage Assessment Checklist for Law Enforcement (TACKLE; James, Myer, & Moore, 2006), and the Triage Assessment System for Students in Learning Environments (TASSLE; Myer et al., 2007). These assessments order crisis events in an expedient manner; however, clinicians who encounter a crisis may not have time to formally assess individuals on site.

While the TACKLE and TASSLE assessments have merit for assisting in situation-specific triage, we believe the TAF assessment is a clear and concise measure adaptable for many crisis situations and is easily understood. The TAF is a brief assessment focused on three dimensions: affective, behavioral, and cognitive. The clinician asks the client a series of questions to evaluate the impact of the crisis on the clients' mood/feelings, actions, and thoughts. An important feature of the TAF assessment is the dimensional domain severity scale. The rating scale (1–10 rating scale, where 1 = No impairment and 10 = Severe impairment) asks the client to select a number that corresponds to each item in each dimension. Total scores are then calculated to determine acuity. The brevity and clarity of this protocol lends itself nicely to crisis situations (Myer, et al., 1992). Instruments, procedures, and strategies not subjected to standardization and a development process are considered *informal assessments*. Informal assessments are used at the site of group crisis or one-on-one with a client. They do not require specialized training, equipment, or standard scoring and are an effective compliment to formal assessments.

Informal Assessment

Most informal assessments involve unstructured interviews, informal observation, checklists, nonstandardized tests, and nonstandardized questionnaires (Drummond & Jones, 2010). An initial informal assessment allows the clinician to determine how to serve the client in crisis and aids the triage process. Questions crisis clinicians consider include, "What is the nature and extent of the crisis?" "Who is likely involved and is it safe to enter this environment?" "What data do I have about the nature, exposure, and proximity of survivors to the crisis?" or "What are the cultural needs of these individuals, this community, or this area?" On site, individuals experiencing a group crisis are typically scattered, overwhelmed, and impulsive, so it is essential that crisis counselors approach these individuals in a manner that provides guidance and safety. A single individual experiencing a crisis may present at your agency, or at your office, on their own or with a support family member or friend. Regardless, members of a group and the individual will benefit from your informal assessment of their concerns.

Whether presenting singly or collectively, you, the clinician, approach those in crisis in a directive and emotionally regulated manner much like the fictional *Dragnet* character L.A. Detective Joe Friday. Friday was well known for his cool and dispassionate demeanor and focus on *just the facts*. Understandably, approaching clients in this manner feels different from your approach in typical counseling sessions, but then again, crisis events are not typical! A more directive and goal-oriented approach does not mean you lack empathy or understanding; you remain warm, compassionate, understanding, and task focused. Examples of more directive messages frequently utilized by clinicians responding to individuals in crisis include; "Tell me what is upsetting you?" "Are you feeling suicidal/homicidal?" "How would you do it?" or "Please slow down and tell me who is involved?" For groups in crisis, "Who here is injured?" "Tell me who was with you, family, friends?" "Please stand up and move away from that area and sit down here." Puleo and McGlothlin (2010) describe directive, nondirective, and collaborative approaches to utilize following an informal assessment. We encourage you to read their work to deepen your understanding.

Holistic Conceptualization of Client Concerns

According to Hood and Johnson (2007), assessment serves to stimulate and provide clarification to clinicians and clients as they consider treatment planning, suicidal intent, and desired outcomes. Informal and formal assessments provide reliable data that enables clinicians and clients to triage client concerns, identify current functioning within several domains, and prioritize need services and supports. In a crisis-counseling context, individuals and their experiences are viewed holistically. It begins with your holistic view of the person or persons in crisis. For example, during individual and group crisis assessment, it is essential for the clinician to determine the meaning of verbal and nonverbal communication (Cavaiola & Colford, 2011) within the client's sociocultural context. A holistic view includes the physical, physiological, psychological, behavioral, relational, and cultural aspects of the person in crisis' experience. These six domains may appear to be discreet categories; they are not. While it is true your assessment must begin somewhere, we urge you to hold the systemic nature of the person in crisis constant as you assess and respond to their needs.

Physical

Individuals who have suffered a crisis may present with physical injury. Ensuring a crisis survivor's immediate physical safety is critical. As mentioned earlier, ethical clinicians do not practice outside the scope of their training. In advance of responding to a crisis event, the clinician secures basic first-aid training and becomes involved with their local emergency preparedness and response organizations. Trainings and continued professional development aid your ability to appropriately assist first responders, consistent with your training.

Physiological

In the immediate aftermath of a crisis, you are likely to encounter individuals who present with one of two reactions: numbing—where the person in crisis' emotions appear to be detached from their thoughts; or emotional dysregulation—where the person in crisis seems unable to control their emotions and may alternating appear frantic, agitated, or tearful. The length of exposure to traumatic situations has consequences for one's brain structures and functioning. According to Bremner (2002), the hormones of adrenalin and cortisol, released during crisis situations, can lead to long-term brain damage. Further, trauma resulting from a crisis may lead to increased irritability in the limbic system, resulting in an abnormal stimulation of the fight-or-flight response. This causes individuals to respond with significant anxiety to almost any crisis-associated stimuli like smells, noises, or bright lights. A small percentage of individuals may go on to meet the diagnostic standards for post-traumatic stress disorder (PTSD) experiencing increased heart rate, blood pressure, and skin conductance (Pitman, Orr, Forgue, De Jong, & Claiborn, 1987) and should be referred for ongoing treatment.

Behavioral and Psychological

Your client's behavioral and emotional states are temporarily overwhelmed as they react or respond to events they deem to be a crisis. According to van der Kolk and McFarlane (1996), trauma is different than other psychological phenomena because of the *subjective* meaning of the experience; in other words, what one experiences as trauma is not necessarily so for another as "the critical element that makes an event traumatic is the subjective assessment by survivors of how threatened and helpless they feel" (p. 6). From a holistic perspective, when an individual deems something as traumatic, their behavior and relationships are most likely also affected. The client's previous exposure and experiences with crisis or traumatic events, specifically, their nature, degree, duration, and idiosyncratic (personal) impact are important to consider and may be contributing to the severity of their symptoms. Assessment of prior events covers aspects such as assault or abuse in childhood or adulthood, criminal activity (DeHart, 2008), and substance abuse and use (Felitti et al., 1998). Bychowski (1968) offered that severe trauma, like surviving the Holocaust, can cause enduring changes in the personality, such as aggression, rage, loss of goal orientation, and inability to act. These issues not only affect the individual experiencing the crisis, it affects current and future relationships.

Relational

Relationships can be severely strained when crisis strikes. Thus, it is important for the clinician to assess and involve the loved ones, family—however defined—coworkers, and peers. Amidst other issues, it appears that there is a strong relationship between PTSD and occurrences of intimate partner violence. Orcutt, King, and King (2003) found that male-perpetrated intimate partner violence was directly related to quality of maternal relationship, war zone stressors, and PTSD symptom severity among 376 Vietnam veteran couples. Similarly, Taft et al. (2005) found, of their 109 participants, men who engaged in partner violence and were simultaneously diagnosed with PTSD evidenced the highest level of risk for future partner violence. A causal link between PTSD and relational violence seems apparent.

Cultural

Samovar and Porter (2001) define culture as the values, beliefs, traditions, and customs that connect a group of people together. These factors play a role in how an individual in crisis experiences, responds, and interprets the meaning of a crisis. Cultural beliefs, stories, rules, norms, and mores create meaning systems that explain crisis, trauma, and disaster. For example, a person experiencing visions, voices, and commands may be responding to a cultural narrative or may be presenting symptoms consistent with schizophrenia. Likewise, a person loudly and publicly proclaiming their grief is expressing their love and loss with their cultural beliefs while another may be decompensating. The determination depends on you *and* your client's context, your intra- and intercultural competencies, and your willingness to avoid judgement and focus holistically on the person in crisis. As part of your assessment, it is critical you ask questions to assess the meaning the person in crisis, and those supporting this person, place on the crisis event. Of importance is your client's perceptions to a crisis involving the death of a loved one as this involves cultural, religious, and philosophical beliefs and values related to death, grieving, and bereavement processes (Athey & Moddy-Williams, 2003).

Evaluation of Vulnerabilities

Vulnerability

With respect to human beings, many commonly view the term *vulnerability* as a personal weakness or character flaw. We find poet, David Whyte's (2015), view consistent with our own and quite apt, he wrote, "Vulnerability is not a weakness, a passing indisposition, or something we can arrange to do without, vulnerability is not a choice, vulnerability is the underlying, ever present and abiding under-current of our natural state." More formally, the International Strategy for Disaster Reduction (2004) defines vulnerability as the predisposition of individuals or societies to be affected and the inability to manage crises. Mitchell (1998) further specifies vulnerability as the potential for loss and causality when exposed to dangerous or threatening stimuli.

You may wish to assess your client's degree of vulnerability through the use of the Connor-Davidson Resilience Scale (Connor-Davidson, 2003; CD-RISC). This 25-item instrument utilizes a 5-point scale to rate an individual's ability to cope with stress and adversity. There are two abbreviated forms of the scale available. The first contains 10 items and the other has 2. The CD-RISC examines an individual's sense of personal competence, tolerance of negative affect, positive acceptance of change, trust in instincts, sense of social support, spiritual/faith, and action-oriented approach to problem solving. High scores reflect a strong sense of resiliency, while lower scores demonstrate areas of vulnerability to stress.

During a crisis, you will not have time or resources to conduct a formal assessment related to the person in crisis' vulnerability; however, Ahmed (2007) identified potential personal characteristics believed to increase one's vulnerability to crisis events. They include identifying as female, having a low sense of safety or social support, being typically described as moody, experiencing a range of emotions more powerfully than others, and perceiving nonthreatening events as threatening. Additionally, these individuals may have preexisting behavioral health concerns and present a negative appraisal of the traumatic event. Further, Ahmed detailed external vulnerabilities related to an individuals' susceptibility to trauma. They include lower levels of formal education, status as an immigrant, a history of previous traumatic events, as well as the severity of exposure or prolonged trauma.

While these factors are helpful to understand, it is an incomplete picture and excludes biologic and genetic elements. For example, a study of prevalence of PTSD comparing monozygotic and dizygotic twins of Vietnam veterans revealed that hereditary factors account for 34% of PTSD symptomology (True et al., 1993). Further, according to Yehuda, Schmeidler, Wainberg, Binderbrynes, and Duvdevani (1998), offspring of Holocaust survivors with a diagnosis of PTSD were more likely to develop the disorder than the children of survivors without PTSD. Lastly, it has been suggested that trauma survivors who develop PTSD are more likely than those who do not to have parents and first-degree relatives with mood, anxiety, and substance use disorders (Davidson, Swartz, Storck, Krishnan, & Hammett, 1985) perhaps indicating susceptibility to emotional disturbances.

We understand and acknowledge the risk in discussing culturally bound, historically inaccurate, and binary gender stereotypes; yet we feel it is important to address these inaccuracies to reduce your risk of carrying them forward into your practices. It is estimated that those who identify as female have a 13% to 20% chance of developing PTSD in comparison to men's 6% to 8% chance (Breslau et al., 1998; Kessler, Sonnega, Bromet, Hughes, & Nelson, 1995) and those who identify as female are reported to be twice as likely to develop PTSD symptoms.

There are a host of possible explanations for these prevalence rates, historic and cultural misogyny, paternalism, threat appraisal, perceived control, peritraumatic dissociation, psychophysiological responses to the event, and coping style (Olff, Langeland, Draijer, & Gersons, 2007), as well as actual biological and genetic predispositions. Thus, we gently remind you there is no consensus related to the effect of gender on one's vulnerability to PTSD; gender is an interesting but not definitive variable.

Evaluation of Resiliencies

Resiliency

If you recall, in Chapter 2, we reviewed the construct of resiliency. Bonanno (2004) defines resilience as the ability to maintain a state of normal equilibrium in the face of extremely dangerous and threatening circumstances. Clinicians can measure client's resiliency through the CD-RISC (Connor, 2006), the Resilience Scale for Adults (Friborg, Hjemdal, Rosenvinge, & Martinussen, 2003), or the Adolescent Resilience Scale (Oshio, Kaneko, Nagamine, & Nakaya, 2003).

We return to the work of Ahmed (2007) to examine internal and external factors believed to promote resiliency in those who have experienced trauma. Internal factors include the client's self-esteem, trust, resourcefulness, self-efficacy, locus of control, attachment style, sense of humor, degree of self-sufficiency, personal agency, degrees of optimism, social problem-solving skills, and impulse control. External factors associated with one's resiliency are: environmental safety, religious affiliation, presence of effective role models, emotional sustenance or understanding, companionship, sense of belonging, and positive regard provided by others to individual in crisis.

Evaluation of Protective Factors

Protective Factors

Fraser, Kirby, and Smokowski (2004) argued protective factors help people resist risk and poor outcomes, deal with crisis, and react to them in proactive ways. While there are few measures of protective factors for crisis or trauma, you can formally assess your client's protective factors with the Scale of Protective Factors (SPF; Ponce-Garcia, Madewell, & Kennison, 2015). This 24-point scale consists of 25 items and provides an assessment of the protective factors contributing to adult resilience. Specifically, the SPF measures social and cognitive protective factors that contribute to overall adult resilience. A benefit of the SPF scale is that it measures a wide range of protective factors.

Like our discussions on vulnerability and resiliency, the following protective factors described by Ahmed (2007), Alvarez and Hunt (2005), Benotsch et al. (2000), and Orcutt et al. (2003) seem to metaphorically inoculate many against the effects of crisis. These factors include active and positive coping skills, preparation to respond to trauma, formal education beyond high school, above average cognitive ability, higher income, increased self-esteem, identification as male, and the capacity to rationalize. It is important to note, many of these factors most likely were determined by culturally bound assessments that privileged those with more access to resources or status. View them with caution. In sum, many coping skills are difficult to assess in the throes of crisis while others are more easily ascertained by asking the person in crisis. We assert the most significant coping skills are active engagement in the process, leaning in rather than leaning out through withdrawal or isolation.

Acute and Short-Term Treatment Planning

Responding to those in crisis, individually and collectively, provides the clinician the opportunity to employ acute and short-term treatment planning and goal setting. In a crisis setting, treatment planning is less formal and often is focused on securing immediate services or resources for your clients. Recall earlier in this chapter we discussed asking Joe, our hypothetical flood survivor, to identify and then take one positive action to secure housing for himself and his family. This informal short-term goal setting and treatment planning differs from the more formal goal setting and treatment planning one does with traditional clients in an office setting. Treatment planning for clients in crisis may include daily review of the treatment plan through the acute phase of the crisis (Jackson-Cherry & Erford, 2010).

Short-term treatment planning addresses the causes of immediate suffering. Treatment strategies following a crisis may include crisis assessment, promoting safety, and the client's readiness to change. Diagnosis is quite different regarding crisis experiences and often are not part of the initial response to a person in crisis.

Consulting and Referring for Ancillary Services

As the clinician, you must be prepared and ready to refer those experiencing a crisis to relevant therapeutic and support services. Following the acute phase and consistent with continuity of care standards, clients may find value in services with a variety of treatment providers including partial hospitalization, inpatient or outpatient trauma treatment centers, vocational or rehabilitation programs, pharmaceutical consultation, nutritionists, housing specialists, community or support groups, faith-based or spiritual systems, and relaxation or a massage therapist.

Client Directed Empowerment and Holistic Healing

Using community resources to help reduce the effects of crisis is common in modern society. Whether a self-help book, a self-defense class, therapeutic massage, or a yoga class, clinicians encourage and support clients to act on their own behalf. Remember, most people who have experience a crisis, trauma, or disaster do not seek formal counseling or therapeutic services and for those that do, your task, our task, is to help them return to self-sufficiency, as they define it, as soon as they are able.

Summary

Clinicians' knowledge, skills, techniques, and assessments and clients' contextual factors play a significant role in the crisis experience and recovery. It is important for all early, mid, and late career professionals to understand that every individual experiences a crisis event in a unique manner and every crisis has an idiosyncratic effect on those exposed or in close proximity to those exposed. These diverse and varied reactions provide the context for tailoring crisis skills, interventions, and treatment plans to the individual, community, and group's unique meaning making experience.

Extended Learning Exercises

Case Illustration: Advanced Graduate Student

Richard, a 42-year-old man, has been in counseling with you at your internship site for the past seven weeks. He describes himself as a proud father of three, a successful banker, and chair of the Latinx Chamber of Commerce. His initial concerns included feelings of sadness, lethargy, and a loss of interest in almost everything for approximately the last six months. In today's session, Richard presented as anxious, moderately agitated, and fighting back tears. After providing support, he recounts how his wife said she was leaving him and had asked for a divorce. He said, "I won't live without my wife and children." Richard says he doesn't know what to do and asks you what he should say to his wife to keep her from leaving him.

Questions to consider:

How do you respond to Richard's immediate concerns?

What skills will you utilize?

What are your priorities with Richard in this session?

Who else may you involve in the conversation?

What additional information or resources are required for you to assist Richard?

What are the desired outcomes for Richard and you in this session?

Describe your assessment and treatment plan.

Case Illustration #2: Advanced Graduate Student

Emma, a 17-year-old high school student, walked into the mental health center where you are doing your internship. You are working on the emergency team, so she is referred to you as a walk-in client. Emma is tearful, shaking, and barely holding it together. Through her sobbing, she tells you she was raped the night before by a boy at a party. She did not know his name. Emma has not told anyone, especially her parents. She is terrified they will blame her because she snuck out of the house after midnight. Emma refuses to go to the police, hospital, school, or home. She appears immobilized.

Questions to consider:

How do you respond to Emma's immediate concerns?

What are your priorities with Emma in this session?

Who else may you involve in the conversation?

What skills will you utilize?

What additional information or resources are required for you to assist Emma?

What are the desired outcomes for Emma and you in this session?

Describe your assessment and treatment plan.

Case Illustration: Novice Professional

Jamar is a 45-year-old African American man who is self-referred to the agency in which you work. The intake paperwork indicates he is seeking psychotherapy to address several life issues, yet his concerns seem vague. The intake worker indicated Jamar reported "feeling depressed and anxious" about life and did not have "anyone in his life to talk to about *this* stuff." In the first session, Jamar vocalizes he is uncertain about being in counseling but does not know where else to go. Over and over he says he feels like he is going to burst. He seems listless and does not identify a particular stressor but agrees to come back for a second session. In the second session, Jamar says he just must tell you something. He asks you not to look at him for a few minutes and during this time. Jamar discloses he has been having feelings he does not understand. He feels confused and ashamed about an encounter he had with another man at work three weeks ago. Jamar said he struggled in the past with

an attraction to men and had gone to a few gay bars. But through his faith, prayer, and family counseling at his church he was able to overcome those feelings and focus on dating women. Jamar said he thought God had cured him, but last week, in a meeting, Micah winked at Jamar. Jamar recalled feeling immediately drawn to Micah but since last week has avoided contact with him. Jamar said all he can think about is Micah and has been fantasizing about a life with Micah. Jamar asks you what you can do to cure him of his homosexuality.

Questions to consider:

How do you respond to Jamar's immediate concerns?

What are your priorities with Jamar in this session?

Who else may you involve in the conversation?

What advanced skills will you utilize?

What additional information or resources are required for you to assist Jamar?

What are the desired outcomes for Jamar and you in this session?

Describe your assessment and treatment plan.

Case Illustration #2: Novice Professional

William is a 68-year-old retired professor of chemistry. He has had a long and distinguished career. His wife, Selly, is 59 years old and still employed. They have four adult children. Last week, William was diagnosed with metastatic melanoma; his prognosis is grave with no reasonable treatment available. William's decline will be rapid, and he is likely to need to be hospitalized within six weeks. His doctors have given him three months to live. They have been referred to your agency two days after the diagnosis by their physician and insurance company. William and Selly report they are "ok" and just feel numb and not sure what to do next. They have not told anyone of William's diagnosis.

> How do you respond to William's and Selly's immediate concerns?
>
> What are your priorities with them in this session?
>
> Who else may you involve in the conversation?
>
> What advanced skills will you utilize?
>
> What additional information or resources are required for you to assist this couple?
>
> What are the desired outcomes for William, Selly, and you in this session?
>
> Describe your assessment and treatment plan.

Case Illustration: Mid-Career Professional

Eva is a single mother of four children who was referred to your private practice by Social Services after a documented history of child neglect and suspected abuse. Eva and her children have been in counseling with you for about three months. Eva is at risk of having all four children placed in foster care due to her struggles with a meth addiction during the past six years. She has been in jail twice for selling meth and once to inpatient treatment. Occasionally Eva attends NA, as she says, "to find a guy to take home to make me feel good." She is currently employed as a housekeeper at a local hotel.

None of the four fathers are currently involved with Eva or the children. The children are Anthony, age 4; Sabrina, age 5; Thomas, age 7;

and Billy, age 9. Billy has learning difficulties and is described as aggressive at school. He has an IEP related to his social and emotional concerns. Thomas and Sabrina are very connected. Both have been described as quiet and withdrawn, moderately detached from interactions with others. Sabrina frequently has Billy speak for her. They both are doing poorly in school. Anthony spent the first six months of his life with Eva's mother while Eva was in treatment. At daycare and at home, Anthony demonstrates unpredictable and destructive behavior toward others, specifically Sabrina. His behaviors are atypical for his age and level of development; Social Services is considering an out-of-home placement for Anthony due to the risk his behaviors pose to other children in daycare and Eva's difficultly in providing him structure.

The course of treatment has been uneven as Eva has canceled two appointments and no-showed for an additional three. Eva vocalizes wanting to get better and wants to keep her family together yet struggles. Today, Eva arrives at your office with Sabrina and Billy for an emergency appointment. She tells you she caught her current live-in boyfriend Mark sexually abusing Sabrina, with Billy in the room watching. Eva's speech is pressured and her thoughts are disorganized. She is sure Social Services will remove her kids and she want you to have Mark arrested and to put Billy in a psychiatric hospital.

Questions to consider:

> How do you respond to Eva's, Sabrina's, and Billy's immediate concerns?
>
> What are your priorities for Eva, Sabrina, and Billy in this session?
>
> Who else may you involve in the conversation?

What advanced skills will you utilize?

What additional information or resources are required for you to assist this family?

What are the desired outcomes for Eva, Sabrina, Billy, and you in this session?

Describe your assessment and treatment plan.

Case Illustration: Professional

Terri is a 15-year-old emancipated youth referred to you by the local school district for increasing anxiety that significantly interferes with her school performance. She describes periods of time when she is tearful, cannot concentrate, feels incredibly scared, and is angry at her parents for "being so screwed up." She says she is "worried about everything all the time." Terri agreed to try a low dose of medication to support her current counseling. She has completed 10 sessions and her anxiety, which appears to be generalized, has become somewhat more manageable.

Terri was legally emancipated from her parents six months ago, after a five-year history of failed foster placements and three attempts at family reunification. She receives supportive services from social services and the local school district. Terri has two siblings, Kara, age 10, and Sam, age 7. She rarely sees them; they have been in foster care for four years. The whereabouts of Terri's parents are unknown.

Last night, the local police came to Terri's apartment due to a noise compliant. The police asked if they could enter the apartment, and in the process of interviewing Terri, some of Terri's friends were found to be in possession of heroin. They were arrested and taken to jail. The officer told Terri he would be informing the Department of Social Services caseworker of the drug bust and that Terri would lose her apartment and would return to foster care until she was 18. Terri expresses feeling guilty and worthless. She presents as restless and inconsolable saying her life is a catastrophe and she is leaving the state for good. She came to say goodbye and is going to find her parents.

Questions to consider:

How do you respond to Terri's immediate concerns?

What are your priorities with Terri in this session?

Who else may you involve in the conversation?

What advanced skills will you utilize?

What additional information or resources are required for you to assist Terri?

What are the desired outcomes for Terri and you in this session?

Describe your assessment and treatment plan.

Additional Resources

Helpful Links

American Red Cross: https://www.redcross
.org/volunteer/volunteer-opportunities/
disaster-volunteer.html

Colorado Crisis Education and Response
Network (CoCERN): https://www.colorado
.gov/pacific/cdphe/colorado-crisis-
education-and-response-network-cocern

Crisis Intervention Teams (CIT)—Designing
CIT Programs for Youth: https://www.nami
.org/citforyouth

Crisis Intervention Continuing Education
Program Courses: https://aihcp.net/crisis-
intervention-ce-courses-program/

How to Help in an Emotional Crisis:
https://www.apa.org/helpcenter/
emotional-crisis

National Child Traumatic Stress Network:
https://www.nctsn.org/treatments-and-
practices/psychological-first-aid-and-skills-
for-psychological-recovery/about-pfa

Psychological First Aid for First Responders:
https://store.samhsa.gov/product/
Psychological-First-Aid-for-First-Responders/
NMH05-0210

The Role of the School Counselor in
Crisis Planning and Intervention: https://
www.counseling.org/resources/library/
VISTAS/2010-V-Online/Article_92.pdf

History and Theoretical Foundations of Trauma

Societies have encountered traumatic and devastating events since the dawn of time. Cave drawings, oral histories, art, literature, religious texts, and more recently, academic writings document the ubiquity of traumatic events, their nature and consequences. René Descartes (1649/1989), in his treatise *The Passions of the Soul*, explained the relationship between disruptive emotions, the resulting fear, and its enduring effect on human interactions and behavior. In contrast to what we believe today, Descartes believed passions, or what we today call emotions, originated from an external stimulus acting on the individual. If understood, these passions could be addressed and controlled. Descartes wrote, "Even those who have the weakest souls could acquire absolute mastery over all their passions if they worked hard enough at training and guiding them" (Bennett, 2017, p. 16). Pivoting slightly from Descartes, the general sentiment that one weakened or made vulnerable by external events could gain mastery over their emotions with understanding, effort, training, and guidance is the central principle of psychotherapy and, particularly, trauma-informed treatment.

It is safe to say most individuals have experienced or witnessed at least one traumatic event in their lifetime. The examination of traumatic events by Benjet et al. (2015) supports this supposition. They reviewed and analyzed 68,894 individual general population surveys drawn from 24 countries. Benjet and colleagues evaluated individuals' exposure to 29 traumatic events, determined prevalence rates, trauma type clusters, correlations with personal characteristics, and traumatic histories including repeated exposures. They found over 70% of individuals had been exposed to at least one traumatic event and 30.5% had been exposed to four or more. Half of the traumatic events identified by respondents came from one of five categories: witnessing death or serious injury, the unexpected death of a loved one, mugging, life-threatening automobile accident, and experiencing a life-threatening illness or injury. The nature, intensity, duration, and scope of tragic and horrific events are traumatizing. In some cases, expected traumatic responding progresses into a more acute or persistent process or psychological disorder. In this chapter, we focus on psychological trauma, differentiate it from crisis and disaster, and explore the historical and theoretical, definitions, and models that inform current conceptual and clinical understandings of trauma.

Learning Objectives

After reading this chapter and participating in the case studies and reflective exercises, you will be able to

- Distinguish trauma from crisis and disaster including the role of perception, proximity, exposure, dose effect, fear, and anxiety

- Understand the historical context, development, and contributions of major theories and theorists of trauma and related concepts including definitions, social/political contexts, and six related controversies

- Articulate key elements related to trauma: clinical presentation, assessments, diagnosis, mechanisms of change, models of treatment

- Differentiate simple and complex trauma and associated prevalence rates

- Apply theoretical and diagnostic knowledge case studies

Lions and Tigers and Bears, Oh My! Differentiating Trauma From Crisis and Disaster

With apologies to Dorothy and the gang from the *Wizard of Oz*, we draw on the above referenced mantra to frame the discussion and distinguish crisis from trauma and disaster. Understandably lions, tigers, and bears are majestic animals that contribute to the ecosystem. Yet, depending on the animal's location—a sanctuary or the wild; your individual temperament—easy/inflexible or curious/fearful; and your history with, proximity to, and length of exposure to lions, tigers, and bears, you may appraise them to be a threat, an awesome creature, or some combination. Context matters *and* your appraisal of that context matters more!

Whether evaluating potential threats from lions, tigers, or bears or attempting to distinguish trauma from crises and disaster, most of you begin, whether you know it or not, by exploring the common and unique elements of the animals or constructs. With respect to treating the traumatized, understanding categorical similarities and differences of crisis, trauma, and disaster (CTD) will help you identify and prepare for clients' needs and inform your case conceptualization and selection of clinical interventions. For example, CTDs involve the perception of threat or harm, are unwanted experiences, and disrupt and disturb previous ways of coping and functioning in many, if not all, domains. Because the clinician understands it is the individual's *perception* of the event, not the event itself, that determines the nature and impact of a CTD, most therapeutic interactions begin with the clinician assessing the clients' perception or experience of the threat. Crises, traumas, and disaster are distinguished by four factors: proximity or how close one was to the event; how long they were exposed to the event; the magnitude of real and perceived threats; and the worsening of troubling or distressing symptoms. Figure 4.1 represents the *Spectrum of CTD* presented in Chapter 1. The braided image presupposes a somewhat linear progression from crisis to trauma to disaster. It also visually represents the interconnected nature of these constructs that are highly correlated, mutually influenced, reciprocal in nature, and influenced by time, proximity, event intensity, duration, and complexity.

Let's apply the concepts presented above to Joe, our hypothetical South Dakotan you met in Chapter 2. Joe and Teri lost their family's home and businesses to a 100-year flood. Revisit the set of circumstances that describe Joe and his family's crisis event. Now let's alter an influencing aspect or two of events and witness the progression and transformation of a crisis into a traumatic event, and subsequently into a disaster. Figure 4.2 presents the essential elements experienced by Joe and Teri as Joe perceived events as a crisis, trauma, and finally a disaster. As you read, reflect on the events and experiences influencing Joe's appraisal and how you might respond as his clinician.

FIGURE 4.1 ● Spectrum of Crisis Trauma and Disaster

Crisis	Trauma	Disaster
Close personal/direct proximity brief to moderate exposure	Very close personal/direct proximity moderate/repeated/prolonged engaging multiple senses	Personal/direct proximity prolonged/severe exposure engaging multiple senses
Low perceived recurrence	moderate to high perceived recurrence	high perceived recurrence

FIGURE 4.2 ● Crisis-Trauma-Disaster Event Progression

	Event progression over time–Crisis to Trauma to Disaster						
Category	Event/Response/Threat Perception	Time Frame for actions	Proximity	Exposure	Perception event will reoccur	Event complexity	Status
Crisis	Joe and Teri receive non-mandatory evacuation order; remain in their home despite neighbors evacuating; low-moderate perception of threat; both feel overwhelmed and uncertain	12–24 hr.	Close/personal	Brief/Moderate	Low: the river rises and falls each spring	Low	Joe and Teri are in crisis because they feel terrified, are immobilized, uncertain about how to respond, worried about kid's safety and business; Joe is short-tempered and agitated; Teri, Max, and Emma withdraw
Trauma	Night of the flood Joe was moving his family to a shelter in town. Along the way, he attempted to rescue Sara, an elderly neighbor, whose truck was surrounded by rising waters. Joe reached the truck, but as he attempted to move her to his vehicle, she was swept away by rushing waters. He feels responsible for her death, Sara's body has yet to be recovered	Ongoing	Very close/Personal	Moderate/High	Low perception event will reoccur. Joe is experiencing intrusive thoughts and images	Moderate to high	Joe is distraught most days and struggles to function. He feels deep guilt related to Sara's death. His attempts to sleep are futile he has frequent nightmares; he re-experiences and relives Sara's hand slipping out of his, her cries and face as she floated into the darkness. Joe is drinking to the point of getting drunk every day. Teri feels helpless and alone
Disaster	Flood occurs, wipes out 2 of 3 of Joe's businesses; destroys the family home; country roads are impassable; Teri cannot return to work; limited state disaster funds are available and there has yet to be a Presidential disaster declaration	1 week to 24 months	Direct/deeply personal	Prolonged/Severe	High: a local dam and several berms were breached; more rain is forecasted	High: Joe and his neighbors experienced devastation; multiple services and systems are inoperable	Joe and Teri are responding to the disaster. Feelings of agitation have transformed into feelings of numbness; Joe is tearful and apathetic about his businesses; they are living, temporarily with Teri's parents

Defining Trauma

The Cultural Context of Trauma

Trauma comes in many forms. Ask laypersons to describe a traumatic event and most will describe horrific or catastrophic events like rape, mass shootings, or abuse while others describe their reaction to the finale of their beloved television mini-series! Our hypothetical laypersons may also offer that traumatic events cause people to "be haunted by their past" and "need counseling" or they will "act crazy or weird" until they "get over *it* and move on." The term *trauma* is also often used interchangeably with *stress*. For conceptual clarity, in this text we distinguish the concepts of stress and crisis trauma.

TABLE 4.1 ● Comparison of Stress and Trauma		
	Stress	**Trauma**
Nature of Event/Situation	onset—acute or chronic less dramatic	onset—acute dramatic, often life threatening
Degree of Control	minor and intermittent loss of control over emotions or thoughts like feeling irritable or momentarily confused	moderate to severe loss of control over thoughts and emotions; experienced as profound sadness, rage, intrusive thoughts, and reexperiencing/reliving the event
Relief	readily achieved as source of stress is addressed or individual diverts attention to other activities	difficult to achieve; without clinical intervention individuals may utilize numbing or avoidance strategies to seek relief from symptoms
Emotional Magnitude	emotional experiences of stress ranges from low to severe; most often is experienced as low grade and chronic	emotional experience of trauma ranges from moderate to severe to debilitating and are persistent

Scholars and clinicians have long sought to resolve controversies related to psychological trauma, particularly its definitions, origins, and interplay of social, biological, physiological, and psychological factors and relationship, if any, to social political contexts. The task seems daunting when one considers the complex history and development of our understandings of trauma, yet it is quite simple when one looks into the eyes of another who seeks our support and skill; they want relief.

Individuals and cultures define and experience traumatic events in multiple ways; it is important to note the commonalities and patterns of trauma-related responding independent of the source of the trauma. In other words, despite many types of traumatic events, humans tend to respond similarly. Descriptions of trauma are commonplace in American culture; they even show up in 1990 in the monologue by comedian George Carlin where he regales the etymology

TABLE 4.2 ● Historical Terms For Psychological Trauma		
Combat Related	**Injury Related**	**Interpersonal Violence Related**
Wind confusion	Railway spine	Psychic shock
Nostalgia	Vertebral neurosis	Traumatic neurosis
Irritable heart	Whiplash neurosis	Traumatic shock
Disordered action of the heart	Accident neurosis	Fright neurosis
Soldier's heart	Accident victim syndrome	Concentration camp syndrome
Da Costa's Syndrome	Compensationitis	Battered wife syndrome
Old Sergeant's Syndrome	Erichsen's diases	Battered child syndrome
War neurosis	Litigation neurosis	Traumatic stress
Combat fatigue	Profit neurosis	PTSD
Neurocirculatory asthenia		
Gas hysteria		
Combat stress neurosis		
Shell shock		
Physioneurosis		
Battle shock		
Neurasthenia		
Effort syndrome		
War sailor syndrome		
Post-Vietnam syndrome		
Effects of Agent Orange		
Gulf War Syndrome		
Desert Storm Syndrome		

Sources: O'Brien (1998); Jones & Wessely (2005); van der Kolk, McFarlane, & Weisaeth (1996).

and history of terms related to traumatic stress (see https://www.youtube.com/watch? v=hSp8IyaKCs0). Table 4.2 contains historical terms, drawn from the professional literature, used to describe psychological trauma. The list of terms in the table is not exhaustive, is culture bound, and reflects the experiences or perspectives of individuals and groups of European and United States origins, particularly Caucasians.

Defining Psychological Trauma

Within the last half century, a robust body of scientific and clinical research has culminated in a more consistent description of trauma and trauma-related responding. Examples include Figley (1995), an American psychiatrist, and Judith Herman, author of the landmark book *Trauma and Recovery* (1992). Herman wrote,

"Trauma events are extraordinary, not because they occur rarely, but rather because they overwhelm the ordinary human adaptions to life" and because they "overwhelm the ordinary system of care that gives people a sense of control, connection and meaning" (p. 33). Karen Saakvitne and her colleagues, who investigated childhood sexual abuse, described trauma as an individual's subjective (personal) experience of an objective event or condition which overwhelms the individual's ability to integrate or cope with the experience perceived as a threat to life, bodily integrity, or caregivers (Saakvitne, Gamble, Pearlman, & Tabor Lev, 2000).

Although there is a fair amount of agreement surrounding the definition of trauma, conditions resulting from exposure and diagnostic criteria for post-traumatic stress disorder in the *Diagnostic and Statistical Manual* (American Psychiatric Association [APA; *DSM–5*], 2013), controversies remain. For example, in 2013, the APA introduced the new category, Trauma- and Stressor-Related Disorders and included a sub-type for children ages six and younger. All conditions in this category require exposure to a traumatic or stressful event as a diagnostic criterion. The eight criteria and two specifications include stressors such as intrusion symptoms, avoidance, negative alterations to cognitions and mood, alterations to arousal and reactivity, duration, functional significance or functional impairment, and exclusion of other factors or causes. Defining characteristics are further refined by consideration of two specifications, response to traumatic stimuli and duration.

Descriptions and defining characteristics of psychological trauma emerge over time and are continuously refined. The concepts, features, and assumptions that underlie the multiple definitions of trauma and trauma-related responding depend on a complex interplay of cultural, socio-political, economic, philosophical, medical, technological, and knowledge factors. In the following sections, you will read how researchers and clinicians, like our hypothetical laypersons, define and describe trauma as unexpected and shocking events that are devastating. Compared to crises, traumas last longer and cause more suffering.

A Brief History of Trauma and Trauma-Informed Counseling

He who loves practice without theory is like the sailor who boards ship without a rudder and compass and never knows where he may cast. —Leonardo da Vinci

History

Da Vinci's words are prophetic, particularly for those of us who study crisis, trauma, and disaster (CTD). Until recently, those developing theories related to trauma and traumatic responding cast about in a seemingly rudderless fashion responding to prevailing winds of public opinion or governmental actions. Being a reflective reader, you might rightly ask, "Why is a theory important?" and, voilà, here's our response! A theory is a constellation of ideas constructed to explain and account for phenomena *independent* of those phenomena. A sound theory has explanatory power, is succinct, describes the relationship(s) between and among components, is testable, predictive, and provides a set of principles, principles that guide real-world application, or in this case CTD treatment approaches. Theories are products of the time and context in which they are set and as such are bounded by the knowledge base, beliefs, and cultural influences during the era in which they were promulgated. Theories provide Da Vinci's rudder and compass to guide researchers and clinicians' knowledge, skill, and treatment of those affected by trauma.

The history and course of trauma theory development, and in particular, post-traumatic stress disorder, are marked by periods of intense interest and study followed inexplicably by extended periods of inattention and disregard. Bessel van der Kolk (2007) summarized, "Psychiatry has periodically suffered from marked amnesias, in which well-established knowledge was abruptly forgotten" and later "...periodically has been fascinated by trauma" (p.19). Other authors have also chronicled the sharp shifts in (Jones & Wessely, 2006; Weisaeth, 2014) the development trauma theories in psychology (Cahill & Foa, 2007; Roberts, 2018; Monson, Friedman, & La Bash, 2014), psychiatry (van der Kolk, Herran, & Hostetler, 1994; van der Kolk, 2007), and the humanities (Alford, 2016, Radstone, 2007). Researchers and scholars have focused on bio-psycho-physiological, social-relational, and vocational aspects of trauma and its impact on individuals, families, and society. In the past two decades, neurobiological and neurocognitive explanations of trauma and trauma-related responses (van der Kolk, 2014) have emerged. Because theories of trauma developed over time and were subject to the influences and controversies of the eras, in this text, we present our understanding of the development of trauma theories chronologically rather than compartmentalizing them in separate sections or chapters. Readers are directed to the works of Alford (2016) and Radstone (2007) for a discussion of trauma theory in the humanities.

Multiple narratives of traumatic events have been chronicled in the literature, creative works, and scholarly writings in many disciplines across many cultures (Antze & Lambek. 1996; Caruth, 1996; Choi et al., 2017; Kurtz, 2014; Herman, 1992; Freud, 1886; Radstone, 2007). Definitions, descriptions, and interpretations emanating from Western cultures are privileged in the development and understandings of the trauma and in our present work. And we recognize the contribution of knowledge and narratives from non-Western cultures. To understand the *human* experience and expression of trauma, scholars and clinicians must continue to seek a global, nonculture bound understanding of the precursors, factors, and mechanisms of trauma. Human experiences and processes involved in acute and chronic expressions (post-traumatic stress disorder; PTSD) of simple and complex trauma also inform and transform the knowledge base. Failure to recognize and confirm cultural variations in the nature and course of trauma across time cosigns us to the shifts of intense focus and periodic amnesias described by van der Kolk. Considering this caution, we endeavored to represent trauma in its multicultural context.

Nineteenth Century Understandings of Trauma

Much of our early understandings of trauma emerged from the experiences of those who experienced the horrors of war and child sexual abuse during the 19th and early 20th century in Europe and the United States. One of the first documented cases of what is now recognized as trauma was recorded in 1813 by Joseph Frank, a Viennese medical professor, at a hospital in Lithuania (Gailiene,

2011). The professor described the acute and repeated dissociative experiences of a 14-year-old girl who witnessed invading soldiers from Napoleon's forces threaten her father's life. Frank was so taken by the girl's account he wrote, "How come no doctor known to me has never before written *ex professo* (as a professional) about the illnesses that spread after wars?" (p. 5). Frank, called into question the absence of medical and psychological professional literature on the mental illnesses associated with citizens who have survived war-torn areas. In the United States, physicians described the anxious, distressed responses of some Civil War veterans as nostalgia. Calhoun (1864) identified four primary causes of *nostalgia* in Civil War solders—rushed enlistments, expectations of a brief war, service far from home, and delays in communication due to use of a nascent postal service challenged by ever-changing battle lines. Calhoun recommended regular leaves to relieve soldiers' psychological anguish. Frank and Calhoun, among others, viewed the origins of what we now call traumatic stress as a psychological, not physical concern.

In the same era in the same war, Philadelphia physician Jacob Mendez Da Costa, working as an acting assistant surgeon during the Civil War, studied over 300 active duty soldiers reporting a variety of soldier's somatic complaints—chest pain, heart palpitations, anxiety, fatigue, tunnel vision, and nightmares. Due to the near universal report of cardiac symptoms, Da Costa informed the Surgeon General's office (Devine, 2014) of these new, *peculiar functional disorder of the heart*. These dysfunctions came to be known as *soldier's heart, irritable heart,* or *Da Costa's syndrome*. Calhoun believed symptoms emanated from soldiers' psychological longing for home in contrast to Da Costa who believed these conditions were due to physiological or organic causes. At this point in history, few medical professionals acknowledged a holistic or systemic understanding of mind-body relationships. This dichotomous view of human functioning provided the foundation for the first of six controversies related to origins and maintenance of trauma and traumatic responding. *Physical or Psychological?* Were the constellations of symptoms or disordered behaviors an illness with an organic/physiological cause or were they due to an emotional/characterological/psychological response? Were the symptoms of *soldier's heart* and other trauma-related responses of psychological or physiological origins? As you read, make note of how this question reverberates through trauma theories for the next century.

Technological advances of the 19th century exposed humankind to an increasing array of traumatic events like pervasive railroad accidents. The next milestone in our understanding of a theory of trauma and trauma-related responding emerged from the medical field, specifically, the 1866 work of John Eric Erichsen. Erichsen authored *On Railway and Other Injuries of the Nervous System* and documented the physical injuries and somatic complaints of railway accident survivors—exhaustion, terror, and chronic pain. Erichsen (1886) believed the psychological symptoms originated from the physical injuries and warned against confusing them with the symptoms of hysteria which originated from psychological processes.

Because railway accidents were so frequent and horrific, in 1864, the English parliament passed the Campbell Act extending liability to railway companies for the physical and *psychological* health and safety of their passengers. For some time, accident survivors with physical injuries were readily compensated, but the presence of physical complaints in survivors with no or limited physical injuries perplexed physicians, particularly when survivors' psychological and physical health continued to deteriorate long after the accident. Those seeking compensation for psychic complaints or injuries relied on medical professionals' explanations, in court, to substantiate their claims. Initial descriptions attributed psychic symptoms to the simulated or microscopic deterioration of the spine, identified post-mortem, in the central nervous systems of deceased accident victims. For approximately two decades (1860–1880), physicians believed the somatic complaints had psychopathologic origins arising out of the survivor's *experience* of the shock rather than an actual shock to the spine. Thus, railway companies were compelled to award significant injury-related compensation to accident survivors with few or no apparent physical injuries. Herein lies the roots of the second controversy related to trauma: *To Compensate or Not*. The primary question was and is "Does compensation represent a just settlement for personal injury and loss or does it encourage malingering among the injured resulting secondary gain like financial, social, emotional support?" By the end of the 1880s, the concept of railway spine had been replaced by that of *traumatic neurosis* (Schivelbusch, 2014). Traumatic neurosis was a term first coined by Oppenheim (1889) who associated trauma-related symptoms with molecular changes in the brain.

Toward a More Scientific Explanation of Trauma

Nineteenth century Europeans heeded societal demands for self-control, emotional restraint, rational thought, and interpersonal diligence. The culture was transitioning away from subjective explanations of phenomena toward the scientific, objective, and rational. In medicine and psychology, this movement is reflected in the words of Sir Francis Galton, "the man of science is deficient in the purely emotional element" (Galton, 1874; p. 207). In contrast, others articulated the necessity for physician to study "mankind as well as medicine," and when treating the afflicted remember that, "they are possessed with hearts and minds that have strong passions, warm sentiments and vivid imaginations, which sway them powerfully both in health and disease" (De Styrap, 1890; p. B1). Divergent opinions extended to advancements in psychological understanding of trauma-related responding. Physicians, including railroad surgeons, neurologists, and physicians like Charcot, Janet, and Freud, investigated and debated the origins and development of emotional conditions resulting from catastrophic injuries. Van der Hart and Brown (1990) credited Albert Eulenburg, a German neurologist, with the introduction of the term *psychic trauma* (Eulenburg, 1878). Eulenburg contrasted psychic trauma to *psychic shock*. Psychic shock described acute, vehement, intense emotions, like terror or horror leading to *commotio cerebri* or disturbances of the brain, disturbances that resulted from physical shock of railway accidents (Caplan, 1995). Thus, Eulenburg may have been the first to hypothesize a biological etiology for psychological trauma. This perspective prevailed for decades. Figure 4.3 denotes first segment of a four-segment timeline summarizing major medical, cultural, psychological, or neurobiological events of 19th, 20th, and 21st

FIGURE 4.3 ●   Timeline Segment 1—The Late 19th Century

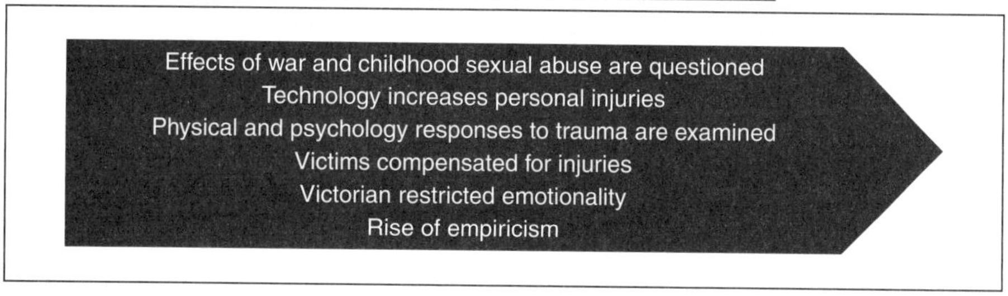

Effects of war and childhood sexual abuse are questioned
Technology increases personal injuries
Physical and psychology responses to trauma are examined
Victims compensated for injuries
Victorian restricted emotionality
Rise of empiricism

centuries. The chapter concludes with an image of full timeline and transition to the Counselor's Toolkit chapter.

The industrial revolution of the 18th and 19th centuries advanced technology and manufacturing and created dangerous and grim conditions for poor and working-class individuals. Exacerbated by physical, sexual, and emotional abuse, women and children were viewed as little more than commodities. Elizabeth Barrett Browning's poem "The Cry of the Children" (1853) and Dickens's novel *Hard Times* (1854) depict the appalling conditions and consequent suffering of the economically impoverished children and women.

Incest, physical and sexual abuse, and rape of children was prevalent across all races and economic and social classes in Europe and the United States (Tardieu, 1862; Brouardel, 1909; Sacco, 2009) yet was rarely acknowledged or its consequences addressed. In the rare cases when it was acknowledged, the acknowledgment did little to correct the distorted attitudes toward and knowledge of sexual abuse, particularly in middle-upper class, typically White families. Lynn Sacco (2009) argued elegantly in her book, *Unspeakable*, that as the number of official reports of child sexual abuse by immigrants, Blacks, and those economically impoverished increased, reports of sexual abuse in middle- and upper-class White families decreased even though female children in the household were assaulted at the same rates. Here again, note how a social injustice portrays the privileged as exempt from abusive and destructive behavior while advancing the notion that *others* (read non-White or those of lesser economic standing) were predisposed to it. Thus, the race, class, status, and gender of the perpetrator and the survivor influenced medical, legal, religious, and public understandings of child sexual abuse until late in the 20th century.

Physicians, social workers, and church groups worked to rescue children from moral danger—starvation, physical abuse, incest, and sexual exploitation. While moralistic and religious dualities of good of the era stimulated sympathy for victims, they also associated child sexual abuse with a perceived flaw in the victim's character, namely moral corruption. Specifically, to explain how adult males could sexually assault child victims, a cultural myth was invoked. The myth posited that child victims possessed advanced sexual knowledge or skills incongruent with their status as children. Therefore, there must be something different or evil about those children who exhibited what we now know to be trauma-related symptoms. The male perpetrator was vexed or tricked into sexual interaction with the child and he, not the child, was the victim. Blaming the victim is the third controversy related to trauma theory development. Trauma-related responding was associated with the character or actions of the victim rather than the nature, intensity, duration, and proximity to the event(s). An example of this line of thought is present in the writings of Paul Brouardel (1909): "Girls accuse their fathers of imaginary assaults on them or other children in order to obtain their freedom to give themselves over to debauchery" (p. 512). The paradox of this era, and today, lies in the discrepancy between the pronounced religious rhetoric of the time and the public denouncement of the sexual abuse and astonishingly low conviction rates (Jackson, 2000) despite increasing rates of sexual abuse cases brought before the court.

As noted earlier, Jean-Martin Charcot, a French neurologist and professor of anatomical pathology at the famed Salpêtrière Hospital in Paris, is recognized for his investigations into the relationships among patient's suggestibility—the ability to be hypnotized, hysteria, and emotional disturbances in women and men. Charcot treated patients suffering from unexplained bouts of paralysis, seizures, and bizarre postures and surmised these symptoms were associated with the patients' response to the physically traumatic event like a railway accident rather than the consequence of the event itself. Charcot's perspectives on the potential of a psychological etiology of trauma stimulated the generation of scholars who followed, including those who focused on one's appraisal of events (Lazarus, 1966; Lazarus & Folkman, 1984).

Psychological Explanations of Trauma

Charcot influenced and advanced the inquiries of many of his contemporaries, most notably Pierre Janet and Sigmund Freud. Janet recognized that his patients diagnosed with hysteria at Salpêtrière's psychological laboratory seemed unable to utilize their personal memories, perceptions, understanding, or knowledge to reduce their symptom reduction or productively engage with their surroundings. According to Herman (1997), historians described the term *hysteria* as a strange disease with incoherent and incomprehensible symptoms. Hysteria was "a dramatic metaphor for everything that men found mysterious or unmanageable in the opposite sex" (p. 10). Janet hypothesized patients' minds were so overwhelmed with emotions that it rendered them incapable of contextualizing current experiences into their previous understandings of their environment. Janet believed accumulated memories resided in what he termed as the *subconscious*, or the hypothesized template for individual meaning and responding (Janet, 1904). One was considered emotionally healthy if they could label and integrate memories, particularly traumatic memories, into their current functioning. Conversely, those afflicted with hysteria stood in stark contrast because they seemed unable to integrate traumatic memories due to overwhelming emotional arousal. The traces of memory remained unintegrated and fixed in the unconscious and outside an individuals' personal self-story (Janet, 1919/1925). These memories, disassociated or outside the voluntary control of the individual, remained in the unconscious until integrated into consciousness. Janet believed this disrupted integration resulted in a *phobia of memory* in which traumatic memories remained inaccessible and disassociated from consciousness despite the intense emotional arousal and related symptoms the patient was unable to resolve. In other words, attempts to avoid or exclude traumatic memories prolongs suffering as these memories interrupt one's functioning in the form of hypervigilance, avoidance, flashbacks, and intrusive thoughts. Van der Kolk, McFarlane, and Weisaeth (1996) summarized Janet's perspective, "As long as these memory traces have not been integrated into a personal narrative, they will continue to intrude as terrifying perceptions, obsessional preoccupations and somatic re-experiences" (p. 309).

Janet sought to understand the relationship between the mechanisms and types of memory, suggestibility, disassociation, and treatments for hysteria. His systematic work placed dissociative processes at the center of 19th century understandings of hysteria. According to van der Hart and Horst (1989), Janet's theory of disassociation built on concepts either introduced or elaborated on by Janet's like psychological automatism, consciousness, subconscious, amnesia, and emotion. For example, Ellenberger (1969) and Jackson (1994) credit Janet with the development of *cathartic psychotherapy*, a method used to provoke emotional release of traumatic memories or mental disinfection through a process called mental liquidation. Blatner (1985), who wrote on catharsis in groups via psychodrama, identified four categories of catharsis: abreaction, integration, inclusions, and spiritual. *Abreaction* involves reexperiencing traumatic events and formerly disowned memories and feelings, bringing into awareness that which was formerly excluded from awareness. *Integration* involves accommodating recently recovered emotions and thoughts through the modification of existing mental schema or mastering a new coping skill. The third category, *Inclusion,* describes the need of affiliation similar to Adler's (1938) concept of belonging or *Gemeinschaftsgefühl.* The final form of catharsis, *significance or spiritual,* focuses on one's awareness of something greater than themselves like the universe or religious deities may be invoked through mediation, breathing, long distance-running, and prayer.

The hypothesized roles of catharsis and the subconscious ruled the early 20th century. For example, Freud embraced many of early works of Charcot and later Janet's concepts of the subconscious processes, particularly extreme emotional charged and yet unintegrated aspects of hysterical episodes. Joseph Breuer and Freud noted in their 1893 paper, *Physical Mechanism of Hysterical Phenomena* (1893/1955), "It is essential for the explanation of hysterical phenomena to assume the presence of a dissociation-a splitting of the content of consciousness" (p. 30). Though Freud and Janet became distanced (Fitzgerald, 2017), Janet's influence on Freud's theories and concepts was profound, particularly as it relates to the nature and function of memories.

In contrast to Charcot, Freud (1896) initially believed hysteria emanated from repressed memories of early or infantile sexual abuse. The foundation of Freud's seduction theory was his belief that children knew nothing of sexuality and sexual desire; thus, neurosis occurred only after the onset of puberty. Symptoms of hysteria arose from the repressed *memory* of the event, not the event itself. Over the course of the next year, Freud urged patients to reproduce and explore repressed memories through psychoanalysis, symbolic interpretation, and abreaction. In

September 1897, Freud documented his growing doubts about the seduction theory in a private letter to Wilhelm Fliess. Freud's reservations centered on "the absence of complete successes" (p. 20) and the theory's requirement that the father, "not excluding my own had to be accused of being perverse," which given the prevalence of hysteria was unlikely. Freud struggled to reconcile the prevalence of childhood sexual trauma with the potentiality that scores of Victorian men, were in his words, *perverse*. Freud came to believe that the unconscious did not represent reality and many of his sexually traumatized patients could not distinguish the truth from fantasy. He went on to write that in "the most deep-reaching psychosis the unconscious memory does not break through," meaning "... the secret of childhood experiences is not disclosed even in the most confused delirium ... if ... the unconscious never overcomes the resistance of the conscious, the expectation that in treatment the opposite is bound to happen" (p. 22).

This was Freud's alternate and, the first author would argue, more convenient explanation. Regrettably, Freud abandoned his belief that children were sexually unaware and now viewed hysteria as an intersubjective experience in which the child's bouts of hysteria were influenced by their parent. From this point forward, Freud's theoretical work focused on infantile sexuality and the origins of impulses, fantasies, and conflicts. Neurotic systems like anger, anxiety, and nightmares were no longer associated with childhood sexual abuse; they were attributed to the child's mind, fantasies, and wishes.

Examinations of trauma associated with childhood sexual abuse seemingly vanished from the professional literature for almost three-quarters of a century, except for Sándor Ferenczi (1949). Ferenczi faced criticism for his sexual abuse trauma theory in which he identified the adult as the aggressor and the child as helpless victim. In his theory, Ferenczi noted the child's primary defense mechanism against the trauma was identification with the aggressor. Freud specifically asked Ferenczi to delay the reading of his paper at the 1932 International Psychoanalytic Society. Undaunted, Ferenczi read his paper leading to a severe lifelong rupture in their relationship and delayed the publication of this paper by almost two decades. Throughout the 19th and 20th centuries, whether it was the tragic carnage and consequence of wars, the utter devastation of sexual abuse, or the corrosive effects of oppression, those with power silenced those with inconvenient truths, be they a theorist, veterans, or victims of childhood sexual abuse.

Researchers and clinicians did not return to investigations of the etiology of trauma related to sexual abuse, sexual victimization, and domestic abuse until the latter half of the 20th century. At that time, Freud faced criticism for his abandonment or suppression (Schimek, 1987; Rush, 1996, Kitzinger, 1996; Masson, 1984) of the seduction theory, but few if any scholar's noted Ferenczi's challenge of Freud. We again witness the *marked amnesia* described by van der Kolk. The role of repressed memories in trauma theories is our fourth controversy. What do you think? Can unintegrated and later reclaimed memories of trauma be trusted as a source of delayed traumatic responding or do the influences of time and subjectivity call these memories into question? Reflect on this question as you read further. Review the timeline in Figure 4.4. Are there other elements you would add?

At the close of the 19th and well into the 20th century, researchers and scholars refined their understanding of the etiology of the trauma neurosis sans the effects

FIGURE 4.4 ● Timeline Segments 1 and 2—Late 19th to Early 20th Centuries

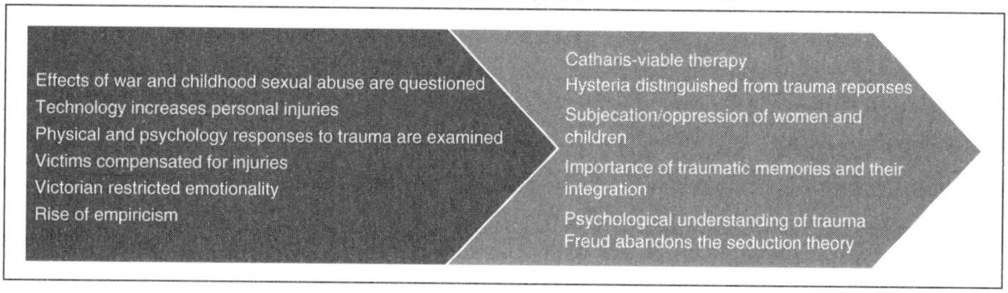

Effects of war and childhood sexual abuse are questioned
Technology increases personal injuries
Physical and psychology responses to trauma are examined
Victims compensated for injuries
Victorian restricted emotionality
Rise of empiricism

Catharis-viable therapy
Hysteria distinguished from trauma reponses
Subjecation/oppression of women and children
Importance of traumatic memories and their integration
Psychological understanding of trauma
Freud abandons the seduction theory

of sexual abuse. Investigating trauma related to sexual abuse and to some degree war-related trauma seemed fraught with political and social taboos. The focus of trauma and underlying theories shifted to examinations of potential predisposing protective and vulnerability factors (Stierlin, 1911) and diagnostic criteria for chronic, rather than acute, psychological suffering. Initial criteria proposed by Jaspers (1913/1997) included an assessment of interplay between one's previous functioning and predisposing physiological or psychological factors, a significant traumatic event, and the time elapsed between the onset of systems and the traumatic event. Jasper's diagnostic criteria remained relevant for roughly 30 years.

The 20th Century: A World at War

The 20th century was marked by two devastating and horrific world wars. Although primarily centered in Europe and later Europe and Asia, the consequences of these wars were felt in most countries. The early 20th century heralded technological advances in the arts, sciences, industry, and warfare. Regrettably, humankind found ever more deadly ways to wage war from the trenches, poisonous gases, automatic rifles, and heavy ordnance of World War I (1914–1918) to the mobility and rapid deployment of troops, advanced weaponry—napalm, and the A-bomb—to the unconscionable treatment of concentration camp causalities and survivors of World War II (1939-1945). Advances in trauma theories and trauma-related responding were associated with traumatic battlefield experiences of soldiers in these wars.

Soldiers in World War I (WWI) faced the horrors of trench warfare as they were *dug in* in squalid conditions for extended periods subjected to relentless shelling. Like their Civil War counterparts, WWI soldiers with no apparent or limited external injuries, presented with fatigue, trembling, paralysis, nightmares, or impairments in hearing and vision had their symptoms attributed to *shell shock*. Recall Oppenheim's (1889) organic explanation for the symptoms, resulting from the concussive consequences of exposure to shelling. Treatment for shell shock included removal from the front line into a nonmilitary hospital. After a short respite, soldiers returned to active combat and the camaraderie of their unit. In the early months of WWI, overwhelming numbers of soldiers experienced shell shock and growing numbers did not recover and were discharged from the service due to a poor prognosis. Psychiatrists stationed closest to the frontline sought more effective treatment and modified the treatment protocol. Rather than sending soldiers home, the standard treatment became retaining shell-shocked soldiers in field hospitals, within proximity to the frontlines, where they could benefit from the order, discipline, and support of military mates, and had the expectation to return to duty with a better long-term prognosis. This treatment protocol, along with Thomas Salmon's five key principles of immediacy, proximity, expectancy, simplicity, and centrality, improved treatment outcomes (Crocq & Crocq, 2000). Although, shell-shocked soldiers were not seen as *defective*, they were expected to recover. Those with persistent symptoms or delayed onset faced questions related to their bravery, honor, character, and individual constitution. For soldiers, it was better to receive treatment for an unbearable situation (the hell of war) than to be accused of an unacceptable impulse (retreat, fear, or cowardice) and its resulting stigma. The change in treatment protocol reduced needless pathologizing of individuals. Now those suffering from shell shock were neither morally or constitutionally deficient not were they cowards. Recovery and a return to the front demonstrated success; failure to recover often meant there *was* something *wrong* with the individual. This leads us to the fifth controversy related to theories of trauma and traumatic responding—why do people exposed to an identical event, react, respond, and recover differently? Why do some respond to brief interventions while others find no relief?

Abram Kardiner treated veterans of World War I and chronicled his findings in *The Traumatic Neuroses of War* (1941). He concluded from his meticulous patient histories that those afflicted with traumatic neurosis or what he termed *physioneurosis* presented with a host of symptoms: extreme physiological arousal, preoccupation with the trauma, anxiety, nightmares, startled responses, fight or flight response, irritability, and persistent environmental vigilance. Kardiner (1941) articulated that soldiers' memories of wartime trauma were generalized to noncombat events and served as a trigger for the reexperiencing of threat during noncombat experiences. As van der Kolk (2007) synthesized, "Central to Kardiner's thinking, as in that of Janet and Freud . . . the subject acts as if the original traumatic situation were still in existence and engages in protective devices which failed on the original occasion" (p. 27). The individual appears fixated on the original traumatic event, unconsciously associates the trigger to the original trauma, and responds to the reexperiencing of thoughts and emotions in a variety of ways—racing heart, difficulty breathing, or aggression. Avoidance, restricted emotions, and emotional numbing serve as defenses against the perceived threat of reexperiencing intense psychophysiological responses. Kardiners is credited for the nascent beginnings of trauma theory integration a setting the stage for the biopsychosocial perspective of PTSD in the *Diagnostic and Statistical Manual of Mental Disorders III (DSM–III)*. Regrettably, physicians practicing forward psychiatry in World War II largely ignored his findings, once again engaging the alternating cycle of intellectual amnesia and intense interest in trauma and trauma-informed treatments. Figure 4.5 represents a trauma informed timeline spanning from late 19th to mid-20th century.

While, physical injuries in World War II (WWII) were attributable to a different type of warfare and weaponry, the resulting psychological impact on soldiers was devastating. Few scholars focused on trauma theory development in the early to mid-20th century, instead their intellectual and clinical energy centered on improving treatment approaches, specifically the reemergence of hypnosis and narcosynthesis. Narcosynthesis is an inpatient procedure, which pairs psychoanalytic techniques of free association and dream interpretation the injection of a

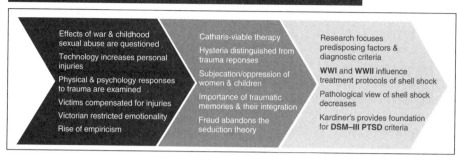

FIGURE 4.5 ● Timeline Segments 1 Through 3—Late 19th to Mid-20th Century

Effects of war & childhood sexual abuse are questioned

Technology increases personal injuries

Physical & psychology responses to trauma are examined

Victims compensated for injuries

Victorian restricted emotionality

Rise of empiricism

Catharis-viable therapy

Hysteria distinguished from trauma reponses

Subjecation/oppression of women & children

Importance of traumatic memories & their integration

Freud abandons the seduction theory

Research focuses predisposing factors & diagnostic criteria

WWI and **WWII** influence treatment protocols of shell shock

Pathological view of shell shock decreases

Kardiner's provides foundation for **DSM–III PTSD** criteria

narcotic like sodium amytal. These treatments provided patients the opportunity to recall aspects of the trauma while in an altered state of consciousness (ASC), which would be addressed and processed later. Much like Janet before them, post–World War II researchers and clinicians believed patients must access *and* transform traumatic memories prior to substituting them; all three processes were necessary for successful treatment. Other notable developments during this era include the use of group treatments for trauma-related responding of soldiers in America (Shalev, 1991) and at the Tavistock Clinic in Britain (Main, 1989) and the study of concentration camp survivors. Krystal (1968) studied over 300 concentration camp survivors recognizing their unrelenting exposure to the monstrous traumas of the concentration camps. For these survivors, threats were multifaceted and interactional, originating from physical, emotional, social, and existential domains resulting in hypervigilance, progressive blocking of emotions and inhibited behaviors. Follow up studies documented associations between the trauma and enduring changes to many survivors' personalities (Eitinger, 1964).

An adequate theory of trauma and traumatic responding would address the variations in response to treatment, particularly dose–effect relationship. To date, researchers and clinicians struggle to demonstrate there is a dose–effect or dose–response relationship in the treatment of trauma. The dose–effect relationship describes the number and intensity of sessions (dose) required to achieve a desired treatment outcome (effect). Effective treatments properly applied, should result in similar levels of recovery for most. Evidenced-based treatment models are presented later in this chapter. In sum, it would be reasonable to believe that once a diagnosis is made, researchers and clinicians could apply the appropriate type of intervention, in the most effective dose over a specified period to reduce distress and improve client's functioning. Regrettably, the science of trauma treatment is not yet to that point, but advancements in empirically supported treatments and neurobiological and neurocognitive trauma responding hold great promise.

The Emerging Influence of Psychological Theories

From Behaviorism to Cognition

Despite previous contributions from theories of learning and conscious thought by scholars like Wundt (1909) and James (1907/1981), behavioral researchers in the early 20th century focused on observable behaviors and eschewed any notion of the influence of cognition on human behavior. Scientific investigations related to anxiety or phobic responding declined. But by mid-century, cognition and learning principles returned to psychology's understanding of human behavior. Wilson (1982) noted:

> During the 1950s and 1960s, the behavior therapies developed within the framework of classical and operant conditioning principles that had originally served importantly to distinguish behavior therapy from other clinical approaches. Over the course of the 1970s, this conceptual commitment to conditioning theory peaked out—some would say even waned. In part this change reflected the shift to more technological considerations governing the increasingly broad application of behavioral techniques that had been developed and refined during the previous period of growth. (p. 51)

Behaviorism continued to be assailed. Noam Chomsky through his critique of B. F. Skinner sought "a more general critique of behaviorist … speculation as to the nature of higher mental processes" (1967, p. 142). Tongue in cheek, Chomsky credited Skinner with a "most careful and thoroughgoing presentation" and regarded Skinner's theory as a "reductio ad absurdum of behaviorist assumptions" (pg. 142). Although Chomsky's (1967) analysis of Skinner's *Verbal Behavior* is often cited as a pivotal moment in the cognitive revolution, cognitive researchers had been investigating schemas (Bartlett, 1958) and content (Heider, 1958; Bruner, Goodnow, & Austin, 1956) of cognitions in the previous decade and foreshadowed investigations in the late 20th century (Beck, Emery, & Greenberg, 1985; Herman, 1981; Herman, 1992; Shapiro, 1995).

Social Influences on Theories of Trauma and Traumatic Responding

Freud's sense of the social order was profoundly disturbed by the scores of female clients who seemed to suffer effects of sexual abuse perpetrated by *perverse* Victorian men. His abandonment of the seduction theory and banishment of Ferenczi are two of the most notable examples of how society rather than science influenced, and some would say impeded, understandings of trauma and its treatment. Social influences also shaped Americans' view of trauma and traumatic responding. Post–WWII America teemed with economic and social mobility in pursuit of the American Dream (Adams, 1931). Returning veterans utilized the GI Bill to purchase homes and advanced their education. Yet, despite serving in WWII, members of historically marginalized groups—Blacks, Latinx, Native Americans, and women—did not share equitably in this prosperity. Their marginalization and oppression led to socio-political movements that influenced theories, research, and treatment of trauma.

The late 1960s and early 1970s were a tumultuous time in America. Daily reports of wartime casualties, anti-war protests, political assassinations, and the fight for women's, civil, and farm workers' rights reflected society's transition and turmoil. In response to societal upheaval, grassroots movements and organizations emerged to meet the specific needs of marginalized groups like Vietnam veterans, women, and persons of color. For example, in contrast to previous returning veterans who were welcomed home as heroes, Vietnam veterans returned to a culture divided and disturbed by the government's conduct of the war. Isaacs (1997) eloquently wrote, "Men who fought in World War II or Korea might be just as haunted by what they had personally seen and done in combat. But they did not come home, as the Vietnam vets did, to a country torn and full of doubt about why those wars were fought and whether they had been worthwhile" (p. 12).

Like soldiers before them, many Vietnam veterans experienced the horrors of war and some returned traumatized and in need of support and treatment. Unlike other veterans, those returning from Vietnam were treated with derision and disrespect and were abandoned and ignored by the very politicians that sent them to war. Americans wanted to move on and in effect moved away from the needs and care required for returning soldiers. Psychiatrists stationed at the front lines treated combat stress much as their WWII predecessors and were perplexed by returning Vietnam veterans who reported a delayed onset of symptoms of hypervigilance, nightmares, and extreme emotional responding. Physicians and researchers limited treatment interventions for delayed onset of symptoms and questioned differences in predisposing or characterological factors of individual veterans until the work of Shatan (1972, 1973), Lifton (2005), and Figley (1978) pivoted the research and clinical communities' attention back to the source of veteran's dysregulation and dysfunction, the stress of war. Shatan and Lifton began *rap sessions* with Vietnam veterans, a form of self-help groups like those simultaneously occurring in the Women's Movement.

Social activists in the Women's Movement of the 1970s redefined gender roles, power differentials, reproductive rights, sexual victimization of, and violence against women and children. The landmark book *Our Bodies Ourselves* (1971) chronicled the myths and impact of rape and self-defense tactics. In 1974, Burgess and Holmstrom published their paper detailing their findings related to *Rape Trauma Syndrome*. Rape victims, they observed, described nightmares, flashbacks, intrusive thoughts, and avoidance. Burgess and Holmstrom connected rape survivors' sequelae to other theories of traumatology, including combat soldiers' experiences (see Webster & Dunn, 2005, for a more detailed history of feminism and trauma). These and other social/cultural forces led to an intense and unanticipated focus on features, nature, and course of trauma-related responding (Andreasen, 2004).

The influence of grassroots movements culminated in the formal recognition of posttraumatic stress disorder (PTSD) and diagnostic classification in the *DSM–III* (APA, 1980) with greater precision and refinements in diagnostic criteria in the *DSM–III-R* (APA, 1987) including reexperiencing, avoidance and numbing, and physiological arousal. Despite the prevalence of traumatic experiences across the globe, some authors (Summerfield, 2004; Hinton & Lewis-Fernandéz, 2011) debate the culture-bound descriptions of trauma-related responding like differences in numbing and avoidance symptoms, meanings attributed to traumatic events, and exposure to types of trauma [genocide]. Others acknowledge striking similarities in trauma-related responding across cultures (North et al., 2005). In 1952, the American Psychiatric Association formally recognized gross stress reaction (GSR:

FIGURE 4.6 ●   Time Line Segment 1 Through 4—19th to 21st Century

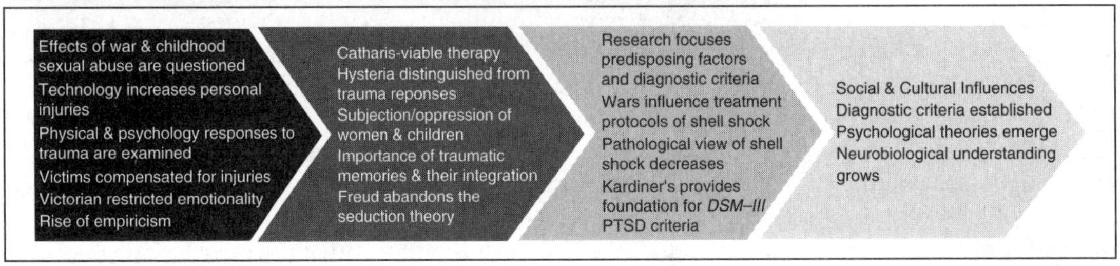

Effects of war & childhood sexual abuse are questioned
Technology increases personal injuries
Physical & psychology responses to trauma are examined
Victims compensated for injuries
Victorian restricted emotionality
Rise of empiricism

Catharis-viable therapy
Hysteria distinguished from trauma reponses
Subjection/oppression of women & children
Importance of traumatic memories & their integration
Freud abandons the seduction theory

Research focuses predisposing factors and diagnostic criteria
Wars influence treatment protocols of shell shock
Pathological view of shell shock decreases
Kardiner's provides foundation for *DSM–III* PTSD criteria

Social & Cultural Influences
Diagnostic criteria established
Psychological theories emerge
Neurobiological understanding grows

APA, 1952, p. 40) and subsumed it under the broader category of transient situational personality disorders. The GSR diagnosis required an absence of premorbid psychopathology, was focused on the acute nature of an unusual stressor resulting from "combat or civilian catastrophe" and that, given time, would naturally resolve itself. The periodic professional amnesia related to traumatic responding, described earlier in this chapter, reemerged in the publication of the second edition of the diagnostic manual (APA, 1968). Curiously, but not surprisingly, the GSR diagnosis was replaced with the category of disorders entitled *transient emotional or adjustment reactions,* specifically adjustment reaction in adult life. This newly classified adjustment reaction was exemplified through one's reaction to an unwanted pregnancy, fear associated with military combat, or receiving a death sentence (APA, 1968; p. 48), a curious combination of events.

PTSD, as a diagnostic category, continues to be a source of controversy as some view it as a bona fide psychiatric disorder while others see it as an artifact of culture. Acute, delayed, and persistent trauma-related responding is not expressed similarly nor does it take an identical course in individuals exposed to the same trauma. Some question the influence of culture on the prevalence, etiology, diagnosis, intensity, and maintenance of trauma-related symptoms, while others attributed refinement of our understanding of trauma on great cultural acceptance of and attention to trauma-related responding, in particular diagnostic criteria for PTSD. What do you think?

Research and clinical investigations into trauma by scientists, scholars, academics, and clinicians flourished in biology, medicine, psychology, and counseling since the mid-1980s. Some focused on the role of memory (Herman, 1992; Shapiro, 1995), differentiating developmental from simple or complex trauma (van der Kolk, 1996, 2005; van der Kolk, Roth, Pelcovitz, Sunday, & Spinazzola, 2005) while others investigated risk factors and longitudinal effects of child abuse and natural disaster (Green, Grace, Lindy, Gleser, & Leonard, 1990; Green et al., 1990; Green, Grace, Vary, Kramer, Gleser, Leonard, 1994) and the neurobiology of trauma (Perry, Pollard, Blakley, Baker, & Vigilante, 1995; Marinova & Maercker, 2015). Advances in our understanding of brain plasticity, (Ericsson et al., 1998) neurogenesis, neuroimaging, neuroendocrinology, and psychopharmacology have contributed to continued refinement of theories of trauma. Whether we examine the supposed contagion effects of war neurosis and railway spine diagnoses or the condemnation and stigma faced by Vietnam veterans and victims of rape, domestic violence, or childhood sexual abuse, it is safe to say, attributions related to the potential influence of culture and cultural events influenced and continue to influence our understanding of trauma.

Theories

The 21st century seemed to usher in trauma and distress at unprecedented levels. Mass shootings, 9/11, wars in Afghanistan and Iraq, anthrax, genocide, and Ebola affected some directly and many indirectly, through an endless news cycle and social media. History and social influences on trauma and traumatic responding continue to emerge and influence our understanding of trauma and the development and maintenance of associated psychological disorders. In the sections that follow, we present theories that form the foundation for current understandings of trauma.

Biological

Biologically based theories of trauma focus on personal and environmental factors, their interactions, and human development to explain the relationships between extreme stress, individual vulnerabilities and predispositions, environmental factors, and psychological distress and disorders. Genetic factors such as neurohormones (oxytocin and vasopressin), neurotransmitters (dopamine, norepinephrine, and serotonin), and brain structures (amygdala, hippocampus, and the hypothalamus) are believed to contribute to the experiencing of trauma and perhaps the progression to PTSD. But heritability and genetics present an incomplete picture. Ryan, Chaudieu, Ancelin, and Saffery (2016) note the variation in responses to traumatic exposure, and risk for PTSD "is likely to be influenced by genetic predisposition and specific characteristics of the stress itself (nature, intensity and duration), as well as epigenetic mechanisms" (p. 1553). Epigenetics is the study of changes in gene expression that occur from environmental interaction. Changes in gene expression do not alter one's genetic code or DNA; it alters the way genes communicate or *read* each other. For example, you may have been born into a family with a low risk for obesity, but if you fail to exercise, eat poorly, and smoke a pack of cigarettes a day, you will likely end up overweight.

Researchers continue to explore the contribution of specific and constellations of genes believed to contribute to traumatic responding, resiliency, and some psychiatric disorders. Ryan, et al. (2016) summarized studies investigating the contribution of 25 genes to PTSD. While a detailed review of genetic studies is beyond the scope of this chapter, we agree with Klengel (2016) who blogged, "We're already confident that genetic variations play an instrumental role in determining individual risk. However, we still need to pinpoint which genes are involved, how they may interact to affect risk, and what are the exact molecular mechanisms behind this. Similarly, we also need to isolate genetic factors that may be responsible for increasing one's resilience to trauma—which is why some individuals do not develop PTSD or other disorders despite considerable exposure to trauma."

The structures in our brain respond and change because of stress. Typical forms of stress can increase awareness, immunity, and determination. Extreme or traumatic stress can lead to significant changes in how we function. Bremner (2006) reported, "Findings from animal studies have been extended to patients with post-traumatic stress disorder (PTSD) showing smaller hippocampal and anterior cingulate volumes, increased amygdala function, and decreased medial prefrontal/anterior cingulate function. These changes influence the regulation of emotion and memory (hippocampus and amygdala) and may disturb empathy, impulse control and decision-making (medial prefrontal anterior cingulate)" (p. 445). Researchers (Ryan et al., 2016; Kendall-Tackett, 2009; Solomon & Heide, 2005) describe our biological response pattern to traumatic stress. A stressor or threat is perceived; in response, the hypothalamus signals the pituitary, which signals the adrenal glands to release hormones—adrenal, epinephrine, and cortisol—which increase glucose levels and heart rate. This is known as the Hypothalamic-Pituitary-Adrenal (HPA) system or axis. Those with a history of prior trauma seemed to be more sensitized to a HPA response and the near immediate release of stress hormones in response to subsequent stressors. This population also has higher rates than the general population for cardiovascular disease, diabetes, cancer, and gastrointestinal disorders (Kendall-Tackett, 2009) and disruptions to their neurologic functioning. Perry et al. (1995) reported as chronic trauma stress persists "there will be 'use-dependent' alterations in the key neural systems involved in the stress response. These include the hypothalamic-pituitary-adrenal (HPA) axis. In animal models, chronic activation of the HPA system in response to stress has negative consequences. Chronic activation may 'wear out' parts of the body including the hippocampus, a key area involved in memory, cognition and arousal" (p. 49).

Mental health clinicians, treating those exposed to trauma, focus on clients' experiences and meanings of traumatic events. To that end, a bioecological understanding of mass trauma (Hoffman & Kruczek, 2011) and a model of biologic pathways for historical/intergenerational trauma (Conching & Thayer, 2019) will inform your approach and treatment of traumatized clients.

Bioecological Model of Mass Trauma

Hoffman and Kruczek (2011) based their bioecological model of mass trauma on the original work of Bronfenbrenner (1979), and Bronfenbrenner and Ceci (1994) extended the model to biological considerations. (See Chapter 6 for a detailed description of Bronfenbrenner's 1979 ecological model.) Bronfenbrenner's original model consisted of five systems (individual-personal characteristics; micro-family and peers; meso-relationship among micro systems; exo-school, community, government, media; and macro-wider environment and economic and social policies). The chronosystem examines patterns of events over one's development and time. Bronfenbrenner and Ceci's inclusion of biological factors like genetic predisposition and temperament provide richer context for Hoffman and Kruczek's adaptation of this model to mass trauma. They note the "expanded model provides an integrated conceptual structure for understanding the effects, intervening in the aftermath, addressing prevention, and researching aspects of large-scale disaster and catastrophes" (p. 5). Hoffman and Kruczek evaluated the influence of traumatic events on individuals' agency, optimism, well-being, sense of meaning and ecological systems to "identify the biopsychosocial extent beyond initial injury and mortality" (p. 3). Using this model, clinicians structure their examination and intervention of clients' traumatic responding in the context of their ecological systems promoting a greater understanding of individual, family, social, community factors and supports, resources, and cultural perspectives.

Biologic Pathways for Historical/Intergenerational Trauma

Historical trauma describes the consequences of oppression, violence, forced incarceration, assimilation, and death experienced by marginalized populations because of colonization, enslavement, subjugation, and genocide. First coined by Maria Yellow Horse Brave Heart in the 1980s, the term *historical trauma* identified the intergenerational transmission of psychological trauma symptom in successive generations of Lakota Sioux (Brave Heart, 2000; Brave Heart and DeBruyn, 1998). Sotero (2006) identified three phases. The first describes the perpetration of mass traumas by the dominant culture resulting in widespread cultural, familial, and economic devastation. Traumatic responding occurring in those originally exposed denotes the second phase. Continued oppression, discrimination, and marginalization of the affected population are the mechanisms that transmit the trauma to successive generations. Brave Heart and DeBruyn examined similarities in the manifestation of historic trauma in Native American and Holocaust survivor populations. They surmised that, independent of type of trauma, marginalized populations' historic trauma responding impacted individuals and communities similarly.

Conching and Thayer (2019) argued that although theories of historical trauma conceptually explain the negative consequences of intergenerational transmission of historical and repeated losses, there is not a model for *how* historical trauma responding HTR negatively impacts later generations. To address this void, they devised a cumulative two pathway model to explain the health effects of HTR in present populations. The first pathway posits that historically oppressed populations are chronically and continually subjected to traumatic events and stressors like low socioeconomic status, discrimination, and historical loss which cause epigenetic changes (discussed earlier) and negatively impact individual and community well-being. In the second pathway, the authors indicate that "biological consequences of historical trauma can be inherited across generations through intrauterine environments, changes in breast milk composition and breastfeeding behavior, and patterns of parental care" (p. 78). As noted previously, we note epigenetic changes do not impact the structure of one's DNA, thus as Conching and Thayer state, the effects are "necessarily permanent and that improvements in environmental conditions could reduce the high prevalence of poor health among historically disadvantaged communities" (p. 72).

Developmental and Neurobiological

In Chapter 2, we discussed human development across the lifespan and developmental crisis events. Developmental theories of trauma and traumatic responding build on the concepts of attachment, attachment styles, developmental tasks, and neural plasticity described earlier and is expanded here to include brain development, neurocognitive aspects of prolonged or chronic trauma, state dependent use, and mechanisms of change.

Humans mature through several periods of social, cognitive, and physical development. These periods describe expected social, cognitive, and physical changes influenced by age-related changes in cognitive and social processes, which influence psychological adjustment following exposure to traumatic events. When there is a supportive enough environment, most development tasks are completed and milestones surpassed. In neglectful and abusive environments, development and performance in any or all these domains is influenced and altered. Treating traumatized children requires a different framework than working with traumatic responding that occurs in adolescence and adulthood.

Brain Development 101

In numerous publications, Perry (1993, 1996; 2000; 2006) notes the brain develops sequentially from the brainstem to the midbrain or diencephalon cerebellum to the cerebrum, which contains limbic, and finally the cortical regions. At each level of the brain, plasticity and complexity increase. The brain is a heterogeneous organ, meaning each region has a distinct organization, purpose, and function. For example, the brainstem region manages communication between the brain and the body and controls basic autonomic functions like breathing, digestion, body temperature, consciousness, and arousal states. The diencephalon cerebellum transmits sensory data between the regions of the brain and controls the autonomic functions of the peripheral nervous system (PNS), which excludes the brain or spinal cord. The cerebrum is comprised of the limbic and cortical regions. Emotion, learning, memory attachment, affiliation, and motivation reside in the limbic region. The cortical region is responsible for abstract and concrete thought, complex language, and decision making. Because the brain develops in a hierarchical, use-dependent manner, development of the upper regions of the brain is influenced by the development of the lower regions.

Each region of the brain contains billions of neurons and ten billion glial cells. A neuron is a specialized cell that transmits electric impulses to other cells in the body. A glial cell supports neurons by providing nutrients, oxygen, and insulation allowing the neurons to sense, process, store, and act on sensory input. Thus, sensory input received by the brain is converted into neural activity. According to Perry (1996) "All neurons change the molecular function in a use dependent fashion. Therefore, patterned sensory input leads to patterned changes in neuronal systems. Patterned neuronal changes allow the brain to make internal representations of the external world." In other words, the more a neural pattern is activated the more the brain builds in that pattern. Experience "creates a processing template through which all new input is filtered. (Perry et al., 1995; p. 275). This process allows infants to respond their internal and external environment. For example, consider the infant who is repeatedly exposed to abuse and neglect. They respond to these threats with hyperarousal—crying or agitation; or disassociation—freezing, or chaotic responses to caregivers. Over time, the repeated aversive stimuli or *state* of hyperarousal becomes a *trait* of the infant's personality. Because the brain organizes in a use-dependent pattern, continued reactivation of an aroused state leads to maladaptive traits and impaired attachment. Because adult brains are developed, exposure to traumatic events results in *states* or periods of hyperarousal rather than traits. (For a detailed discussion, please see (Perry et al., 1995.) Figure 4.7 summarizes the theory.

FIGURE 4.7 ● Impact of trauma on brain development

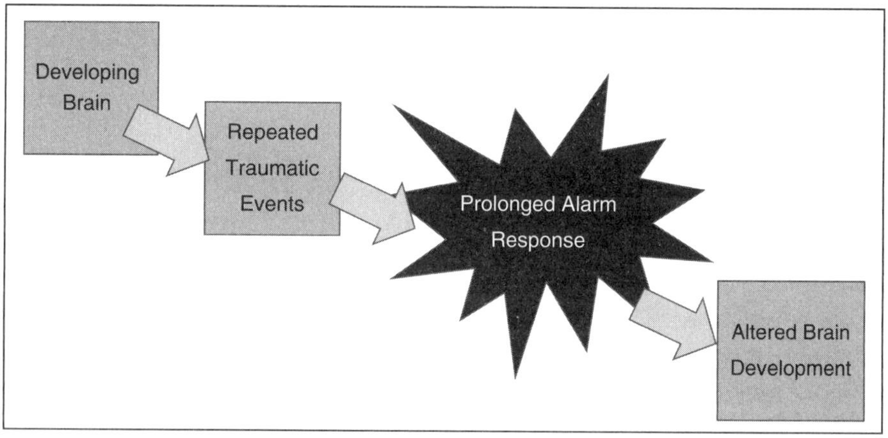

Behaviorism

Theories of behaviorism and psychological understandings of trauma rose to prominence during the 20th century, particularly theories of classical and operant conditioning. Ivan Pavlov, the director of the Institute of Experimental Medicine, examined the physiology of digestion in dogs and, in 1904, his research resulted in a Nobel Prize. Pavlov continued his work and in 1927 published the principles of classical conditioning. Proponents of operant conditioning, most notably Thorndike and Skinner, examined the stimulus-response relationship in nonreflexive responding including the *law of effect, schedules of reinforcement, shaping, and stimulus discrimination* through the use of animal models. For a fuller discussion of these concepts, see, McSweeney and Murphy (2014). The initial phases of theory development related to trauma focused on anxiety reduction through classical or operant conditioning. Orval Hobart Mowrer (1951/1960) explained the development and maintenance of phobias. He purported a two-factor theory combining learning principles from classical and operant conditioning. Mowrer believed phobias developed because of a paired association between a neutral stimulus and feared stimulus (i.e., they were classically conditioned). However, classical conditioning theory did not fully explain the maintenance of the phobic behaviors like fear, avoidance, and the desire to escape or enduring impairments in psychological, relational, and social functioning. Mowrer turned to the concepts in operant conditions to explain the maintenance of the phobia. Consider the two-factor theory in the following example. A woman is mugged during her nightly run. After the attack, she experiences debilitating panic attacks when she is outside after dark. Thus, darkness, formerly a neutral or unconditioned stimulus, is now associated with being attacked, a conditioned response, which in turn results in fear/panic or a conditioned response. By avoiding going outside after dark she is *rewarded* with less anxiety, thus the avoidance becomes her dependable coping strategy.

Wolpe (1954) also examined potential interventions for anxiety experienced by clients. He believed anger and aggression were discordant with the emotional states required for assertiveness. This led him to develop the techniques of reciprocal inhibition and later systematic desensitization. Systematic desensitization, like reciprocal inhibition, is based on the principles of classical conditioning, specifically counter-conditioning. Over time and in successive steps, the fear response is substituted with a relaxation response. Throughout the mid-20th century, systematic desensitization techniques matured beyond the initial clinical setting are distinguished from the two other types of exposure therapies in vivo and imaginal flooding.

The intersections of operant and classical conditioning theories fueled advancements in our theoretical understandings of trauma-related and post-trauma-related responding. Kilpatrick, Veronen, and Resick (1979) compared fear responses of victims of rape to nonvictims. The results of their longitudinal study revealed a possible relationship between the process of classical conditioning and victims' stimulus generalization and ensuing attempts to avoid thoughts, feelings, and behaviors related to the event. For example, traumatic responding was believed to result from original traumatic cues like unexpected touching or unexplained noise being generalized to subsequent occurrences of the same cues. The generalized cue stimulates emotions, thoughts, and bodily responses independent of the original trauma. Kolb (1987) hypothesized that the reflexive responding present in classical conditioning may explain the conditioned fear response and proposed the amygdala's role in the exaggerated reaction to stimuli, connecting psychological and physiological. The amygdala is a structure in the brain that facilitates the experience of emotions and memory functions involved in conditioned fear responses. Specific to the development of theories of trauma, Monson, Friedman and La Bash (2014) cite the contributions of operant conditioning to our understanding avoidant behavior as a negative reinforcer as, "avoidance maintains the originally learned anxiety associations because it prohibits exposure and habituation of conditioned responses" (p. 54).

Using Perry's framework, therapists can precisely target their work to whatever stage a child was in when trauma took place. Treatment begins with assessment. Traumatized children "need patterned repetitive experiences appropriate to their development needs, needs that reflect the age at which they missed important stimuli or had been traumatized, not their current chronological age" (Perry & Szalavitz, 2007; p. 138). For children and adolescents, treatments target regions of the brain and its functioning impacted by the trauma. The neurosequential model of therapeutics is presented later in this chapter.

Cognitive

Cognitive theories hypothesize and describe how humans process information. The process involves our perception, selection, and attention to personal experiences and how we store, organize, and retrieve those memories. Over time, memories develop into schemas or frameworks that are more efficient at interpreting and organizing external stimuli. Traumatic experiences (TE) are believed to influence schemas and, by extension, one's cognitive interpretation and organization. Dalgleish (1999) conducted a review of cognitive theories of posttraumatic stress disorder (PTSD) and identified five common features. First, individuals hold sets of beliefs about themselves, others, and the world. Most often this is referred to as the *just world belief* or *good things happen to good people and bad things happen to bad people*. The frame of individuals whose beliefs are primarily negative is *the world is not safe. I can't trust anyone*. Second, when one experiences a TE, the experience is incompatible with their previous beliefs. Traumatic events alter and disrupt individuals' core beliefs because the unexpected event alters beliefs about self, others, and their environment in an extreme way (Resick, et al 2007). The incompatible information leads to distress. The third common element describes the individual's attempt to relieve their distress by integrating the TE into their belief system through assimilation, accommodation, or overaccommodation. The integration is difficult and results in the fourth common element—emergence of PTSD phenomena or symptoms like fear, hypervigilance, irritability, and sleeplessness. The final common element addresses resolution. With successful resolution, distressing symptoms remit; when unsuccessful, distress increases as the traumatic information continues to conflict with the individual belief system. The goals of cognitive theories of trauma are to help traumatized clients activate and correct faulty beliefs in order to view themselves, others, and their environment more realistically and to process and acknowledge the traumatic event and associated emotions. Of the plethora of cognitive and cognitive-behavioral theories of trauma, we detail three that contribute to your understanding of fear networks, threat appraisal, and maintenance of PTSD.

Integrated Emotion Processing Theory

Foa and Kozak (1986; EPT) based emotional process theory on Lang's (1977) bioinformation theory and Rachman's (1980) emotional processing theory. Foa and Kozak (1986) noted fear structures become maladaptive through a process in which formerly neutral elements of traumatic events are subsequently perceived as threatening, activating flight or fight responses, and associated physiological responding (increased heart rate, rapid breathing, dilated pupils). Elements of the traumatic event, traumatic-responding, and their meaning comprise the fear structure. These types of fear responses are incongruent with the context and circumstances, are in excess of what is required to manage the event, and their meaning is mistakenly perceived and encoded into memory as a source of danger. During times of trauma or extreme stress memories are stored in a fragmented, chaotic, and incomplete manner. Thus, when all elements of a traumatic event are associated with permeating fear, individuals walk around in a constant state of readiness (hypervigilance). EPT conceptualizes chronic PTSD as a failure to adequately process the trauma memory due to extensive avoidance of thoughts and situations that are trauma reminders. (Foa, 2011). In sum, emotional processing theory proposes that the intervention involves the emotional process of traumatic memories so that they can be modified or replaced (Foa & Kozak, 1986; Foa, Huppert, & Cahill, 2006).

Emotional Processing Theory was expanded to Integrated Emotional Process Theory by Foa and her colleagues (Foa & Meadows, 1997; Foa & McNally, 1996; Foa & Riggs, 1993; Foa & Rothbaum, 1998). They emphasized the nature of disorganized traumatic memories and detail the role of memories, schemas, and posttraumatic reactions to self, others, and the environment. In essence, a traumatic event results in a fear network which contains all information about the event. These networks are strongly associated with fear and are bolstered by multiple stimuli and responses. Extensive fear structures are associated with signs of danger or fear and subject to overgeneralization of threat—almost anything can pose a threat. Dalgleish (2004) viewed the Foa's expanded theory as one of the most comprehensive to date.

Janoff-Bulman's Cognitive Appraisal Model

Like other cognitive theories, Janoff-Bulman's (1992) theory, sometimes referred to as the shattered assumptions theory, describes a mental template or model from which the individual views the world and makes decisions. Three basic assumptions ground Janoff-Bulman's model—the world is benevolent or *I am safe*; the world is meaningful or *we get what we deserve . . . good behavior and character leads to good outcomes; poor behavior and character lead to poor outcomes;* and finally the third assumption, the self is worthy or *I am good and can control events in my life.* Thus, traumatic experiences shattered one or more of these assumptions. The world is experienced as senseless, chaotic, and disorganized in the cognitive appraisal model. In this theory, a return to coping means rebuilding assumptions thorough prolonged exposure therapy or cognitive processing therapy—both explained later.

Ehlers and Clark's Model of the Maintenance of PTSD

Ehlers and Clark theorize a model of PTSD in which two core cognitive abnormalities exist. The first is the individual's appraisal and meanings of the TE are excessively negative and viewed as a serious threat. Because they overgeneralize the threat, the individual engages behaviors like safety seeking, intending to reduce the threat. Regrettably, the behavior is maladaptive and sustains the disorder by preventing change. The second cognitive abnormality involves disturbances in one's memory of themselves and the TE. Those with chronic or persistent PTSD have memories that are poorly elaborated and lack context, are strongly associative (the smell of gunpowder evokes the terror of war), and respond quickly to perceptual priming. Ehlers and Clark (2008) recommend a variety of cognitive therapy approaches to address the concerns of those with persistent PTSD.

Models of Trauma Treatment

The history and theories presented in the previous section are the foundation for models of treatment and intervention for those exposed to trauma. Consistent with our focus on development, we present the models of treatment from childhood through older age.

Children

Trauma-Informed Care

Hopefully you have been exposed to trauma-informed care in your graduate program or through professional development. The National Child Trauma Stress Network indicates that trauma-informed systems of service are those in which providers routinely screen for traumatic exposures and its symptoms; use culturally responsive and evidence-based protocols; and provide resources/psychoeducation to children and families about trauma exposure. Clinicians in these comprehensive systems also identify, discuss, and address resilience and protective factors in children and their families; address caregiver/parental trauma and its systemic impact on others; and attend to the wellness of clinical staff and takes steps to reduce secondary traumatic stress. These activities are undertaken in a context of mutuality, respect, and collaboration between service providers and families. Services providers also acknowledge and address issues of intersectionality across all identities.

Neurosequential Model of Therapeutics

Perry and Hambrick (2008) describe the Neurosequential Model of Therapeutics (NMT) as "a developmentally sensitive, neurobiologically informed approach to clinical work" not a set of skills or interventions (p. 38). The NMT rests on three principles, in the form of rhetorical statements that inform one's clinical practice: "Where the child has been" "Where the child is" and "Where the child should go." "The brain is a historical organ" (Perry & Hambrick, 2008; p. 40), and as such the *NMT Assessment* begins by cataloging the nature, severity, and duration of "key insults, stressors, and challenges" and when they occurred in the developmental process. These traumatic events are reviewed and scored to an approximate amount of trauma incurred to determine how and in what manner the brain was compromised (Perry, 2001). Relational health history is a *Functional Assessment* of attachment, resiliency, and vulnerabilities. Along with the neurodevelopmental history, the functional assessment provides an estimate of which brain areas are associated with which neuropsychiatric symptoms or child's strengths. An interdisciplinary team synthesizes the data into a functional brain map that is used in treatment with child and caregivers. The brain map is the foundation for the third component, *Specific Recommendations*. Perry and Hambrick note the functional assessment "helps determine a unique sequence of developmentally appropriate interventions that can help the child reapproximate a more normal developmental trajectory" (p. 42). Neurosequential intervention based on the NMT model requires a engaged and reliable team of individuals to create the needed environment. It is not something the clinician should attempt on their own.

Child–Parent Psychotherapy (CPP)

According to Lieberman, Van Horn, and Ghosh-Ippen (2005), child–parent psychotherapy is an effective evidence-based treatment approach for children under six years of age. The treatment is flexible and allows for incorporation of a discussion of cultural values and culture-related experiences. CPP is based on attachment, psychodynamic, developmental, trauma, social learning, and cognitive behavioral theories. This approach focuses on safety, improving the child–caregiver relationship, joint construction of trauma narrative, affect regulation, and helping the child return to a normal developmental trajectory. CPP has been empirically validated through four randomized controlled trials. These trials included a sample of children who witnessed intimate partner violence (Lieberman, Van Horn, & Ghosh-Ippen, 2005); maltreated preschooler's attachments (Toth, Maughan, Manly, Spagnola, & Cicchetti, 2002); the adjustment of maltreated children's attachment classification (Cicchetti, Rogosch, & Toth, 2006); and low-income Spanish speaking women and their babies (Lieberman, Ippen, & Van Horn, 2006).

Initial CPP therapy sessions are attended by the parent/caregiver and focus on developing an understanding of the nature and magnitude of the traumatic experience. Following these initial sessions, the parent and child attend together. Subsequent sessions focus on working with the child, in a play therapy format, to create a narrative regarding the traumatic experience. The primary therapeutic goal is to assist the caregivers' reengagement in the protective role with the traumatized child (Lieberman, Van Horn, & Ghosh-Ippen, 2005) and to aid the understanding of trauma and its effects on the child.

Parent-Child Interaction Therapy (PCIT)

Parent–Child interaction therapy (PCIT), developed by Sheila Eyberg (1988) and advanced by McNeil and Hembree-Kigin (2010), incorporates components of behavior therapy, play therapy, family systems, and social learning theory into a time-sensitive (12–20 sessions; average 14) dyadic behavioral intervention. PCIT focuses on improving the quality of the parent-child relationship, particularly attachment; decreasing child behavior problems (defiance, aggression) while increasing prosocial behaviors (helping, caring, comforting); improving parenting/relational skills through the use of **p**raise, **r**eflection, **i**mitation, **d**escription, and **e**nthusiasm (PRIDE) and positive discipline; and decreasing parenting stress. Originally created for children ages 2 to 7, some authors restricted the target population (Lenze, Pautsch, & Luby, 2011) to children ages of four and seven while others (Chaffin et al., 2004) have researched PCIT's application to children as old as 12.

Children and their caregivers are seen together in PCIT. The clinician observes typical interactions between the parent and child, then instructs parents on the above-referenced skills and asks them to use them with their child in a playroom while coached by a therapist. Clinicians coach from an observation room with a one-way mirror into the play or consultation room using a wireless or Bluetooth communication system to support the parent as they play with their child. Coaching provides parents immediate feedback on their use of the new parenting skills enabling them to apply the skills correctly while experiencing success designed to support acquisition and mastery. At the end of each session, the therapist and caregiver, together, decide which skill to focus on during daily five-minute home practice sessions the following week. The caregiver must have regularly daily contact with the child as homework is often assigned as a regular part of treatment.

As the clinician, you will spend most of the session time observing, evaluating, and coaching caregivers in the application of specific therapeutic skills. In addition to the initial clinical interview or intake completed, you may also wish to use a number of inventories to assess, monitor, and document treatment outcomes. Assessments you may wish to consider include:

- Achenbach's Child Behavior Checklists https://aseba.org/preschool/; https://aseba.org/school-age/

- Eyberg Child Behavior Inventory™ (ECBI™) along with its companion inventory Sutter-Eyberg Student Behavior Inventory-Revised™ (SESBI-R™) https://www.parinc.com/WebUploads/samplerpts/Fact%20Sheet%20

- ECBI-SESBI-R.pdf and or the Parenting Stress Index™, Fourth Edition Short Form (PSI™-4-SF) https://www.parinc.com/products/pkey/335;

- Eyberg Child Behavior Inventory™ (ECBI™) and its companion inventory Sutter-Eyberg Student Behavior Inventory-Revised™ (SESBI-R™) https://www.parinc.com/WebUploads/samplerpts/Fact%20Sheet%20ECBI-SESBI-R.pdf; or the

- Parenting Stress Index™, Fourth Edition Short Form (PSI™-4-SF) https://www.parinc.com/products/pkey/335;

- Eyberg Child Behavior Inventory™ (ECBI™) its companion inventory Sutter-Eyberg Student Behavior Inventory-Revised™ (SESBI-R™) https://www.parinc.com/WebUploads/samplerpts/Fact%20Sheet%20ECBI-SESBI-R.pdf; and

- Parenting Stress Index™, Fourth Edition Short Form (PSI™-4-SF) https://www.parinc.com/products/pkey/335

PCIT outcomes have been empirically validated through multiple investigations. Chaffin et al. (2004) found PCIT significantly reduced the amount of negative parent–child interactions with 110 parents who physically abuse their children. Not only did the PCIT group demonstrate a significant reduction in abuse behavior, but long-term follow-up demonstrated clear evidence that the changes were maintained. Similarly, Hood and Eyberg (2003) researched the long-term maintenance of changes following PCIT. They utilized a sample of young children demonstrating behaviors of oppositional defiant disorder. Evidence suggested that the positive changes demonstrated in children and caregivers persisted. Finally, PCIT has demonstrated efficacy in a randomized dismantling field trial. Dismantling designs are used with therapies that have multiple components of treatment and seek to either identify active mechanisms of change or the degree to which additional specific features contribute to the degree of change attributable to those components. Discreet components may be studied in isolation or in combination with other components of the intervention, typically in a sequential manner. For example, Chaffin, Funderburk, Bard, Valle, and Gurwitch (2011) found that a motivation–PCIT package, self-motivation (SM) combined with PCIT, reduced child abuse recidivism compared to a services as usual (SAU) sample of 192 parents whose children had been removed from the home, had six prior child welfare referrals, and were receiving parenting services at a community-based agency in Oklahoma. Cases were followed for a median of 904 days. Results from this study supported a synergistic SM + PCIT benefit and reduced future child welfare reports, particularly when children were returned to the home sooner rather than later.

Play Therapy

According to Erikson (1950), "Play is a function of the ego, an attempt to synchronize the bodily and social processes with self" (p. 214). While many adults may conceptualize play as something children do to pass time, in reality, children use play to express their inner-world symbolically. Kottman (2010) defined play therapy as "an approach to counseling young children in which the clinician uses toys, art supplies, games, and other play media to communicate with clients using the 'language' of children—the 'language' of play" (p. 4). Play therapy assists children suffering from trauma by offering them a process to symbolically play out their experience and is believed to directly impact the sensory experiences stored in the brain (Green et al., 2010). The Association for Play Therapy (Ray & McCullough, 2015; [APT]) recommends play therapy for children ages 3 to 12.

During play, children have control over the extent to which they come into contact with the traumatic experience. The play therapist utilizes warm and empathic skills to encourage the child to feel a sense of safety and empowerment as they project their emotions, thoughts, and experiences on the various play mediums (toys, paint, sand art, dress-up). Play therapy is offered in different formats (individual, co-joint, familial), however it is typically best suited for children three to nine years of age.

Ray and McCullough (2015) describe the effectiveness of play therapy for children based on Paynter's (2009) research credibility pyramid for the social sciences. Paynter presents a four-level hierarchy of evidence researchers can use in evaluating mental health interventions. This hierarchy parallels but is not as detailed as the work of Chambless and colleagues (1996, 1998) and the American Psychological Association's 2006 presidential task force's statement on evidenced-based practice. The pyramid is comprised of four levels; at the top are systematic reviews and meta-analyses of findings from multiple studies from a narrowly defined treatment approach or intervention. Systematic reviews and meta-analyses and randomized controlled trials discussed in the next section are considered the *gold standard* of efficacy studies. Next are studies designed as randomized controlled trials (RCTs). RCTs compare two groups whose membership is randomly assigned. One group receives the intervention under study; the other group is a control group whose members receive a placebo or no treatment. RCTs reduce research bias through standardized methods and control over variables of interest, thus findings can be generalized to the population from which the sample was drawn. The third level of the pyramid includes observational studies-quasi-experimental studies (manipulation of the independent variable without random assignment, less control over variables of interest, limited generalization), correlational designs (which cannot attribute causation) and single-case experimental designs. The better evidence comes from cohort studies which identify a variable of interest and associate it with an outcome (prospective) or examine a group exposed to a variable (like exposure to trauma) and determine if they experienced the outcome. Studies at this level of the pyramid may have statistically significant results but do not yet provide sufficient evidence to be considered in the gold standard. Finally, the base of the pyramid describes case reports or case studies, which may include qualitative and anecdotal evidence and can include individual quantitative data, on the use of a particular intervention. Similar to quasi-experimental designs, case studies provide valuable information on the efficacy of treatments but do not yet rise to the level of gold standard set for cognitive behavior therapy (CBT). For full review of the evidence base for play therapy interventions please see Phillips (2010) and Ray and McCullough (2015).

Adolescents

Cognitive Behavioral Intervention for Trauma in Schools (CBITS)

According to Feldman (2007) CBITS is a 10-session, school-based group intervention, developed for children (5–11) and adolescents (12–14) to reduce symptoms related to PTSD, complex trauma, depression, and general anxiety. Jaycox, Langley, and Hoover (2018) structure the intervention as follows: two group sessions; introductions in session one, followed by education and relaxation techniques in group session two. Next, the child then completes three individual sessions that focus on processing the trauma memory narrative. Group sessions 5 though 10 focus on an introduction to cognitive therapy, combating negative thoughts, an introduction to real-life exposure, two sessions on exposure to stress or trauma memory, problem solving, social problem solving, and concludes with relapse prevention and graduation. Through this treatment protocol, clinicians help adolescents cope with the trauma symptomology and develop more prosocial and adaptive coping skills. CBITS has been tested in a randomized controlled study with children diagnosed with PTSD (Jaycox, et al., 2002). Research findings indicated that the intervention group had significant improvement in PTSD and symptoms of depression.

Trauma-Focused Cognitive Behavioral Therapy (TF-CBT)

Trauma-focused cognitive behavioral therapy (TF-CBT) is comprised of four components: exposure, cognitive processing and reframing, stress management, and parental treatment (Cohen, Mannarino, Berliner, & Deblinger, 2000). TF-CBT is a 12-week model developed for children and adolescents (ages 3–18). This model has also been adapted for toddlers and preschoolers (Scheeringa et al., 2007). Children and adolescents are often well suited for TF-CBT due to their ability to clearly recall the traumatic event (the focus of treatment). TF-CBT is a holistic model that integrates interpersonal, behavioral, cognitive, and family therapy theoretical tenets. Cocreating the therapeutic relationship, learning skills to cope and understand trauma, and fostering the parent–child bond are all salient to the TF-CBT model. The acronym PRACTICE refers to the major components of this model: **p**sychoeducation, **r**elaxation skills, **a**ffective expression, **c**ognitive coping, **t**rauma narration and processing, **i**n vivo mastery of trauma reminders, **c**onjoint child–parent sessions, and **e**nhancing safety.

Trauma theory focuses on the appraisal and experience of crisis or traumatic events accompanied by devastating or paralyzing fear alter emotional and psychological functioning (Perry, 1993). In a percentage of cases if suffering and anguish persists, posttraumatic stress disorder (PTSD) may develop. Thus, clinical interventions target the realignment of emotional and psychological responses to trauma-related thoughts, memories, and recollections. Interventions, like Trauma

Focused Cognitive Behavioral Therapy (TF-CBT), are based on trauma and social cognitive (Beck, 1985) theories. TF-CBT components include creation of current and future safety plans, psycho-education, relaxation training, identification and regulation of emotions, coping and cognitive processing, and trauma narrative. Like CBITS referenced above, TF-CBT includes parent psychoeducation and skills training, as well as conjoint child-parent sessions. The effectiveness of TF-CBT is well established for victims of sexual abuse (Silverman et al., 2008). The parent–child or caregiver–child relationship and attachment seem critical to positive treatment outcomes. For example, Lieberman et al. (2005) found that a 50-week child/parent therapy program, based on attachment theory, reduced symptoms of traumatic stress and improved behavior when compared to case management and individual psychotherapy. Cohen, Mannarino, and Iyengar (2011) used a randomized controlled design to compare Child Centered Therapy (CCT) with a brief version of TF-CBT and found children in the TF-CBT group demonstrated fewer PTSD symptoms and anxiety when compared to those in the CCT group. Clearly, parental or caregiver involvement in treatment influences children's ongoing risk, capacity for resiliency, and recovery from traumatic or neglectful events. TF-CBT is one of the most well-supported forms of therapy for children and adolescents with severe PTSD symptoms and complex trauma (Stein et al., 2003).

Adults

Effective clinicians take a holistic approach with traumatized individuals understanding their psychological, social, emotional, and behavioral expressions of trauma as well as their physical and somatic reactions. This includes the use of evidence-based treatments and guidelines that aid your selection and utilization of specific treatment protocols matching your client's specific needs. In addition to what we presented in the section on child treatment, Foa, Keane, Friedman, and Cohen (2009) stated that for CBT treatments, guidelines are based on the systematic and metanalytic reviews to examine and establish the efficacy or *grade* of each intervention. Grades range from A to D. A grade of A demonstrates the treatment approach is strongly supported by empirical evidence and positive client outcomes, while a grade of D indicates a treatment with little to no empirical support and ineffective or harmful client outcomes.

Empirically Supported

A number of evidence-based treatments (EBT) have been identified as the gold standard for treatment of trauma, most notably for PTSD and other trauma-related problems (CATS Consortium, 2007; Ebert, Amaya-Jackson, Markiewicz, Kisiel, & Fairbank, 2012; Ebert, Amaya-Jackson, Markiewicz, & Fairbank, 2012; Karlin et al., 2010). The most notable trauma-based treatments include trauma-focused cognitive–behavioral therapy (TF-CBT) discussed earlier, prolonged exposure (PET), cognitive processing therapy (CPT), cognitive behavioral therapy (CBT), psychological debriefing, critical incident stress debriefing (CISD), eye movement desensitization and reprocessing (EMDR), art-assisted therapy, and brainspotting (BSP). TF-CBT and CPT can be offered in a group-counseling context.

Prolonged Exposure Therapy (PET)

Prolonged Exposure therapy (PET) is one of the most well-known empirically based treatments for adults with chronic PTSD arising out of single or multiple traumas. Developed by Edna Foa, this approach is recognized as a Level A treatment and is supported by hundreds of studies demonstrating its efficacy. PET is grounded in emotional processing theory (EPT), which focuses on how fear is organized, structured, and stored in one's memory. As noted previously in this chapter, fear responses or structures can be adaptive or maladaptive, meaning that when threats are real, the experience of fear moves the individual to react by avoiding danger adapting in a context-congruent manner.

Prolonged exposure therapy is aptly named. The goal of treatment, generally 8 to 15 90-minute sessions, prepares the client for prolonged and sustained exposure to the feared situations through a combination of psychoeducation, retelling, and revisiting the trauma. First, clients are educated about typical reactions to trauma, rationale for and explanation of treatment protocol, including the types of exposure, and PTSD and physiological and emotional management strategies like relaxation techniques and breathing retraining. Clients are asked to practice relaxation techniques between sessions. Next, the client, in collaboration with the clinician, ranks trauma-related stimuli from least feared to most feared. Then the client is intentionally and systematically exposed, at a pace they determine, to trauma-related events, elements, and associations via in vivo (direct experience with feared situations) and imaginal (repeated verbal recounting and revisiting the trauma) exposure. Following each exposure, the client and clinician process the experience to explore the client's reactions, identify errors in thinking, dispute previous beliefs ("The world is a dangerous place" "I am completely incapable"), and challenge avoidance of triggering situations. Clients are asked to monitor between-session traumatic responding and report back in session. The repeated retelling, revisiting, and discussion of trauma-related memories or experiences are believed to aid in the consolidation and clarification of more accurate memories and associations. Foa (2011) reminds us that encouraging clients "to elaborate on new insights and making them explicit is likely to facilitate emotional processing and modification of the pathological emotional structure" (p. 1045). Prolonged exposure therapy has been contraindicated for clients with PTSD, co-morbid suicidality, psychotic, dissociative, and anxieties disorders (Becker, Zayfert, & Anderson, 2004), and multiple childhood traumas (van Minnen, Hendriks, & Olff, 2010). Yet, van Minnen, Harned, Zoellner, and Mills (2012) found prolonged exposure could safely and effectively be used with these populations and is often correlated with a decrease in PTSD and co-morbid behaviors or disorders. For greater detail on EPT, please see the manual Prolonged Exposure Therapy for PTSD: Emotional Processing of Traumatic Experiences, Therapist Guide (Foa et al., 2007).

Cognitive Processing Therapy (CPT)

Originally developed by Resick and Schnicke (1993), CPT is a version of CBT originally designed for the treatment of those traumatized by rape and subsequently has been expanded to treat members of the military. Like PET, CPT is recognized as a gold-standard treatment by International Society for Traumatic

Stress Studies (ISTSS) PTSD Treatment Guidelines (Foa et al., 2009) and in the clinical practice guidelines from the Veteran's Administration and Department of Defense (Management of Post-Traumatic Stress Working Group, 2010). The theoretical foundations for CPT rest upon Lang's (1977) information processing theory, extended into the treatment of trauma by Foa, Steketee, and Rothbaum, (1989) and social cognitive theory. In essence, for CPT, these theories propose an individual's view of themselves, others and the world frames their experience and interpretation of each; either positively or negatively. Those with a positive frame see the world as a just place and believe in their ability to influence it; those with a negative frame see the world as unjust and believe they have little agency to change events or outcomes. Traumatic events are believed to disrupt the individual's core beliefs particularly when they are incongruent with their personal frame. Resick et al. (2008) argued individuals attempt to undermine their experiences through the processes of assimilation (memories or cognitions are altered to fit current beliefs), accommodation (beliefs are altered to fit experience; often consider the most health response), or overaccommodation (belief about self, others, and the world are altered to an extreme extent).

Treatment typically occurs over 12 sessions beginning with psychoeducation about depression and PTSD, a brief description of the most traumatic event, cognitive perspective of PTSD, and expectations and commitment to treatment compliance, treatment rational—including stuck points and written work, and homework in the form of an impact statement. In the impact statement, the client is asked to write why they think this event happened to them and how has it changed their views about themselves, others, and the world. In the second session, the client reads the impact statement and discusses it meaning. The clinician introduces the connection between events, thoughts, and feelings, and concludes the session with an introduction of the A B C *Worksheets* (Activating Event, Belief and Consequence). Sessions 3 and 4 focus on cognitive restructuring; at the end of Session 3, clients are asked to document their traumatic experience including thoughts, feelings, and sensory inputs. CPT Sessions 5 through 12 use a combination of daily assignments, cognitive restructuring, and domain specific concerns (safety, trust, power, intimacy; sessions 8 through 12). Like PET discussed above, CPT is contraindicated for those individuals experiencing dissociative states. Six empirical studies, four of which were randomized control trials, demonstrated the efficacy of CPT. For more detailed information on CPT, please see the therapist training manual available at https://www.apa.org/ptsd-guideline/treatments/cognitive-processing-therapist.pdf.

Cognitive Behavioral Therapy (CBT)

Cognitive behavioral therapy (CBT) is a well-known empirically supported treatment for trauma, complex trauma, and PTSD (Adler-Nevo & Manassas, 2005; La Greca & Silverman 2009; Stallard, 2006). CBT targets trauma-related symptoms in 12 to 16 sessions via individual or group counseling. Cognitive behavioral therapy approach is a sophisticated set of procedures aimed at ameliorating cognitive and behavioral trauma symptomology. Cognitive techniques center on restructuring unproductive cognitions through ameliorating faulty schemas, assumptions, automatic thoughts, and cognitive distortions. Typical techniques include, but are not limited to, Socratic questioning, downward arrow, and psychoeducation. Behavioral interventions are generally aimed at decreasing maladaptive behaviors and increasing adaptive ones through intervention based on learning theory, operant conditioning, and classical conditioning.

Eye Movement Desensitization and Reprocessing (EMDR)

EMDR is a comprehensive therapeutic modality, encompassing eight phases of treatment (Shapiro, 2001) based on several theoretical perspectives: cognitive-behavioral, psychodynamic, interactional, and body-based (Shapiro & Maxfield, 2002). EMDR is an adaptive information-processing model of treatment designed to ease the suffering linked with traumatic memories (Shapiro, 1989). EMDR treatment is structured into eight stages; stages three through eight occur throughout treatment. The eight stages begin with *client history and treatment planning* followed by *preparation*—which includes education about the nature of trauma, treatment rationale, and procedures specific to EMDR and coping skills instruction (relaxation training, emotional regulation); *assessment*—where targeted trauma memories and associated negative beliefs, physical sensations, and their location in the body are revealed; desensitization and reprocessing—where the individual simultaneously holds negative beliefs, disruptive trauma memories, and the location and type of any bodily sensations while visually tracking the clinician's rhythmic movements across the visual field. Shapiro (2001) hypothesized that while client's work with a clinician on attending to traumatic memories, they should also experience brief alternating bilateral stimulation via eye movement, audio stimulation, hand tapping, or vibrating pads. These two experiences, done simultaneously, create an adaptive resolution to the traumatic experience and new associative links are developed. These new associations, guided by the clinician, result in a variety of healing experiences, including information processing, eliminating emotional distress, new learning, and empowerment. The EMDR therapist will also collaborate with the client on creating imaginal templates of future experiences and the skills needed for adaptive behavior. The fifth stage, *installation of positive thoughts* or cognitions, occurs after the client's report of a 0 or 1 on the subjective units of distress (SUDs) assessment where 0 = no distress and 10 = very distressing. The client is asked to hold the new positive belief in mind while again tracking the clinician rhythmic movements and to scale their perceptions of the new positive belief as not at all valid to completely valid. In the sixth stage, *body scan*, the client surveys their body for problematic physical sensations (rapid heartbeat, sweating, muscle tension, aches of unknown origins), acknowledges them, and repeats the visual tracking (or tactile stimulation-finger tapping) procedure with the clinician. *Closure* marks the seventh stage in which direct coping skill instruction (relaxation, visualization) is provided. Clients are encouraged to practice these skills to combat disruptive memories or images. The final stage, *reevaluation*, provides the client and clinician opportunities to review and assess treatment goals, the degree of their attainment, and the potential emergence of additional concerns.

According to Nardo, Hogberg, Looi, Larsson, and Hallstrom (2010), when someone experiences a traumatic incident, the brain's limbic system fires off chemicals that direct our bodies to fight, flee, or freeze. Memories from the traumatic event are kept within the brain's limbic system and midbrain, and are eventually processed within the prefrontal cortex. However, at times, trauma-based experiences are not processed within the prefrontal cortex. Instead, they are stuck within the neurons of the limbic system and mid-brain. When clients experience EMDR treatment around a traumatic event, the neurons within their limbic system start to become rewired. This rewiring moves the trauma-based information from the limbic system and mid-brain to the prefrontal cortex and experiences are processed. The desensitization and prefrontal processing of the traumatic event ultimately leads to a more cognitive-based response to trauma-related stimuli and reduces common trauma-based symptomology akin to hyperarousal, flashbacks, and memory failure (Ecker, Ticic & Hulley, 2013; Lilienfeld & Arkowitz, 2008).

EMDR has an A-level rating from the International Society for Traumatic Stress Studies (Foa et al., 2009) and the Management of Post-Traumatic Stress Working Group (2010), which means it is as effective as other exposure-based treatments. Despite this rating, the function of eye movements bears further investigation as some (Spates, Koch, Pagoto, Cusack, & Waller 2008) have found that eye movements were not associated with positive treatment outcomes, while others (Schubert, Lee, & Drummond, 2011) found benefits associated with eye movement. Clinicians must become certified in EMDR through a 50-hour EMDR Basic Training (previously titled EMDR 1 and 2). Formal training and supervision include supervised practice, and 10 documented consultation hours. More information is available at https://www.emdr.com/us-basic-training-overview/.

Psychological Debriefing

Psychological debriefing is a type of post-traumatic care centered on preventing trauma symptoms directly after a crisis event. Psychological debriefing typically includes a single session, group-format debriefing, thought- and fact-based information and processing, coping skills education, and symptom information, and the dissemination of referral information. One approach to psychological debriefing that has garnered considerable attention is Critical Incident Stress Debriefing (CISD; Mitchell & Everly, 1996; Everly, Lating, & Mitchell, 2000). CISD is a seven-phase structured small-group model that takes approximately one to three hours to conduct. The seven phases are introduction phase—a description of the debriefing process and meeting the facilitators. This first phase is an intentional thoughtful presentation of the process that sets the stage and expectations of the session (individuals can choose to *pass* on a question), highlights problem areas, and invites active participation from the group members. Second is the Fact phase during which participants share their experiences of the traumatic event. A common opening inquiry may be: "Would you each give us (the team) a brief summary of what occurred from your point of view. Third, the Thought phase, participants share their thoughts about the incident and begin the transition into emotional processing. A typical inquiry might include, "What was your first thought after the event?" Fourth, the Reaction phase includes unstructured group processing of the traumatic event. As a facilitator you may ask, "What is the worst thing about this event, for you?" Fifth, the Symptom phase is where facilitators ask participants to identify symptoms occurring since the event. The symptom phase facilitates participants' transition from emotional back to cognitive processes. Sixth, the Teaching phase allows the team to normalize the symptoms identified participants. The team provides psychoeducation related to those symptoms and coping skills are reviewed. Handouts may be distributed. Re-entry is the seventh and final phase where the team provides summary statements and referrals. One-on-one sessions are frequent after the CISD ends.

Critically, it is important to note that CISD is a *group* intervention and is contraindicated for individuals. Individual applications of CISD have been a source of controversy. Several researchers have demonstrated that CISD did not have empirical support for its efficacy (Foa, et al., 2009) and in some cases has made individuals worse (Bisson, McFarlane, Rose, Ruzek, & Watson, 2009). Mitchell (2003), responding to these criticisms, noted that CISD was "not a stand-alone process" (p. 192) and should only be "employed within a package of crisis intervention procedures under the Critical Incident Stress Management umbrella. Without exception, every negative outcome study on CISD to date has not used trained personnel to provide the service and they have violated the core standards of practice in the CISM field" (p. 191) as some have used the CISD for individuals instead of homogeneous groups. The Cochrane Review (Wessely, Rose, & Bisson, 1998) summarized the negative outcome studies on CISD. In that review, 100% of the studies were performed on individuals. When a group process designed for homogeneous groups is used on individuals, it changes the inherent nature of the process itself and also what is being measured. In addition, the negative outcome studies applied a group process model to individuals for whom the CISD process was never intended.

Art-Assisted Therapy

Art therapy is a trauma-based treatment that is centered on clients utilizing drawing, painting, collage, and sculpting to create awareness of trauma-based experiences and to latent memories and thoughts. Art therapy is often categorized as *creative art therapy* (along with music, dance, and psychodrama therapies). Clinicians typically augment a traditional, empirically based approach to trauma (EMDR, TF-CBT, CBT) with art-assisted therapy or it is part of a multidisciplinary inpatient or outpatient treatment program (Droždek, Bolwerk, Tol, & Kleber, 2012). The overarching goal of art therapy is to help client's process emotions, cognitions, and latent processes to work through, process, and symbolically express trauma symptoms through art mediums (Gantt & Tinnin, 2009). According to Foa, Keane, Friedman, and Cohen (2009), art therapy reduces trauma symptomology (alexithymia [an inability to identify and describe emotions], dissociation, anxiety, nightmares, and insomnia).

Brainspotting (BSP)

Grand (2013) describes BSP as a brain-based dual-attunement model of trauma therapy. While EMDR emphasizes bilateral eye movements, BSP has client's hold a gaze in an area that causes the eye to wobble. Clinicians initially utilize a pointer and music while having the client follow the pointer until they reach a place where they are stuck. Without being asked to talk about their trauma, clients are encouraged to initiate activation around a problem issue and work through whatever is getting them stuck in that particular eye position. Repeatedly working through these brain spots facilitates rapid discharge and resolution of traumatic experiences that are embedded in the brainstem. According to Hildebrand, Grand, and Stemmler (2017),

> By slow eye tracking, either with one eye or with two eyes, locations for BSP are identified. To find these locations, the techniques of either "Inside Window" or "Outside Window" can be used. The "Inside Window" utilizes the client's felt sense, the "Outside Window" helps to locate this location by observation of clients' reflexive response such as blinks, eye twitches or wobbles or quick inhalation, by the therapist. (p. 4)

Scant empirical evidence exists in support of Brainspotting, yet Corrigan and Hull (2015) describe it as an advancement in psychotherapy that works at a deeper level, perhaps the midbrain.

Summary

History, context, and individual characteristics or perceptions influence our understandings of trauma and traumatic responding in clients and ourselves. They provide a foundation for further advancements in theories, research, interventions, clinician training, and ultimately, client care. Originally, trauma theories focused on the body's physiologic responses to physical insults. Over time, the number of theories has increased and, as a group, has matured, become more integrated, robust, and culturally relevant. Succinct theories with high explanatory power led to trauma-informed treatment models and interventions which resulted in relief for those who suffer. Dynamic fields of study, like trauma, are rife with controversies and powerful prevailing social or economic influences. Hopefully, this dynamism continues to support intellectual curiosity and rigor that advances the needs of our clients rather than the periodic professional *amnesias*.

Extended Learning Exercises

Questions for Review

1. List the six controversies related to the development of trauma theories and their effect on diagnosis and treatment.

2. Discuss the concepts of the unbearable situation and unacceptable impulse.

3. Compare and contrast psychiatric and psychological theories of trauma.

4. Describe the contributions of cognitive behavioral understandings of trauma.

5. How does the concept of malingering influence our understanding of trauma and trauma-related responding?

6. Describe the cultural influences refinement of trauma-related responding and diagnosis in the diagnostic manuals (*DSM–I through DSM–V*).

Additional Resources

Helpful Books

Cahill, S.P., & Foa, E. B. (2007). Psychological theories of PTSD. In M. J. Friedman, T. M. Keane, & P. A. Resick (Eds.). *Handbook of PTSD: Science and Practice* (pp. 55–77). New York: Guilford.

Herman, J. L. (1992). *Trauma and recovery: The aftermath of violence—From domestic abuse to political terror.* New York: Basic Books.

Kolb, L. C. (1987). A neuropsychological hypothesis explaining posttraumatic stress disorders. *American Journal of Psychiatry, 144,* 989–995.

van der Kolk, B. A. (2014). *The body keeps the score: Brain, mind, and body in the healing of trauma.* New York: Penguin Group, LLC.

Helpful Websites

Adverse Childhood Experiences Study: http://www.acestudy.org/

The Child Trauma Academy: http://www.childtrauma.org

Community Connections (includes TREM, M-TREM): http://www.communityconnectionsdc.org/

International Society for Traumatic Stress Studies: http://www.istss.org/Home1.htm

Mc Silver Institute for Poverty Policy and Research: http://mcsilver.nyu.edu/search/search_by_page/trauma%20of%20racism

National Child Traumatic Stress Network (NCTSN): http://www.nctsnet.org/

PTSD Alliance: http://www.ptsdalliance.org/

SAMHSA National Center for Trauma-Informed Care: http://www.samhsa.gov/nctic/

Seeking Safety: http://www.seekingsafety.org/

Sidran Institute: http://www.sidran.org/t3

Training: think-teach-transform: http://www.center4si.com/training/index.cfm

Trauma Focused Cognitive-Behavioral Therapy (TF-CBT) Training: http://tfcbt.musc.edu/

Trauma-Informed Response: http://www.traumainformedresponse.com/Home.html

Trauma Stewardship: http://traumastewardship.com/

Traumatic Stress Institute: http://traumaticstressinstitute.org/

Veterans Administration: http://www.ptsd.va.gov/

5

Caring for Those
Affected by Trauma

Those affected by trauma present with a variety of symptoms and concerns. Some symptoms appear connected to the traumatic event while others do not. In this chapter, we discuss the knowledge, skills, awareness, and resources used to treat those affected by trauma. These treatment components help you contextualize clients' experiences, specifically the nature, extent, and magnitude of present and prior traumatic exposure(s). This includes direct and indirect exposure, socially just treatment, and the process of recovery and restoration.

Traumatic exposure (TE) in childhood is interpersonal, disrupts attachment, and is associated with more complex forms of trauma, like PTSD. Consequences of direct or indirect exposure can and often are immediate, multidimensional, and enduring (Herman, 1992; van der Kolk, 1996; van der Kolk, Roth, Pelcovitz, Sunday, & Spinazzola, 2005; Courtois, 2008). Traumatic responding impairs one's ability to regulate their emotions and relate effectively to others and increases the risk of future traumatic exposures, psychiatric disorders, and a host of medical and social issues. In Chapter 9, you will read about the trends in *DSM* diagnostic criteria (See Table 5.1) and note how understandings of post-event traumatic responding have been refined and advanced. Changes to *DSM* criteria related to extreme stress or trauma have primarily been based on the experiences of adult males returning from combat. Given what we knew about developmental influences on traumatic responding, it was clear potential differences in traumatic responding by children and women needed to be explored and understood (Herman, 1992; Courtois, 1988). Herman's (1992) synthesis of current research offered an "unsystematized but extensive empirical support for the concept of a complex posttraumatic syndrome in survivors of prolonged, repeated victimization. This previously undefined syndrome may coexist with simple PTSD but extends beyond it" (p. 387). For almost two decades, researchers, clinicians, and a dedicated workgroup argued for a distinct classification of complex posttraumatic stress, but to no avail. The exclusion of complex trauma from the *Diagnostic and Statistical Manual of Mental Disorders, Fifth Edition* (*DSM–5*) was described as *arbitrary* and *curious* (Phillips, 2015) while others saw complex trauma as subtype of PTSD (Sar, 2011). We agree with Ford and Courtois (2014) who distinguish complex psychological trauma from other stress disorders as complex psychological trauma that is marked by exposure to repetitive and prolonged stressors, involves harm or abandonment by caregivers, and occurs during critical periods of brain development. This type of traumatic exposure and experiences result in "changes in the mind, emotions, body and relationships" as "problems with dissociation, emotion dysregulation, somatic distress or relational or spiritual alienation" (p. 13). We explore complex trauma in the last section of this chapter.

Learning Objectives

After reading this chapter and completing the reflective exercises, you will be able to

- Understand the major types of trauma
- Integrate treatment with the developmental level of the trauma survivor
- Understand general and advanced skills and awareness
- Provide a case conceptualization and assessment
- Consider a variety of techniques to clinical vignettes

The Counselor's Toolkit

As you recall, in Chapter 3, we reviewed the knowledge, skill(s), awareness, technique(s), and resources clinicians required to assist those experiencing crises. In contrast to Chapter 2, here we present the elements of the *Toolkit* in a more integrated rather than sequential manner. We begin with knowledge component, segmented by the client's developmental level, and incorporate the associated skills and techniques within each intervention or treatment approach. Consistent with Chapter 2, a table summarizing the knowledge, skills, awareness, techniques, and resources related to treating those affected by trauma is presented. The chapter concludes with extended learning opportunities designed to enhance your learning about trauma counseling.

Knowledge

Approaches to Care and Treatment

Trauma affects families, groups, individuals, and communities. Clinicians treat trauma in a variety of therapeutic formats: individual, group or couples and family counseling, parent consultation, play therapy, and advocacy. When an individual is affected by a traumatic event, multiple family or community members share in that suffering and care must be coordinated. At times, family therapy is not recommended due to a variety of factors such as acute individual symptomology, severe comorbidity with substance abuse, and the existence of intimate partner violence. Families not directly involved in treatment should be provided referral information and informed of self-help groups and support groups and encouraged to participate in such groups (Rosenfeld, Caye, Lahad, & Gurwitch, 2010).

When communities are affected, plans should include provisions for a fully coordinated response. Community stakeholders and leaders ensure plans address delivery mechanisms for immediate practical assistance, multiple channels of communication with neighboring communities, mobilization and coordination of first responders, and trauma specialists who use evidence-based assessment and treatment services. Healthcare providers and the clients they serve benefit from clear roles and responsibilities, which are behavior specific in nature (Rosenfeld, Caye, Lahad, & Gurwitch, 2010).

In regards to trauma-based contextual factors, the emotional and physical proximity to danger, degree of perceived control, duration, and exposure to the traumatic event, individual's appraisal of the event, others' reactions, and the type of traumatic event (interpersonal violence, war, suicide, neglect, sexual abuse, terrorism, mass shooting) impact an individual's reaction and recovery process. According Courtois and Ford (2009), an individual's response to trauma is complex and almost impossible to predict. A person's age, gender, past exposure to trauma, social support, race, ethnicity, culture, individual and family psychiatric history, and general psychological well-being are contextual factors related to individual response to trauma.

After posttraumatic stress disorder (PTSD) was introduced into the third edition of the *Diagnostic and Statistical Manual of Mental Disorders* (*DSM–III*; American Psychiatric Association, 1994) treatment guidelines were developed in a variety of formats ranging from outpatient/inpatient to residential rehabilitation programs to support groups. Because of the social movement and political influences referenced in Chapter 4, PTSD treatment initially focused on adults returning from war then on women's experiences with sexual or interpersonal violence rather than children. While some elements of treatment cross over, many do not because of children's and adolescents' levels of development and cognitive maturation which influence their perceptions and responses.

Treatment by Individual's Developmental Level

Children and adolescents respond to traumatic events differently. Their reactions are influenced by their developmental level, individual functioning, cultural contexts, previous exposure to traumatic events, available resources, and preexisting child and family concerns. However, nearly all children and adolescents express distress or behavioral change in the acute phase of recovery from a traumatic event. Ford and Courtois (2014) rightly note that children who are exposed to complex trauma experience a "violation of and challenge to the fragile, immature and newly emerging self" (p. 16) as well as distorted and insecure attachment processes. Some examples of distress are new fears, behavioral disruptions, separation anxiety, sleep disturbances, nightmares, somatic complaints, and irritability. Not all acute responses are problematic as some behavior changes may reflect adaptive attempts to cope. Where symptoms are mild and have been present for less than four weeks after the trauma, watchful waiting is recommended (Siegel, 1999).

Early Childhood Trauma

The psychological health of pregnant women may have a direct impact on the health of the fetus (Kinsella & Monk, 2013). Fetal development—cellular, physical, and neurological—is intimately intertwined with the health and functioning of the mother. During this time, the fetal brain is changing more rapidly compared to any other point in development (Cognitive Neuroscience Society, 2018; CNS). The CNS researchers used functional magnetic resonance imaging (fMRI) and discovered fetal brain organization, development, and efficiency were influenced by maternal stress independent of the environment into which the child was born. Maternal stress was defined as mothers from low-resourced urban settings who experienced elevated stress levels like anxiety, depression, and worry. These findings, as well as others, demonstrate the effects of stress on human psychobiological development and functioning—perhaps even our response to traumatic stress.

Early childhood traumatic responses are evaluated using the same triad of categories used for adults: reexperiencing, avoidance, and hyperarousal. However, a notable difference is young children need to evidence only one symptom in each diagnostic category to be diagnosed with PTSD. Recall the first three years of life are the most intensive period for acquiring speech and language skills. These skills develop best in an enriched environment filled with predictable sounds and sights and consistent nurturing care. Traumatized infants and children are ill equipped to understand and process these events. A child's preverbal experience of traumatic events is just as, if not more, impactful compared with any other phase of development. Some argued that infants and toddlers, who were unable to verbally express their response to trauma, were not affected later in life (Perlman & Doyle, 2012). Subsequent research (Green et al., 2010; van der Kolk, 1994) has since confirmed that there are *indeed* long-term implications. Experiences of trauma are stored in the infant's brain as sensory experiences. The consequence of frequent preverbal traumatic sensorimotor experience is often a disorganized attachment style (Markese, 2007).

As noted in Chapter 4, empirically based treatments for infants, toddlers, and young children include parent(s)–child dyadic therapies and play therapy. Evidence-based treatments are founded on scientific rigor and a robust body of evidence to support their claims. Child–parent psychotherapy (CPP) and parent–child interaction therapy (PCIT) are evidence-based treatments (EBTs) for childhood trauma. Significant evidence for the effectiveness of Play Therapy (PT) is growing.

Skills and Techniques

Treatment approaches for children share several core counseling skills like observation, immediacy, reflection of content, feeling and meaning, encouragers and clarification, facilitation of decision-making, and empathy. Psychoeducation related to effects of child maltreatment or abuse, effective parenting strategies, open-ended questions, and coaching are specific skills associated with CPP and CPIT. Ray (2004) noted nonverbal and verbal skills in play therapy. Nonverbal skills include culturally appropriate eye contact, physical proximity with the child during play, leaning forward, and moving with the child around the play therapy space. Verbal skills include a verbal tone congruent with the child's affect, tracking, or narration of the child's actions and intent, facilitating creativity, esteem building, and relationship building. Below are additional examples of child-centered play therapy skills and techniques utilized to help children work through traumatic experiences. While some of the below skills are associated with those promoted by Axline (1969), we expand on her initial recommendations to include skills endorsed by other scholars (Kottman, 2010; Ray, 2011; Vernon, 2009).

Play Therapy Skills

In the initial session, clinicians briefly describe the playroom. After that and in each subsequent session, they remind the child that play therapy is a time when most things can be done. For example: *Clinician:* "This is our playroom and this is a place where you can play with toys in a lot of the ways you would like to. This is a place where you can do most things."

Tracking

Concretely describe or narrate the activities of the child as the child presents them. You do not label or judge the child's behavior, as labeling imposes your perspective. The goal of play therapy is to encourage and support the child's frame of reference. For example: *Clinician:* "You covered the horse with sand."

Restating Content

This technique balances using age-appropriate language and not parroting the child. When you engage a child in play therapy, you will get on the floor or will sit alongside the child to engage them on their physical level and talk directly to or through a toy or process. For example: *Client:* "I'm building a big castle and a big wall with these blocks . . . I will use this blue stuff to make a river." *Clinician:* "You are building a castle and it's important to have a wall and water around it."

Reflection of Feeling

In a play therapy setting, reflections of feeling are proffered in a more tentative manner allowing the child to hear from you the feelings they are expressing. The structure of the reflection begins with *you are* followed by the feeling word and a brief description of the story line of the play. It is important to use age-appropriate feeling words and avoid words that children may not understand. For example, stating "you are dismayed" would be difficult for most four-year-olds to understand. Clinicians do not ask how or why questions as this may lead the child to be guarded or defensive. For example: *Clinician:* "You seem scared of the snake crawling into the house."

Providing Choices

Children in play therapy benefit from the opportunity to develop problem-solving and decision-making skills. Providing children the opportunity to make age-appropriate choices provides a measure of control, the experience of natural logical consequences of their choices, and appropriate testing of limits. For example: *Clinician:* "You can paint on the easel or the table, which do you choose?" This statement allows the child to *buy into* the choice and avoids a power struggle.

Setting Limits

This skill is often mistaken by parents and referring agents as a form of discipline. They are often anxious to have you attempt this with the child. It is important that you understand that limit setting is employed within the context of a therapeutic relationship and is a combination of reflection of feeling and providing choices. Structurally, you acknowledge the child's feeling, in a neutral tone of voice, set a limit on the unacceptable behavior, and offer choices for more appropriate responses or activities. For example: *Clinician:* "You feel frustrated and want to destroy all the dolls in the dollhouse. However, dolls are not for breaking. You can hit the pillows with the hammer or jump up and down on the bubble wrap."

Returning Responsibility

Clinicians return responsibility by using metaphor, minimal encouragers, restating content, reflecting feeling, and applying the whisper technique. For example: *Client:* "Where should the mouse hide? The cat is coming." *Clinician* (softly) "The mouse can decide for itself the best place to hide from the cat."

Dealing With Questions

In the play therapy setting, you strategically choose how or if to ask and respond to questions. Typically, direct questions from the clinician are not utilized in play therapy, yet therapeutic opportunities may present themselves. For example, if the child asks, "How does this tool work?" you might respond, "How can we make it work?" or if the child says, "Do you have kids?" you may wish to politely ignore the question and if the child persists, respond with the statement, "You are curious about my family," and finally should the child ask: "Did your mom hit you?" you may respond softly, "Hit me?" Clinicians use questions in play therapy skillfully to engage children more deeply and to expand their opportunities to share.

Process Play

Clinicians focus on the process of the child during play, not just tracking discrete behaviors. You give voice to the toys and give voice to the process the child is demonstrating. At times, it is effective to do this in a curious manner. For example: *Client:* Places 10 of the same cars on one side of a toy wall. *Clinician:* "You like having the same things together in the same place. They like being together?"

Narration of Therapist's Actions

As you move around the play therapy space with the child occasionally, you will articulate your actions to maintain engagement with the child. For example: *Clinician:* "I am moving closer to you to see what you're doing with the dinosaur." To deepen your learning related to play therapy, we provided an extended learning exercise at the end of this chapter. *Extended Learning Exercise #1* focuses on Axline's eight basic play therapy principles and asks you reflect on your perspectives and practice.

Child and Adolescent Trauma

As noted earlier, stressful maternal events negatively influence fetal brain development. We encourage you to be mindful of the intersections of physical, cognitive, social, linguistic, moral, and familial development as you work with children and adolescents. Kempe (1987) recognized traumatized children's need for nurturance, resolution of trust-mistrust struggles, impact of low self-esteem, emotional dysregulation, an inability to express emotions, and ineffective or not yet developed problem-solving skills. Continual exposure to traumatic events disorders children's attention, learning and memory, emotional regulation, and relationships. School-aged children, affected by trauma, exhibit a variety of behaviors such as poor social or academic adjustment, low frustration tolerance, and problems in concentration like distractible or obsessive behaviors. They also may be highly dependent, detached or emotionally unpredictable, mistrustful of adults, and act out. These maladaptive responses or reactions are out of proportion of the context or perceived dangers.

As children progress toward adolescence and sexual maturation, the quest for identity and independence take center stage. Traumatized adolescents may demonstrate maladaptive strategies similar to children as well as those related to their increased autonomy, like dropping out of school, running away from home, delinquency, and sexual acting out. Interpersonally, adolescents affected by trauma may exhibit mistrust of self and others, emotional lability, poor self-esteem, or narcissistic or antisocial behaviors like sexually acting out or joining a gang. These potentially lethal behaviors hold the promise of meaningful, although distorted connections and exemplify the lengths adolescents will go to belong. Treatment of traumatized adolescents focuses on safety, trust, moderated emotional expression, self-regulation, and impulse control.

Mandated Reporting for Child Abuse and Neglect

While not typically considered a treatment or a therapeutic intervention, in most states clinicians are mandated reporters of the suspicion of child maltreatment. Reports can be therapeutically disruptive yet may be the most impactful intervention a clinician can offer. The decision to retain or remove the child in the home lies with the child welfare agency, not the clinician. State child abuse laws and duties vary in their definition, scope, procedures, and mandates for reporting. At the time this text was published, the most updated nationwide resource on state-by-state statutes is https://www.childwelfare.gov/topics/systemwide/laws-policies/state/. We urge you to know local laws and policies that govern your practice.

The Child Abuse Prevention and Treatment Act (CAPTA) passed in 1974 brought child abuse into the national spotlight, and by 1986, most states mandated teachers, nurses, social workers, and mental health professionals as reporters (Fraser, 1986). Experts estimate that the actual incidence of abuse and maltreatment is as much as three times higher than what is reported (USDHHS, Administration on Children, Youth and Families, 2017). In 2014, child abuse resulted in 1,580 reported fatalities. While important progress has been made, in 2014, approximately 3.6 million reports involving 6.6 million children were referred to U.S. Child Protective Service Agencies. We have a long way to go. Below we describe various forms of child abuse and neglect and provide information on the informal assessment of childhood neglect and physical, sexual, and emotional abuse. Confirm your reporting responsibilities as defined by your local and state statutes.

Physical

According to Wolfe (1999) child physical abuse is the intentional or unintentional infliction or the intended or threatened but unrealized infliction of physical harm to a child by an adult. Abusive behaviors include punching, kicking, biting, burning, or shaking. In most settings, clinicians are asked to report the *suspicion* of abuse and are neither expected nor trained to conduct a formal investigation. Unexplained bruises, welts, abrasions on face, lips, mouth, torso, back, buttocks, or thighs are indicators of potential physical abuse. Observant clinicians, who report their suspicions to child-welfare workers, document the pattern, age, and extent of injuries. Abuse may also come in the form of unexplained surface burns from a cigar, cigarette, or lighter or immersion burns that are sock-like, glove-like, or doughnut shaped, and broken or fractured bones, particularly of extremities or the face or head. Clinicians take special care when multiple or spiral fractures are present. Lastly, unexplained lacerations or abrasions to the mouth, lips, gums, and eyes are quite uncommon for youth and when seen should be thoroughly assessed (Capstick & Fraenkel, 2004).

Sexual Abuse

Finkelhor (1979) described sexual abuse as any sexual activity with a person when consent is not or cannot be given. Child sexual abuse is any form of penetration (penile, digitally, or with an object), intercourse, fondling a child's genitals or breasts, exposing a child to genitalia, or commercially exploiting a child through pornography or prostitution. Clinicians are aware of their state's age of statutory consent laws. At the federal level, it is a crime to engage in a sexual act with a person who is at least four years younger and who is between the ages of 12 and 16. At the state level, criteria upon which the statute is based varies. An interactive map is available at https://www.ageofconsent.net/states and was accurate at the time of this book's publication. Physical indicators of child sexual abuse include but are not limited to difficulty walking or sitting, pain or itching in genital area, genital or anal bruises or bleeding, sexually transmitted infections, especially in preteens, and pregnancy. Unexplained withdrawal from family activities, refusing to publicly change into athletic wear, unusual demands for privacy, marked change in eating or sleeping patterns, public masturbation, unusual sexual behavior, and reports of sexual assault are behavior indicators of sexual abuse (Capstick & Fraenkel, 2004).

Emotional Abuse

According to Capstick and Fraenkel (2004), child emotional abuse compromises the child's psychological health. Although all abuse exacts an emotional toll, certain emotionally abusive intents and consequences like close confinement (a child in a closet, restrained to a bed), verbal or emotional assault (repeated insults, name-calling), and other or unknown abuse (withholding food, assigning excessive responsibilities) often leave less visible injuries. Furthermore, unexplained speech disorders, lags in physical development, failure to thrive, emotional detachment or reactivity, abrupt changes in emotional regulation, age-inappropriate interpersonal boundaries, age-incongruent vocabulary, and impaired social skills may indicate emotional abuse.

Neglect

Unlike child abuse, child neglect is commonly thought of as an act of omission rather than of commission (Dubowitz et al., 1993). Neglect occurs when children's basic needs are not met for a period of time. Physical and emotional neglect are the two most common forms. Capstick and Fraenkel (2004) identified 14 types ranging from educational neglect to refusal to provide mental health care. Indicators of child neglect are persistent or consistent hunger, poor hygiene, inappropriate dress, consistent lack of supervision, especially in dangerous settings for long periods, and unattended physical problems or medical needs.

Adult Trauma

"Because trauma affects every aspect of human functioning from the biological to the social, treatment must be comprehensive" (Herman, 1997; p. 156). Adults affected by trauma are typically able to access their emotions, verbal skills, and resources better than children or adolescents, yet the disruption they face is often exacerbated precisely because they are *aware* of the nature, scope, and extent of the personal, social, and emotional changes or losses. Traumatic events distort one's sense of safety. The resulting hypervigilance and anxiety cause many to discredit themselves and distrust their environment. They feel unsafe everywhere—within their body, their relationships and their environment. Herman (1997) notes three phases of healing from trauma: safety, remembrance and mourning, and reconnection. She cautions that because trauma syndromes are "oscillating and dialectical in nature" (p. 155), the process of recovery is iterative, complex, and often fraught with disappointment and confusion for the client *and* the therapist. Stage one, *safety*, focuses on the client's psychological, emotional, and physical safety needs and concerns. It is the most essential element in trauma-focused therapy because it provides the basis for intra- and interpersonal stabilization. Without safety, healing is impossible. Before treatment can proceed, a sense of safety needs to be (re)established within the individual and in relation to others. Elements of safety are supported by the creation of an engagement in a treatment plan focused on self-care and, where necessary, referrals. The second stage, *remembrance and mourning*, involves verbal exploration of the multisensory details and personal meanings of the trauma story, as well as mourning the previous self, lost to the trauma (Herman, 1997) with all the accompanying emotions. Decisions related to the timing, depth, and extent of traumatic recollections lie with the client, not the clinician. Each telling and retelling of the trauma story provides greater detail and supports the transformation of transient, fragmented, or distorted recollections into a more coherent narrative, a narrative which can be integrated, over time, into an individual's memory and belief systems. The trauma and narrative or story provides an explanation, not an excuse for the experiences related to the trauma, not the event itself. The process intentionally structures and focuses recovery on one's adjustment to a *new normal*.

As recollections and remembrances multiply, losses associated with the trauma are ever-present, haunting, and terrifying in nature. No wonder Herman (1997) notes, "The descent into mourning is at once the most necessary and the most dreaded task of this stage of recovery" (p. 188). Losses due to trauma may be physical, psychological, relational, status, or religious/spiritual. Though readily apparent to others, they are the source of profound and permeating grief. Facilitating and supporting the client's process of grieving invites the exploration, examination, and integration of a full range of emotions that they avoided or sought to numb, sans a safe, therapeutic space. Your therapeutic stance is critical, again Herman (1997) indicates, "It is not enough for the therapist to be 'neutral' or 'non-judgmental'. . . . The therapist's role is not to provide ready-made answers, which would be impossible in any case, but rather to affirm a position of moral solidarity with the survivor" (p. 178).

There is work to be done and some degree of client reluctance and resistance is expected. Traumatized clients fear unending grief and are overwhelmed. They may view grieving as a form of submission or acknowledgment that the perpetrator or cause of the trauma *has won*. Or fueled by feelings of helplessness, they seek revenge, which is a form of catharsis. Revenge fantasies allow clients the opportunity to discharge the powerful emotions like fear, dread, and shame by vanquishing the perpetrator. Reluctance and resistance can take the form of forgiveness, revenge, or compensation fantasies (Herman, 1997) or missing sessions, rationalization, or self-recriminations. Moving through this phase of recovery can be powerful for those suffering from trauma because it can allow them to "discover [their] indestructible inner life" (Herman, 1997, p. 188).

The final phase, *reconnection*, is akin to adaptation and asks the individual to actively incorporate new experiences into their current and future selves, in essence, who are they and how do they function posttraumatic event. Tedeschi and Calhoun (2004) introduced the concept of posttraumatic growth (PTG). Essentially, PTG posits demonstrable positive psychological changes result from one's response to trauma or adversity. According to Tedeschi and Calhoun, PTG is defined by the presence of a significant adversity or trauma, demonstrable changes that are an "outcome or ongoing process" and not the illusion of change and may "require a significant threat or the shattering of fundamental schemas" (p. 4). Some (MacFarlane & Alvaro, 2000; Frazier et al., 2009) criticize PTG, noting a lack of empirical support. (See Tedeschi & Calhoun, 2004, for greater detail). As a clinician, you can monitor clients' post-event perspectives through questions like, "Given what you have and are experiencing, how have you changed?" "In what ways has your overall functioning improved?" or "What coping strategies do you use now, that you did not before?" The therapeutic process centers on you, the clinician, helping the client to reestablish a sense of self-control. "In accomplishing this work, the survivor reclaims her world" (Herman, 1997, p. 197). This can be a challenging stage of recovery because being asked to intentionally control one's self and one's emotions may feel foreign to those who have experienced long-term trauma. At its core, trauma is the profound absence of self-control.

Reconnection builds on the accomplishments of the previous two phases and establishes or embeds a foundation of safety. From this foundation, the individual reclaims their power and control over their own life. The results of these phases provide those affected by trauma a context in which more adaptive physiological responses to perceived fear and danger can be constructed and practiced. Individuals are supported to challenge their assumptions about their previous coping skills, for instance, how they may have interfered with their recovery without taking the culpability away from the perpetrator. It is important to remember that while there are certainly phases and milestones in trauma recovery, there is no full recovery from trauma, only healing (Herman, 1997). Through treatment, clients understand that concerns related to traumatic events may reappear at certain life stages, or after certain life experiences, and their improved coping skills should help them better identify the issue and navigate its consequences.

Adjuncts to Treatment

Individual Case Management in Support of Treatment and Recovery

Van der Kolk, McFarlane, and Weisaeth (1996) noted that trauma is different than other psychological phenomena because of the subjective meaning of the experience. In other words, what one experiences as trauma is not necessarily so for another, "The critical element that makes an event traumatic is the subjective assessment by victims of how threatened and helpless they feel" (p. 6). Given the subjective nature of traumatic experiences, individuals make different meanings based on several factors like previous life experiences, prior exposure to traumatic events, attachment style, and self-efficacy. Personal meaning making of a threatening situation or traumatic loss can lead to a major change in one's internal processes and perceptions (van der Kolk, 1989). Given the multiple personal meanings and the related negative consequences of fear—depression and anxiety—treatment and recovery must be uniquely tailored to the client's experience of the potentially traumatic experience.

Trauma has profound effects on one's self-esteem, resilience, and ability to function. Wiggall and Boccellari (2017) described the holistic nature of case management as one of the most important innovations in mental health counseling. There have been many models created for the effective case management of those who have experienced trauma (Ziguras & Stuart, 2000); however, one central tenet regarding successful trauma case management is consistent and clear communication among all members of the team. Herman (1997) described stabilization and safety as the foundation of trauma treatment. In addition to intra- and interpersonal psychological and behavioral stabilization, we urge you to consider clients' needs for a stable environment. A case management approach to treatment begins by helping clients secure housing or temporary shelter, public assistance, food and clothing, and medication. The second step is the comprehensive and collaborative assessment of needs. The clinician and client evaluate the whole client and their environment, identifying, prioritizing, and documenting services that promote safety and stabilization *and* the client's ability to access or engage those services. Once identified, clients are provided a detailed resource list, including phone numbers, locations, and contact persons, and self-selected deadlines to make contact. Case management services may include: complementary or alternative therapy formats, support groups, legal services, childcare, housing, food, medical/medications, hospitalization, transportation, vocational, and religious or spiritual support. Clients' needs change as they progress through treatment; the skilled clinician reassesses clients' needs at each interaction.

Team Approaches in Support of Treatment and Recovery

Treating traumatized clients presents challenges and opportunities. Clients present with a host of symptoms, needs, and concerns that may initially overwhelm you and your skill set. Just as we recommend holistic assessments and treatment approaches for your clients, so, too, do we urge you to take a holistic or team approach to treatment. Treatment teams, when well coordinated, provide multiple perspectives, distribute the workload, and, we believe, reduce the risk for burnout and compassion fatigue.

Multidisciplinary and Integrated Primary and Behavioral Health Teams

Multidisciplinary treatment teams and integrated primary and behavioral health initiatives demonstrate the importance of comprehensive and efficient treatment for clients. According to Epstein (2014), in-hospital or agency-based multidisciplinary teams are considered a best practice designed to improve client outcomes and reduce adverse events. Benefits of working within a well-organized team of profession-based experts are many and include: the comprehensive nature of client care, a holistic approach, accessibility to specific professional expertise, expedited referral process, synergy of new ideas and processes, and creativity. In short, delivering excellent client care often emanates from a foundation of cohesive teamwork.

When managed well, multidisciplinary teams challenge discipline-based *silos* and professional hierarchies. Poorly managed teams result in professional *in fighting* and detracts from client care. Clinicians are mindful of potential pitfalls of multidisciplinary teams such as professional competition and status-seeking behaviors like dismissing or limiting the perspectives of others. Unprofessional behavior results in power struggles, single decision-making models, ambiguous accountability, and poor time management. Generally, effective pathways of communication as well as clear roles and responsibilities minimize potential pitfalls.

Integrated primary and behavioral health care is a significant advancement in team treatment and support. Integrated behavioral health care assigns medical, behavioral, substance abuse, school, community, food and nutrition professionals, and health educators to *one* physical location. Professionals form an *integrated* team that works collaboratively and holistically to identify and address clients' concerns and document interactions, interventions, and communications in one record. Integrated care extends beyond previous notions of case management, multidisciplinary teams, or collaborative care as it is *simultaneous* rather than sequential care. The Substance Abuse and Mental Health Service Administration (SAMHSA) Integrated Care denotes three common levels of integration and collaboration: care coordination, co-located care, and integrated care. Together, these three strands emphasize communication, physical proximity, and practice change. Read more about the integrated behavioral health care movement at https://www .integration.samhsa.gov/ or Patient-Centered Medical Home and Collaborative Care at https://www.nimh.nih.gov/health/topics/integrated-care/index.shtml.

General and Advanced Skills and Awareness

Safety, Intake, and Triage

When an individual experiences trauma, they seek to adapt. Some seek no services, while others process concerns with lay helpers or family and, for yet another group, adapting to posttrauma experiences is an enormous challenge for which they seek professional support and treatment. A traumatic experience can inhibit cognitive and psychosocial development and lead to the development of psychiatric disorders, altered personalities, and changes in behavior patterns. Criteria in the *Diagnostic and Statistical Manual* has evolved over time to include dissociation and proposes that, fear, helplessness, and horror may not be as prominent at the *initial* traumatic experience (American Psychiatric Association, 2013). Despite the scores of persons exposed to and suffering from trauma, many do not meet the criteria for any psychiatric disorder.

Clients' Hierarchy of Needs, Safety, and Stabilization

As discussed previously, Maslow's (1943) theory is an important perspective treatment of traumatized individuals. The first two levels of Maslow's hierarchy of relative prepotency are centered on physiological and safety needs. Clinicians assess client's needs and meet them where they are. Levers and Buck (2012) notes the impossibility of clients expending energy in self-actualizing activities prior to meeting their basic safety or physiological needs. Self-preservation takes precedence and is context dependent.

Judith Herman's (1997) classic model describes the importance of safety in the first stage of treatment. Maslow (1943) would place these needs in the first two categories of his hierarchy of relative prepotency. During the *Safety and Stabilization Stage*, clients often test boundaries to assess the durability of the therapeutic relationship, perceptions of their self-worth, and the likelihood of therapist abandonment. Clinicians focus on support, safety, and coping skills instruction to aid the client's development of more adaptive strategies to increase a sense of safety, address self-harm, suicidal ideation, substance misuse or abuse, and to create a safe network of supportive family members and peers (Peck, 2012).

Safety also refers to the pace of therapeutic processing. This is especially critical during Herman's second phase, remembrance and mourning, where trauma-based memories are shared, explored, and integrated. Clinicians educate clients on how to slow or stop their emotional processing when feelings become too overwhelming or intense. This includes instruction in self-soothing, grounding, and containment skills (Ford, Connor, & Hawke, 2009) in the early phases of the therapeutic relationship. For example, pairing self-soothing skills with traumatic thoughts could assist clients in cognitively understanding overlooked aspects of the traumatic event. Over time, this desensitizes the client to the stimuli and assists in further processing of perceptions and memories. For example, *Clinician:* "Bob, I was thinking about our session last week. I wondered if you would be interested in using the focused breathing process you've been practicing when you feel tightness in your chest." *Bob:* "Okay." *Clinician:* "It should help you stay in the moment a bit longer, which is a goal of yours. Remember, you take a deep breath, hold it momentarily, locate a focus point. Focus on it as you exhale and say to yourself, 'everything's okay, I am safe.' What are your thoughts about trying focused breathing today, should you need to?" This hypothetical dialogue demonstrates the intentional, graduated, and sensitive introduction of a clinical intervention—focused breathing—while maintaining or respecting boundaries regarding the client's right to determine the nature and extent of their disclosures.

Triaging Individuals and Groups—Acute Versus Long Term Needs

When one has a traumatic experience, the clinician's first step is to assess their needs, prioritize services, then help the individual access to needed services. Triage is "the process of evaluating and sorting victims by immediacy of treatment needed and directing them to immediate or delayed treatment. The goal of triage is to do the greatest good for the greatest number of victims" (NIMH, 2002, p. 27). While professional responsiveness is important, it is essential to first determine whether the individual exposed to trauma *wants* assistance or is exhibiting signs of traumatic responding. If they are receptive to services, determine the nature, order, intensity, and likely duration of each service.

Individuals and groups respond to traumatic events differently; there is no one size fits all approach. The American Psychological Association (APA) recommends further assessment, beyond an acute response to the event, to determine whether the individual's response to the event involves "intense fear, helplessness, or horror (in children, the response must involve disorganized or agitated behavior)" (2013, p. 463). The application of trauma-based interventions to those not properly assessed can cause harm and create the conditions for a self-fulfilling prophecy of feeling broken or unnecessary dependency. Prematurely treating a client violates at least three of the five moral principles (Kitchener, 1984): nonmaleficence (do no harm), beneficence (do good, contribute to client welfare), and fidelity (principles which underlie most ethical codes of conduct and numerous ethical standards).

Brock, Sandoval, and Lewis (2001) reported that the normal reaction to a crisis is to recover without therapeutic assistance. During the screening process, it is quite likely a good percentage of those exposed will not seek help or support beyond the acute phase. Reactions and responses needing referral for ongoing service may present as maladaptive coping behaviors like taking unexplained risks, agitation, aggression, isolation, or withdrawal. Certain symptoms or constellation of symptoms require a mental health referral, symptoms like peritraumatic dissociation or hyperarousal occurring around the time of the trauma, persistent reexperiencing of the crisis event, and avoidance of crisis reminders, significant depression, and psychotic symptoms. Individuals demonstrating these behaviors should be referred to a provider who specializes in trauma-based disorders and approaches treatment in a trauma-informed manner. If they are referred to you, you will want to ensure you have support and safety protocols in place to support the advanced needs of your client. When individuals are in significant distress, a greater level of care is needed, perhaps intensive outpatient program or short-term inpatient hospitalization for stabilization and treatment planning (Brock, Sandoval, & Lewis, 2001).

Screening and Assessing Exposure to Traumatic Experiences

Traumatic events and their consequences have devastating effects on individuals, families, and society. Traumatic responding, the sequelae of psychological trauma, and the overlap in symptom presentation with other disorders may result in delayed or misdiagnosis. Screening and assessment processes and instruments aid initial client stabilization, evaluations of threats to self or others, clarification of symptomology, differential diagnosis, and refinement. The American Psychological Association's Division 56 Trauma Psychology documented their recommendations for assessing trauma in an unpublished manuscript. The authors encouraged clinicians to inform themselves about the various trauma reactions, specifically individual responding, appraisal, and meaning making (Center for Substance Abuse Treatment, 2014). Remember, the results of formal trauma assessments do not *verify* the exposure to a Criterion A traumatic event, the results illustrate to what degree the respondent's responses are consistent with typical reactions to trauma.

Clients are screened at first contact and throughout treatment. Clinicians document clients' current functioning and responses to traumatic events that include screening for suicidal ideation and behaviors, prior history of trauma, substance use or abuse, and emotional and physical discomfort. Screening and assessment, particularly in the early phases of contact, are an integrated part of treatment, and as such clinicians refrain from asking for detailed accounts of the traumatic events. The focus of assessment is how traumatic symptoms affect the individual's current functioning and how the results will be used to construct a treatment plan and identify previously effective coping skills (Harris & Fallot, 2001). As with any client, clinicians ensure client safety and readiness to depart each session. When a client's safety is in doubt, clinicians immediately screen for safety and reiterate or engage previously established safety plans.

The National Center of PTSD created a comprehensive list of empirically validated assessment and screening measures for trauma. To view the list in its entirety, visit the website (www.ptsd.va.gov). Additionally, a brilliant resource for assessment is available at https://www.apa.org/ptsd-guideline/assessment/ with links to interview and self-report instruments that are used for screening, diagnosis, treatment outcomes, and research. Below we detail clinician-administered and self-report assessments you may final useful in your practice.

Assessments for Children and Adolescents

The Assessment-Based Treatment for Traumatized Children: A Trauma Assessment Pathway (TAP) Model, developed by the Chadwick Center for Children and Families (2009), with funding from the Substance Abuse and Mental Health Services Administration. It was designed for children 0 to 18 years of age who have experienced any type of trauma and who may or may not be in the child welfare system. TAP is a multifaceted assessment process to screen and triage child clients who may have or are believed to have been exposed to trauma. The four components of TAP are triage, assessment, unique picture of the child, and treatment. During the triage process, the clinician assesses and determines the level of the child's risk to self, to others, and from others. Triaging clinicians also take time to determine the child's needs, social supports, and symptom severity. The results of the triage assessment inform the future services and referral needs. *Assessment* involves the use of the clinical interview process and appropriate standardize measures like the PTSD Semi-Structured Interview and Observation Record for Infants and Young Children (Scheeringa & Zeanah, 1994; [PTSDSSI]) a semi-structured caregiver report for children aged 0 to 7. The PTSDSSI measures the presence of 11 trauma symptoms described in the DSM-IV. The UCLA Child/Adolescent PTSD Reaction Index for *DSM-5* is a semi-structured interviewed based on *DSM–5* criteria for children/adolescents aged 5 to 18. The third phase, creating a *unique client picture* from the individual's trauma history, involves synthesizing the information from assessments like symptom presentation, systemic issues. and relevant contextual history into a coherent view of the client and their experiences. Your conceptualization influences the nature, length, and type of treatment intervention, including referrals.

A second assessment process for children is the Child and Adolescent Needs and Strengths (CANS)—Trauma Comprehensive Version. The CANS-Trauma is a flexible, multi-purpose tool utilized in different capacities depending on the needs of a particular child-serving system (Kisiel, Fehrenbach, Small, & Lyons, 2009). The CANS methodology gathers information on a range of domains relevant to the functioning of the child and caregiving system, information like the client's trauma experiences, stress symptoms, emotional and behavioral needs, risk behaviors, strengths, and caregiver needs/strengths (Kisiel et al., 2018). The information is integrated into individualized treatment and care plans.

The final assessment for children is Spaccarelli's (1994) transactional or interactive model, which examines factors related to the abuse of the child, as well as those associated with the investigation like disclosure events and related events occurring after the investigation (e.g., placement outside the home and court hearings). This model incorporates demographic descriptors and personality factors; social support; and previous coping styles and cognitive appraisal schemes. Spaccarelli assumed that "cognitive appraisals and coping responses mediate the effects of these traumatic events and developmental and environmental factors may moderate relationships between sexual abuse stressors and victim responses, and that victims' initial responses may effect subsequent levels of abuse-related stress" (Spaccarelli, 1994; p. 340). Although not widely researched, this model shows some promise (Spaccarelli, 1994; Spaccarelli & Kim, 1995).

Researchers utilize longitudinal research designs to focus on the emergence and accumulation of different types of abuse and related stressors such as disclosure-related stress, initial response pattern to abusive events, and protective and contextual factors. Adverse Childhood Experiences (ACEs) profoundly impact children, their families, and communities. Effective assessment and treatment hold the most promise for recovery. For additional reading, check out the Centers for Disease Control (CDC) website on child abuse and prevention https://www.cdc.gov/violenceprevention/childabuseandneglect/acestudy/index.html?CDC_AA_refVal=https%3A%2F%2Fwww.cdc.gov%2Fviolenceprevention%2Face study%2Findex.html.

Clinician-Administered Adult Assessments

Clinician-administered assessments are interactional and are like a semi-structured interview. The clinician asks the client a series of questions from a protocol which also may include drawings or activities. The Clinician-Administered PTSD Scale for DSM-5; (Weathers, et al., 2017; [CAPS-5]) was developed by clinicians at the U. S. Department of Veteran Affairs. This 30-item assessment is designed to evaluate the frequency and severity of current and past PTSD symptoms. The assessment takes 45 to 60 minutes and is administered by a trained clinician. The International Society for Traumatic Stress Studies refers to the CAPS-5 as the *gold standard* in PTSD assessment, while others note limitations like the length of time to administer, limiting of norming populations like military veterans, and restriction to one traumatic event. Weathers et al. (2017) provide a thorough review of CAPS-5 psychometric properties.

The PTSD Symptom Scale Interview (Foa et al, 2016; Foa, Riggs, Dancu, & Rothbaum, 1993; Powers, Gillihan, Rosenfield, Jerud, & Foa, 2012; [PSS-I and PSSI-5]) allows clinicians to assess clients' PTSD-related symptoms occurring in the previous month. The semi-structured interview contains 24 questions, 20 of which focus on symptoms and four of which address the distress and disruption in daily life and symptom onset and duration. Through the assessment, the clinician confirms the presences of *DSM–5* PTSD Criterion A. When clients report multiple traumatic events, the clinician confirms the most distressing event (index trauma) and evaluates the remaining criteria in light of the most distressing event. The PSSI–5 compares excellently to the CAPS-5, Posttraumatic Diagnostic Scale for *DSM–5*, PDS–5, and PTSD Checklist—Specific Version (PCL-S).

Finally, the Structured Interview for PTSD (SIP or SI-PTSD) originally developed to align with the *DSM–III* criteria was subsequently revised for *DSM–III-R* and *DSM–IV* (Davidson, Malik, & Travers, 1997; Davidson, Kudler, & Smith, 1990). During this semi-structured interview, the clinician uses 17 items to evaluate the severity of the clients' symptom during the previous four weeks and two additional items assess survival and behavior guilt or clients' self-blame and lack of control during the traumatic event. Data drawn from the SIP helps to refine clients' diagnosis. Clients rate each item on a 0 to 4 scale that represents "a composite of frequency, severity and functional impairment" (Davidson, Malik, & Travers, 1997; p. 127). The SIP takes 20 to 30 minutes to administer. It correlates with other measures of PTSD, but not measures of combat exposure (Riggs & Keane, 2006), demonstrates psychometric utility in culturally diverse populations (Kim et al., 2009) and combat veterans.

Self-Report Measures for Adults

Self-report measures are efficient and convenient tools to gather client perspectives and data. These types of measures provide quantifiable information directly from the client and limit observational bias. Alternatively, the data garnered from self-report measures also warrants caution. Disadvantages such as forced or fixed choices or confusing items may limit clients' expression and increase the propensity for social desirability bias or response bias—particularly acquiescing (habitually answering yes). As Demetriou, Ozer, and Essau (2015) noted, "Self-report instruments may not be sufficient for determining an individual's specific diagnosis but are necessary to assess their experience" (p. 1).

The Impact of Event Scale–Revised (IES-R) refined by Weiss and Marmar (1997) is an excellent tool to support a preliminary diagnosis of PTSD. The IES-R is a 22-item self-report instrument that corresponds to *DSM–IV* symptoms of PTSD. Weiss and Marmar added five items to Horowitz's original Impact of Event Scale (Horowitz, Wilner, & Alvarez; 1979 [IES]) to better reflect *DSM* criteria. The IES-R is a brief, easy-to-administer scale intended to measure the subjective experiences related to traumatic experiences of older adults including nightmares, avoidance, hyperarousal, intrusive thoughts, imagery, and intrusive feelings. For each item, individuals indicate how much they were distressed or bothered during the past seven days on a scale from 0 (not at all) to 4 (extremely). Creamer, Bell, and Failla (2003) noted an analysis of the IES-R yielded a two-factor solution, meaning it most accurately identified symptoms of intrusion/hyperarousal and avoidance. Some (Larsson, 2000; Shevlin, Hunt, & Robbins; 2000) questioned the IES's ability to distinguish PTSD from one general distress factor. Beck and colleagues (2008) noted, "Although the IES-R was not developed as a diagnostic tool, examination of its discriminative validity suggests that the measure can differentiate between individuals with and without PTSD" (p. 11).

Like the IES-R, the PTSD Checklist for DSM-5 (PCL-5) developed by staff at the Veteran's Administration National Center for PTSD, (Blevins, Weathers, Davis, Witte, & Domino, 2015) is used to support a provisional diagnosis and to monitor symptom change. The PCL-5 is a 20-item self-report, paper and pencil assessment that takes five to seven minutes to complete and is scored by the clinician. Checklist items correspond with 20 PTSD symptoms identified in the *DSM–5*. Clients endorse the presence and degree of severity of symptoms within in the last month on a 0 to 4 scale where 0 = *not at all* and 4 = *extremely*. Since the initial development of the military version (PCLM), two others were created to assess stressful experiences of civilians (PCLC) and experiences associated with a specific traumatic event (PCL-S). The versions differ with regard to the nature of the anchoring event and the terms used to describe the event. The psychometric properties of all three versions found the PCL—civilian, military, and specific trauma—to be a well-validated measure (Bovin et al., 2015; Kendall, Wilkins, Lang, & Norman, 2011).

Treating Trauma via Group Process

According to Klein and Schermer (2000), the curative factors applied in group counseling apply directly to the treatment of trauma. Because isolation is such a common effect of trauma, the ability of groups to provide support and social connection for members is particularly important for survivors. Group therapy is a cost effective way to provide for many recovering from trauma support (Ford, Fallot, & Harris, 2009). Group placement depends on the structure and goals of the particular group and the characteristics of the particular individual under consideration. Depending on the heterogeneity of the group, potential members are screened for level of acuity or chronicity, nature of traumatic event, and other salient factors. In the immediate aftermath of trauma, an individual may feel overwhelmed and not able to relate to a group. At these times, individual treatment is recommended until the individual feels able to interact with others (Ford, Fallot, & Harris, 2009). Once potential participants resume activities of daily living and practice behaviors that are self-nurturing, they are likely well suited for group therapy. Clinicians and group members create a clear therapeutic agreement and decision on the overall goal of the group therapy experience.

General trauma, PTSD, and complex trauma group therapy can offer members an honest, respectful, safe, and private opportunity to experience and be experienced by other survivors. This atmosphere can offer much needed relief from the shame, guilt, and alienation and can provide a profound sense of empowerment and encouragement. In addition, group therapy provides a platform for psychoeducation and social role learning experiences.

Group interventions offer unique advantages in addressing the areas in which traumatized individuals have been the most affected (Klein & Schermer, 2000). Group leaders provide guidance and group members provide modeling around understanding emotions, thoughts, and differentiating between competing emotional experiences. For those exposed to mass trauma, concerns related to survivor's guilt may be present. Survivor's guilt is a condition that occurs when a person believes they have done something wrong by surviving a traumatic event when others did not (American Psychiatric Association, 2013). Trauma groups are designed to provide a shame-free atmosphere to process unique and common concerns.

Group Leadership Skills and Techniques

Group leaders must balance asserting leadership and creating a safe and welcoming group experience. Having thorough knowledge on the topic of trauma is critical for group leadership and informs psychoeducational group encounters, maintaining a level of safety and appropriate client disclosures. Ford, Fallot, and Harris (2012) poignantly described the interpersonal dynamics group leaders address while engaging members of PTSD and complex trauma-based groups. They note the example of emerging relational dynamics that negatively affect group members throughout their personal development. Group leaders must work with these heightened dynamics that continually resurface during trauma-based group process. Below are definitions and examples of group counseling skills utilized to help trauma survivor's work through traumatic experiences. The skills and techniques are promoted by various authors (Berg & Landreth, 2017; Corey, 2011; Yalom, 1995).

Linking

Linking is when a clinician connects members' process or experiences to common themes in the group. This promotes member-to-member interactions and encourages the development of cohesion. *Clinician*: "April, you're echoing the feelings of many of the group members. Others here feel helpless and confused by their partner's abuse."

Reflection of Feeling

Reflection of feeling is when a clinician communicates an understanding of the content of feelings. Consistent with individual counseling, clinicians let members know they are heard and understood beyond the level of words. Specific to the treatment of trauma, skilled clinicians recognize the need for an expanded and descriptive feeling word vocabulary to capture the horrors of trauma. Consider the following statements: *Clinician 1:* "You are sad your partner left." *Clinician 2:* "You're terrified of being abandoned again."

Holding the Focus

Holding the focus has to do with the clinician redirecting group members back to the topic of the group. *Clinician*: "I wonder what caused the group to talk about food shopping when we were just talking about Mark's sister's suicide. I wonder how uncomfortable each of you are. Let's stay with Mark's and others feelings for a few more minutes."

Cutting Off

Clinicians keep the group on topic and give everyone a chance to share. This skill must be used with care to avoid creating an unsafe group climate. Using a calm, matter-of-fact tone and a slight physical gesture, the clinician may say,

"Sharon, please stop for a moment, let's see what other members think of Jill's statement that suicide was her only option."

Drawing Out Members

Clinicians invite quieter group members to participate as befits their process. Invitations to speak in group balances participation, reminds participants of their value to others, and promotes mutuality. We remind you to balance the needs of the group with individual perception of safety. *Clinician:* "Andy you have been quiet all group. I wonder if you are processing or would like some time to check in. You decide."

Gossiping

Co-therapists talk to each other about what they are observing in front of the group to remain connected and to evoke a response from the group. This technique allows the group members to regroup and get a feel for what is happening in the session. *Clinician A:* "I don't know about you, Chris, but I'm sensing something different about the group today. *Clinician B:* "Yeah, Steve, it seems something has happened that caused everyone to get quiet and uncomfortable around each other. Hmmm . . . I wonder what it could be."

Providing Feedback

This skill allows the clinician to express concrete and honest reactions to members' behaviors and group dynamics based on observations and immediacy. Group leaders offer an external view of how the person appears to others and can pose questions about members' behaviors or responses. The intent is to increase the client's self-awareness while maintaining a safe environment. *Clinician:* "Sally, you took a huge risk telling the group about your sexual abuse. I see Frank and Jennifer are moved to tears. Your courage to share the terror and humiliation you experienced shows your growth and strength. This room is full of support for you."

Traumatic experiences and one's pattern of responding hold unique and common elements. Unique in that personal appraisal and coping are determined by a host of individual factors and common in that many exposed to trauma experience similar, but not identical, symptomology. It is difficult for others to truly understand one's experience of trauma but group counseling and the associated skills create a sense of mutuality and validation for those suffering from trauma.

Community Culture

Clinicians help individuals who experience collective trauma. According to Rosenfeld, Caye, Lahad, and Gurwitch (2010),

> collective trauma occurs when a disaster or trauma damages the bonds that connect people and destroys the basic tissues of social life and the prevailing sense of community. Moral anchors are lost; morale plummets. People feel disorientated. . . . They no longer perceive the world as safe. (p. 39)

When communities suffer traumatic experiences, citizens depend on community leadership and nongovernment institutions to systematically implement trauma-informed responses like triage, psychological first aid, communication, and provision of a range of services. Certain traumatic experiences lend themselves to intervention better than others. Rosenfeld et al. (2010) described community-based crisis events as evolving from either immediate crisis situations or from larger more persistent problems like the economic collapse or hate crimes. According to Levers and Buck (2012), during a community crisis event, clinicians try to alleviate the effects of trauma, thereby thwarting the progress of more serious circumstances. Citizens' response to danger and violence are understood more effectively through the lens of a complex and integrated system of normal human reactions to abnormal events. Culturally traumatic events affect all aspects of our lives. Existential and spiritual reactions are likely based on the complex structure of a normal human response. If only maladaptive behaviors, rather than their sources, are considered, the mental health system becomes a source of institutional cultural oppression. Trauma recovery is a process of individuals taking time to regain a sense of self, creating a collective meaning of the experience, and taking control of their lives.

Assessment and Case Conceptualization

We have explored a variety of assessment measures and issues in crisis and trauma-based counseling. In this section, we extend your learning by demonstrating how assessments are integrated into the conceptualization of the client's concerns. Courtois and Ford (2009) urged clinicians to conduct formal as well as informal assessments to refine the diagnosis of trauma. Specifically, when clinicians observe symptoms related to PTSD or complex trauma, they invest time and engage in clinical interviews or empirically validated assessments prior to making a formal diagnosis. Staff in agencies or hospitals typically embed trauma assessments within the initial intake assessment/history. Regrettably, this type of assessment can feel invasive to the recently traumatized individual because the context lacks the safety described as a necessity by Herman (1997). Traumatic experiences are frightening and tender to talk about sans the safety and trust established through the therapeutic alliance.

During the clinical interview, traumatized clients are approached in a respectful and intentional manner. Some are cautious or unable to disclose much about themselves let alone the traumatic event, while others need help structuring or slowing down the process of disclosure. A structured and supportive process with predictable steps aids clients hesitant to discuss significant trauma or victimization and reduces the possibility of becoming overwhelmed with emotion. Clinicians approach these situations with openness and sensitivity from a position of supportive neutrality (Courtois, Ford, & Cloitre, 2012). Unfortunately, clinicians are not often formally trained to approach trauma survivors with such sensitivity. Attending to nonverbal behavior and understanding invitational skills (Young, 2013) are extremely important. Below are examples of important invitational skills and examples utilized to help clinicians approach traumatized individuals with support, openness, and sensitivity. While some of these skills are associated with those promoted by James and Gilliland, we expand their recommendations to include skills cited by other scholars (Cormier, Nurius, & Osborn, 2009; Flynn & Hays, 2015; Ivey, Ivey, & Zalaquett, 2010; Young, 2013).

Observation

The clinician observes and conveys awareness of differences between the clinician and client's verbal and nonverbal behavior within key areas like grooming, posture, physical proximity, and eye contact. Contextualize observations through a multicultural lens and understands culturally bound verbal and nonverbal behavior.

Nonverbal Communication

The clinician uses culturally and contextually appropriate eye contact, gaze, facial expression, posture, gestures, spatial distance, and the maintenance of an open and relaxed posture. Observing and being immediate about clients' responses and reactions to the therapeutic process informs how the clinician responds.

Encouragers

The clinician uses nonverbal minimal encouragers including elaborating/attending behavior, relaxes, natural style of encouragement, mirrors or matches client's physical movements (leaning forward, level of energy, head nodding). Clinicians use well-timed verbal minimal encouragers like Oh, So, Then, And, Umm-hmm, and Uh-huh, or repetition of key words used by the client to elicit additional information and context.

Vocal Intonation and Pacing

The clinician's vocal intonation and pacing are congruent to the content and valence of the client's trauma story and are appropriate for the goals of each session. Traumatized clients experience hypervigilance and may infer or perceive judgment, pity, or harshness in the clinicians' responses. Clinicians communicate warmth, caring, acceptance, and congruence appropriate to the session.

Silence

This is a profoundly powerful skill. The clinician uses pauses or periods of silence to manage the pace of the session, reduce activity, provide the client time to think, and return responsibility to the client. Silences are context dependent and culturally bound. When used haphazardly or inappropriately silences can be (re)experienced as punishment, hostility, or abuse by traumatized clients.

TABLE 5.1 ● Knowledge, Skills, Awareness, and Resources Needed for Trauma Counseling by Client Type and Level of Professional Development

	Knowledge	Skills	Awareness	Techniques	Resources
	Advanced Graduate Students and Novice Professionals				
Individuals	Hierarchy of needs (Maslow) Developmental processes Cultural context and individual differences Treatment by developmental levels Case management Formal and informal clinical interviewing for PTSD Psychological first aid Psychological debriefing Child abuse and neglect Cognitive behavioral therapy Herman's three phase model	Informal assessment—basic needs Informed decision making related to triage Data gathering Clinician's emotional regulation Nonverbal communication Encouragers Silence Vocal tone Observation	Sympathy vs. empathy Clinician's personal history of trauma Multicultural competencies 4 core Multicultural attributes Culturally bound assumptions Vicarious trauma Mandatory reporting Limits to confidentiality	Triage Debriefing model Informal assessment of child abuse and neglect Mandatory reporting Limits to confidentiality	Referral list of clinicians specializing in the treatment of PTSD and complex trauma Referral list of pro bono providers Personal support/debriefing for the clinician Access to psychiatric hospitalization Local medical support
Groups	Stages of a group Purpose of the group Group process Group roles Group leadership/co-leaders Support vs. Treatment groups Ethical decision making	Active listening Modeling Linking member's content and feelings Initiating and facilitating communication	Self-awareness Intersectionality Allow member self-identification Protect clients Protect boundaries Guard against universality	Scanning-eye contact (as is culturally appropriate) with each member Set a support and goal-oriented tone Modeling desired behavior	Referral list for trauma specialists Local shelters for those experience ongoing trauma Food pantry Local medical support

	Cutting off Holding the focus Drawing out members Gossiping Reflection of feeling Providing feedback	Cross-cultural communication	Ice-breakers-initial activities designed to promote member to member sharing Dyads and triads-promotes more focused conversation linking or bridging-members comments to each to demonstrate mutuality	Referral list First responders list Community psychotherapy and addictions groups Shelters Local Medical support
Communities	Local health and safety organizations Community emergency communication/disaster plan			
Experienced Professionals*				
Individuals	All those listed above Learn supervision Case management to support treatment and recovery Advanced training in trauma informed methods			
	All those listed above Reflective listening for meaning and intent	Personal and professional humility Coping skills aimed at protecting the clinician from vicarious trauma	All those listed above Advanced techniques associated with the various EBTs	Local information on services, health and safety, social, housing, counseling, financial, food, religious/spiritual supports

(Continued)

TABLE 5.1 (Continued)

	Knowledge	Skills	Awareness	Techniques	Resources
		Experienced Professionals*			
	Play therapy Child–parent psychotherapy Parent–child interaction therapy Art assisted therapy Trauma-focused cognitive–behavioral therapy Cognitive processing therapy Eye movement desensitization and reprocessing Cognitive exposure therapy	Appropriate self-disclosure Therapeutic patience-inventions timed for maximum impact/learning Advanced skills associated with the various EBTs	Anxiety no longer impacts performance Looks inward for guidance Engages in reflective practice and professional development Role model for advanced graduate students and novice professionals		Personal support/debriefing for the clinician; Provide support and debriefing for clinicians Local medical support
Group	Addressing complex and layered group dynamics Facilitating complexity and conflict in groups Using conversations rather than directives to effectively facilitate Understanding your style and patterns in group facilitation Reflective practice—how you relate to groups and personal triggers Managing disruptive members' behaviors Facilitating emergent agendas and change				

Communities					
Using Fishbowls and other experiential tools Promoting group's self-directed learning	Leadership and command structure of trauma responders Regional resources History of previous crisis events, particularly natural and human caused events Local health and safety organizations Community emergency communication/disaster plan	Advanced practice Supervision Leadership Organization Advocacy Networking	Public health and safety Communication plans Public Affairs including medical needs, food and housing announcements Recognition of underserved communities Nonhuman (animals and wildlife) and environmental concerns Immediate, short- and longer-term planning	Panel discussion Community listening sessions/forums Engaging regional or national service organizations (short term)	State and local referral list Pro bono services Community trauma survivor groups Local medical support

History of Multiple Traumas

Ford and Courtois (2009) describe multiple traumas—two or more separate trauma injuries, one of which placed the client's life in danger—and their influence on symptom presentation, assessment, and potential treatment interventions. Complex trauma is different from multiple traumas in that it is defined by the repetitive, prolonged exposure to trauma. Clients demonstrating a history of PTSD and trauma often demonstrate a plethora of symptomology, which can overwhelm even seasoned clinicians. A hallmark of complex trauma and multiple traumas is dissociation. Dissociation includes an internal disconnect from reality, where thoughts, feelings, and experiences are outside the client's awareness. Repeated traumatization and dissociation can significantly interfere with daily functioning and one's ability to process thoughts and emotions (American Psychiatric Association, 2013).

McFarlane and de Girolamo (1996) separated traumatic stressors into several different categories: long-term exposure, time-limited events, and sequential. An expected emotional response of fear can have a significant impact on one's ability to make accurate perceptions of events. Another commonality amongst the three stressors is the notion that individuals can become stuck in their trauma, causing them to fixate on the event and eventually become consumed. This fixation may lead the person to relive or reexperience the event. With each repetition, it becomes generalized into their everyday experiences.

Lewis (2005) noted the roots of complex traumatic stress disorders are survival-based neural patterns. These patterns result in complex emotional reactions causing *global stabilization*, in which circumstance appraisal becomes rooted in the belief that one's survival is in constant jeopardy—one is under constant threat. This form of cognitive process has been aptly entitled *survival brain*. Survival brain is reactive and guides the individual by anticipating and reacting to perceived threats, instead of taking time to reflect on self-awareness and learning. Within the brain, there is a rapid alternating between appraisals and coping, which comes from constantly preparing for and avoiding danger.

Impact of Multiple Traumas

Evidence of trauma has a history dating back to ancient times. In the *Iliad*, Homer wrote of Achilles suffering from recurrent and intrusive thoughts, as well as sleep disturbance (Homer, 2011, p. 563, as cited in Ben-Ezra, 2010). While we have explored well-known symptoms of hypervigilance, avoidance, and flashbacks, contemporary evidence suggests that complex trauma and PTSD affect learning, attention, memory, arousal patterns, cardio physiology, vigilance, and sleep patterns (American Psychiatric Association, 2013).

Attention

Attention is involved in several cognitive processes, including vigilance, alertness, orientation, capacity, arousal, and continuous mental effort (Zillmer, Spiers, & Culbertson, 2008). Traumatic events impact the individual's ability to sustain and focus attention through selective attention. This is important because selective attention is activated when sensory memories are encoded into short-term memory. Traumatic responding is believed to impede the individual's sustained and focused attention; the consequence can be likened to selective attention, which is used when processing sensory memories into short-term memories (American Psychiatric Association, 2013; Jenkins, Langlais, Delis, & Cohen, 2000). Degraded focused attention may result in fragmented or incomplete encoding of memories.

Memory

The experience of complex trauma and PTSD can directly affect a survivor's memory. Memory loss may be a temporary way to help survivor's cope with the trauma or it may be permanent (Vasterling & Brailey, 2005). As noted previously, early exposure to extreme stress affects children's neurocognitive development, specifically intelligence, verbal capability, and school achievement. The extent of such effects may be a function of the duration and severity of the stressor (Zillmer et al., 2008).

Arousal Patterns and Vigilance

During a stressful event, the sympathetic nervous system activates the fight, flight, or freeze response. The stress hormone cortisol is released. Normally, when the stressor is low, the parasympathetic nervous system responds and returns the body to normal. When a traumatic event occurs with extreme stress, excess cortisol is released in the body (American Psychiatric Association, 2013; Zillmer et al., 2008). Individuals exposed to traumatic events are often hyperaware of potential danger. Hypervigilance, however, is an exaggerated state of awareness and is one of the hyperarousal symptoms of PTSD. Hyperarousal interferes with the survivor's ability to make rational cognitions and interferes with the processes of resolution and integration of the trauma. Individuals demonstrating symptoms associated with vigilance will be motivated to maintain an increased awareness of their surrounding environment, sometimes even frequently scanning their settings to identify potential sources of threat (American Psychiatric Association, 2013; Zillmer et al., 2008).

Cardio Physiology

Trauma and PTSD leads to overactive nervous system, poor immune response, and activation of the hormone system that controls blood pressure. These changes eventually contribute to the result of increased cardiovascular disease risk. Persons with complex trauma or PTSD may also experience hypertension, hyperlipidemia, obesity, and cardiovascular disease (American Psychiatric Association, 2013; Zillmer et al., 2008).

Sleep Patterns

Because of hyperarousal patterns and elevated states of vigilance, those with complex trauma often experience disturbed sleep patterns. During sleep, hyperarousal occurs, which creates the emotional experiences hypervigilance and paranoia. These experiences contribute to sleep disturbances. For example, Beth was raped twice in adolescence. As a college freshman, she feels uncertain in her new residence hall and her fears of being raped are escalated and omnipresent. She is unable to get to sleep, wakes up with nightmares, and fears every noise in the hallway. Beth's presentation is experienced by many with complex trauma. They have difficulty getting to sleep, sleep lightly, and are aware of unanticipated noises in their home. This stress may lead to persistent insomnia or sleep paralysis. These episodes consist of reexperiencing the traumatic event. Night terrors are vivid, and often are continually experienced when awakening. This may result in accidental violent or even injury-provoking behaviors (American Psychiatric Association, 2013; Zillmer et al., 2008).

Summary

This chapter provided information on the assessment, treatment, and care coordination for those who have experienced trauma. It is important to note that while the knowledge, skills, techniques, awareness, and resources presented may be ones with which you are familiar, application and utilization of them, in real time, with a vulnerable human being can be quite daunting as well as moving. Knowledge, skills, techniques, awareness, and resources are continually updated and modified; thus, we urge you to continue your professional and personal development long after your formal training; your clients are counting on it!

Extended Learning Exercises

Exercise 1: Axline's Eight Basic Play Therapy Principles

Consider the basic principles promoted by Axline (1969). Rank them in the order of importance to you as the clinician. For the child client, what cultural considerations apply? Which principle appears to be the most challenging principle for you to follow? What makes it challenging?

- The therapist must develop a warm, friendly relationship with the child, in which good rapport is established as soon as possible.

- The therapist accepts the child exactly as they are.

- The therapist establishes a feeling of permissiveness in the relationship so that the child feels free to express their feelings completely.

- The therapist is alert to recognize the feelings the child is expressing and reflects those feelings back to the child in such a manner that they gain insight into their behavior.

- The therapist maintains a deep respect for the child's ability to solve their own problems if given an opportunity to do so. The responsibility to make choices and to institute change is the child's.

- The therapist does not attempt to direct the child's action or conversation in any manner. The child leads the way; the therapist follows.

- The therapist does not attempt to hurry the therapy along. It is a gradual process and is recognized as such by the therapist.

- The therapist establishes only those limitations that are necessary to anchor the therapy to the world of reality and to make the child aware of their responsibility in the relationship.

Exercise 2: Limits to Confidentiality

Review the below example of a limits to confidentiality script written for a clinician practicing in the state of New Hampshire. Look up your own state-specific limits to confidentiality and create your own script.

Limits to Confidentiality

Everything that happens in counseling is strictly confidential and protected under the law. I will not discuss anything about your therapy, or even identify that you are a client, unless you give me written permission. There are some instances when I will talk with someone about your case *without* obtaining your consent that is allowed under the law. These include reviewing your case during Clinical Supervision or Peer Consultation.

There are some instances in which I am mandated under New Hampshire state law to break confidentiality. These include

- If you make significant threats to self, others, or property

- If I witness or suspect the abuse and/or neglect of a child

- If I witness or suspect the abuse of an incapacitated adult

- For Health Information Portability and Accountability Act (HIPAA) regulation compliance

- If there are certain rights you may have waived when contracting for third party financial coverage

- If I am ordered by the courts to disclose information from our sessions

What questions, thoughts, or feelings do you have about what I just mentioned to you?

Case Illustration 1: Advanced Graduate Student

Anastasia, a 17-year-old female, was referred by her school clinician to you after failing several classes. During your intake session, she disclosed she was sexually assaulted by an acquaintance four months before. Prior to the sexual assault, Anastasia was a straight-A student and in the top 10 of her class. Since the assault, she is failing three of her four classes, cannot concentrate, and struggles to remain in class or at school. She feels that everyone knows. Anastasia reported a history of panic attacks before the sexual assault, but the frequency and intensity remitted significantly with counseling.

Anastasia reported that since the sexual assault, she cannot sleep and feels irritable and hopeless all the time. She does not want to do anything at home and ends up fighting with her mom. She does not want to see her friends, and in particular, her best friend, Kami. Kami is the ex-girlfriend of the young man who assaulted Anastasia.

Anastasia was previously diagnosed with an unspecified anxiety disorder, but at this point, you are not sure if this is relevant to her current concerns. Lynn, Anastasia's mom, is her primary support. Lynn, at intake, acknowledges that Anastasia has reported the sexual assault, and wonders why she can't just *get over it* like she did when she (Lynn) was raped by her uncle. Lynn thinks therapy will only make things worse and believes Anastasia should be able to work this out on her own, because *that's what women do.*

Questions for you to consider:

How do you respond to Anastasia's immediate concerns?

What skills will you utilize?

What are your priorities with Anastasia in this session?

Who else may you involve in the conversation?

What additional information or resources are required for you to assist Anastasia?

What are the desired outcomes for Anastasia and you in this session?

Describe your assessment and treatment plan.

Case Illustration 2: Novice Professional

Jane is a 44-year-old female who is having a hard time. She struggles most days to get through the day, with grocery shopping, laundry, and taking care of her kids. She works at the local hospital as a nurse and has been calling in sick two to three times a week for the past three months. Jane's supervisor, Janis, is concerned about Jane and speaks to Jane privately about her appearing disheveled, distracted, overwhelmed, and unfocused at work. Jane handles medications for patients and there have been two incidents where patients were given the wrong meds, only to have another nurse catch the error. Jane was put on probation. Janis refers Jane to the hospital's employee assistance program for assessment and maybe counseling.

Jane shares with you that she feels stuck. She is married for a second time to Ben, her high-school sweetheart. Ben and Jane have a blended family consisting of Jane's two children from her first marriage and Ben's daughter from a previous relationship. Jane was *disfellowshipped* from her faith and shunned by her parents and two sisters because she no longer practices her faith as a Jehovah's Witness. Jane feels deeply alone and rejected. She reports she has no desire to cook or go out dinner with friends, an activity she usually enjoys. Jane is even less interested in going on nightly walks with her husband and neighbors; they have noticed her absence. Jane says she just feels listless, struggles to get out of bed in the morning, could care less about how she appears to others, and is just trying to survive. Jane adds, she struggles to get to and stay asleep, is rarely hungry, and just feels numb, most days just prefers to stay in bed with the covers over her head.

Jane is cutting herself off from her friends and family. She says doesn't want to burden them with her problems and prefers to keep things to herself. Jane is terrified she is going to lose her job, particularly because of the probation. She is not sure she even wants to be a nurse anymore. She says quietly, "I am not sure I even want to go on." Jane believes that if she is going to get fired, there is no point of even showing up to work despite Janis telling her she really wants Jane to get the help she needs. Janis does not want to fire Jane because she is a respected nurse and has been a great asset to the hospital.

Jane says she feels rejected and abandoned by her church, her family, and now her employer. She says it feels like she is reliving the whole *disfellowship* experience all over again and in no time other nurses will shun her too. She sighs and says, "It really isn't worth going on, is it?"

Questions for you to consider:

How do you respond to Jane's immediate concerns?

What skills will you utilize?

What are your priorities with Jane in this session?

Who else may you involve in the conversation?

What additional information or resources are required for you to assist Jane?

What are the desired outcomes for Jane and you in this session?

Describe your assessment and treatment plan.

Case Illustration 3: Mid-Career Professional

Sam brought his children into counseling because the family is having troubles. He seems very expressive about the problems in his family. He says he is *being pulled in too many directions.* He reports his son José has been acting up a lot lately and was given a warning by the police for skateboarding in a restricted area. Sam notes José is typically *a good kid*, but recently he's hanging out with an older group of boys skateboarding and playing *Fortnite,* a popular computer game. José seems obsessed with *Fortnite.* Sam believes the computer game has begun to affect José's schoolwork and dominates almost every conversation he has with Sam and José's sister, Natalia. Sam mentions this is only the tip of the iceberg and goes on to describe how Natalia, who is *a great kid*, made some poor decisions as of late. According to Sam, Natalia recently sexted a picture of her

bare chest to a close friend, as a joke. After the friend received the picture they forwarded it to 15 others who also sent it on to others. In short, Natalia's picture was seen by most of her peers by the next day. When Natalia came to school the next day, she received hateful texts and salacious looks from various boys. Natalia was devastated and spent the better part of the next two weeks in tears, locked up in her room. She is demanding to enroll in a new high school, soon. Tearfully, Natalia mentions that her Nana, grandmother and family matriarch, called her *a little slut* when she found out. Natalia says she hates her grandmother and feels like *a loser.* José mentions that he is doing well and he doesn't like hearing about Natalia's issues, because it is *girl stuff.* During the sessions, you notice that Sam and Natalia avoid discussing the sexting incident. They both seem embarrassed about the incident and take up the session with a lot of other issues.

Questions for you to consider:

How will you structure your time with this family?

Will you see them all together, separate them out, or something else?

How would you work with this issue?

Describe an intervention you might use to break the ice?

Who else may you involve in the conversation?

What additional information or resources are required for you to assist Natalia?

What are the desired outcomes for Natalia in this session?

Describe your assessment and treatment plan.

Additional Resources

Helpful Links*

Clinician Administer PTSD Scale for DSM-5; Past Week Version: https://www.ptsd.va.gov/professional/assessment/documents/CAPS_5_Past_Week.pdfNational Coalition against Domestic Violence https://ncadv.org

The National Domestic Violence Hotline: http://www.thehotline.org

Love Is Respect: http://www.loveisrespect.org

Psychology Today: https://www.psychologytoday.com/us/blog/the-time-cure/201211/your-brain-trauma

PTSD Scale-Self Report for DSM-5 PSS-SR5: https://www.div12.org/wp-content/uploads/2014/11/PSS-SR5.pdf

Trauma Checklist for Youth: https://depts.washington.edu/hcsats/PDF/TF-%20CBT/pages/1%20Assessment/PTSD%20Measures/Trauma%20scale%20child%20version%20.pdf

Trauma Recovery: http://trauma-recovery.ca/recovery/phases-of-trauma-recovery/

*Confirm your responsibilities regarding copyrighted materials. Reproduction or redistribution, in whole or in part, in any manner, without the prior written consent of the copyright holder, is a violation of copyright law

Helpful Books

The Body Keeps the Score: Brain, Mind, and Body in the Healing of Trauma (2015). Bessel van der Kolk

Trauma and Recovery (1997). Judith Lewis Herman

Waking the Tiger: Healing Trauma (1997). Peter A. Levine

The Body Remembers: The Psychophysiology of Trauma and Trauma Treatment (2000). Babette Rothschild

Healing Developmental Trauma: How Early Trauma Affects Self-Regulation, Self-Image, and the Capacity for Relationship (2012). Aline Lapierre & Laurence Heller

DVDs

Gone Baby Gone (2007)

Goodwill Hunting (1997)

Precious (2009)

Mommy Dearest (1981)

The Invisible War (2012)

What I've Been Through Is Not Who I Am (2011)

Paper Tigers (2015)

Resilience (2016)

Private Violence (2014)

Power and Control: Domestic Violence in American (2010)

Disaster

Disaster disrupt, dislocate, devastate, and destroy. World history is replete with the tragedy of human and environmental suffering on a local, regional, national, or multinational scale. Some examples include, the volcanic eruption of Mount Vesuvius in 79 AD (20,000 persons presumed dead/missing); the Black Death pandemic (Byrne, 2004) of 1347 -1351 (75 to 200 million dead); the 1556 earthquake in China's Shanxi Province (830,000 dead); the 1986 Chernobyl plant nuclear meltdown in Ukraine (4,000 estimated dead and approximately 100,000 km² of land significantly contaminated with radioactive fallout); and the 2014 mass shooting in Kenya at Garissa University College (Zirulnick, 2015), where 148 were killed.

All who experience disaster are impacted to some degree. The type, intensity, chronicity, and duration of the impact vary due to a multitude of factors like individual premorbid physical and psychological functioning; the scope, duration, and magnitude of the event; witnessing the dead and injured; proximity and exposure to the event; and the acuity and timeliness of response and recovery efforts. Compared to crisis and trauma, our scholarly and empirical understanding of disaster is in its infancy. Much of the knowledge base of what is now referred to as disaster mental health (DMH), disaster psychology, and disaster psychiatry emerged since the late 1980s. In this chapter, we examine the relatively recent history and development of disaster counseling and DMH.

Learning Objectives

After reading this chapter and participating in the extended learning exercises, you will be able to

- Distinguish the foundation of DMH responding from trauma and crisis-counseling including the role of proximity, exposure, locus and nature of individual-in/and with community treatment and the progression of emotional responding

- Understand the historical context and development of DMH frameworks, as well as definitions, the role and history of disaster organizations and federal legislation, and ecological context of disaster

- Articulate key elements related to DMH responding like clinical presentation, individual and group assessment, diagnosis, mechanisms of change, integrated planning, and development of multi-disciplinary community/regional teams

- Apply theoretical, diagnostic, and clinical concepts

Defining Disaster

Disaster is unplanned, catastrophic events that occur at specific locales during a specific timeframe to a specific group of individuals. Disaster degrade the abilities of individuals, groups, communities, and societies to function in the short term because their typical coping mechanisms and resources are overwhelmed by the magnitude of devastating losses. Losses occur across all categories of human experience—physical, psychological, spiritual, economic, vocational, and material. By their very nature, disaster are abnormal events experienced by most as an acute crisis and by some as persistent traumatic reactions after the event. In the acute phase, survivors' clinical presentation may include numbness, tearfulness, anxiety, hypervigilance, and depression, which are normal reactions given the abnormal conditions of the disaster. Most survivors with the passage of time and comprehensive support return to their previous level of functioning. But for some, the symptoms persist or worsen, manifesting into physical and psychological disorders like anxiety, depression, or post-traumatic stress disorder.

Categories of Disaster

Three categories of disaster, human-, nature-, or technology-initiated, are presented in Table 6.1. *Human-initiated* disaster are those caused, intentionally or unintentionally, by humans. The individuals' actions may be deliberate or due to negligence, but regardless of intent, they cascade into a natural or technological disaster. *Nature-initiated* disaster are the result of events or processes that occur in nature. Human- and nature-initiated disaster are differentiated by the element of human intent, negligence, or responsibility that leads to human suffering.

TABLE 6.1 ● Categories and Types of Disaster

Categories of Disaster		
Nature	**Human**	**Technological**
Drought, crop failure	Bombing, terrorism	Chemical spills
Earthquakes, landslides	Cyber or Internet based	Nuclear power plant failures
Flooding	Financial collapse	Oil spills: Deepwater Horizon
Snow, avalanches	Mass shootings	Bridge/building failures
Viral pandemics: Ebola, Influenza, Zika	Pollution: Love Canal, Bhopal India	
Volcanic eruptions	War, genocide, terrorism	
Weather: hurricanes, rain, tornadoes, wind		
Wildfires		

A *technology-initiated* disaster is a failure of a technological structure or some human error in operating technology. Although displayed here in a discreet format, it is important to note that disaster may originate in more than one category.

Distinguishing Disaster

Disaster is differentiated from crisis and trauma in numerous ways. The knowledge base regarding disaster is less well developed when compared to crisis or trauma studies. Current DMH models, theory, research, and practice are promising, yet not fully developed. Academic, empirical, and clinical understandings and interventions also continue to emerge. While DMH clinicians and researchers rely heavily on crisis intervention models and assessment and treatment protocols, the nature and scope of a disaster demands a differentiated knowledge and treatment base consistent with the disaster contextual factors. As Halpern and Tramontin (2007) stated, "A disaster could qualify as a crisis, but not all crises are disaster" (p. 2). Second, disaster are not chronic. They are encapsulated events, with beginnings and ends, and are broad in scope and scale. Crisis and traumatic events are typically narrower in scope, impact the individual or small group, occur intermittently, and are primarily, but not exclusively, human-initiated. Third, the origin of the disaster matters to survivors and their recovery. Research findings indicate that the nature and course of survivors' short- and long-term psychological recuperation may be associated with the cause or category of the disaster. The course of recovery does not seem to be associated with the cause of the crisis or psychological trauma. Some human-initiated disaster mirror natural disaster in scope and scale and are the direct and often purposeful result of another human being. Nature-initiated disaster is not intentional. Like human-initiated disaster, technology-initiated disaster involve human mismanagement and are sometimes categorized as a human-initiated disaster. Categorization as a human-initiated disaster is an important distinction because there is an *identifiable cause* of the disaster *directly* attributable to a person or persons. Knowing that *someone* is responsible for the pain and misery challenges our understanding of what it means to be human and humane. Patterns of responding seem to generalize across disaster of different origins and types. Initial research findings indicate a relationship between variations in the category and type of disaster and survivors' long-term psychophysiological reactions (Neria, Nandi, & Galea, 2008; US Department of Justice, 2000). Psychological effects of a disaster may be chronic and may not occur in the acute phase of the disaster. Fourth, unlike crisis or traumatic events, in some types of disaster, a pre-disaster period exists. An example of a pre-disaster period is the severe tornado warning. The warning signals the impending threat affording time to anticipate and prepare to avoid injury or loss of life. Consider those disaster that occur without warning. They are understandably overwhelming because individuals and communities are caught off guard. Slow to develop events, like floods or severe weather, provide time for a warning and preparation. These events can be experienced much like human-initiated disaster in that loss and injuries are believed to be preventable if individuals heed the warning. When warnings go unheeded and people die, someone is to blame because the deaths are attributed, rightly or wrongly, to human mismanagement. The psychological impact of human-initiated disaster may be more detrimental (Goldsteen & Schorr 1982) than other types. Technology-initiated disaster may have a longer recovery period due to litigation (Picou, Marshall, & Gall, 2004); widespread economic devastation in the region—like the Deepwater Horizon oil spill (Grattan et al., 2017); and incessant broadcast and social media reports, which exacerbate already heightened stress and trauma (Morris, Grattat, Mayer, and Blackburn, 2013). Fifth, in contrast to crisis or traumatic events, the phases of emotional responding in a disaster are distinct. The progression of the emotional responding (HHS; SAMSHA, 2000) is presented in Figure 6.1 and illustrates the common reactions of individuals and communities from pre-disaster warnings through the one-year anniversary of the event. These reactions are described in detail in the subsequent section.

Sixth, the focal point of disaster response, intervention, and treatment is, by necessity, the individual-in/and with community. Individual-in/and with community model describes the ecological, systemic, and contextual nature of disaster and depicts the simultaneous and interconnected elements of disaster response, intervention, treatment, and recovery for individuals and their communities. When compared to crisis and trauma, disaster responding is greater in scope in terms of victims and number and variety of response agencies, and is more public. An ecological, systemic, and contextual model of in- and with-community response, adapted from Bronfenbrenner's (1995) ecological model of child development, is presented later in this chapter. Finally, the phases of disaster responding are less linear, more recursive and continuous, and extend beyond etiology and treatment. The phases have multiple foci—prevention, assessment, response, and recovery—and necessitate the use of a multi-disciplinary team of responders.

History and Emerging Theories of Disaster Mental Health and Disaster Responding

The academic and empirical study of disaster, and in particular DMH, is a relatively recent development. Historically, disaster occurred in a localized area and local residents responded, many of whom were also casualties of the disaster. Those affected reacted; there was no state or federal response or rescue. They assessed and secured the well-being and safety of those closest to them, family and loved ones, then attended to individuals in next closest proximity. They evaluated and treated physical injuries and wounds and located the missing or dead. The second reaction or priority was to ensure the individuals' security, safe and suitable shelter, nourishment, and sanitation. As basic needs were met, communities developed cohesion and turned toward recovery and rebuilding.

The absence of community or federally based relief agencies meant those affected by disaster were pretty much on their own in terms of immediate and long-term response, recovery, and rebuilding. In Europe and the United States, formal disaster relief organizations emerged in response to the devastation of regional and global wars. The Swiss Red Cross (1863), American Red Cross (1881), International Federation of the Red Cross and Red Crescent Societies (IRFC; 1919) played critical roles in responding to the physical injuries of soldiers and civilians. Interestingly, psychological and emotional wounds like soldier's heart or shell shock were largely ignored or were attributed to physical causes until the Vietnam War.

Formal organizational responding began in 1866 with the Swiss-initiated global Red Cross, founded by Henry Dunant, a Swiss businessperson. Dunant came upon soldiers of the Battle of Solferino in 1859 and was appalled at the poor conditions and profound lack of medical care for the over 40,000 who lay injured and dying. He offered comfort and aid to the wounded and in 1862 chronicled his experiences in *A Memory of Solferino*. Because of these experiences, Dunant and others proposed a permanent relief agency for humanitarian aid during war supported by a formal government treaty confirming the nonalignment and neutrality of aid agencies allowing them to respond to those in the war zone. Dunant's efforts resulted in the established of the Swiss Red Cross in 1863 and influenced articles of the Geneva Convention in 1864.

The Geneva Convention is a series of treaties and protocol establishing international law and standards for humanitarian treatment during times of war. For his efforts, Dunant received the first Nobel Prize in 1901. Encouraged by the efforts of the Swiss, Clara Barton and others called for the formation of the American Red Cross (ARC) in 1881 amidst the American Civil War. Nine years later, a congressional charter formally recognized the ARC. Over the decades, the ARC and its volunteers have provided a range of public health, education, and disaster relief efforts in the United States and across the globe. The most recent version of the charter, adopted May 2007, restates the ARC's traditional purposes: providing relief to and serving as a medium of communication between members of the American armed forces and their families and providing national and international disaster relief and mitigation. In the United States, additional relief agencies and federal legislation were created throughout the 20th century in response to naturally occurring disaster.

Federal legislation paved the way for funding and services like the Center for Disease Control, created in 1946; the Disaster Relief Act of 1950; the Federal Civil Defense Act of 1950; the Federal Emergency Management Agency Act of 1970; and organizations like the Mercy Corps. James and Gilliland (2017) note, "Although the federal government has been involved in disaster relief since the 19th century, until recently it has paid very little attention to the psychological aftershocks of a disaster" (p. 579).

The Development of DMH Theories and Models

At first blush, the absence of a catalogue of coordinated theoretical, practical, and scientific understanding related to disaster seems curious given the development of numerous relief agencies and the plethora of theories, research, and interventions in crisis and trauma counseling. James and Gilliland (2017) identified a confluence of four influences they believe contributed to the development of advanced theoretical and conceptual study as well as clinical and community intervention in DMH. The first was the establishment of the *Community Mental Health Act of 1963,* also known as the Mental Retardation and Community Mental Health Centers Construction Act of 1963. This legislation and subsequent improvements in mental health care radically enhanced the delivery of mental health services. Those in need of comprehensive mental health services would now receive them their local communities rather than being dispatched to institutions far from home. Local mental health centers provided five essential services: inpatient services, outpatient services, day treatment, emergency services, and consultation and education services. Second, as you read in Chapter 4, in 1980, post-traumatic stress disorder (PTSD) was classified by the American Psychiatric Association as a legitimate psychiatric disorder (3rd ed.; *DSM–III*; American Psychiatric Association [APA], 1980). Though controversial at the time, the APA's attribution of a catastrophic stressor like war, disaster, or rape as the source of trauma was momentous. No longer would psychological trauma be associated, at least by researchers and clinicians, as a personal failing or character flaw or weakness. Survivors diagnosed with PTSD after the trauma of a catastrophic event were differentiated from those who experienced the pain and stress of daily living—bereavement, divorce, or changes in financial status. Mental health professionals understood those affected by disaster may exhibit transitory or enduring symptoms like reexperiencing, hypervigilance, anxiety, nightmares, and intrusive thoughts. Their clinical presentation would be similar to soldiers. The third influence, the development of a national cadre of DMH trained professionals, emerged from the aftermath of Hurricane Hugo and the Loma Prieta Earthquake, two fateful sequential disaster in the fall of 1989. The extent of these tragedies had the American Red Cross (ARC), Federal Emergency Management Agency (FEMA), and other disaster relief organizations reeling. The Government Accountability Office (U.S. Government Accounting Office, 1991) documented that the ARC, despite providing the greatest number of volunteers, did not have "enough people to manage the shelter facilities adequately" (p. 37) and had "difficulty assigning adequate numbers of qualified personnel to disaster response activities" (p. 40). In its separate self-assessment, ARC officials documented that response personnel attending to California earthquake survivors "were not adequately trained to deal with the needs of ethnic minorities" and that ARC "staff was culturally insensitive to victims, and did not have appropriate bilingual skills to serve some communities" (p. 41).

Documented dissatisfaction and widespread ARC staffing shortages were present *prior* to the twin 1989 disaster, and now Hurricane Hugo and Loma Prieta ARC volunteers were faced with deeply intense and stressful disaster relief work with little to no reprieve or recognition of vicarious traumatization. A stressed system of critical responders was further stressed. In response, the ARC convened a task force to determine if an internal formalized DMH program (Halpern & Tramontin, 2006) was warranted. The task force's findings led the ARC to distinguish the "disaster mental health program from its disaster nursing program and created a corps of mental health volunteers" (Morris, 2011, p. 279) and a mental health certificate program. The final influence identified by James and Gilliland was the women's movement of the late 1960s and 1970s. As noted in Chapter 4, the women's movement increased cultural and societal awareness of the plight of women. In 1974, Burgess and Holmstrom published their findings related to Rape Trauma Syndrome. Rape victims, they observed, described nightmares, flashbacks, intrusive thoughts, and avoidance. Burgess and Holmstrom connected rape survivors' sequelae to other theories of traumatology experiences. Increased cultural awareness on the impact of trauma on individual women set the stage for understanding the impact of disaster on women and their families.

We add four additional influences to the four identified by James and Gilliland (2017). They include the demand for coordinated disaster response services and recognition of mental health consequences of mass disaster, particularly in rural areas; the rise in global terrorism; the expansion of intervention teams; and the intersections of federal legislation and executive orders designed to address disaster relief.

Coordinated Disaster Response

In 1972, three rural communities experienced flooding of historic proportions; Logan County, West Virginia, on February 26; Rapid City, South Dakota, on June 9 to 10; and Wilkes-Barre, Pennsylvania, on June 14. These nature-initiated disaster resulted from excessive rain over several days. The Logan County flooding occurred when a dam burst while the Rapid City flooding was caused by excessive rainfall. Wilkes-Barre faced flooding from the aftermath of Hurricane Agnes. These communities had critical and overwhelming needs yet could not benefit from resources promised by the *Community Mental Health Act* of 1963 because they lack the appropriate level and type of resources such as organized DMH support and triage, sufficient numbers of responders for the physically injured, morgue services, and general volunteers. The magnitude and scope of the disaster and lack of adequate and organized acute and ongoing aid led members of Congress to meet with representatives from these three communities to craft federal legislation aimed at improving and coordinating disaster relief. Federal-level responding provides direct aid and generates conceptual and practical knowledge related to disaster responding and DMH counseling.

Rise in Global Terrorism

The Global Terrorism Database defines a terrorist attack as "the threatened or actual use of illegal force and violence by a non-state actor to attain a political, economic, religious, or social goal through fear, coercion, or intimidation." (START Center, 2018, p. 10). Terrorist acts are intentional and involve coercion, violence, or the threat of violence against people, property, or in cyberspace. The goal of terrorism is to intimidate, influence, and harm individuals and the policies and actions of their government. The GTD documents acts of terrorism worldwide; from 1990 through 2016, 770 acts of terrorism occurred in the United States. The constancy of terrorist threats and action may give rise to the cultural detachment, at times witnessed in the United States, as responses to these events become normalized and approximate the feelings of "routine emergency" described by Pat-Horenczyk (2005).

The Expansion of Intervention Teams

The International Critical Incident Stress Foundation (ICISF), founded in 1989, provides leadership, education, training, consultation, and support services in comprehensive crisis intervention and disaster behavioral health services to the emergency response professions, other organizations, and communities worldwide. Members of the ICISF do not respond to disaster, rather they focus their interventions on first responders. In contrast, the National Organization of Victim Assistance (NOVA), founded in 1975, has direct and indirect services to disaster survivors. Like the ICISF, NOVA provides education, advocacy, and professional credentialing as well as Crisis Response Teams (CRT). CRTs are comprised of individuals specifically trained to provide trauma mitigation, education, and emotional first aid in the aftermath of small-scale or mass-casualty events. The focus on first responder education, training, and well-being and the expansion of intervention teams have professionalized emergency responding and DMH.

Disaster and Emergency Response Legislation

Prior to the 1970s, over 100 federal agencies and thousands of agencies at the state and local level had jurisdictional control and involvement in emergency responding and management. Coordination, collaboration, and communication, if present, were woeful. We note four significant pieces of legislation or executive orders that created, augmented, or influenced disaster responding. This, by no means, represents an exhaustive list of disaster relief legislation. Rather we note them due to their significance in advancing resources and research in DMH. First, the *Disaster Relief Act of 1974* emerged from dialogues with emergency responders from the three tragic floods of 1972 and was reformulated and reauthorized as the *Stafford Disaster Relief and Emergency Assistance Act of 1988*. The Stafford Act included specific language related to augmented mental health services during disaster relief. It was again amended and reauthorized in 2016. Second, in the early 1970s, federal disaster relief and recovery efforts were assigned to the Federal Disaster Assistance Administration (FDAA) unit located in the Department of Housing and Urban Development (HUD). This unit, the precursor of FEMA, was established by executive order in 1978. The FDAA oversaw disaster response until its incorporation into FEMA in 1978. Prior to FEMA, disaster response services were fragmented, decentralized, and confusing. Services were often duplicated resulting in ineffective emergency management. Thus, FEMA's mandate was and continues to be one of coordination and communication amongst all federal agencies. Third, the *Homeland Security Act of 2002* established the Department of Homeland Security (DHS) as a new entity within the government. The intent of this act was to restructure units with the federal government after the terrorist attacks of September 11, 2001, into the new DHS. Title V of the *Homeland Security Act* consists of nine sections that ensure the efficient response time, interagency coordination, and increased preparedness for providers responding to terrorist attacks, major disaster, and other emergencies.

The Department of Homeland Security was severely tested in 2005 during Hurricane Katrina, the largest natural disaster in recent U.S. history. The demands placed on FEMA exposed areas of improvement in cross-agency communication, coordination and logistics, and care of the displaced and injured. The final significant federal legislation was National Response Framework (FEMA, 2008; [NRF]). Much like the 1975 *Disaster Relief Act,* the authors of the NRF utilized stakeholder feedback after a series of disaster, their assessments of adequate and inadequate responses, and subsequent lessons learned to develop their framework. The framework enhanced the principles of the *National Response Plan of 2004* and its precursor the *1992 Federal Response Plan.* Most notably, the 2008 NFR articulates that effective incident response is a shared responsibility of all levels of government, the private sector, nongovernmental organizations (NGOs), and individual citizens. Inadequate disaster response, at all levels of government, highlighted the continued need for improved preparation for both nature- and human- initiated disaster. The foundations of our academic, empirical, and clinical understandings of DMH have emerged out of tragedies and terror; hopefully, those of us involved in DMH continue to learn and improve services to those affected by disaster as lives depend on it.

Disaster in Context

In 2000, the Substance Abuse and Mental Health Services Administration (SAMHSA), an agency within the U.S. Department of Health and Human Services (HHS), published the second edition of a training manual for mental health and related personnel working a major disaster. An element of this helpful resource described the six-phase evolution of collective reactions of individuals within communities affected by disaster (see Figure 6.1). The first five phases are hypothesized to take place during the first year after the event and the final phase after the one-year anniversary of the event.

Phase 1, *Pre-Disaster,* describes the period of time just prior to the disaster event in which individuals and communities do or do not receive advanced warning of the disaster. Advanced warnings typically include the type, scope, timing, and potential magnitude of calamitous events with predictable degrees of destruction as well as recommendations or mandates to evacuate for safety. While survivors

FIGURE 6.1 ● Progression of Emotional Responses to a Disaster

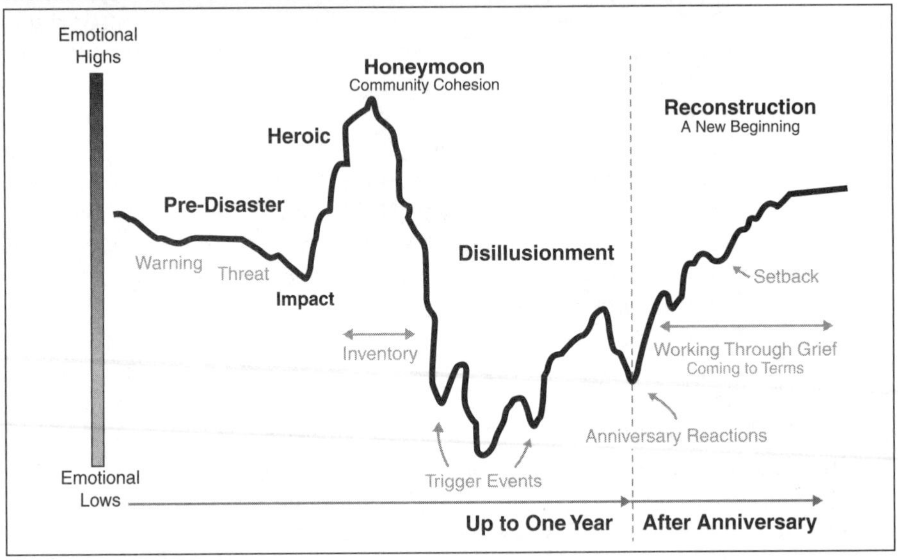

Source: DeWolfe, D. J., 2000.

who heed the warnings may suffer property damage or loss of income, they experience a measure of control as they reduced the likelihood of injury or protected themselves and their family. Survivors who were aware of but did not heed the warnings are likely to experience self-blame and remorse, particularly if they or their loved ones are injured or die because of their inaction. When no warning occurs in the *Pre-Disaster* phase, survivors are likely to experience feelings of vulnerability, fear, insecurity, anxiety, and powerlessness due to the sudden and arbitrary nature of events.

The *Impact Phase* immediately following the pre-disaster phase takes one of two courses. The first event is abrupt and violent, like an earthquake or mass shooting. The second is described as a slowly gathering event, starting at a low level like weather-related events. The hallmark of this phase is variability. Psychosocial responding is associated with the type, magnitude, and scope of the destruction related to the event. The greater the loss, the greater the potential for deep, longer-lasting psychosocial aftershocks.

Phase three, the *Heroic Phase*, occurs in the immediate wake of the disaster. Marked by acts of individual or collective heroism, this phase is all about rescue and survival, survival of the individual and their loved ones, and rescuing others. This type of emotional responding may occur in professional as well as lay helpers, first-responders, and survivors of the disaster. The *Cajun Navy,* the impromptu group of Louisiana boat owners who rallied to rescue survivors of Hurricanes Katrina and Harvey, is a prime example of heroic emotional responding. Their remarkable acts of altruism, and likely adrenaline-stimulated behaviors, put some of them at great personal risk.

The progression of emotional responding described in this model appears to reach its zenith in Phase 4, the *Honeymoon Phase*. Survivors of disaster experience this phase in a variety of ways depending on the location of and accessibility to the disaster, the magnitude of destruction of human life, and to community infrastructure. Those who receive disaster relief, timely and sufficient community, mental health, and volunteer assistance are more likely to experience a sense of community cohesion, momentary optimism, and the hope to return to *normal*. Individuals who experience delayed, insufficient, or fragmented disaster relief suffer community fragmentation, helplessness, anger, and dismay. Consider the *Honeymoon Phase* for individuals impacted by the 2017 hurricane season and the differential response. Review the U. S. government's response to the 2017 hurricanes in Texas compared to Puerto Rico (https://www.nytimes.com/2017/09/27/us/politics/trump-puerto-rico-aid.html) and contemplate how the recovery of Texas' survivors compares to those in Puerto Rico.

The mutuality, relief, and support experienced by many during the *Honeymoon Phase* gives way to the discouragement and disappointment experienced in Phase 5, *Disillusionment*. After the immediate threats of the disaster have passed and emergency responders and volunteers have left, disaster survivors face the enormities of their *new normal*, their post-disaster reality. During this phase, most survivors catalog and inventory the extent of their losses and the disparity of timely and adequate resources. Individuals consider care for the injured, grief for the dead, relocation to or repair of living spaces, financial hardships, homelessness, food insecurity, and inadequate infrastructure support like inconsistent electricity, no water treatment or sanitation. Others consider new or worsening of previous medical or mental health conditions and competing demands. Stress abounds during this time leading to anger, fatigue, family conflict, and disillusionment among those who continue to struggle. Individuals and communities who believe they received inequitable or fewer resources compared to others experience rancor, dissension, and resentment at their unequal treatment.

The sixth and final phase, *Reconstruction,* coincides with the one-year anniversary of the event. This phase may continue for multiple years post disaster. During this time, most survivors and communities have begun to restore and recover from the effects of the disaster and, more importantly, realize that resources and support to recover, thrive, and grow come from within the individuals and local community, not from external sources. Early in the *Reconstruction* phase, there is the simultaneous recognition of losses, readjustment to present circumstances, and gratitude for survivorship. A disaster is a life-altering event whose meaning and purpose are dependent on the perceptions of the effected individuals and their communities.

Individual and Community Responses

Individual Responses

The U.S. DHHS, Substance Abuse and Mental Health Services Administration (2000) notes that most affected by disaster return to premorbid psychological functioning without external intervention. That sentiment notwithstanding, vulnerable populations may be at greater risk during a disaster. Vulnerability comes in many forms and may be a function of age, degrees of ability, preexisting circumstances or concerns, cultural or ethnic groups, historic marginalization, and disaster relief workers. Vulnerable populations require assistance to understand and physically respond to a threat, engage personal agency, marshal resources, and aid in the recovery effort. Consider infants, children, and seniors who need assistance in responding to danger or those with low or no vision, limited physical mobility, deaf or hard of hearing who can respond if communicated with appropriately, or those with pre-existing physical or psychological circumstances like medical dependency, serious and persistent mental conditions, or limited cognitive abilities. Additionally, immigrants, those with low or no English language proficiency, and undocumented individuals may not seek care due to language and legal barriers. Members of vulnerable populations are at greater risk during a disaster than members of the general population because of decreased access to resources, reduced degrees of independence, or ability to understand the magnitude and urgency that often accompanies disaster.

Regardless of vulnerability or manner of responding to a disaster, survivors have universal needs. As noted earlier, in the aftershock of a disaster, the need for safety and basic survival are paramount. Survivors experience fear, anxiety, confusion, and distress as they locate loved ones, grieve the dead and loss of valued or meaningful possessions. Once the immediate danger has passed, survivors may experience dread, sleeplessness, nightmares, reimaging the disaster, and relocation concerns. Those affected by disaster need to tell their stories over and over again in an attempt to make sense of overwhelming events and to feel part of the community. The severity of emotional and psychological reactions can be depicted graphically. Figure 6.2 was adapted by the first author from the Center for Disease Control's (2012) *Disaster Mental Health Primer* and serves as a reminder that given support and time, many disaster survivors improve and return to full functioning.

FIGURE 6.2 ● Psychological Reaction After a Traumatic Event

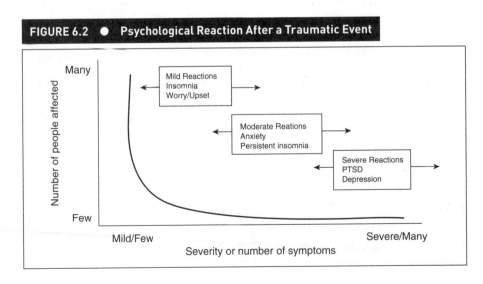

A number of survivors will require longer-term and perhaps more intensive levels of mental health support in terms of counseling, medications, and case management. Symptoms requiring additional services include disorientation, depression, anxiety, inability to care for one's self, substance misuse, violence toward self or others, and or hallucinations of any type. Chapter 7 details skills and interventions for those exposed to disaster.

Disaster survivors also have unique needs. As mentioned earlier, all touched by disaster are affected in some way. Individual responses, in the short and long term, vary and depend on the survivor's proximity to the disaster, their appraisal of the disaster's impact, available intra-and interpersonal resources, and premorbid psychological functioning. In vulnerable populations, individual coping with the aftereffects of the disaster vary widely (Bonanno, 2004; Linley & Joseph, 2004; Walker & Chestnut, 2003). Like what you read in Chapter 4 related to PTSD, researchers continue to investigate the personal and contextual variables that influence differential responding to a disaster. The question remains why, after a short period of crisis responding, do some individuals improve and return to health while others develop PTSD (Norris, Friedman, & Watson, 2002)?

Lewis and Roberts (2001) encouraged clinicians to examine survivor's perceptions of the stressor, its relationship to the source of the crisis, available coping processes, available resources, relevant cultural norms, and psychosocial and emotional functioning. It is important to distinguish coping processes from coping styles. As noted in previous chapters, we rely on the work of Lazarus and Folkman (1984), who identified the importance of the interplay between the person and environment-coping processes and distinguished them from coping styles that are more associated with personality traits and characteristics. Later in this chapter, we draw the reader's attention to the appraisal of coping and stress for the individual disaster survivor within their ecological, systemic, and contextual settings.

Community Response to Disaster

The community's response to disaster reflects their level of preparedness. After a disaster, numerous critical activities must happen immediately and efficiently. Communities that lack or have outdated disaster response plans or have inadequate levels of first responders will struggle. The struggle and confusion delays rescue and recovery efforts worsening an already terrible situation for residents. The magnitude and scope of response and recovery efforts is determined by how the disaster begins—abruptly or gradually, its duration, degree of threat, scale of the devastation, and potential for evacuation. Communities with skilled and prepared emergency responders who work from a coordinated disaster plan aid individual and community recovery. A disaster plan, or emergency preparedness, is designed and tested and retested *prior* to a disaster. The plan prioritizes and sequences communication between responders and the community. Clear, accurate, and timely communication aids rescue, triage, and care of the injured; policing and fire response; management of the deceased; and threat assessment and management—particularly roads and bridges, downed electrical lines, potable drinking water, access to food, and the provision of shelter or temporary housing.

As described earlier, disaster are distinguished from crises and traumas in that individuals and communities develop plans for the management of disaster. FEMA recognizes four phases to emergency management for communities: mitigation, preparedness, response, and recovery. *Mitigation* takes place before and after disaster and can best be described as actions that prevent future disaster or minimize the aftereffects should one occur. Examples of mitigation are improving the community's drainage system, testing the evacuation routes, or having redundant water treatment facilities. Second, community disaster education and response plans are critical. Community vulnerability and threat assessments are regularly conducted and acted upon resulting in improved infrastructure. The *Preparedness* phase occurs continuously and is in *advance* of the disaster. *Preparedness* activities include design and constant updating of the community's disaster response plan. This plan designates roles, responsibilities, and communication plans among all emergency responders, hospitals, utilities, transportation systems, volunteer agencies, and state disaster coordinators. Emergency responders conduct training and exercises to test the plan including warning sirens and notifications. The *Response* phase occurs during the disaster as first responders engage in mass rescue to save lives, reduce property damage, and stabilize the incident. Response activities are those activities identified and practiced in the disaster response plan including the initiation of evacuations and shelters. The final phase, *Recovery*, occurs after the acute phase of the disaster and focuses on health and social services, economic recovery, debris management, and temporary or permanent housing. The *Recovery* phase can last from months to years depending on the nature and extent of devastation and the level of one's resources. Consider the aftereffects of a tornado that rips through a small- to medium-size community on the eastern plains of Colorado. Everyone survives with minor physical injuries, but the devastation to homes and businesses range from no damage to broken windows and roof damage to complete destruction. Vital establishments, the grocery store, the hospital, the high school, and 30% of the homes are destroyed. The community plan determines that they will restore the hospital prior to extending assistance to local businesses or homeowners. For many individuals who experience the destruction of their homes or businesses, serious financial, emotional, and security issues abound.

Community-based or collective emotional and psychological responses to a disaster must begin with a communication plan that shares factual and timely information across numerous platforms in a variety of languages, including sign language. In the acute phase of a disaster, access to traditional modes of communication like radio, television, and newspapers may be limited or unavailable. It is imperative that communities have a centralized communications command, cellular and social media venues, and in rural venues, a central location for the distribution of information at regular intervals. Dependable and accurate communication reduces rumors and inaccuracies and promotes recovery. Along with relief agencies, community mental health centers can facilitate opportunities for those affected by disaster to come together to express a range of feelings like anxiety, fear, anger, hope, mourning, blessings, comfort, and encouragement. The mutuality and support expressed within and among community members provides the foundation for meaning making and interpretation during a time when little seems to make sense. Post-disaster planned community gatherings focused on hope and restoration demonstrate to survivors they are not alone; help, support, and resources are available and recovery will take time.

Ecological, Systemic, and Contextual Model of Individual In- and With-Community Response

Bronfenbrenner (2008; 1994) wrote that human development "occurs in the midst of a vibrant, complex environment" which is "largely defined by social and cultural practices and institutions" (p. 14). We live dynamic, interdependent lives in which a multitude of systems are influenced, intersected, bolstered, and dampened by a host of personal, cultural, and contextual variables. At times, it is overwhelming to consider. These individual variables and dynamic systems collide violently with the disaster and its aftermath leaving you, the clinician or first responder, to aid survivors in picking up the pieces. Our goal for this section is to present an ecological, systemic, and contextual model of disaster that aids your understanding of the ever-changing interplay of the individual disaster survivor, their family, community, culture(s), and biopsychosocial variables that influence functioning and systems. These interact and influence responses to disaster. Understandably, the systems, their influences, and individual and community needs will change over time and in intensity. We provide you a solid foundation from which to consider these intersecting perspectives.

A general ecological, systemic, contextual (ESC) model drawn from Bronfenbrenner's work rests on several assumptions. First, individuals are influenced by their unique biopsychosocial, physiological, economic, cultural-language, belief systems, norms, and assumptions and vocational variables. Individual variables, *along* with the environment, form the basis of interactions between and among individuals and groups. Interactions occur at each level of the ESC model and are developmental, reciprocal, and grow increasingly more complex over time. Interactions develop over time into relationships of various quality that are multifaceted and demonstrate various degrees of reciprocity. Second, meaningful and effective interactions are influenced by proximity. In short, the closer we are physically to individuals, groups, or environments, the more immediate and repetitive our interactions are. Myer and Moore (2006), describing their ecological model of crisis in context, wrote, "crises do not happen in a vacuum but are shaped by the cultural and social contexts in which they occur" (p.139). Their statement extends our understanding beyond a primary focus on the individual disaster survivor to the contexts and systems in which they live.

Bronfenbrenner's ecological model (Figure 6.3) and Myer and Moore's Crisis in Context (CCT) model describe layers and interactions of crises and their impact. The layers of a crisis are determined by the individual's physical proximity and reactions to the event. Interactions between individuals and systems involved in the disaster are reciprocal in the CCT model. Direct and indirect interactions occur in primary and secondary relationships and are impacted by the degree of change or disruption resulting from the disaster. The passage of time and anniversary dates significantly related to the disaster influence post-disaster responding. Myer

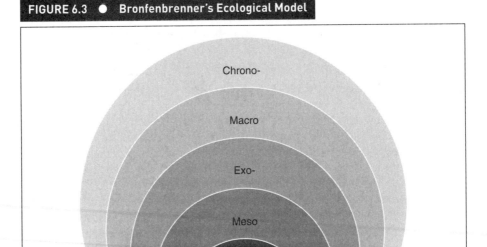

FIGURE 6.3 ● Bronfenbrenner's Ecological Model

and Moore synthesized their theory into a succinct formula where the impact of a crisis is a function of interaction of individual variables mediated by time.

$$\text{IMPACT} = \frac{f(\text{proximity, reaction, relationship, change})}{\text{time}}$$

Recall Myer and Moore's (2006) model was detailed in Chapter 2. Finally, in the ESC model, individuals engage and construct their environments; the environment is not static, rather it is the result of individuals' actions and inactions. This concept holds true for individuals and groups within the community.

Bronfenbrenner based his work on Lewin's (1935) theory of psychological fields, which later was dubbed *field theory*. Lewin investigated the interaction pattern between an individual and the total environment or field and change theory (unfreezing change refreeze). There are five nested systems within the environment: the micro, meso, exo, macro, and chrono. The *micro*-system is the immediate environment of the individual including family members—defined by culture not biology—and intimates. With respect to the aftermath of disaster, individuals would be most likely to find the greatest safety at this level. Interpersonal interactions are typically deep, meaningful, in close proximity, and vary from harmonious to conflicted. Myer and Moore (2006) detailed that actions and interactions post-disaster in the micro-system may enhance or worsen the crisis.

The direction, nature, and intensity of individuals' response to the aftermath of the disaster are contingent upon their proximity, relationship to, appraisal, and perceptions of the event. Recall the progression of emotional responding presented earlier in the chapter; those in the hero phase are most likely to rescue individuals in their micro-system first, followed by individuals in the meso-system. The *meso*-system includes all the interactions, linkages, connections, and elements of the micro-system and extends the environment to work, school, religious, and recreational settings. The extension and interactions of communication between the micro-, exo-, and macro-systems allow for increased and differentiated interactions and produce growth or conflict. In terms of disaster and its aftereffects, the communication channels contained in the meso-system must ensure dependable or redundant, clear, efficient communications are shared or transmitted in multiple languages across multiple platforms from an interdisciplinary group of emergency responders to individuals and their communities, the exo-system.

For Bronfenbrenner (2008/1994) the *exo*-system included linkages and processes between two or more individuals, groups, institutions, and settings that are further removed from those engaged in the micro-system. In a disaster, this may include local, regional, or state relief agency personnel and services. For the individual disaster survivor, the quality of communications between the exo-, meso-, and micro-systems are critical and affect individuals' appraisal and perceptions of the disaster's aftermath. One need only consider the differences in the immediate post-disaster experiences of Hurricane Katrina survivors relocated to the New Orleans Superdome to those who reside in the French Quarter—much of which was not flooded. For individuals, engagement in DHM services provided at this level are critical as the risk of PTSD has been repeatedly shown to be associated with severity of exposure to the disaster across numerous studies (Green et al. 1990, 1994; Joseph, Yule, Williams, & Hodgkinson, 1994; Sungur & Kaya, 2001; Galea et al. 2002; Neria, Gross, Marshall, & Susser, 2006).

On a community level, the aforementioned disaster response plan resides in this level and is at its best when it is integrated horizontally across a broad representation of community agencies (e.g., police, fire, hospitals, media, behavioral health centers, relief agencies, utilities and sanitation and water plants, cellular providers, educational institutions, etc.) and vertically from local to state to federal levels within the same category (local/state/federal law enforcement organizations). The *macro*-system encompasses the total context in which individuals live (Bronfenbrenner, 1995). This includes the intersection of norms, beliefs, ways of being, laws, mores, customs, rituals, practices, behaviors, activities, and interests. In a disaster, the macro-system expands beyond the family community, state, or region to the nation and its resources. For example, consider the October 1, 2017 mass shooting in Las Vegas, Nevada, where 59 were killed and 851 were injured. This human-initiated disaster initially overwhelmed local and regional emergency responders. Advanced disaster planning allowed Las Vegas officials to rely on the Rescue Tasks Forces that were developed out of the Multiple Assault Counter-Terrorism Action Capabilities. National organizations, such as ARC, NOVA, and International Association of Fire Fighters, responded with aid and support for survivors and first responders. James and Gilliland (2017) note the importance of the macro-level because disaster by their nature frequently overwhelm a community's ability to marshal sufficient resources and impact the national consciousness. The access to and the magnitude of federal-level resources assists individuals' and communities' transition from an acute rescue phase to taking stock and initial recovery. The final ecological system is the *chrono*-system. According to Bronfenbrenner (1995), it involves the configuration, nature, consistency, and change of individual and societal events over time as well as contextual factors. In a sense, it extends the environment into a third dimension (Bronfenbrenner, 2008/1994), time. In DMH, clinicians address individual, family, small group, and community sufferings that are experienced in both acute and chronic progressions. Contextualizing post-disaster traumatic responding through the lens of the chrono-system allows clinicians to identify the progression of individual and community emotional responding (recall Figure 6.2) as well as the progression of individual sequelae. Chapter 7 presents the knowledge, skills, and dispositions for the clinician across the professional lifespan including assessments for those affected by disaster. It is our hope you integrate the knowledge from these chapters into your understanding of the spectrum of crisis, trauma, and disaster to advance your services to clients and for your own well-being.

Summary

Disaster mental counseling builds on the concepts and techniques found in crisis and trauma-informed counseling. It is also emerging as a specialty, with distinct theoretical understandings, models, and research base. The three categories of disaster present individuals, groups, and communities a host of miseries and amazing opportunities for collaboration and connection. Set in an ecological context, community-based responding incorporates the best of systemic planning, integration of helping professions, and delivery of services.

Extended Learning Exercises

Professional Development

Disaster mental health counseling has its roots in preparation. Your readiness to serve in this role demands that you are familiar with the systems in your community, region, and state. Starting with your city or county, identify the local emergency preparedness office and confirm the range of services provided. Next conduct the same inquiry at the state level. With each inquiry, determine the roles and responsibilities of providers. What are they for clinicians? Complete this exercise by constructing a professional development plan that addresses the education, experience, and involvement you need to become a DMH clinician.

Advocacy

Contact your local office of emergency preparedness and ask for their plan for your community. As you examine the plan, notice the location of resources like fire stations, hospitals, police stations, etc., in your community relative to the population and the demographics of the population. What do you notice? Are there redundant services in some areas and a scarcity in others? How does the plan account for those with vulnerabilities or special populations? Once you have a sense of the plan's strength and weakness, do something about it—raise the issue in class, write a letter, and seek to change the plan. Advocacy takes many forms . . . you can choose yours.

Reflection

What professional skills and dispositions do you possess, or can you develop, that would contribute to your success as a DMH clinician? What personal ones? What personal or professional factors might impede your success? Make a list of these factors and evaluate them relative to your current training and experience and determine what if any you wish to address? How will you address them? What will demonstrate your success?

Additional Resources

Emergency Planning—templates, examples and resources: http://www.emergency-response-planning.com/blog/bid/72134/The-Evolution-of-Emergency-Management-and-Disaster-Response

Disaster Relief/Emergency Response

American Red Cross: http://www.redcross.org/

Centers for Disease Control (CDC): https://stacks.cdc.gov/welcome

Doctors without Borders: https://www.doctorswithoutborders.org/

International Red Cross and Red Crescent Societies: https://www.icrc.org/

International Critical Incident Stress Foundation: https://icisf.org/

Mercy Corps: https://www.mercycorps.org/

National Organization for Victim Assistance (NOVA): https://www.trynova.org/crisis-response-program/

Ready.Gov: Plan Ahead for Disaster: https://www.ready.gov/

Disaster Relief/Emergency Educational Organizations

Substance Abuse and Mental Health Services Administration: https://www.samhsa.gov/

Disaster Assistance Federal Student Aid: https://studentaid.ed.gov/sa/about/announcements/disaster

Salvation Army: https://disaster.salvationarmyusa.org/training/

Caring for Those Affected by Disaster

McFarlane and Norris (2006) defined a disaster as a "potentially traumatic event that is collectively experienced, has an acute onset and is time delimited . . . and may be attributed to natural, technological, or human causes" (p. 4). Individuals affected by natural disaster, conditions of war, and other catastrophic conditions need immediate and, at times, long-term therapeutic care. Much like crises and traumas, one's experience of a disaster is influenced by its origin or type, scope or extent of impact, scale or severity, duration, and individual appraisal of threat. Unlike crises and trauma, disaster are, as McFarlane and Norris (2006) noted, collectively experienced, and simultaneously impact members of a community (Bowman & Roysircar, 2011) rather than being primarily experienced by an individual. In a disaster, all are affected, and the consequences extend to, among, and between individuals in a community. Consequently, we order our focus from the community and group to individual experiences of nature-, human- and technology-initiated disaster.

Learning Objectives

After reading this chapter and participating in the extended learning exercises provided, you will be able to

- Distinguish crisis, trauma, and disaster by unique and common features
- Comprehend early- and mid-stage disaster mental health (DMH) interventions
- Understand in-depth DMH interventions
- Know basic assessment procedures and protocols related to DMH counseling
- Consider a variety of techniques to clinical vignettes

The Counselor's Toolkit

The DMH *Toolkit* presented in this chapter focuses on the treatment of communities, groups, and individuals suffering from the devastation of a disaster. Many of the skills, awareness, and techniques used in DMH are identical to those used in a crisis or trauma and thus are referred to but are not repeated here. Rather, we extend your knowledge and awareness related to DHM thorough the presentation of early and mid-stage as well as in-depth (DMH) interventions and DMH resources.

Knowledge

According to Kanel (2012), "Disaster mental health is a crisis intervention method that stabilizes, supports and normalizes people in an effort to strengthen their coping abilities, and hopefully, prevent long-term damage such as PTSD, substance abuse, depression, and family and relationship problems. It is not meant to be treatment" (p. 21). A disaster is characterized as a *traumatic crisis event* regardless of its origin. Disaster occur without warning, are devastating to individuals and communities, and typically require a large-scale response. To assist communities, local, state, and regional response networks like the American Red Cross Disaster Mental Health Services, Medical Reserve Corps, and National Center for Posttraumatic Stress Disorder react to the disaster site with professional staff and trained volunteers.

The Bureau of Justice Statistics (2016) found that approximately 5.7 million people were violently traumatized in 2016. According to Bromet et al. (2016), the results of a 24-country survey discovered that 70% of participants ($N = 68,000$) reported exposure to a traumatic event and over 30% were exposed to four or more. Those exposed to a disaster had a greater likelihood of developing PTSD and were at a higher risk that premorbid mood disorders would reemerge with higher acuity (Mitchell, Griffin, Stewart, & Loba, 2004). Along with the increase chances of worsening mental health, individuals' basic needs, post-disaster, may be severely degraded due to widespread destruction and suffering, loss of life, food insecurity, and homelessness. For example, large-scale, nature-initiated disaster like Hurricane Irma, Harvey, or Katrina resulted in numerous fatalities, countless injured, and scores in unsafe conditions without shelter, food, or potable water. The aftermath of these disaster temporarily or permanently displaced many evacuees from their homes. As you can imagine, the lack of safety and security resulting from one's temporary displacement or permanent homelessness, increases a survivor's risk of trauma and psychological disruptions or disorders (Watson, Brymer, & Bonanno, 2011).

Early and Mid-Stage Disaster Mental Health Interventions

Bonanno, Westphal, and Mancini (2011) stated most individuals that encounter a disaster will not need or benefit from counseling intervention. Furthermore, there is some evidence indicating that they may be harmed by therapeutic interventions since it interrupts their natural ability to cope (Watson, Brymer, & Bonanno, 2011).

This section provides an overview of disaster interventions, techniques, and guiding principles, supported by pertinent examples.

During disaster response efforts, clinicians should not work outside of their professional competency and training. Disaster environments are initially chaotic and disorganized. Many individuals have multiple, serious, and immediate needs. Recalling our focus on prepotent needs within the affected community, some individuals will seek first to satisfy physiological needs—food, shelter, and water, while others seek safety and security. Most will do this through social collaboration and consultation discussed in Chapter 2. In a DMH context, the response to basic needs is provided by local, regional, and national emergency response teams or networks of which you may be a member. Attainment of psychological and self-fulfillment needs occurs post disaster. It is absolutely essential for DMH clinicians to know and utilize an effective triage strategy to align individual's needs with available resources. Again, much of the work in DMH is triage, informal assessment, connection with basic services, and post-disaster counseling interventions look more like crisis- or trauma-informed counseling.

Not everyone is qualified to become a DMH clinician or responder. For example, the American Red Cross (ARC) eligibility requirements for DMH volunteers include registering as a volunteer, completing the health screen and background check, attending ARC volunteer and psychological first aid (PFA) training, possession of master's degree or higher from a mental health profession (e.g., professional counselors, social workers, psychologists, psychiatrist, school counselors/psychologists) and current state professional licensure. You will need to determine your personal and professional readiness to serve as volunteer or DMH volunteer in the aftermath of a disaster. If you possess the desire and abilities to function in service to others under conditions of ambiguity, chaos, and devastation, DMH may be your calling. Alternatively, clients and communities need clinicians with crisis and trauma intervention knowledge and skills to address post-disaster functioning and recovery.

Resiliency, Protective Factors, and Risk Factors

Prior to discussing disaster specific skills, techniques, and principles, it is important for you to gain foundational knowledge related to disaster survivor's traits, behaviors, and experiences associated with resiliency, protective, and risk factors. In the throes of a disaster, one does not have time to formally assess those impacted, however knowledgeable DMH clinicians notice themes in survivors' behaviors, responses, and reactions that inform their work. Watson, Brymer, and Bonanno (2011) describe common traits of resilient individuals believed to serve as protective factors and vulnerabilities of underlying risk factors.

Risk Factors

Their analysis of the DMH literature points to a relationship between the severity of exposure and the level of post-disaster stressors as predictors of persistent post-DMH disturbances like anxiety, irritability, and hypervigilance. Additional risk factors associated with the development or exacerbation of mental illness post-disaster include: severe exposure, living in a traumatized community, being female, trauma in childhood, preexisting mental health issues, and low social support being evacuated or displaced from one's home (Watson, Brymer, & Bonanno, 2011). For example, consider the residents of New Orleans. Their lives and homes were shattered by Hurricane Katrina, devastated by delayed or nonexistent emergency response, and degraded by the weight of the traumatic event, persistent unmet needs, and lack of resources. Sastry and Van Landingham's (2009) examination of New Orleans residents who survived Katrina found prevalence rates for mental illness in excess of those found in other disaster. The prevalence of mental illness remained high in the year following Hurricane Katrina, in contrast to the pattern found after other disaster. They "determined that nearly 40% had probable mental illness 1 year after the storm, and half of these illnesses were classified as severe" (p. S730). Sastry and Van Landingham's findings highlight the importance of acknowledging and accounting for the intersections between social injustices and higher rates of death and serious mental illness. They note the

> major reason for the higher levels of serious mental illness (SMI) among Blacks in New Orleans in the aftermath of Hurricane Katrina was that they were much more likely to have their dwelling in the city severely damaged or destroyed. The likelihood of having a home damaged or destroyed by Katrina was significantly ($P< .01$) higher for Blacks in the sample (81%) compared with Whites (47%). (p. S729)

In this study, SMIs were present when the respondent met the criteria of at least one anxiety or mood disorder based on *Diagnostic and Statistical Manual of Mental Disorders, Fourth Edition* (*DSM–IV*) criteria and reported severe impairment within the past 25 to 30 days.

Resiliency and Protective Factors

Common resiliency factors for those exposed to disaster are similar to the ones described for individuals experiencing crisis or trauma. They include a secure attachment, little to no history of significant trauma, optimistic attributional style, internal locus of control, sense of humor, impulse control, strong role models, positive social skills, and emotional sustenance. Milojev, Osborne, and Sibley (2014) examined the stability of the Big Six personality traits in a sample of 3,914 New Zealanders affected by the Christchurch earthquake. The Big Six traits are emotional stability, extraversion, openness, conscientiousness, honesty-humility, and agreeableness. Their findings indicate that personality traits were resilient over a two-year test–retest time frame. The one exception was a minor decrease in emotional stability which may signal vulnerability to depression and anxiety for some respondents.

Protective factors like resiliency are not unique to exposure to a disaster. Watson et al. (2011) indicated positive predisaster functioning, religion or spirituality, effective coping skills, advanced education, being male, and limited experience with trauma and loss served as protective factors. The capacity for hope and optimism, agreeableness, emotional stability, and self-efficacy related to coping skills are also considered individual protective factors (Bosmans & Van der Velden, 2015; Bosmans, Benight, Knaap, Winkel, & Velden, 2013; Cherry et al., 2015). Individual adaptive skills such as application of flexible, contextualized coping skills, seeking social support, positive reframing after the disaster, and meaning making (Henslee et al., 2015; Shing, Jayawickreme, & Waugh, 2016) help those recovering from disaster take action and experience personal agency.

Protective factors also extend to our social groups and communities. Being connected with others allows individuals to reduce feelings of isolation, share recovery and coping information, be accepted and understood by those who have a common experience or traumatic bond, and receive group support. In communities, social connectedness extends to looking out for others, particularly the elderly or those with limited mobility or cognitive impairments and advocacy for those who may not have access to decision makers. Watson et al. (2011) examined the literature on community resiliency and found that at the community level, resiliency is associated with financial stability, dependable emergency responding and relief, and effective communication. Functioning communities with equitable distribution of wealth; vibrant economies; trusted, competent leadership and communication; and a sense of place are more resilient than their peers who lack these factors.

Triage

We presented the concept and process of triage in multiple chapters. Consequently, in this chapter, we describe unique elements of triage associated with DMH. In 2014, approximately 45% of U.S. citizens with a diagnosable mental condition sought professional treatment (SAMHSA, 2014). More than half of those identified as needing professional treatment did not seek it. If not provided with appropriate direction, disaster survivors may not be aware or choose proper services. Like crisis and trauma, the more readily one addresses their reaction to and impact of a disaster event and returns to previous functioning, the lower the probability that they will develop more persistent symptoms or psychological disorders.

Particular to DMH, effective triage is of the utmost importance. Some may be inclined to engage those afflicted in critical incident stress debriefing (CISD). As discussed in Chapter 4, CISD is a group intervention typically provided after the acute phase of a crisis or disaster event. Studies have demonstrated that psychological debriefing is contraindicated in DMH, ineffective in preventing or treating PTSD, and in some cases, significantly worsened client's symptoms (Rose, Bisson, Churchill, & Wessely, 2002). Effective triage could help identify those with worsening symptoms and refer them for longer-term psychological or psychiatric services. Triage assists in helping individuals injured (physically and psychologically) find the most appropriate type and level of care.

According to Linzer, Sweifach, and Heft-LaPorte (2008), DMH triage is the most efficient process to prioritize survivors' needs and align them with scarce resources. As an approach, mental health triage is, at its core, the stewardship of needed resources. Triage differs from most mental health programs providing referrals in that it is preceded by an active screen and referral pre-established services or providers with a high probability of resolving the client's need. Within a DMH context, triage helps those affected by the disaster to return as quickly as possible to normal functioning and self-sufficiency. Efficient triaging also serves others as more individuals are responded to and can move through the system of care with fewer barriers.

Birch and Martin (1985) developed a three-pronged approach to DMH triage. The three groups are the *referral*, *return*, and *retain* groups. The *referral* group is comprised of those not expected to respond to immediate intervention. Members of this group include those with long-standing mental health concerns, homeless individuals, and those who are intoxicated. They receive care coordination and are referred to appropriate community resources. The *return* group is populated with individuals who demonstrate minor or moderate mental health concerns which do not warrant hospitalization. These individuals may be treated with emergency medication, brief therapy, and a referral to a community mental health center. The *retain* group consisted of individuals who were considered unsafe to self and others or suffering from acute psychiatric classification and may be experiencing hallucinations or delusions. These individuals are hospitalized for evaluation and, where appropriate, treated.

Psychological First Aid

North and Pfefferbaum (2013) assert that crisis counseling "shares many fundamental elements with psychological first aid" and "can be delivered to individuals or groups to help survivors understand their reactions, enhance coping, consider options, and connect with other services" (p. 514). These authors and others (Allen et al., 2010) recognize psychological first aid (PFA) as an integral and early intervention in the aftermath of a disaster. Recall that the goal of PFA is to create human connection in a compassionate and nonintrusive manner. According to Hobfoll et al. (2007), PFA, as it relates to DMH, is centered on five principles: (a) instilling hope; (b) promoting connectedness; (c) instilling a sense of self and community efficacy; (d) creating a calming atmosphere; and (e) promoting a sense of safety.

While PFA offers a myriad of interventions it is important to understand that these are considered *early DMH interventions* utilized by first responders and mental health providers alike. PFA utilizes clear and effective communication skills through a sequential series of actions: *contact and engagement, safety and comfort, stabilization, information gathering, practical assistance, connection with social supports, information on coping, and linkage with collaborative services* (Ruzek et al., 2007). Although presented in Chapter 2, to reduce repetition, we present a brief description of each action along with example statements from the DMH clinician. For a complete review of PFA, please review the most recent edition of *Psychological First Aid Field Operations Guide*; the definitions and examples below are drawn from the second edition (Brymer et al., 2006).

Contact and Engagement

The DMH clinician makes contact and engages survivors in an empathic and respectful manner to increase the survivor's openness to help. DMH clinicians do not assume the individual wants or needs help. For example: *DMH Clinician:* "Hello, my name is Bryan. I am here to help you find food, shelter, and resources.

I can also be a safe person to share your thoughts with. If you need help, I'm here to listen." Or *DMH Clinician*: "You can decide whether or not you want help, and if you want help, what kind you want. If you're interested, we have blankets, food, and we have nurses on hand."

Safety and Supports

The goal of this step is to offer emotional and physical safety and comfort. For example: *DMH Clinician:* "I know you are looking for your dog. Please stay calm and maintain significant distance from the river." "Please notice the electric wires in front of you. If you touch them you will be electrocuted, and it could kill you." Or *DMH Clinician:* "There is a bomb shelter right there. Please return to it and stay in the shelter until the siren stops."

Stabilization

Stabilization asks the DMH clinician to demonstrate emotionally calming behaviors and to orient survivors. This includes a calm but firm vocal tone, awareness of physical gestures, and calm clear directives spoken directly to individuals. Those responding to a disaster experience intense emotions like tearfulness, anger, or confusion. Extreme reactions like numbing, pervasive anxiety, state switching, and hyperarousal are not. Those exhibiting intense emotions typically respond well to a clinician who is calm, physically and emotionally present, in close proximity, and who possesses helpful information. *DMH Clinician:* "You look worried and a bit frantic. What do you typically do to calm yourself?" Or *DMH Clinician*: "I know you're very frightened; however, in order to help you we need to know the last time you saw your daughter. Take a few deep breaths and try to remember when you lost sight of her."

Information Gathering

In this step, the DMH clinician helps individuals access services and resources in line with their needs. DMH clinicians align needs and services based on information from the triage process and additional information gathered from the client. *DMH Clinician:* "I understand you've been through a lot. What do you and your family need first to feel safe and secure? What information about services, resources, or earthquakes do you need?" *DMH Clinician:* "What happened to you and your family? Are your children safe? Do you need housing or shelter information?"

Practical Assistance

Practical assistance is delivered in a positive, empowering, and hopeful manner. Due to the nature of disaster events, you communicate in a more direct and instructive manner. *DMH Clinician:* "I understand your number one goal is finding your family; however, let's get to safety first, this area is not secure." Or *DMH Clinician:* "Bob, it appears that your leg is broken. I'm going to call an EMT.

They will stabilize your injury. Once that's done, we'll work on reconnecting you with your wife." Or *DMH Clinician:* "Amit, your head is bleeding. Sit down and put this compress on it. I will get the nurse."

Connection With Social Supports

Throughout this text we have discussed the importance of social connection or support for those affected by crisis, trauma, or disaster. Connecting those affected to supportive persons, family, or social services is key to recovery. *DMH Clinician:* "I understand that talking about your experience is tough. However, if you open up about how you feel, it tells others it is 'okay' to talk about the shooting. Others in the family may start feeling safe in doing the same." "No doubt, talking about the wildfire seems like complaining, yet *not* talking about makes it seem like it never happened. I think the kids need to talk about being homeless and what is going to happen to the horses and rabbits." Or *DMH Clinician:* "Johnny, I want to thank you for reaching out to your dad for help. The more you can communicate your needs, the sooner you may start feeling better."

Information on Coping

DMH clinicians provide individually tailored coping information to assist individuals in overcoming intense emotional experiences and returning to adaptive functioning. *DMH Clinician:* "Veronica, what you describe sounds like flashbacks. Often, when one has a traumatic experience, like watching your neighbors' house explode in the tornado, they have a strong emotional and physiological reaction to sights or sounds that remind of them of the event. Like just now, the thunder and gust of wind took you back to this morning's tragedy. Let's do a deep breathing exercise. I will show you how." Or *DMH Clinician:* "Before the shooting, what did you do to reduce your anxiety besides drink until you were drunk? Drinking may let you feel numb for a moment, but it causes you a host of other miseries. Tell me what worked before. Let's see if we can have you take one step in that direction."

Linking With Collaborative Services

The previous steps have helped the individual feel safe and emotionally supported, address their basic needs, begin the process of stabilization, and consider how to reorder their life. In this final step, the DMH clinician transitions the client to ongoing services and care for the near term. *DMH Clinician:* "It sounds like you've found housing for you and the kids through next weekend. I have located longer-term housing options that you may wish to contact. Also, have you made contact with the food bank?" *DMH Clinician:* "Mike, it sounds like you're not able to sleep and you are having significant issues with your memory. I am going to provide a list of clinicians with trauma expertise. These individuals are all local and have openings for new clients." Birkhead and Vermuelen (2018) put it best, "Helping survivors feel safe, reducing stress-related symptoms, and fostering positive coping strategies enable responders to better meet survivors' basic needs and ensure their linkage to critical resources and social support" (p. S381).

The Five Essential Elements

Hobfoll et al. (2007) described five empirically based DMH intervention principles in their landmark article, "Five Essential Elements of Immediate and Mid-Term Mass Trauma Intervention: Empirical Evidence." The authors conceptualize five principles of early and mid-stage DMH interventions that promote "a sense of safety, calming, a sense of self and community efficacy, connectedness, and hope" (p. 284).

Safety

Those who have survived a disaster feel unsafe and as if their lives are at continued risk. They fear for the safety of their family and often experience fight, flight, or freeze reactions. According to Balaban et al. (2005), the frequent psychophysiological and neurobiological reactions that disaster survivors experience can eventually lead to mental health disorders, including PTSD, acute stress disorder, anxiety, somatization, sleep disturbances, and depression. Hobfoll et al. (2007) reported that after survivors find initial safety, locate their family members, and meet their basic needs, DMH clinicians can employ a variety of techniques to help them extend their sense of safety. Techniques may include breathing retraining, deep muscle relaxation, yoga, mindfulness meditation, and music (Bernstein & Borkovec, 1973; Carlson, Speca, Patel, & Goodey, 2003; Foa & Rothbaum, 1998). Each of these activities is designed to help clients regain a measure of control over their reactions, relaxation, and awareness.

While relaxation, mindfulness, yoga, and breathing exercises are useful after the acute phase, DMH clinicians may not have an adequate amount of time or staff, or have staff with the appropriate level of expertise for these interventions.

DMH clinicians consider the physical and psychological safety of survivors. Techniques associated with this element are maintaining a calm and compassionate tone of voice to demonstrate care and concern. Where appropriate, the therapeutic dialogue focuses and refocuses on safety and the reduction of immediate threats. This means you work with clients to limit their exposure to graphic accounts of the disaster online, in the news, or in their social media feeds. Helping the client to use grounding techniques highlights their relative safely, initiates coping skills and adaptive cognitions or self-talk (Hobfoll et al., 2007).

Calming

The effects of initial trauma exposure can be intense and range from heightened levels of arousal to numbing and state switching. Consequently, the second intervention principle is calming those affected by disaster. According to Hobfoll et al. (2007), frightening levels of arousal dominate a survivor's psyche following the aftermath of a disaster. This intense emotional state contributes to panic attacks, dissociation, PTSD, agitation, depression, somatic problems, and long-term complex trauma (Bryant, Moulds, Guthrie, & Nixon, 2003; Hobfoll et al., 2007). Interventions designed to aid the client in self-soothing strategies to calm themselves are stress inoculation training, cognitive behavioral therapy, and enhancing survivors coping ability through self-talk, positive thinking, thought stopping, and deep muscle relaxation (Hembree & Foa, 2000; Meichenbaum, 1974).

DMH clinicians responding to catastrophe focus on engaging the response team, receiving their assignment, and beginning the process of triage. Interventions address immediate concerns, safety, and stabilization. DMH clinicians are prepared to swiftly assess survivors' needs, apply the appropriate intervention, or disseminate information and assess the outcome. Survivors need factual and accurate information to resolve immediate concerns. DMH clinicians and first responders clearly describe the status of the disaster, location, and well-being of family members, if known, and the location and staging of relief services—food, phone banks, or temporary housing. In addition, large-scale community outreach and education efforts are recommended. Succinct psychoeducation materials provide common short-term survivor reactions to the disaster event, tips on anxiety management, understanding of the role of media exposure in survivor's recovery, and warning signs of persistent distress and how to access professional help. As much as possible, after the acute phase of a disaster, those affected should be encouraged to engage in uplifting activities not associated with the disaster (Hobfoll et al., 2007).

Self and Community Efficacy

The third principle is the promotion of a sense of self and community efficacy (Hobfoll et al., 2007). It is helpful for those affected by disaster to reclaim their sense of self-efficacy and control over their environment. Self-efficacy is the belief that one's action will lead to a particular outcome (Bandura, 1997; Benight & Bandura, 2004). Benight and Harper (2002) add that in addition to a sense of efficacy, it is important that survivors believe they can cope with the catastrophe. Hobfoll et al. (2007) promote the utilization of individual and group cognitive behavioral therapy (CBT) to enhance the individual and community sense of efficacy following a disaster.

The shock, trauma, and destruction of a community, can have an enormous impact on the individual and community-based self-efficacy. Individual efficacy can be enhanced through taking stock of and reversing the loss cycle. Implementing and encouraging individuals to engage in community activities, including mourning and remembrance rituals, working with local helpers, survivor support groups, and religious activities begin to address the cycle of loss. Furthermore, self-efficacy is enhanced when survivors feel they have a voice in the collective healing of the community. Involvement in activities such as citizen decision making related to the needs, public policy, and restoration of important community resources (e.g., schools) demonstrates positive change. Lastly, individuals and community members experience increased self-esteem when preventative efforts transform into disaster and community vocational skills training (e.g., first aid, CPR, EMT; Hobfoll et al., 2007).

Connectedness

Attaining and maintaining social support from family, friends, professionals, and fellow disaster survivors is of critical importance. These relationships and connections provide survivors emotional support, information, and resources.

Attaining social support greatly enhances emotional well-being and can have a healing effect on individuals with PTSD (Solomon, Mikulincer, & Hobfoll, 1986). Some DMH clinicians function, in part, as emergency care coordinators. They provide up-to-date lists of resources, their location, and hours of operation. Resources include local shelters, food pantries, medical and mental health providers, religious services, child and elder care, disability services, and police (Hobfoll et al., 2007). Following a disaster, those affected may choose to or may become isolated. DMH clinicians assess survivors' needs and preference for connection, offer opportunities, describe the benefits of participation, and encourage engagement with service agencies and resources.

Hope

The fifth and final principle is instilling hope. It may seem like common sense that survivors of a disaster would achieve better outcomes if they have a sense of hope and optimism about their future. According to Saul (2013), survivors engage in a meaning-making process that frames their perceptions and reactions to the disaster event. If the meaning they make is extremely negative—shattered worldview or a sense of doom—it can degrade their overall mental wellness. Endless news cycles, graphic details, rumors, social media, and inaccurate information trigger emotions recollection and fears related to the disaster and have a profound effect on survivors' outlook. The key is to create consistent, honest, and authentic meanings within the affected community that contextualize survivors' experience. Meanings attributed to the event are individual and collective, are a form of adaptation, and when affirming limit, the worsening of negative symptomology and subsequent crises (Hobfoll et al., 2007).

For disaster survivors, hope is established when their basic needs are met and they are linked with essential services. Thorough risk assessment, setting positive goals, reducing self-blame, and enhancing problem-solving efforts are of the utmost importance (Hobfoll et al., 2007). Infrastructure that helps survivors reclaim their lives is essential. Disaster survivors need assistance with housing, employment, relocation, finding household necessities, rebuilding destroyed possessions, and understanding the bureaucratic process related to insurance reimbursement and state and federal relief programs. It is of the utmost importance that local stakeholders develop systems that empower traumatized survivors' recovery from the acute phase of a disaster and establish a path to restore their lives and livelihoods.

In-Depth Disaster Mental Health Interventions

While it is helpful to have an understanding of in-depth mental health procedures, DMH clinicians possess specific skills. Rosenfeld, Caye, Lahad, and Gurwitch (2010) indicated DMH clinicians attend to and empathize with the survivor's perception of the experience. They accept that survivors express their post-disaster fear, anger, and confusion in different ways. DMH clinicians provide an informal assessment of disaster-related stressors—temporary homelessness, food insecurity, and lack of privacy; provide social support for adaptive coping methods naturally employed by the survivor and their family; address traumatic responding; and facilitate the grief and mourning process, where relevant. The following section describes in-depth support related to the survivor's recovery. As noted earlier, these interventions are applied post-event.

Stress Inoculation Training

Two in-depth behavioral approaches for the management of anxiety associated with disaster-related trauma include stress inoculation training (SIT) and exposure therapy. Behavioral approaches such as these are typically time-sensitive interventions and provide direct coping skill instruction through cognitive restructuring, relaxation training, thought stopping, and positive self-talk. Donald Meichenbaum (1974) created SIT as a program to manage trauma-related anxiety and was initially empirically investigated in the treatment of rape victims (Veronen & Kilpatrick, 1983). Stress inoculation training is a three-phase treatment approach that begins with *conceptualization and education* followed by *skill acquisition and rehearsal* and concludes with *application and follow through*. In the conceptualization and education phase, clients are taught the potential reasons they may be experiencing distress, hyperarousal, hypervigilance, anxiety, or flashbacks and what may occur if the symptoms and their associations are not addressed or are partially addressed. For example, you might discuss the physical reactions to a disaster event like increased heart rate, anxiety, confusion, avoidance, and the release of hormones in preparation to respond. Nontechnical descriptions of the function and purpose of the sympathetic and parasympathetic nervous systems relative to a perceived threat informs clients how their bodily systems are activated to avoid danger (sympathetic) and to protect them from constant arousal and turmoil (parasympathetic).

During the second phase of SIT, the client learns stress inoculation skills and rehearses them. They develop a repertoire of specific coping skills to reduce disaster-based symptoms and apply general skills to enhance daily task performance. Common coping activities and skills include guided imagery, role play, self-talk, and thought stopping (Saunders, Driskell, Johnston, & Salas, 1996; Stebnicki, 2017). The final phase, application and follow through, asks the client to practice and transfer the recently learned skills into the real world. They are encouraged to apply the new skills gradually, across aspects of their daily life (Saunders, Driskell, Johnston, & Salas, 1996).

Exposure Therapy

Exposure therapy, discussed in Chapter 4, is used by itself or combined with other therapeutic techniques. For example, trauma-focused cognitive behavioral therapy (TF-CBT), prolonged exposure therapy, and CBT incorporate elements of exposure therapy (Zoellner et al., 2011). For the purpose of this chapter, we focus on in vivo exposure therapy and imaginal exposure therapy.

According to Zoellner et al. (2011), "Imaginal and in vivo exposure are the primary tool in reducing client avoidance of memories, emotions, and situations and in correcting unhelpful thoughts and beliefs about the self, others, and the world that maintain PTSD" (p. 301). In vivo exposure asks clients to create a fear hierarchy from least feared to most feared events. In DMH, this means the survivor and clinician determine situations the survivor avoids due to residual post-disaster trauma. With the clinician, the client identifies and practices several techniques to reduce their anxiety like focused breathing, deep breathing, or affirming self-talk. The client engages the least feared event out in the world. When anxiety or distress emerges, they practice anxiety-reducing technique to combat and eventually master their anxiety. Relaxation is incompatible with distress. The client progressively works up the hierarchy until the most feared or avoided events are approached and mastered and feelings of anxiety remit. Imaginal exposure is the repeated and detailed exploration of traumatic stimuli within the survivor's imagination. Similar to in vivo exposure, distressing events are rank ordered and paired with relaxation techniques. Imaginal exposure typically takes place in the clinician's office during a 30- to 40-minute session. The DMH clinician asks the client to remember the distressing narrative in a comprehensive and thorough manner, reflecting on all five senses. The narrative is repeated multiple times and anxiety-reducing techniques are applied to address emerging anxiety. Following imaginal exposure, the DMH clinician processes the client's experience and anxiety reduction. Over time, clients manage and master their distress related to disaster events.

Grief Counseling

According to *The Human Cost of Natural Disaster: A Global Perspective* (Center for Behavioral Health Statistics and Quality, 2015) report "Between 1994 and 2013, EM-DAT recorded 6,873 natural disaster worldwide, which claimed 1.35 million lives or almost 68,000 lives on average each year. In addition, 218 million people were affected by natural disaster on average per annum during this 20-year period" (p. 7). Nature-initiated disaster cause a significant death toll. According to James and Gilliland (2017), disaster-based traumatic death increases the frequency of complicated grieving. The American Psychiatric Association's (2013) *Diagnostic and Statistical Manual 5th Edition (DSM–5)* includes a section on "Conditions for Further Study." Within this section is a proposed future disorder entitled Persistent Complex Bereavement Disorder (PCBD). The proposed PCBD criteria includes a deep desire to be united with the deceased individual to the extent that it causes physical or emotional suffering, obsession with the departed, and intrusive recurring images of the death, including 13 additional symptoms:

1. Difficulty accepting the individual is dead

2. Persistent yearning

3. Disbelief that the individual is dead

4. Bitterness or anger over the loss

5. Maladaptive appraisals about oneself in relation to the deceased or the death

6. Excessive avoidance of reminders of the deceased

7. Avoidance of reminders of the deceased

8. Desire to die in order to be close with the deceased

9. Mistrust of others

10. Feel isolated

11. Thought that life has no meaning

12. Loss of interest in usual activities

13. Diminished sense of identity

Overall, this emerging disorder brings much-needed attention to a phenomenon that DMH clinicians frequently encounter, but never knew how to identify.

Grief counseling has a long history in the helping professions. Traditionally, clinicians relied on phase or stage models to understand the grieving process; however, recently grief is viewed as a unique experience. It is important to acknowledge the unique elements of the grieving process that each individual experiences. Stage theories, like Kubler-Ross's (1969) five stages,—denial, anger, bargaining, depression, and acceptance—were once commonly referenced yet are empirically unsupported and do not fit the experience of many.

Beyond stage and phase models, clinicians can rely on models associated with particular theoretical orientations. A few common models for grief counseling include attachment theory (Stroebe, 2002), adaptive grieving styles (Doughty, 2009), dual process model (Servaty-Seib, 2004), and constructivism (Neimeyer, Prigerson, & Davies, 2002). In regard to the efficacious treatment of prolonged grief disorder (PGD), a meta-analysis of controlled and randomized trials of counseling styles for adults with PGD revealed that the most effective treatment modality for reducing PGD symptomology was cognitive behavioral grief-targeted interventions (Wittouck, Van Autreve, De Jaegere, Portzky, & van Heeringen, 2011).

Given the wide variety of interventions and models aimed at grief counseling, we focus our efforts on explaining key elements of cognitive behavioral grief-targeted interventions (CBGTI). CBGTI includes a large catalog of interventions and features of other interventions combined with a cognitive or behavioral approach like imaginal and in vivo exposure. Additional behavioral approaches include guided mourning and the engagement in health-promoting behaviors. Cognitive elements include attributional theory, the cognitive promotion of letting go of the deceased and not forgetting about them, assimilation of grief activities with normal daily living, meaning making related to the loss, and writing about the loss (Matthews & Marwit, 2004).

Treatment Considerations for Children and Adolescents

Post-disaster, the lives and memories of children are forever changed. As discussed in Chapter 2, children thrive when they have consistency, predictability, and routine in their lives. Unfortunately, disaster is a significant disruption in children's routines. After a disaster, children may be temporarily homeless, reside in a new home, change schools, lose their social group, make new friends, and struggle with mental illness. Starting over is difficult for children and adolescents, however, the abrupt and devastating nature of disaster creates chaos, confusion, and disequilibrium, making adaptation, healing, and coping difficult.

While most children and adolescents experience difficulties post disaster, all do not develop mental health disorders. As previously discussed, there are a myriad of protective, risk, and resiliency factors that can cause positive or negative responses following a disaster. While not all children and adolescents develop trauma, DMH clinicians should understand the common reactions youth demonstrate when facing traumatic shock. The National Institute for Mental Health (NIMH; 2001) identified common reactions to trauma based on development level. Children 5 years and younger often demonstrate fear, anxiety, and separation anxiety while experiencing trauma. Elementary school-aged children 6 to 11 years of age feel the same level of fear and anxiety that younger children exhibit, however, their reaction can appear more defiant. For adolescents 12 to 17 years of age, there is often a higher level of acuity-numbing nightmares.

During the immediate impact of a disaster, responders are focused on finding children and adolescents social support and helping them with the meaning making of the disaster situation (Dingfelder, 2006). Social support often includes being reconnected with displaced family members, finding support from professional DMH clinicians, depending on adults to provide safety. An important factor is ensuring children and adolescents are not being isolated or left behind. While individual treatment may be indicated for some, most children and adolescents are helped in family or group sessions to ensure mutuality and support. In the immediate aftermath, group counseling, traumatic grief groups, and support groups are helpful in counseling child and adolescent survivors regarding disaster experiences. From a theoretical perspective, CBT groups generally produce favorable results (for a comprehensive review, see La Greca, Silverman, & Lochman, 2009).

TABLE 7.1 ● Knowledge, Skills, Awareness, and Resources Needed for Disaster Counseling by Client Type and Level of Professional Development

	Knowledge	Skills	Awareness	Techniques	Resources
	Advanced Graduate Students and Novice Professionals				
Individuals	Hierarchy of human needs (Maslow) Developmental processes Cultural context and individual differences Triage Psychological First Aid The Five Essential Elements Protective, risk, and resiliency factors	Informal assessment—basic needs Informed decision making related to triage Data gathering Management of personal emotion Compassion Empathic listening Compassion and hope Observation Closed- and open-ended questioning Reflection of content, feeling, & meaning Restatement, summary clarification of client statements Personalizing clients' feelings to promote their ownership, Collaborative owning statements,	The common themes in disaster community process (e.g., hero) Understanding federal, statewide, and local response system Triage hierarchy Common signs of trauma Various ways in which people will respond Sympathy vs empathy Personal need to rescue clients 4 core Multicultural attributes Culturally bound assumptions Emic and etic models of helping Locus of control	Instilling hope Promoting connectedness Instilling a sense of self and community efficacy Creating a calming atmosphere Promoting a sense of safety Immediacy Interpretation Focusing Creating awareness Silence Expanding the clients view Reframing Normalizing Emphasizing what's manageable Summarizing	List describing assistance being provided on the federal, state, and local level Information pertaining to shelter, food pantry, and clean water supplies List of displaced individuals that have lost family members Local information on services, health and safety, social, housing, counseling, financial, food, religious/spiritual supports Referral list of pro bono providers Personal support/debriefing for the clinician

		Disowned statements, conveying understanding Positive reinforcement Limit setting Facilitative listening		Implementing order Psychoeducation Promoting mobilization Care coordination Providing support Providing protection Providing guidance Advocacy Triage
Groups	Stages of a group Purpose of the group Group process Group roles Group leadership/co-leaders Ethical decision making	Active listening Modeling Linking member's content and feelings Initiating and facilitating communication Blocking Summarizing	Self-awareness Intersectionality Allow member self-identification Protect clients Protect boundaries Guard against universality Cross-cultural communication	Scanning—eye contact (as is culturally appropriate) with each member Set a support and goal oriented tone Modeling desired behavior Ice-breakers—initial activities designed to promote member to member sharing Round Robin—each member shares their perspective or may pass Dyads and triads—promotes more focused conversation Linking or bridging—members comments to each to demonstrate mutuality

(Continued)

TABLE 7.1   (Continued)

	Knowledge	Skills	Awareness	Techniques	Resources
	Advanced Graduate Students and Novice Professionals				
Communities	Understanding federal, statewide, and local response system; history of previous disaster events, particularly natural and human caused events Local health and safety organizations Community emergency communication/disaster plan		Federal resource allocation, unique needs of children and adolescents, volunteers, integrative collaborative teams, and federal government personnel Flow and tone of local and national news of the event		Referral list First responders list Disaster information based on developmental level
	Experienced Professionals				
Individuals	All those listed above and how disaster events can result in a trauma response Specialized focus on special populations (children, adults, police, educational settings)	All those listed above Reflective listening for meaning and intent Appropriate self-disclosure Therapeutic patience-inventions timed for maximum impact/learning Cognitive complexity Relativistic thinking	General and advanced disaster assessment methods Personal and professional humility Anxiety no longer impacts performance Looks inward for guidance	Exposure therapy Stress inoculation training Grief counseling Interpretation Advanced accurate empathy—deepens clients' experience via metaphor stories, analogies Empathic confrontation	Local information on services, health and safety, social, housing, counseling, financial, food, religious/spiritual supports Personal support/debriefing for the clinician; Provide support and debriefing for clinicians

(Continued)

Grief theory and counseling methods				
Trauma theory and methods to alleviate symptomology				
Cognitive behavioral theory and counseling methods		Engages in reflective practice and professional development		
Behavioral theory and counseling methods		Role model for advanced graduate students and novice professionals		
General and advanced disaster assessment methods				
Learn supervision				
Advanced training in trauma informed methods				
Partnerships with local psychiatrists, psychiatric treatment centers, and continuum of care				

TABLE 7.1 (Continued)

	Knowledge	Skills	Awareness	Techniques	Resources
			Experienced Professionals*		
Group	Grief theory and counseling methods				
	Trauma theory and methods to alleviate symptomology				
	Cognitive behavioral theory and counseling methods				
	Behavioral theory and counseling methods				
	Addressing complex and layered group dynamics				
	Facilitating complexity and conflict in groups				
	Using conversations rather than directives to effectively facilitate				
	Understanding your style and patterns in group facilitation				
	Reflective practice—how you relate to groups and personal triggers				

Managing disruptive members' behaviors Facilitating emergent agendas and change Using Fishbowls and other experiential tools Promoting group's self-directed learning						State and local referral list Pro bono services Serve on local and state crisis and disaster response teams
	Communities	Understanding federal, statewide, and local response system Leadership and command structure of DMH clinicians Regional resources History of previous crisis events, particularly natural and human caused events Local health and safety organizations Community emergency communication/disaster plan	Advanced practice Supervision Leadership Organization Advocacy Networking	Public health and safety Communication plans Public Affairs including medical needs, food and housing announcements Recognition of underserved communities Nonhuman (animals and wildlife) and environmental concerns Immediate, short- and longer term planning	Panel discussion Community listening sessions/forums Engaging regional or national service organizations (short term)	

Assessments in Disaster Mental Health

Effective treatment begins with quality assessment and conceptualization of concerns. In DMH North and Pfefferbaum's (2013) systematic diagram of psychiatric assessment guides DMH clinicians through three components: identification of psychopathology contrasted normative emotional distress, triage and referral to appropriate care, and provision of targeted interventions identified through an assessment. The diagram displays the sequence of work for disaster clinicians in two-week intervals, decision points, and determination of future and more intensive services. See North and Pfefferbaum (2013, p. 5) for greater detail.

In previous chapters of this book, we explored the mental status exam, triage assessment system, evaluation of resiliency, case management, crisis assessment, and suicide. These formal and informal assessments are useful to the DMH clinician. In this chapter, we focus specifically on disaster-based assessments like the *Impact of Events Scale*, *Level of Exposure Scale*, and the *Inventory of Complicated Grief.*

Perhaps the most common and important disaster-assessment protocol takes place on an informal basis. The primary purpose of post-disaster assessment and screening is to determine if the survivors are attaining the most relevant and appropriate care. In addition, DMH clinicians ensure that those who may have developed more significant concerns like PTSD, generalized anxiety, or acute stress disorder (ASD) are receiving the appropriate care. According to Rosenfeld et al. (2010), DMH clinicians are looking, informally, for clues that provide evidence of more significant mental health needs. DMH clinicians are mindful of several broad considerations like preexisting mental health issues, survivor perceptions of hopelessness or impending doom, and behaviors like numbing, or state switching, and the severity of disaster-related deprivations.

DMH clinicians consider 10 factors when assessing a disaster survivor's well-being and whether a significant traumatic reaction has occurred (Connor & Butterfield, 2003). The 10 factors include legal system, stressors, psychosocial context, personal characteristics, behavioral and health risks, military history, trauma symptoms, dissociative symptoms, safety, and trauma history. While these factors are important to assess for, there is evidence that traumatized survivors often refuse to seek help (Rosenfeld et al., 2010). Consequently, perhaps the most a DMH clinician can do is provide a list of resources related to the observed symptoms and plant a seed for future potential help-seeking behavior. In the following section, we provide an overview of three assessment measures aimed understanding the impact and severity of a disaster and the complicated grief that may ensue.

Impact of Events Scale–Revised (IES-R)

The Revised Impact of Events Scale (IES-R; Horowitz, Wilner, & Alvarez, 1979; Weiss & Marmar, 1997) is a 22-item scale designed to measure subjective distress as it relates to the three domains of PTSD—reexperiencing, avoidance, and hyperarousal—for children, adolescents, and adults. Survivors are asked to indicate, on a five-point Likert scale, how many times symptoms happen over the past week. It has been reported, that the IES-R has good internal consistency (Cronbach's alpha = .79–.94) and strong test–retest reliability (.89–.94) (Creamer, Bell, & Failla, 2003; Weiss & Marmar, 1997).

Traumatic Exposure Severity Scale (TESS)

One of the most prominent disaster risk factors for the development of a traumatic reaction is the proximity, impact, and duration of a traumatic event. Given the finding that those who directly face the terror of a nature-, human-, or technology-initiated disaster for an extended period of time often experience the highest level of acuity. The Traumatic Exposure Severity Scale (TESS; Elal & Slade, 2005) is a 28-item adult measure designed to assess the scope of exposure to a disaster. Survivors are asked to indicate, on a dichotomous response scale, if they experienced a negative experience related to the disaster. If they acknowledge a particular event, they are asked to rate the degree it was distressing, on a five-point Likert scale. The six subscales are Disruption of Life/Being in Need, Material Loss and Damage, Physical Injury to Self or Significant Others, Threat to Life of Self or Significant Others, Exposure to the Grotesque, and Loss of Loved Ones. It has been reported that the TESS has good internal reliability and validity (Elal & Slade, 2005).

Inventory of Complicated Grief (ICG)

Catastrophic events result in large death tolls. Due to the sudden and unpredictable nature of death due to disaster, the bereavement process can be more difficult (Kaltman & Bonnano, 2003). Survivors of a disaster who are also coping with the deaths of loved ones often have elevated mental health symptomology due to coping with their own trauma and the bereavement process (Neria & Litz, 2004). Consequently, complicated grief often ensues. Complicated grief is conceptualized long-term dysfunction that is separate from bereavement-related sadness and depression. Reports of prevalence rates range from 2.4% to 4.8% (American Psychiatric Association, 2013). The Inventory of Complicated Grief (ICG; Prigerson et al., 1995) is a 19-item measure that evaluates the emotional, behavioral, and cognitive issues related to complicated grief. Survivors are asked to respond to 19 statements concerning their bereavement-related symptoms. There are five response options ranging from never to always. The concurrent validity ($r = 0.67, 0.70,$ and 0.87) and internal consistency reliability (Cronbach's $\alpha = .94$) were fairly high and high respectively (Prigerson et al., 1995). Research confirms the equivalent five-factor structure of the ICG in a sample of 232 participants reporting symptoms related to complicated grief (Fisher et al., 2016).

Summary

In this chapter, we described the context in which DMH clinicians learn and develop skills and interventions related to DMH counseling. Crisis, trauma, and disaster events have unique and common elements, distinct histories, and modes of treatment. Unique elements related to DMH include the connection of various government support systems, the community process, disaster-based psychological first aid and guiding principles, early- and mid-stage disaster interventions, in-depth protocols, and basic disaster assessment protocols and procedures.

Extended Learning Exercises

Exercise 1: Recent and Historic Nature-Initiated Disaster

Pick and explore a recent or historic, large-scale nature-initiated disaster and answer the below questions.

1. What was the aftermath of the disaster—death toll, destruction, evacuation efforts, media coverage, government and local-based help efforts?
2. What were the post-disaster supportive and rebuilding efforts?
3. How and to what degree were DMH clinicians involved?
4. Utilize a Google and EBSCO search and retrieve information on the physical and mental health consequences of the disaster.
5. Evaluate the DMH response.

Exercise 2: Government-Based Entities

Consider the roles of FEMA and other government-based entities. Utilizing scholarly literature, report on the federal government's response to three disaster (e.g., natural or man-made). In addition, answer the following questions related to government processes.

1. Name the government entities involved in the disaster response efforts.
2. What patterns do you notice in regard to the federal process related to disaster decision and response efforts?
3. How do government-based entities collaborate to create response efforts?

Exercise 3: SAMHSA Guiding Principles of Trauma-Informed Care

SMHHSA (2014)

Review the below SAMHSA's (2014) Guiding Principles of Trauma-Informed Care. Describe how each principle relates to disaster-based interventions. For example, consider the different forms of safety needed for flood, earthquake, and tsunami survivors.

Guiding Principles of Trauma-Informed Care

1. **Safety**—Throughout the organization, staff and the people they serve feel physically and psychologically safe.

2. **Trustworthiness and transparency—** Organizational operations and decisions are conducted with transparency and the goal of building and maintaining trust among staff, clients, and family members of those receiving services.

3. **Peer support and mutual self-help—** These are integral to the organizational and service delivery approach and are understood as a key vehicle for building trust, establishing safety, and empowerment.

4. **Collaboration and mutuality—**There is true partnering and leveling of power differences between staff and clients and among organizational staff from direct care staff to administrators. There is recognition that healing happens in relationships and in the meaningful sharing of power and decision-making. The organization recognizes that everyone has a role to play in a trauma-informed approach. One does not have to be a therapist to be therapeutic.

5. **Empowerment, voice, and choice—** Throughout the organization and among the clients served, individuals' strengths are recognized, built on, and validated, and new skills developed as necessary. The organization aims to strengthen the staff's, clients', and family members' experience of choice and recognize that every person's experience is unique and requires an individualized approach. This includes a belief in resilience and in the ability of individuals, organizations, and communities to heal and promote recovery from trauma. This builds on what clients, staff, and communities have to offer, rather than responding to perceived deficits.

6. **Cultural, historical, and gender issues—**The organization actively moves past cultural stereotypes and biases (e.g., based on race, ethnicity, sexual orientation, age, geography), offers gender responsive services, leverages the healing value of traditional cultural connections, and recognizes and addresses historical trauma (SAMHSA, 2014).

Case Illustration 1: Advanced Graduate Student

Tim, a 52-year-old man, has been in counseling with you at your internship site for the past 13 weeks. He describes himself as a successful dentist with a thriving practice who has recently been displaced because of a large-scale flood. He mentions that his house has been destroyed and all of his possessions were lost. He states that he is from Texas and has no family in the area. He has no family of his own and recently had a divorce with his wife of 15 years. His initial concerns include flight of thoughts, heart palpitations, feeling that "everyone is out to get him," and insomnia. These symptoms have been occurring for approximately three weeks. In today's session, Tim demonstrated a flat affect, and mentioned that he had another night of little sleep. He said, "I feel like it is me against the world." He mentions that his work is starting to suffer and he has made a few dentistry errors due to his exhaustion and preoccupied thoughts.

Questions to Consider:

How do you respond to Tim's immediate concerns?

What skills will you utilize?

What are your priorities with Tim in this session?

Who else may you involve in the conversation?

What additional information or resources are required for you to assist Tim?

What are the desired outcomes for Tim and you in this session?

Describe your assessment and treatment plan.

Case Illustration 2: Novice Professional

You are on the front line of a DMH evacuation effort following a large-scale flood. Chloe is a 25-year-old African American woman who is triaged and sent to you for help. When you ask her how she is doing, she states that she is "lost and freaking out." When you ask her about her family and support network, she states, "I can't find anyone and I am lucky to have escaped with my life." You notice that she has several large cuts on her arm and she is not making eye contact with you. When you ask her what she needs, she states, "I just want to see my mom and dad. I can't believe our home is gone."

Questions to Consider:

How do you respond to Chloe's immediate concerns?

What are your priorities with Chloe's triage process?

Who else may you involve in the conversation?

What skills will you utilize?

What additional information or resources are required for you to assist Chloe?

What are the desired outcomes for Chloe?

Case Illustration 3: Experienced Professional

Chris is a 15-year-old teenage survivor of a local school shooting. He is referred to you by the local school district for disturbing verbal and nonverbal behavior, which significantly interferes with his school performance. He describes periods of time when he is tearful, cannot concentrate, feels angry, and fears being alone because he "doesn't know what he'll do." His mother mentioned to you that she is "worried, he is reckless and still hasn't healed from losing his good friend." Chris agreed to try a low dose of medication to support his current intense bouts of anxiety. Chris mentions that he wants to stop thinking about watching his friend dying. He stated that he desperately wants to take revenge on the guy that shot him and knows just what he would do to him. School officials and his parents cannot determine if he will act on these statements.

Questions to Consider:

How do you respond to Chris's immediate concerns?

How will you protect Chris and others he may feel violent toward?

Who else may you involve in the conversation?

What intervention will you utilize to help ameliorate his anxiety?

What additional information or resources are required for you to assist Chris?

What are the desired outcomes for Chris and you in this session?

Describe your assessment and treatment plan.

Additional Resources

Helpful Links

American Academy of Child and Adolescent Psychiatry (AACAP): www.aacap.org

The American Academy of Experts in Traumatic Stress (AAETS): www.aaets.org

American Counseling Association (ACA): www.counseling.org

ACA Trauma and Disaster Mental Health Resources: https://www.counseling.org/knowledge-center/trauma-disaster

American Psychiatric Association (APA): www.psych.org

American Psychological Association (APA): www.apa.org

American Red Cross (ARC): www.redcross.org

To Volunteer with the Red Cross: http://www.redcross.org/become-a-disaster-mental-health-volunteer

Centers for Disease Control and Prevention (CDC): www.cdc.gov

National Association of School Psychologists (NASP): www.nasponline.org

National Association of Social Workers (NASW): www.naswdc.org

National Institute on Mental Health (NIMH): www.nimh.nih.gov

National Mental Health Association (NMHA): www.nmha.org

Substance Abuse Mental Health Services Administration (SAMHSA): www.samhsa.gov

U.S. Department of Veteran Affairs Center for PTSD: https://www.ptsd.va.gov/public/treatment/therapy-med/disaster_mental_health_treatment.asp

Helpful Books

Disaster Mental Health: Theory and Practice (2007). James Halper & Mary Tramontin

Mental Health Response to Mass Emergencies (1988). Mary Lystad

Mental Health and Disaster (2009). Yuval Neria, Sandro Galea, & Fran H. Norris

Disaster Mental Health Counseling: Responding to Trauma in a Multicultural Context (2017). Mark A. Stebnicki

The Crisis Counseling and Traumatic Events Treatment Planner, with DSM-5 Updates, 2nd Edition (2012). Tammi D. Kolski, Arthur E. Jongsma, & Rick A. Myer

Community-Based Psychological First Aid: A Practical Guide to Helping Individuals Communities During Difficult Times, 1st Edition (2016). Gerald A. Jacobs

When Their World Falls Apart: Helping Families and Children Manage the Effects of Disaster (2010). Lawrence B. Rosenfeld, Joanne S. Caye, Mooli Lahad, & Robin H. Gurwitch

DVDs

When Helping Hurts: Sustaining Trauma Workers. (1998). Distributed by Gift from within, 16 Cobb Hill Road, Camden, Maine 04843

Children in Crisis: 3 Video Series. (2005). Calamari Productions

When Their World Falls Apart: Helping Families and Children Manager the Effects of Disasters (2010). NASW Press.

Caring for Those Who Care

Clients recovering from a crisis, trauma, or disaster (CTD) necessitate significant care and commitment from clinicians. A commitment, if not handled properly, may lead to stress, professional burnout, compassion fatigue, or vicarious trauma. This type of work-related stress occurs among CTD counseling professionals, particularly for those with a personal history of trauma (Pearlman & Mac Ian, 1995). "There is a cost to caring" (Figley, 1995, p. 1).

Crisis- and trauma-informed therapies involve intensive therapeutic work to address destabilized and devastated clients. Clinicians encounter clients in their most vulnerable and fragile states. Clients' significant, multiple, and complex needs coupled with limited coping skills or resources leave them feeling helpless, panicked, or immobilized. Their world is upside down. The catastrophic nature of clients' experiences and the intensity and iterative nature of treatment challenge clinicians' coping skills and well-being. In some cases, the challenges result in physical and mental exhaustion, and if left unaddressed, result in vicarious trauma or compassion fatigue.

Learning Objectives

After reading this chapter and participating in the reflective exercises provided, you will be able to

- Understand how CTD clinicians find balance
- Differentiate burnout, impairment, compassion fatigue, secondary trauma, and vicarious trauma

(Continued)

(Continued)

- Understand the counselor's orientation to helping and wellness in crisis, trauma, and disaster context

- Recognize personal and professional boundaries in CTD work

- Conceptualize how a counselor's personal history of trauma, vulnerabilities, and sense of resilience impacts therapeutic work

- Become familiar with the neurobiological basis of psychological distress

- Consider a variety of techniques to clinical vignettes

The Counselor's Toolkit

As in previous chapters, we present you with a toolkit to augment your understanding related to the pragmatic aspects of counselor wellness. In this chapter, we categorize the social, emotional, physical (Meyers, Luecht, & Sweeney, 2004; Roscoe, 2009), and pragmatic techniques for enhancing counselor wellness. The Toolkit presents common procedures for enhancing wellness within the established categories.

Finding Balance

Nationally, the severity of mental health issues is increasing in acuity and prevalence. For example, the Center for Disease Control (2018) staff reported in the 2017 Youth Risk Behavior (YRBS) Survey that mental health issues among youth are increasing. In a nationwide sample, 19% of respondents experienced bullying; 7.4% were forced to have sex; 17.2% reported serious thoughts about attempting suicide; 13.6% made a suicide plan, and 7.4% attempted suicide. Recall, 70% to 80% of the U. S. population will experience exposure to at least one traumatic event in their lifetime; now more than ever, skilled clinicians are needed to skillfully counsel clients.

Counseling, at its core, is transactional. You provide therapeutic services to clients and receive compensation. Clients provide crisis or traumatic concerns and seek relief. Done well, counseling is a mutually beneficial professional relationship. Yet, for many, counseling, particularly trauma-informed counseling, is more than a mere transaction. Trauma-informed counseling is a deep therapeutic interaction in which clinicians somewhat selflessly and compassionately attend to clients. In this exchange, clinicians temporarily suspend their needs/process to advance treatment. Therapy is filled with meaning, purpose, and intent. In this chapter, we present a balanced perspective and promote relativistic thinking (Perry, 1970) related to the demands of trauma-informed counseling.

Altruism and Self-Interest

Counseling is simultaneously a transaction—a service is purchased; a skewed, yet reciprocal relationship—where *give and take* occurs between participants with differing degrees of risk and responsibilities and an interaction—where participants demonstrate some level of investment and action. For the clinician, the therapeutic enterprise contains elements of altruism and self-interest. Altruism is defined as the practice of and concern for the welfare of others. It is akin to the ethical principle of beneficence or promoting good for one's client. Self-interest, also an important concept in counseling, focuses practices and concern on the *self* before considering others. In appropriate measure and balance, altruistic- and self-interested beliefs and practices promote healthy living. When either or both are absent or excessive, individuals may feel confused, overwhelmed, isolated, or disconnected.

Cultural rewards and risks exist that are associated with altruistic or self-interested behaviors. Generally, altruistic individuals are described positively as noble, selfless, warm, kind, and thoughtful. Negative portrayals describe individuals as do-gooders, saps, or martyrs. Specific to clinicians, altruistic individuals may be viewed as wonderfully empathic professionals or a variation of Bemak and Chung's (2008) *Nice Counselor Syndrome* (NCS)—which, by the way, is not a compliment. Bemak and Chung argue that school clinicians exhibiting NCS primarily value being viewed by others as *nice*. To maintain this perception, they avoid conflict and confrontation and strive to promote harmony rather than advocate for real change. Positive associations with self-interest include admiration for engaging in self-care, maintenance of personal boundaries, and *doing good by doing well* (personal success allows me to help others). In contrast, negative portrayals of self-interest describe individuals as selfish, narcissistic, egocentric, and self-absorbed.

Altruism is associated with biological, physiological, cognitive, and social rewards. For example, helping others avoid threat or death promotes survival of the species—a biological imperative. While helping others activates the brain to release neurotransmitters like dopamine, physiologically, it feels good to help others. Cognitively, helping others reduces distress and promotes self-efficacy. And finally, socially engaging in altruistic acts advances relationships and results in recognition. Risks associated with altruism include increased stress related to focusing on others, resentment from unmitigated communion (UC) or an interpersonal style where one is too involved in caring for others that they have no reciprocal relationships, and burnout. Rewards for self-interested behavior parallel those present in altruism except that they are associated with and revert to the individual rather than others. For example, biological rewards center on personal versus group survival, which some describe as winning. Similarly, social gains focus on the individual's action or contribution over the group's or others. Risks associated with excessive or inappropriately timed self-interest are mediated by one's cultural context and may include isolation due to actual or perceived violation of social norms and misattribution that may be viewed as lacking empathy, understanding, and other awareness and detachment from others due to lack of actual or perceived social reciprocity. The second author has explored the dynamic interaction between altruism and self-interest in a helper (Flynn 2009; Flynn & Black, 2011, Flynn & Black, 2013). Flynn argues for a self-augmenting single construct entitled *altruism–self-interest*. The holistic understanding of this phenomenon can assist clinicians as they engage in CTD counseling. Specifically, responding to a crisis or disaster takes energy, focus, and commitment. Failure to maintain a balance between altruism and self-interest may impede a clinician's ability to perform tasks properly in the field due to exhaustion and burnout resulting in exploitive or unethical behaviors, ineffective or inappropriate personal boundaries with clients, or may result in the counselor exiting or being forced to exit the profession prematurely.

Wellness and Resilience

The profession of counseling and psychotherapy provides clinicians amazing opportunities for meaningful and life-altering work and simultaneously presents threats to their well-being. Those moments when you experience your clients' successes are humbling and heartwarming. Alternatively, clients' persistent anguish, suffering, and failure to make progress can take a toll on you and erode your confidence. Clinicians who overutilize empathy, have large caseloads (James & Gilliland, 2013), and fail to attend to their wellness may experience impairment, overtime, and burnout. The magnitude of client concerns, external and self-imposed pressure to achieve treatment results in less time, and fatigue also contribute to burnout (Craig & Sprang, 2010). But there is hope and help in the form of active engagement in wellness activities. To promote and maintain wellness, you can engage in personal counseling, yoga, or meditation; set and maintain personal and professional boundaries; get a life outside of work; or restore yourself by eating right, getting adequate sleep, or involving yourself in spiritual or religious groups. Frequent engagement in these activities is believed to enhance the resilience and hardiness practitioners exhibit when working with clients experiencing a CTD (Dass-Brailsford, 2010) and is an ethical imperative of most helping professions.

According to the American Psychological Association (APA), *resilience* is defined as "the process of adapting well in the face of adversity, trauma, tragedy, threats or even significant sources of stress" (2011, para. 4). Buckwalter (2011) adds, "There is one defining characteristic of resilience that everyone seems to agree on—resilience is evident when we are confronted with significant trauma and stress. It's hard to assess resilience when things are going well." He notes "resilience determines how quickly we get back to our "steady state" after the air has been knocked out of us, when we must push through life circumstances that challenge our very being." (para 3). Much of the research on resiliency examines global factors like the quality and nature of one's relationship, presence of a support system, positive self-image, and optimism. Buckwalter and his research team are investigating more specific subcomponents of resiliency that include one's ability to regulate, articulate, and openly express emotions. Others' research indicates that more emphasis on resilience and stress management could help professionals thrive in both the clinical and academic settings (Mathad, Pradhan, & Rajesh, 2017; Smith & Yang, 2017; Turner & McCarthy, 2017).

As emphasized throughout this book, CTD counseling can be taxing. Regardless of your level of professional development, clinical supervision of CTD cases is a must. Supervisors with training and experience in CTD are familiar with and experienced in the relevant symptomology, interventions, risk assessment, and social justice issues that individuals exposed to CTD experience on a day-to-day basis (Lonergan, O'Halloran, & Crane, 2004; Paige, 2015; Turkus, 2013). As discussed in Chapter 1, supervision supports the clinician and provides perspective, but most importantly it protects clients' welfare.

Burnout, Impairment, Compassion Fatigue, Secondary and Vicarious Trauma

Concerns about the well-being of psychotherapists have been evident since the inception of the profession. In 1982, Farber and Heifetz articulated concerns about a "paucity of research" on psychotherapist stress and burnout. Their concerns still resonate today; they wrote,

> there is, however, a notable paucity of research on stress and burnout in psychotherapists. This gap exists despite the fact that over 40 years ago Freud (1937/1964) wrote of the "dangers of analysis" for analysts, despite the fact that the inner experience of the therapist has come to be acknowledged as an important variable in the psychotherapeutic process (Burton, 1972), and despite, too, the fact that the manpower shortage in the mental health field (Albee, 1959, 1968; Hobbs, 1964) critically increases the need to maximize the job satisfaction and efficiency of available personnel (p. 293).

Today, despite a plethora of research, multiple and highly correlated terms, and multiple definitions, we seem no closer to predicting or understanding which clinicians experience burnout, under what conditions, the impact on clients, and what we do to intervene.

Burnout

Burnout, as defined by Pines and Aronson (1988), is physical, mental, and emotional fatigue caused by a helping professional being placed in long-standing, high-impact situations. It is a process that develops over time. Burnout is characterized by physical exhaustion, powerlessness and hopelessness, discouragement, negative thoughts of self, and a negative attitude toward most aspects of one's life. Similarly, Ogresta, Rusac, and Zore (2008) defined burnout as "a sustained response to chronic work stress and includes emotional exhaustion, negative attitudes and feelings toward the recipients of the service (depersonalization) and a feeling of low accomplishment and professional failure" (p. 365). Negative attitudes and cognitions are believed to cause a significant loss of energy that hinders a practitioner's ability to cope and serve clientele effectively. In sum, burnout puts clinicians and clients at risk.

Philosophically, practitioners experiencing burnout often have a difficult time finding relief due to professional expectations that a counselor's ability to demonstrate unconditional positive regard, empathy, altruism, and perception of self are central to the therapeutic alliance and client change. Clinicians repeatedly empathize with individuals experiencing a significant helplessness, discouragement, and disappointment as they realize that they may not be able foster change for all or even most individuals exposed to crisis and trauma. Burnout has been linked to turnover, absenteeism, and low organization morale (Lanham, Rye, Rimsky, & Weill, 2012).

In a crisis and disaster mental health context, practitioners are required to be fully engaged, alert, competent, and respond in an acute and urgent setting where decisions are made rapidly with low information. Clinicians who experience burnout are likely be too physically and mentally fatigued to successfully conduct CTD assessments and interventions resulting in the unintended consequences that result in risk for negative client outcomes and harm, especially when there is the threat of actual physical danger.

During trauma-informed therapy, clients often repeatedly reexperience the traumatic event (Herman, 1997). This form of therapy requires clinicians to systematically guide clients through the trauma experiences and simultaneously safeguard their psychological safety in the process. The deep and thorough nature of trauma work cannot be done by potentially impaired practitioners.

Impairment

Therapeutic *impairment* takes place when there is a significant decline in a clinicians' competence or ability to proactively intervene with clients. Clinician's impairment is often associated with substance abuse, chemical dependency, mental illness, crisis, and physical illness (Figley, 1995). When impaired clinicians do not consistently attend to their wellness, they put their clients and themselves at risk. Consider the effective practitioner who encounters a challenging life circumstance like the death of a family member, divorce, or layoff. If the clinician copes by using excessive amounts of alcohol or develops insomnia, this once competent counselor becomes physically and emotionally exhausted, is unable to focus or manage their emotions, and is not present for their clients. Overtime and without intervention, the clinician's lack of effective coping skills impacts the care they deliver to their clients. Impaired clinicians may ignore physically dangerous environmental conditions, misunderstand the issues related to triage and assessment, and take advantage of vulnerable and traumatized individuals. If intervention procedures are not accurately and effectively executed, clients could be further traumatized and their symptoms could escalate (Figley, 1995; James & Gilliland, 2013).

Compassion Fatigue, Vicarious Trauma, and Secondary Traumatic Stress

Compassion fatigue, vicarious trauma, and secondary traumatic stress (STS) are three overlapping constructs. According to Figley (1995), compassion fatigue is an emotional residue and feeling of sadness for someone else's suffering, supplemented by the clinician's strong wish to remove the suffering. Similarly, vicarious trauma is the impact that an unconditional empathic connection with client pain has on the counselor. Effective, empathic, and aware clinicians connect with their clients as clients describe and reexperience the torment and pain associated with the trauma. Witnessing and absorbing these experiences can have a toxic impact on a practitioner. Further, there is often a tension or preoccupation with the stories shared by clients (Pearlman & Saakvitne, 1995), which may simultaneously attract and repel the counselor's engagement and interest. Whereas vicarious trauma is centered on a practitioner suffering due to multiple painful and graphic client narratives, STS has been described as the emotional sensitivity and vulnerability to the knowledge of trauma affecting someone else. The vulnerability leads to a trauma-like response (Figley, 1995).

Compassion fatigue, vicarious traumatization, and STS are a significant concern among clinicians working in CTD contexts. The rapid nature of certain crisis and disaster therapeutic experiences, compassion fatigue, vicarious trauma, and STS may become more prominent (Dass-Brailsford, 2010; Dworkin, Sorell, & Allen, 2016). Large caseloads, access to clinical supervision, and clinician's personal factors have been associated with the variability in incidents of STS (Dworkin, Sorell, & Allen, 2016).

Vulnerabilities to Secondary Traumatic Stress and Vicarious Trauma

Vicarious traumatization and STS are associated with repeatedly listening to first-hand accounts of trauma and the consequent absorption of another's emotional, spiritual, psychological, and traumatic pain. This process results in the secondary experience of the trauma-based reaction. Vicarious trauma is believed to be a reaction to multiple exposures to other's trauma and emotional hurt, whereas STS can occur immediately after one encounter (Figley, 1995). Symptoms related to vicarious traumatization and STS closely resemble those of PTSD. Typically, clinicians do not experience flashbacks and night terrors related to clients' stories, but the clinician's personal traumatic history, if present, may be activated resulting in reexperiencing of a more personal nature. Regardless, those who experience vicarious trauma or STS report exhaustion, feeling overwhelmed, isolation, hyperarousal, and general dissatisfaction with one's life.

While definitions can offer distinction, the reactions can be conceptualized as indirect exposure to trauma through listening to one or multiple trauma-saturated narratives. Like direct trauma, not everyone who listens to trauma-saturated narrative(s) develops vicarious trauma or STS. Individuals who are directly affected by trauma have experience with the traumatizing phenomena. For example, when a child is abused by an adult or witnesses a sibling being abused by a trusted adult, they experience direct trauma. This traumatic experience could impact their view of the world, relationships, and themselves. A counselor may experience STS if the child, in the above example, provides a detailed account of their abuse and the helper listens and responds empathically.

Clinician's Orientation to Helping

As a CTD clinician, you will be challenged by three significant issues throughout your career: managing the multiple professional duties like assessment, triage, linking services, and counseling; exhaustion from the amount of your personhood, skill, energy, and focus required to work with verbal and nonverbal trauma states during EMDR or later stages of trauma-focused cognitive behavioral therapy; and the responsibility to remain professionally up to date (Daniels, 2010).

While trauma-informed counseling typically happens within an office or agency, the early stages of community-based crisis and disaster counseling most often take place in the field. Office settings lend themselves to organization, coordination, and support because of the access to information, predictability, and professional peers. Community crises or disaster situations often require the clinician to work alone with few resources and support. We encourage clinicians to have a *go bag* ready with food, water, resources, and referral information. In other words, by failing to prepare, you prepare to fail. Clinicians must also prepare themselves mentally and emotionally. This includes emotional regulation, recognizing the short-term nature of crisis and disaster responding, and trusting your training and your teammates; you are not in this alone.

Within this text, you were presented a myriad of techniques, skills, and dispositions related to CTD counseling. Interventions range from core counseling skills, modalities, and interventions developed for specific to CTD. In addition to therapeutic skills and interventions, basic crisis and disaster management skills are necessary for clinicians to understand. Developmentally speaking, experience matters, and you will be able effectively execute CTD counseling with repeated experience in the field, supervision, and ongoing professional development.

Given the advanced nature of CTD skills, we recommend pairing your skills with clinical interventions. The advanced graduate student is prepared to conduct suicide assessments but may require support from a colleague to assess homicidal intent. Early career professionals are prepared to treat those responding to the crisis of divorce or death of a loved one but may need additional training and supervision to treat an adult client recovering from childhood sexual abuse. Mid- to late-career professionals typically distinguish themselves through specialization and may secure issue-specific training, like EMDR or trauma informed counseling. We encourage these professionals to utilize ongoing clinical supervision to guard against rescue narratives like *I am the only one who can save them*. Burnout, emotional numbing, or callousness typically emerge during the mid to late phases of one's career. Engaging in professional development and enhancing one's skill level through reading, training, experience, supervision, and consultation is critical in this ever-changing profession.

Responding to Crisis, Trauma, and Disaster

As discussed in Chapter 7, Hobfoll et al. (2007) described five empirically based disaster mental health intervention principles. The principles are instilling hope, promoting connectedness, instilling a sense of self and community efficacy, calming, and creating a sense of safety (p. 284). Similarly, we discussed Judith Herman's (1997) initial stage of adult trauma treatment—stabilization and safety. We believe clinicians create safety and stabilization through a variety of skills and interventions. Reflective practice, while not associated with acute responding, provides clinicians perspective and insight into their actions and reactions and advances their skills and wellbeing (Meier & Davis, 1997). Meier and Davis note it is essential for clinicians to fluidly move between a professional and personal mindset. The intersection of professional and personal processes helps clinicians hone their skill, achieve excellence, and maintain their wellness.

Occasionally, clinicians live in a community affected by a CTD. With respect to personal wellness and resiliency, it important for them to acknowledge they have been exposed and may respond like others feeling fear, dread, and dislocation. Some clinicians may question their sense of professional competence, worth, and effectiveness. We believe it is essential to maintain a professional mindset while helping those exposed, if possible, or to excuse oneself from treating others to attend to personal needs. For those who can maintain a professional presence, after the acute phase, we urge a return to a non-caregiving role to receive care, recognize personal needs, and permit others to provide care. We all deserve time to reflect, receive care, and replenish.

The Role of Personal and Professional Boundaries

Boundaries can be conceptualized as an individual barrier that separates a professional from a client in a manner that creates the appropriate amount of connectedness and autonomy. Creating appropriate space between oneself and a client can, at times, help professional clinicians achieve a sense of wellness and avoid issues such as burnout and impairment. The 2014 *American Counseling Association* (ACA) *Code of Ethics* section on Managing and Maintaining Boundaries and Professional Relationships (A.6.a. and A.6.b.) indicates clinicians are thoughtful about how they extend previous nontherapeutic relationships and work with someone in a counseling context. For example, a friend from your church asks you to treat their son who was sexually abused by a neighbor. The friend is desperate and his son has failed with three therapists and he trusts only you—you are the only one who can help his child. What do you do? Your compassion and previous relationship may induce you to accept the child but your respect for the client, professional boundaries, and ethical code influence you to listen empathically, acknowledge the father's concern, and suggest you work together to find another therapist.

Boundaries between the clinicians and individuals or clients can become blurred during crisis- and disaster-counseling situations. Determining how to intervene is important to consider. For example, assume a crisis or disaster occurred in your community and you responded to a location with mass casualties. Upon arriving you see the husband of a dear friend who is clearly distraught and has blood on his shirt. He grabs you and says his partner is dead; he does not know what to do or where they have taken his body. You are shocked and devastated. You know you are supposed to report to the command center, but your emotions are swirling, and neighbor is unable to let go of you. What do you do? Do you stay and comfort him or tell him you need to report? Do you try to connect him to a first responder and compartmentalize your shock? There is no easy or singular response. Your challenge is to balance responding compassionately to your neighbor, dealing with the unexpected death of a close friend, and determining whether you can be of service to others.

A clinician's personal and professional boundaries may be challenged by a client's interest in their life or experiences. For example, a client may ask, "Were you ever raped?", "Have you ever been sexually abused?", or "How did you overcome the trauma you've experienced in life?" While a client's curiosity about their clinician is somewhat normative, it is the responsibility of the clinician to maintain appropriate boundaries regarding what, if any, information to share. In a situation like this, the clinician might use the skill of immediacy to address the client's question. This may include a response like: "You wonder if I understand what it is like to be raped and knowing if I had might help you trust me." The clinician may also choose to redirect the client back to the purpose of counseling. For example, "While I understand why you're curious about my personal background, it is generally not appropriate for me to disclose such information. Our main goal is to help you work through your trauma."

Clinicians who had previously been traumatized in some manner that relates to the client's trauma-saturated narrative may experience countertransference (Murphy, 2013). Countertransference may manifest for those who have not sought therapy or supervision for issues related to past trauma and who respond to a client's disclosure of trauma as an opportunity to share their own experiences. Countertransference can affect clinicians across the professional lifespan, yet early career professionals are more susceptible (Williams, Judge, Hill, & Hoffman, 1997). Murphy (2013) indicates engaging in frequent clinical supervision and personal counseling can reduce the incident of countertransference.

Starting a new therapeutic relationship with a previous acquaintance who is now in crisis or experiencing traumatic responding may challenge your professional boundaries. You may wonder, "How do I help this person given my previous relationship with them?" or "Will this new role hurt the other relationship I have with them?" You may live in a community with few mental health providers; if another counselor is available who does not have a previous relationship with the client, a referral should be made. Alternatively, if resources are limited, you should address your concern up front, discuss options, ask for permission to work in this new manner, and establish guidelines for in-session and out-of-session interactions (Heaton & Black, 2009). Following the first therapeutic encounter, you ask the client if they understand the boundaries of the therapeutic relationship and if they would like to continue seeing you.

Working Within Your Scope of Practice

Skills and interventions related to CTD counseling require regular updating and development to maintain professional competency and to insure practice within the scope of one's training. In a crisis, and certainly a disaster, you may be called upon to provide a wide range of services. In chaotic and crisis situations, most of us want to jump in and help, but as a professional, you are held to a different standard than a lay helper. This means you need to evaluate each request and say *no* to those that are outside of your practice. For example, during a disaster you can provide aid and comfort, but it is beyond the scope of your practice to recommend anxiety medication to those who are suffering.

Working within one's scope of practice also involves self-awareness. Clinicians who engage or consider engaging in practices outside their training lack sufficient self-awareness, may desire to be viewed as important, or may have activated their rescue fantasy. These problematic behaviors put clients, the clinician, and the profession at risk. Through training, supervision, and personal counseling (Murphy, 2013), clinicians can become more aware and discontinue these behaviors.

The *Professional Competence* section of the ACA Code of Ethics (2014) outlines clinicians' responsibility to be aware of and manage the boundaries of professional competence (C.2.a. and C.2.b.). Attention to the limits of one's skill and training means being informed about education, practice, supervision, and ethical requirements of credentials like state licensure or those offered by the American Academy of Experts in Traumatic Stress (https://www.aaets.org/tss.htm) and successfully completing. Ongoing professional development and experience allow professionals to maintain and advance their skills and awareness, develop a specialized practice, and meet ethical and licensure requirements.

It is important to distinguish clinician competency from clinical competencies. Broadly, clinician competency refers to the professional's ability and acumen and clinical competencies are expected standards of achievement within a domain, like social justice competencies. Clinicians, and for that matter clients, have little guidance on how to measure and confirm a clinician's competence. Professional competency is typically comprised of four factors: knowledge, skill, attributes, and performance. For us, competency is the interaction of one's *knowledge*—both general (counseling processes), and specific (trauma-informed therapy); skills—implementation of core, advanced and technique specific, like EMDR; attributes—personal characteristics (demeanor, culture, personal experiences); and performance—ability to integrate and utilize knowledge, skill, personal characteristics in the delivery of quality psychotherapeutic services.

Counselor's Personal History, Vulnerabilities, and Resilience

Professional counseling has been described as a "high touch profession" that is a career where one frequently hears painful experiences (Skovholt, 2017). Individuals who work in CTD settings and are repeatedly exposed to the pain of others experience vicarious traumatization, compassion fatigue, are prone to burnout, and, at times, leave the field due to impairment (Lee, Cho, Kissinger, & Ogle, 2010; Skovholt, 2017). The effects of repeatedly witnessing, listening, intervening, and processing client's pain from CTD experiences are cumulative. So, it is not surprising they suffer from burnout, compassion fatigue, vicarious traumatization, secondary traumatization, and impairment (James & Gilliland, 2013). In addition to wellness and self-care, we believe it is essential for the clinician to have a sense of humor and share collectively regarding their experience in this work. Whether it be a consultation or a supervision group, it is immensely helpful to share and to have an appropriate sense of humor about the complex nature of this sort of work.

Personal Histories

Who you are influences what you do. Your dispositions and the fullness of your individual genetic, relational, and intergenerational history interact with those around you and, in particular, your clients. Consider what occurs for a clinician with a personal history of trauma who chooses to serve CTD clients. As you might guess, they may be able to use their experiences as a basis for empathy and understanding clients or they may be triggered and reexperience their own traumatic experiences or some combination of the two. It is important for us to stop for a moment and note, that it is not solely the *presence* of a trauma history that contributes to a clinician's vulnerability; it is the presences of and lack of attention to mitigating the effects of one's traumatic history that puts a clinician at risk. Those clinicians, impacted by a history of trauma, may blur client/clinician boundaries, overidentify with clients' suffering and struggles, experience countertransference, or see a reemergence of a host of symptoms like hyperarousal, hypervigilance, intrusive thoughts, and state switching (Lawson & Myers, 2011). For some clinicians, this leads to professional and perhaps personal impairment.

According to Carl Jung (1966), a wounded healer is a helping professional who is motivated to help others because of their own emotional hurt and psychological distress. Thus, clinicians with unfinished business may unintentionally influence a client's therapy due to their history. Client's helplessness, pain, and fear are a few of the many foci in CTD counseling. Clinicians with an unaddressed history of trauma who are repeatedly exposed to clients' trauma, at best may experience emotional arousal in or after sessions, at worst they develop burnout and compassion fatigue (Figley, 1995; Lawson & Myers, 2011).

Unfortunately, some clinicians believe they should be able to overcome personal difficulties without the assistance of therapy and conclude they are immune to mental health concerns (Lawson & Venart, 2005). According to Flynn's (2009) participants, they often neglected their personal needs, did not seek therapy when they needed it, and described *wounded healers* as untrustworthy (See Theme 11; Professional Mistrust). They acknowledged fear associated with the disclosure of their mental health concerns or disorders and believe others would see them as impaired. This sense of professional mistrust can create a viscous cycle of self-statements such as: "I provide genuineness and unconditional positive regard, yet when I let my guard down, fellow colleagues attack." Conflicting messages such as this can create professional isolation, which can lead to burnout and clinicians attempting to get their needs met in inappropriate ways.

Environmental Vulnerabilities

Where we work and how we feel at work matter. Feeling involved and respected contributes to our wellbeing. For example, evidence (Dworkin, Sorell, & Allen, 2016) suggests that aspects of the caregiver's environment have a profound effect on their well-being, such as feeling a sense of control and decision-making power in the workplace (Ceschi, Demerouti, Sartori, & Weller, 2017) along with sense of meaning (Niessen, Sonnentag, & Sach, 2012). Paterson, Luthans, and Jeung (2014) stated that employee resiliency results from feeling supported and valued by fellow workplace colleagues. Specifically, employees who do not feel a sense of control, meaning, and support fail to thrive and often find themselves unhappy, alone, and anxious and some come to depend on their clients to get their needs met. Environmental factors contributing to counselor burnout include large caseloads of clients with severe pathology (Rupert & Kent, 2007) or high-risk behaviors (Sim, Zanardelli, Loughran, Mannarino, & Hill, 2016) and working with traumatized clients with little or no training (Craig & Sprang, 2010). Membership in historically disadvantaged groups (Jacobson, 1989), a history of personal trauma (Nelson-Gardell & Harris, 2003), and one's need for trust, safety, control, intimacy, and esteem in their environment (Foreman, 2018) increase the chance of caregiver distress.

Resilience

While it is important to recognize factors or vulnerabilities that contribute to burnout, it may be more helpful to consider how a counselor may build their resilience and wellness (Osborn, 2004). Resilience is comprised of one's behaviors, thoughts, and action. Because it is not a trait, it can be taught and improved. When faced with a CTD event, people experience distress and have a host of emotions including fear, sadness, and hopelessness. Often, gains in resiliency result from periods of emotional distress. Resilience is akin to bouncing back from a stressful and difficult event and is considered a form of adaptation.

Factors contributing to resilience include the presence of love and security in supportive relationships, self-esteem, capacity for emotional regulation, encouraging role models, and cultural narratives about responding to adversity. To build or support resilience, researchers recommend investing in positive relationships that nurture, stay engaged during times of adversity rather than detaching, engage optimism, and practice self-care (Myers & Sweeney, 2005). Regardless of your strategy, it is important to identify and engage in activities that meet your needs. In addition to practices that increase resiliency and wellness, clinicians can and often do engage in compassion satisfaction (Figley, 1997) like spending time with loved ones or having a balanced caseload with clients with less acute issues (Lawson & Myers, 2011). Resiliency plans help clinicians identify specific behaviors, thoughts, and actions that can support their ability to bounce back. We encourage you to consider creating a plan specific to their needs. Table 8.1 describes a wellness toolkit for CTD clinicians organized around eight domains.

The Neurobiological Basis of Psychological Distress

In response to a perceived threat, the autonomic nervous system responds with a fight, flight, or freeze reaction. During these experiences and in preparation for fight or flight, one's muscles tense and heart rate increases; the sympathetic branch of the autonomic nervous system has been activated. The adrenal glands release norepinephrine, epinephrine, and cortisol (Baranowsky, Gentry, & Schultz, 2005). The limbic system's amygdala is the primary controller of emotional reactivity to client trauma narratives. For example, the amygdala coordinates the release of norepinephrine, cortisol, and epinephrine when faced with a traumatic story. Golkar et al., (2014) discovered that there is a weaker functional connection between the amygdala and the medial prefrontal cortex (mPFC) in individuals suffering from work-related stress. This finding indicates that burnout is largely based in the limbic system.

Psychological distress includes "memory and concentration problems, sleeplessness, diffuse aches, profound fatigue, irritability, anxiety, and a feeling of being

TABLE 8.1 ● Wellness Toolkit for Crisis, Trauma, and Disaster Clinicians

Social	Emotional	Physical	Intellectual	Spiritual	Occupational	Financial	Environmental
Respectful conversations	Breathing exercises	Daily exercise	Learning new skills	Engaging in spirituality and religion	Engaging in a satisfying work environment	Understanding one's financial circumstances	Respecting the external environment
Cooperation	Positive self-talk	Healthy diet	Daily mental activities (crossword puzzles)	Yoga	Following a professional calling	Setting and accomplishing reasonable financial goals	Avoid littering
Community engagement	Open communication	Walking whenever possible	Video/computer games	Introspecting on one's beliefs	Commitment to one's chosen career	Creating long-term financial plans	Protecting fragile environments
Dating	Positive mental imagery	Dancing	Taking classes	Discussing meaningful topics with colleagues	Engaging in meaningful aspects of one's career	Maintaining a balanced budget	Supporting causes that protect the environment
Serving on committees	Adopt daily rituals and routines	Less sitting	Developing new hobbies	Developing a rich inner world	Work–life balance	Advocating that one's pay matches one's education and training	Minimizing one's carbon footprint
Social media		Joining a sport or club team	Reading	Counseling			
Casual get-togethers		Counting steps	Writing	Attending a retreat			
Joining clubs		Massage therapy		Mindfulness			
Expressing gratitude		Sleeping					
		Chiropractic adjustment					
		Following medical advice					

emotionally drained" (Golkar et al., 2014, p. 9). These symptoms appear in those exposed to trauma-saturated narratives overwhelming the limbic and autonomic nervous systems. According to Golkar et al. (2014), when individuals experience psychological distress, they attempt to down-regulate negative emotional reactions. At this point, the parasympathetic nervous system is activated and produces better self-regulation and increased physical comfort (Baranowsky, Gentry, & Schultz, 2005). We provide this information to help you better understand how your nervous system and brain are involved in your emotional dysregulation. It is our belief that most clinicians suffering from work-related psychological distress are interested in finding a sense of balance and working toward self-regulation. Not understanding your neurobiology is like a mechanic working on the engine of a car without ever opening the hood.

Maintaining Healthy Relationships and Work–Life Balance

Many clinicians feel a calling to their chosen profession and are passionate about helping others. Yet, it is very difficult to care for others when you have neglected yourself. Whether it be spending time with loved ones, attending to your personal wellness, advancing your career, or engaging in religious or spiritual organizations, clinician's need to be mindful of their work and life balance. Crisis, trauma, and disaster counseling are critical services for clients and society and may come at a cost to you. We believe it is important to remember the interactive and interdependent nature of giving and receiving. Truly, you can only give to the extent that you feel nourished, happy, and well (Flynn & Black, 2011).

Summary

In this chapter, we explored a variety of constructs related to caring for the caregiver—finding a sense of balance, vulnerabilities, resilience, wellness, and use of appropriate self-interest. The importance of understanding how burnout, impairment, compassion fatigue, and secondary and vicarious traumatization develop are paramount and mediated by growth-producing behaviors, thoughts, and actions. Clinicians intentionally engage in self-care and wellness, not only for themselves; they do so for their clients and the profession.

Extended Learning Exercises

Case Illustration: Advanced Graduate Student

Burnout or compassion fatigue is most often associated with mid- to late-career professionals. Because most advanced graduate students have not had the number and type of clinical cases associated with compassion fatigue, no case illustration is provided. The wellness and self-care strategies discuss previously are useful for the general stress and fatigue encountered in graduate school.

Case Illustration: Novice Professional

Marybeth is a 44-year-old woman who is serving in the role of crisis counselor on the emergency room (ER) wing of a hospital. Recently, there has been a heavy client flow in the ER. Marybeth has been working with many individuals returning from war. These men and women have mostly been diagnosed initially with substance abuse and later PTSD. Marybeth's supervisor noticed she was calling into work two to three times a week and, after a conversation with Marybeth, recommended personal counseling. Marybeth shared she had difficulty getting to sleep and feels more anxious than she ever remembered. On the days Marybeth is at work she appears unfocused, unmotivated, and disheveled. Her supervisor noticed Marybeth frequently sitting alone in the staff lunch area. When others try to connect with Marybeth she is talkative and appears jovial, remarking that "nothing is wrong."

Questions to Consider

As a colleague, how do you respond to Marybeth?

What suggestions or skills will you utilize to help her achieve wellness?

What are your priorities with Marybeth as a fellow employee?

When you speak to Marybeth, who else may you involve in the conversation?

What additional information or resources are required for you to assist Marybeth?

What are the desired outcomes for Marybeth?

Describe any thoughts you have about Marybeth's supervisor's course of action.

Case Illustration: Mid-Career Professional

You are a 39-year-old supervisor of a disaster mental health response team, helping citizens in a flood situation. Individuals are waiting on rooftops to be evacuated. Your team is asked to help evacuate residents by boat; you want to pitch in but are concerned about their capacity to rescue others. Over the course of the next two days, you notice a steady decrease in one team member, Bob's, functioning. He seems distracted and at times disorganized in his thinking. Rather than executing his duties, Bob has been engaging in casual conversations with rescued residents. Each night, he and a few other disaster response team members go out and drink heavily. Bob has come back to work severely hungover and is detached. He is exhausted and unable to focus. As the supervisor, you have asked Bob what is going on and suggest his drinking is disrupting his ability to do his work; he agrees to stop drinking. However, in the days that follow, he continues to report for work hungover. At this point, you would like to ask Bob to go home; however, due to the few numbers of disaster team members, you are hesitant.

Questions to Consider

As a field supervisor, how would you respond to this concerning situation?

What do you think may be contributing to his behavior?

How would you intervene and what are the potential positive and negative consequences of your intervention?

What ethical and legal aspects of this case must be considered?

When you confront Bob about his behavior, would you want anyone else with you? Why?

What are your desired outcomes for Bob?

Additional Resources

Helpful Books

The Resilient Practitioner: Burnout Prevention and Self-Care Strategies for Counselors, Therapists, Teachers, and Health Professionals (2017). Thomas Skovholt

Simple Self-Care for Therapists: Restorative Practices to Weave Through Your Workday (2015). Ashley Davis Bush

Burnout: The Cost of Caring (2003). Christina Maslach

Compassion Fatigue: Prevention and Resiliency (2005). Eric Gentry

Counseling for Wellness: Theory, Research, and Practice (2005). Jane Myers & Tom Sweeney

Coping With Secondary Traumatic Stress Disorder in Those Who Treat the Traumatized (1995). Charles Figley

9

Emerging Trends

Scientific and clinical understandings of crisis, trauma, and disaster (CTD) continue to evolve and transform. This chapter presents emerging trends in the areas of diagnostics, technology, and clinical training as they relate to the treatment of individuals, families, and groups. Clinicians and researchers enhance the knowledge base through empirical investigations, theory building, epidemiology, and innovations and integration of medicine, culture, and psychology. These advancements lead to more effective treatments and interventions, improved outcomes, and greater refinements in the education of the next generation of researchers and clinicians. The trends presented here are neither exhaustive nor comprehensive; rather, we aspire to provide you, the reader, an appreciation of what lies ahead.

Because this chapter focuses on emerging trends, we do not provide *Extended Learning Exercises* or the *Counselor's Toolkit*.

Learning Objectives

After reading this chapter you will be able to

- Identify the emerging trends in CTD mental health counseling and treatment as they relate to diagnostics and client evaluation, technology, and clinical education

- Understand emerging trends in context and mental health and community frameworks

- Acquire specific knowledge to extend your awareness, knowledge, and skill in the treatment and support of those who have experienced or continue to experience CTD

- Recognize the need for continued personal and professional development specifically as it relates to CTD mental health

Diagnostics and Client Evaluation

Diagnosing stress and trauma-related conditions present numerous opportunities for researchers and clinicians. In this section, we explore developments in diagnostic criteria and associated processes like appraisal and coping, idiosyncratic memory, and comorbidity considered by clinicians and researchers. Subsequent versions of the *Diagnostic and Statistical Manual* (American Psychiatric Association, 1980, 1987, 2000, 2013) ushered in changes and refinements designed to increase diagnostic accuracy, resolve inconsistent and imprecise terminology, improve conceptual clarity, and reduce diagnostic instability. Indeed, as North, Suris, Smith, and King (2016) note, the "DSM-5 has corrected several major ambiguities and errors of the former editions that are fundamental to the construct of PTSD . . . but problems remain in *DSM*-5 trauma criteria, especially inconsistencies between exposure criteria and the definition of trauma." (p. 197). The diagnostic criteria for PTSD and perhaps its legitimacy as a psychiatric diagnosis will continue to trend as research and technology advance.

In Chapter 4, we discussed the challenges and controversies related to the diagnosis of stress and trauma-related disorders, most notably the American Psychiatric Association's inclusion of Posttraumatic Stress Disorder (PTSD) in the *Diagnostic and Statistical Manual III* (*DSM–III*); (American Psychiatric Association [APA], 1980). Initial diagnostic criteria recognized that traumatic responding emanated from various types of traumatic incidents and that those affected responded to similar treatment regimens, despite the origins of their trauma(s). Inclusion of PTSD in the diagnostic nomenclature reignited the centuries-old debate about the validity, origins, nature, and course of psychological trauma as a psychiatric disorder.

Almost four decades after the formal recognition of PTSD and the creation of diagnostic criteria presented in the *Diagnostic and Statistical Manual* (American Psychiatric Association [APA; *DSM–5*], 2013), the existence and diagnosis of PTSD continues to provoke disagreement and debate. Some view the continual changes as an overdue step in the right direction because many who suffer from exposure to traumatic events and chronic trauma do not experience standard PTSD symptoms. They experience symptoms associated with depression, anxiety, dissociation, or borderline personality disorder. The changes to the *DSM–5* are a positive indicator of the necessary refinements for distinct diagnoses. These refinements may help differentiate simple and complex traumas and identify the constellation of symptoms in an individual whose symptoms worsen into PTSD from those who do not. Alternatively, others argue continued changes in criteria foment the historic controversy surrounding PTSD. They question the legitimacy of PTSD as a distinct psychiatric disorder. Some decry the lack of an agreed-upon definition of trauma, arguing the conceptual constructs of trauma and stress are often conflated leading to over- or underdiagnoses, depending on which version of the *DSM* is used. Hoge et al. (2016) warn the changes will lead to unintended and negative consequences. They believe with no empirical basis for the revised criteria, clinical utility is reduced and clients or patients who previously met the criteria are excluded (Hoge, Riviere, Wilk, Herrell, & Weathers, 2014; O'Donnell et al., 2014).

Those critical of the changes in *DSM–5* criteria note the criteria fail to distinguish trauma from other complex stress disorders; disturb epidemiological research; and present decontextualized, confusing, and, at times, contradictory definitions of trauma, PTSD symptom clusters, and sequelae. Researchers and clinicians, who continue to debate the clinical criteria for syndromes and disorders, may wish to take note of Voltaire's (Besterman, 1969) caution of the perfect being the enemy of the good or in other words, the outcome of *DSM* debates should arrive at a *good enough* set of agreed-upon criteria, but given our history, this does not seem likely.

The present controversy and related trends center on the removal of A2 criteria and reducing subjectivity reflected in the *DSM–5*. The actions signal a significant change in *how* clinicians diagnose disorders. Typically, syndromes or disorders present a set of characteristics drawn from client histories, symptoms, and responses to treatment or the phenomena of the disorder. To arrive at a diagnosis, clinicians gather the client's concerns and experiences through a social and symptom history, paying special attention to the onset, intensity, chronicity, expression, and duration of the symptoms. Yet, a PTSD diagnosis is different. It requires clinicians to first establish the client's prior exposure to an *identifiable and qualifying* stress-inducing event and link it to the presenting and specific symptoms of concern. Symptoms, existing prior to the traumatic exposure like nightmares or hypervigilance, are not considered in the present diagnosis unless related specifically to the traumatic event. In comparison to previous versions, the *DSM–5* criteria further discriminate between the occurrence of and exposure to a traumatic event. Without the prior qualifying *exposure*, the remaining criteria for a PTSD diagnosis are irrelevant, regardless of the similarity of symptoms. Breslau, Chase, and Anthony (2002) underscored the connection between an individuals' exposure to intensely threatening events and PTSD symptoms. For them, the connection is the *critical* diagnostic criteria. Thus, the association of symptoms to the traumatic exposure is correlational not causal or put another way, "PTSD symptoms are conditionally linked to trauma exposure" (Pai, Suris, & North, 2017; p. 3). Exposure to a traumatic experience is the prerequisite event that differentiates PTSD from all other psychiatric and medical diagnoses.

Revisions to the diagnostic criteria from *DSM–III* to *DSM–5* were due, in part, to advocacy of social movements (see Chapter 4), academic and clinical/medical research, factor analytic reviews of *DSM* symptom clusters and improved clinical interviewing. Table 9.1 presents an overview of the diagnostic criteria for PTSD from *DSM–III* to *DSM–5*.

Pivotal changes in *DSM–5* diagnostic criteria related to trauma heralded a shift in the trajectory of mental health treatment and theory (Friedman, Keane, & Resick, 2014) as they are much more explicit and expansive about how one responds to traumatic events. This results in a more comprehensive diagnostic profile.

The *DSM–5* criteria stand in contrast to the PTSD criteria presented in the forthcoming *International Classification of Diseases (ICD–11)*. The ICD is used by the 194 members of the World Health Organization (WHO). The *ICD–11* diagnostic manual, currently in development, presents a more focused constellation of symptomatology and emphasizes the central role of re-experiencing fear.

TABLE 9.1 ● Trends in DSM PTSD Criteria from 1980 to 2013

Category	DSM-3 (1980)	DSM-3-R (1987)	DSM-4 (1994)	DSM-5 (2013)
	Anxiety Disorder	Anxiety Disorder	Anxiety Disorder	Trauma & Stressor Related Disorders
Criteria	A–Identifiable stressor outside range of common experience that would be markedly distressing to almost anyone B–Re-experiencing–intrusive, distressing recollections, dreams, intense psychological distress at exposure to events symbolic of the trauma C–Avoidance of events, thoughts, feelings, detachment, restricted range of affect, foreshorten future and/or partial event amnesia D–Arousal-sleep disturbance, irritability, hypervigilance, startle response, problems in concentration E–Duration > 1 month	A–Identifiable stressor outside range of common experience that would be markedly distressing to almost anyone B–Re-experiencing–intrusive recollections, dreams, intense psychological distress at exposure to events symbolic of the trauma C–Avoidance of events, thoughts, feelings, detachment, restricted range of affect, foreshorten future and/or partial event amnesia D–Arousal-sleep disturbance, irritability, hypervigilance, startle response, problems in concentration E–Duration > 1 month	A–Experienced, witnessed, or was confronted event(s) —actual or threatened death or serious injury, or a threat to the physical integrity of self or others and responded with fear, helplessness or horror B–Persistent re-experiencing– thoughts, dreams images, perceptions, reliving, intense psychological distress at exposure, physiological reactivity C–Avoidance–of events, thoughts, feelings, detachment, restricted range of affect, foreshorten future and/or partial event amnesia D–Arousal-sleep disturbance, irritability, hypervigilance, startle response, problems in concentration E–Persistence > 1 month F–Functional impairment from significant distress or impairment	A–Exposure to actual or threatened death or serious injury or sexual violence B–Intrusion recollections, nightmares, flashbacks, physiological reactivity C–Avoidance-persistent and effortful-thoughts, feelings, people, events D–Negative alterations in cognitions; partial event amnesia; negative beliefs and expectations; trauma related emotions distorted self or other blame E–Alterations in arousal-irritable; self-destructive, startle response, sleep disturbance, F–Persistence > 1 month

Subtypes	Specify delayed onset	Specify delayed onset	– Acute < 3 months – Chronic symptoms last > 3 months – With Delayed Onset > 6 months before symptom present	**G**–Functional impairment from significant distress or impairment **H**–No other causes – Dissociative – Preschool – Delayed expression
Types of Exposure	Direct	Direct	– Direct – Witnessed – Indirect	– Direct – Witnessed – Indirect – Repeated/extreme indirect—not through media
Required for diagnosis	3 of 12 symptoms	6 of 17 required	6 of 17 required	6 of 20 symptoms

Note: See manuals for specific required number of symptoms or duration for diagnosis.

Although initial examinations of the two diagnostic systems (O'Donnell et al., 2014) indicate nonsignificant differences in prevalence rates, levels of comorbidity with depression, and functional outcomes, competing diagnostic systems, and by extension methods of treatment, present difficult and confusing trends for researchers, clinicians, and the clients they treat. Research comparing *DSM–5* and *ICD–11* based criteria for PTSD is urgently needed as two diagnostic systems may result in differences in who receives a diagnosis (Friedman, 2013) and ultimately treatment.

The findings from the World Mental Health Survey Consortium (Benjet et al., 2016) indicate over 70% of respondents reported exposure to a single traumatic event and 30.5% reported exposure to four or more events. Most individuals who encounter CTDs return to their previous level of functioning after a period of recovery. Refining diagnostic criteria, predicting who develops PTSD and interactions among and between the aforementioned variables will require research that is multidimensional and longitudinal. The evolution in diagnostics will lead to more clarity about whom, how, and under what conditions one progresses from an acute response to traumatic exposure to PTSD. This should result in improved assessments, potential modes of prevention, and early intervention. As our understanding of individual and perhaps cultural variations underlying the numerous clinical presentations of PTSD—simple and complex trauma—are refined, researchers will need to explore the contribution of the appraisal or perception processes related to threat, anxiety, and fear, idiosyncratic appraisal and memories and preexisting or comorbid disorders.

Appraisal of Threat and Fear

Crisis, trauma, and disaster events evoke feelings of fear, anxiety, and threat in individuals and communities. Each of us responds according to our perception and evaluation of the degree of harm resulting from the event, its idiosyncratic meanings, and resources available. The threat appraisal and coping are anchored in the work of Lazarus (1966), who integrated Selye's (1956) theory of stress as response and research findings of stress as a stimulus (Holmes & Rahe, 1967) into an interactional theory of dynamic appraisal of stressful events or environments. In his later work, Lazarus, along with Folkman (1984), further refined appraisal as the "process of categorizing an encounter, and its various facets, with respect to its significance for well-being" (p. 31). They believed one's appraisal was a critical determinant of the nature and type of one's response to and coping with said event. As discussed in Chapter 2, Lazarus and Folkman proposed three forms of cognitive appraisals—primary, secondary, and reappraisal believed to influence *how* individuals enacted coping behaviors when confronted by stressful events (Folkman & Lazarus, 1985; Lazarus & Folkman, 1984; Lazarus, 1991). Recall that cognitive appraisal occurs when one assesses, somewhat simultaneously, the degree of threat posed by immediate exposure to the stressor—primary appraisal—and resources available—secondary appraisal—to address or mitigate the stressor and concomitant stress. One's ability to cope with a CTD seems profoundly influenced by the meaning of a stressor and one's perception of available resources. Reappraisal is a recursive process of assessing the nature of the stressor and available resources for coping over time.

Ehlers and Clark (2000) and Meiser-Stedman (2002) evaluated the appraisal process in light of information processing models of anxiety and traumatic stress. These researchers posited that the appraisal process led to strategies, which likely contributed to or exacerbated posttraumatic symptoms. Within the last decade, researchers have extended these models to children, noting particularly the impact of development on cognition, learning, and memory (Dalgleish, Meiser-Stedman, & Smith, 2005; Salmon & Bryant, 2002). This is a promising trend in research.

The process of appraisal has long been associated with PTSD (Ozer, Best, Lipsey, & Weiss, 2003) and with elevated and enduring PTSD symptoms. Like Ehlers and Clark's (2000) cognitive model, O'Donnell, Elliot, Wolfgang, and Creamer (2007) indicate exacerbated negative self-appraisal and its feedback loop increased an individual's anxiety and perception of threat. Further, they hypothesized it may increase the number of PTSD symptoms and perhaps the development of PTSD. Threat appraisal research is complex and confounded by improvements in mapping physiological response patterns like arousal; avoidance behaviors; comorbid functioning; information processing patterns—including attention and cognition; prior learning; and neural responding (Britton, Lissek, Grillon, Norcross, & Pine, 2011).

Neuropsychology and Neuroimaging

These incremental and stepwise investigations enrich our understanding and yield innovations in assessment, diagnostics, and treatment of acute stress and acute and chronic psychological trauma. For example, trends in cognitive science reveal researchers who investigate threat appraisal, extinction, and coping processes with cutting edge medical technology. Schlund, Brewer, Richman, Magee, and Dymond (2015) utilized functional magnetic resonance imaging (fMRI) to investigate the role that two brain structures, the dorsal anterior cingulate [adACC] and the dorsal medial prefrontal cortex [dmPFC]. play in the appraisal and discrimination of threatening events. Specifically, they examined the role of avoidance and extinction on threat appraisal and activation of these structures to determine what specific *features* of threatening situations activate these structures. They were interested in the way avoidance modifies appraisal and reduces the perceived threat and activation. These researchers considered how prevention of potentially stressful or traumatic events impacts responding. Neuroimaging studies of those diagnosed with PTSD have reported less activation of the medial prefrontal cortex (Markowitsch et al., 2000; Shin et al., 2001). According to van der Kolk (2006) "Neuropsychology and neuroimaging research demonstrate that traumatized individuals have problems with sustained attention and working memory, which causes difficulty performing with focused concentration, and hence, with being fully engaged in the present" (p. 280). The integration of knowledge between researchers and clinicians continue to advance our systemic and holistic understandings of trauma.

Idiosyncratic Appraisal and Memory

Evidence related to group and individual differences in crisis and traumatic responding is emerging. Researchers and clinicians continually strive to understand

and predict who and why some exposed to CTDs improve without intervention, some improvement and recover with intervention, and still others see their symptoms develop into persistent PTSD. Ehlers and Clark's (2000) cognitive model of persistent PTSD may aid our future understanding of the etiology and hence diagnosis of this disorder. They identified two primary cognitive abnormalities—an excessively negative appraisal of the traumatic event steeped in personal meanings creating a sense of a serious, current threat and idiosyncratic memories and their relationship to other personal memories. In this model, the traumatic exposure is processed in a way that results in excessively negative appraisals associated with disturbances in personal, vague, fragmented, or apparently random memories. These idiosyncratic memories seem automatically triggered by cues similar to the traumatic event. Problematic appraisals and the associated memories are believed to induce a range of maladaptive safety-seeking behaviors like carrying a weapon, numbing, avoidance, or vigilance and cognitive strategies like avoiding thoughts about the trauma, rumination, or keeping busy. Behaviors designed to minimize the serious and current threat. Regrettably, these actions appear to maintain the problem by directly producing PTSD symptoms (hypervigilance) or preventing change in the negative appraisals and the nature of the trauma memory. Ehlers and Clark's theoretical model continues to generate research and critical literature challenging models of PTSD and the beliefs surrounding the cause and maintenance of PTSD (Rubin, Berntsen, Ogle, Deffler, & Beckham, 2016; Berntsen, Rubin, & Johansen, 2008; Monroe & Mineka, 2008; Brewin & Andrews, 2016; Rigoli, Silva, de Oliveira, Pergher, & Kirstensen, 2016). For clinicians, it is an exciting time to engage the burgeoning professional literature and clinical debates; be a part of it!

Understanding Preexisting and Comorbid Disorders

Enduring traumatic reactions and responses have long been associated with acute or complex stress reactions or PTSD. The scope of the problem is staggering. Grinage (2003) indicated, "Approximately 80 percent of patients with PTSD have at least one co-morbid psychiatric disorder" (p. 2401). Comorbid disorders include substance abuse, depressive or anxiety disorders, neurocognitive problems, personality disorders, and impairments in physical health. Diagnosing and treating comorbid disorders requires skill, experience, and feedback as clients may deny, fail to associate, or may diminish a connection between current symptoms and previous exposure to traumatic events.

Researchers and clinicians assess clients for enduring symptoms. Often, these symptoms fail to respond to established treatments or may present after exposure to a traumatic event. Some clients use drugs or alcohol to facilitate a numbing response further complicating the diagnostic picture. Understanding the interplay between individual and socio-cultural factors requires advancements in clinical research, the neurobiology of traumatic responding, and improvements in integrated care.

Data emerging from numerous studies (Kessler, Chiu, Demler, Merikangas, & Walters, 2005; Kessler, Sonnega, Bromet, Hughes, & Nelson, 1995) point to the importance of understanding the contribution of preexisting and comorbid disorders emanating from medical, neurocognitive, or psychological disorders. Additional considerations of comorbidity include prior traumatic exposure, proximity to the traumatic event, threat appraisal, resiliency, and socio-cultural factors.

Depressive disorders, specifically major depression, are the most conspicuous among the psychological disorders comorbid with the development of PTSD symptoms in veteran and civilian populations (Erikson, Wolfe, King, King, & Sharkansky, 2001; O'Donnell, Creamer, & Patterson, 2004; Perlman et al., 2011; Bowman, 1999; Paris, 2001). Breslau, Davis, Peterson, and Schultz (2000) examined retrospective and prospective data contained in an epidemiologic study of 1,007 young adults to estimate the risk of major depression for those diagnosed with PTSD. They noted "Preexisting major depression increased the risk for subsequent exposure to traumatic events twofold and increased the risk for PTD among exposed persons more than threefold" (p. 906). This means PTSD and major depression, in those exposed to trauma, were not influenced by separate vulnerabilities. Kilpatrick et al. (2003) utilized a national household probability sample of 4,023 telephone-interviewed adolescents ages 12 to 17 to examine the prevalence of comorbidity and risk factors for PTSD, substance abuse, and major depressive episodes. Their results are significant because they indicate a high percentage of adolescents are exposed to traumatic events resulting in significant traumatic responding, particularly for those who have physical or sexual assault or have witnessed violence. These factors are believed to increase the risk of PTSD, major depression, and substance abuse and comorbidity.

Trends in Technology: Artificial Intelligence and Virtual Reality

Innovative diagnostic and treatment technologies continue to emerge as researchers and clinicians gain a more sophisticated understanding of the interplay of individuals' neurobiopsychosocial responses to traumatic events. New technologies, specifically digital phenotyping (Torous, Onnela, & Keshavan, 2017), provide access to a wide range of client data. Digital phenotyping, or the collection of data, may be done actively by direct input by the client or passively through the monitoring of sleep patterns or heart rates by smartphones or wearable health tracking or monitoring devices like the Apple Watch® or Fitbit®. Compiled data is analyzed relative to preselected variables (labels) through a computerized machine learning (ML) process commonly referred to as artificial intelligence (AI). The analysis generates predictions based on the variables of interest like behaviors, activity, or physiological responses. This is not unlike your DVR or TiVo®. Clinicians and researchers use the results to refine diagnoses and treatment.

While additional research needs to be performed, recent investigations utilizing ML and attempting to predict PTSD in trauma survivors (Karstoft, Galatzer-Levy, Statnikov, Li, & Shalev, 2015) and predeployed military personnel (Karstoft, Statnikov, Andersen, Madsen, & Galatzer-Levy, 2015) yielded encouraging results. Other researchers (Kessler et al., 2014) utilized large data sets (i.e., 47,446 individuals drawn from 24 countries) to develop a predictive model of PTSD. Variables included prior exposure to a traumatic event, a description of the nature and type of traumatic events, sociodemographic information, history of prior and cumulative exposure to traumatic events, and preexisting psychiatric disorders based on the *DSM–IV*. Kessler and his colleagues demonstrated that a sensitive risk algorithm could be generated using data collected in the immediate aftermath of a traumatic event. To demonstrate clinical utility in a practice setting, Kessler et al.'s algorithm requires further refinement and validation to produce a reliable protocol to identify those most at risk to develop PTSD. Models derived from ML processes are an encouraging step toward development of a personalized prediction of PTSD risk based on analytics and knowledge. Finally, Freeman et al. (2014) assessed the occurrence of paranoid thinking and of symptoms of posttraumatic stress disorder (PTSD) in 106 participants who had experienced a previous assault with the prior month. Participants engaged in a neutral virtual reality (VR) experience—a train ride. Paranoid thinking about the neutral computer-generated characters and the occurrence of PTSD symptoms in VR were assessed. The results indicated responses to VR predicted the severity of paranoia and PTSD symptoms as assessed by standard measures six months later.

Virtual Reality

Virtual reality (VR) or computer-generated, interactional simulation of three-dimensional environments seem to be everywhere, from gaming systems to virtual tours of homes to training applications like nursing, surgery, or flight simulators. Using specialized sensory equipment like gloves, helmets, motion chairs, goggles, headsets, and computer programs, VR systems present to the user a believable, interactive, and explorable atmosphere that is immersive. The VR equipment tracks head movement while the VR program responds. The user is presented a seamless and responsive environment that creates a sense of immersion. The environment is detailed. Events and one's reaction to them occur in real time.

Virtual reality systems simultaneously engage multiple senses and cognitive processes in realistic, controlled, and safe settings, not unlike many exposure therapies. Clinicians who regularly utilize exposure therapies like flooding, systematic desensitization, and imaginal or prolonged exposure (Keane, 1995) and Eye Movement Desensitization and Reprocessing (Rogers & Silver, 2002) understand the importance of a realistic therapeutic environment.

Exposure techniques vary in manner and timing. For example, the flooding technique uses in vivo exposure or actual exposure to the feared stimulus as one engages the previously learned relaxation techniques. This hierarchical process is designed to assuage symptoms of panic or anxiety. Alternatively, prolonged exposure techniques have clients confront their anxiety by first discussing it with the counselor—imaginal exposure, then progress to confronting actual reminders of the trauma in vivo. Virtual reality exposure (VRE) is a modality garnering increased utilization and empirical support. For clinicians, researchers, and their clients, this is an exciting opportunity to use innovative technologies and advance the next generation of exposure therapies. Virtual reality exposure creates an evocative environment designed to augment the client's memories and imagination while pairing them with multisensory VR experiences. Typically, in this form of therapy, clients describe as fully as is possible the details of the traumatic experience while engaged in a VR simulation. Clinicians monitor and analyze clients' physiological and psychological responses. The goal of this treatment is based on repeated, engaged, and prolonged exposure to the traumatic experiences. It is believed exposure helps clients engage newly developed appraisal processes, coping skills, self-soothing behaviors, and protective strategies designed to challenge previous maladaptive beliefs.

Prolonged exposure is based on emotional processing theory. According to Foa and Kozak (1986), emotional engagement during imaginal exposure is critical to a positive clinical outcome. Lack of emotional engagement predicts poor treatment outcomes (Jaycox, Foa, & Morral, 1998). Foa and Kozak hypothesized that two conditions were necessary: The memory of the traumatic event needed to be activated through emotional engagement and corrected information or knowledge needed to be encoded and incorporated into memory. Thus, some (Reger et al., in press) propose that VRE presents the *trauma-relevant, multisensory stimuli* necessary to increase emotional engagement which increases the likelihood of positive clinical outcomes.

Recent empirical studies seek to explore VR-based interventions. For example, in 2005, the Office of Naval Research funded a series of investigations focused on different forms of VR-based treatments for veterans of Afghanistan and Iraq. McLay et al. (2011) examined Virtual Reality–Graded Exposure Therapy (VR-GET) for active duty service members with combat-related post-traumatic stress disorder. VR-GET differs from other VR-based interventions in that VR-GET combines graded exposure, skills training, and monitoring of the fight or flight response. McLay et al. stated, "This is designed to allow a participant to more fully confront and tolerate simulated memories and fears within the VR environment" (2011, p. 224), particularly those clients who may not be able to fully verbalize their experiences. Incremental or graded exposure in virtual reality experiences is designed to provide clients a measure of control, deepening their emotional engagement, and decreasing autonomic and cognitive reactivity like angry outbursts or intrusive thoughts. It also supports the development of mental models for self-management which can be applied in other areas of clients' lives. The results from McLay et al.'s small, randomized trial ($N = 10$) indicate that 7 of 10 participants who received VR-GET improved by 30% or greater while only 1 of the 9 returning participants in the treatment-as-usual control group showed similar results. This study has clear limitations yet demonstrated clinically and statistically significant results. VR-GET was an effective treatment for participants.

Trends in Clinical Training

Clinicians are at the very heart of treating those who have experienced trauma. At best, providing treatment is challenging and exciting. Skilled clinicians aid client outcomes through use of evidence-based interventions. At worst, providing treatment is a complex enterprise fraught with challenges. Treatment delivered by underskilled and inadequately trained practitioners has the potential to harm clients and continue their suffering. Inclusion of CTD-specific curriculum and clinical experiences occurred, in most counselor training programs, only *after* the Council for Accreditation of Counseling and Related Educational Programs (CACREP, 2009) required it. It is curious that despite the ubiquity of traumatic exposure, particularly the last two centuries, counselor education programs failed to dedicate a portion of the curriculum and field experiences to the treatment of those suffering from trauma in all its forms. Further, we agree with Fairburn and Wilson (2013) who noted it was extraordinary that despite a focus on evidence-based treatments, scant attention or research has focused on the outcome of therapists' education and competence. This calls into question whether clients are receiving the best possible treatment from competent, and often state licensed, practitioners. We also question the depth and breadth of the content studied in training programs. Are students exposed to trauma-informed treatments, neurosequential models of intervention, integrated-care models including use of psychopharmalogical agents, and community versus individual levels of responding? Without adequate research to inform training practices, it is not surprising; we have no way to assess the competence of therapists and counselors.

Thankfully, things are changing. A compelling review by Rosen, Ruzek, and Karlin (2017) presents the challenges and opportunities of evidence-based training for PTSD providers. They describe three distinct training models training in three distinct settings, the Veteran's Administration (VA), the National Child Traumatic Stress Network, and the Improving Access to Psychological Treatment initiative. It is notable this training occurred outside of institutions of higher education despite the CACREP standards, the five core competencies, the scientific basis of trauma therapy, evidenced-based assessment and treatment practices, ethics, and the nine cross-cutting competencies recommended by a consensus group of the American Psychological Association (Cook & Newman, 2014). No methods or means of assessing training outcomes or therapist competence were included.

Rosen, Ruzek, and Karlin's (2017) review documenting VA training was based on competencies tied to improved clinical outcomes for clients through a case conceptualization model grounded in ongoing consultation and supervision. Pedagogical elements included a three- to four-day intensive experience involving role-plays, demonstration of clinical procedures, and a review of videotaped client interactions. Most notably, trainees were exposed and expected to deliver evidenced-based treatments with competence, integrity, and fidelity. Initial studies appear to demonstrate positive outcomes for clinicians (Karlin & Cross, 2014) and their clients (Stewart et al., 2015).

The National Child Traumatic Stress Network (NCTSN) intended to foster a large-scale collaboration on evidenced-based treatment for traumatized children between the academy and community agencies. The NCTSN model, much like the VA model, involved intensive workshop training, supervisor or consultant interactions, and direct instruction in evidenced-based treatments. Unlike the VA program, the NCTSN model included an emphasis on supervision, long-term sustainability, and greater scalability. Regrettably, there is scant outcome data on the results of this training program limiting the generalizability of this model.

The final model reviewed by Rosen and his team is the Improving Access to Psychological Treatment Initiative in the United Kingdom. Begun in 2007, the initiative was heralded as a beneficial and cost-effective method to address mood disorders through a continuum of care titrated from low-intensity, low-cost services provided by trained paraprofessionals, to self-help and supportive interventions, to the costliest level of intervention—evidenced-based treatment by a trained cognitive behavioral therapist (Clark, 2012). Although, recent outcome data from this model demonstrates low correlational support between client outcomes and provider competence (Rosen, Ruzek, & Karlin, 2017), the model has provided greater access to care, stimulated research, and an effective training framework for citizens of the United Kingdom.

Summary

Emerging trends in CTD counseling take many forms. As you consider how you develop as a counselor, it is critical to understand the importance of personal and professional development. Fairburn and Wilson (2013) noted the gravity of this task when they considered the specialized training necessary in eating disorders; they wrote, "The daunting task is how to train all those therapists who require training, not just those who work in a particular organization, state or country, but worldwide. The current method of training is not suited to this task" (p. 517–518). The same is true of your training in crisis, trauma, and disaster counseling. We implore you, continue your training, read widely, seek supervision, attend to your wellness, focus on proven treatments, and monitor your clients' outcomes; they deserve no less.

• References •

Chapter 1

Adams, S. A., & Riggs, S. A. (2008). An exploratory study of vicarious trauma among therapist trainees. *Training and Education in Professional Psychology, 2,* 26–34. http://dx.doi.org/10.1037/1931-3918.2.1.26

American Counseling Association. (2014). *2014 ACA Code of Ethics* Retrieved July 6, 2016. http://www .counseling.org/docs/ethics/2014-aca-code-of-ethics .pdf? sfvrsn=4

American Psychological Association (APA). (2002). Ethical principles of psychologists and code of conduct. *American Psychologist, 57,* 1060–1073.

American Psychological Association. (2010). *Ethical principles of psychologists and code of conduct.* Retrieved July 6, 2016. http://www.apa.org/ethics/code/

Appell, M. L. (1963). Self-understanding for the guidance counselor. *Personnel and Guidance Journal, 42, 143–148.*

Bernard, J. M., & Goodyear, R. K. (2009). *Fundamentals of clinical supervision.* (4th ed.). Columbus, OH: Merrill.

Borders, L. D., Glosoff, H. L., Welfare, L. E., Hays, D. G., DeKruyf, L., Fernando, D. M., & Page, B. (2014). Best practices in clinical supervision: Evolution of a counseling specialty. *The Clinical Supervisor, 33,* 26–44.

Boud, D., Keogh, R., & Walker, D. (1985) *Reflection: Turning experience into learning.* London: Kogan Page.

Boyd, E. M., & Fales, A. W. (1983). Reflective learning: Key to learning from experience. *Journal of Humanistic Psychology, 23,* 99–119.

Cashdan, S. (1988). *Object relations therapy: Using the relationship.* New York: W.W. Norton.

Cavanagh, A., Wiese-Batista, E., Lachal, C., Baubet, T., & Moro, M. R, (2015). Countertransference in trauma therapy. *Journal of Trauma Stress Disorders and Treatment, 4,* 4. doi:10.4172/2324-8947.1000149

Center for Behavioral Health Statistics and Quality. (2015). Receipt of services for behavioral health problems: Results from the 2014 national survey on drug use and health. Retrieved April 14, 2016. http:// www.samhsa.gov/data

Collins, S., & Arthur, N. (2010). Culture-infused counselling: A model for developing multicultural competence. *Counselling Psychology Quarterly, 23,* 217–233. doi:10.1080/09515071003798212

Collins, S., Arthur, N., & Wong-Wylie, G. (2010). Enhancing reflective practice in multicultural counseling through cultural auditing. *Journal of Counseling & Development, 88,* 340–347.

Connelly, F. M., & Clandinin, D. J. (1988). *Teachers as curriculum planners: Narratives of experience.* New York: Teachers College Press.

Corey, G. (2013). *Theories and practice of counseling and psychotherapy* (9th ed.). Belmont, CA: Brooks/ Cole-Cengage Learning.

Court, D. (1988). Reflection-in-action: Some definitional problems. In P. P. Grimmett & G. L. Erickson (Eds.), *Reflection in teacher education* (pp. 143–146). New York: Teachers College Press.

deJong, T., & Ferguson-Hessler, M. G. M. (1996). Types and qualities of knowledge. *Educational Psychologist, 31,* 105–113.

Dewey, J. (1933). *How we think. A restatement of the relation of reflective thinking to the educative process* (Revised ed.). Boston: D. C. Heath & Company.

Dupre, M., Echterling, L. G., Meixner, C., Anderson, R., & Kielty, M. (2014). Supervision experiences of professional counselors providing crisis counseling. *Counselor Education and Supervision, 53,* 82–96.

Duval, T. S., & Wicklund, R. A. (1972). *A theory of objective self-awareness.* New York: Academic.

Edwards, G., & Thomas, G. (2010). Can reflective practice be taught? *Educational Studies, 36,* 403–414.

Finlay, L. (2008). Reflecting on 'reflective practice'. *PBLB paper, 52*. Retrieved August 18, 2016. http://www.sencer.net/Symposia/SSI2015/documents/Finlay-2008-Reflecting-on-reflective-practice-PBPL-paper-52.pdf

Fosshage, J. L. (2005). The explicit and implicit domains in psychoanalytic change. *Psychoanalytic Inquiry, 25*, 516–539.

Furr, S. R., & Carroll J. J. (2003). Critical incidents in student counselor development. *Journal of Counseling & Development, 81*, 483–489.

Goleman, D. (1995). *Emotional intelligence*. New York: Random House.

Gray, L. A., Ladany, N., Walker, J. A., & Ancis, J. R. (2001). Psychotherapy trainees' experience of counterproductive events in supervision. *Journal of Counseling Psychology, 48*, 371–383.

Grayer, E. D., & Sax, P. R. (1986). A model for the diagnostic and therapeutic use of countertransference. *Clinical Social Work Journal, 14*, 295–309.

Guiffrida, D. A. (2005). The emergence model: An alternative pedagogy for facilitating self-reflection and theoretical fit in counseling students. *Counselor Education and Supervision, 44*, 201–213.

Hanna, F. J. (1994). A dialectic of experience: A radical empiricist approach to conflicting theories in psychotherapy. *Psychotherapy, 31*, 124–136.

Hill, C. E., Charles, D., & Reed, K. (1981). A longitudinal analysis of counseling skills during doctoral training in counseling psychology. *Journal of Counseling Psychology, 28*, 428–436.

Hill, H. R. M, Crowe, T. P., & Gonsalvez, C. J. (2015). Reflective dialogue in clinical supervision: A pilot study involving collaborative review of supervision videos. *Psychotherapy Research, 26*, 263–278. http://dx.doi.org.unco.idm.oclc.org/10.1080/10503307.2014.996795

Ho, D. Y. F. (1995). Internalized culture, culturocentrism, and transcendence. *The Counseling Psychologist, 23*, 4–24.

Hogan, R. A. (1964). Issues and approaches in supervision. *Psychotherapy: Theory Research and Practice, 1*, 139–141.

Jarvis, P. (1992). Reflective practice and nursing. *Nurse Education Today, 12*, 174–181.

Johns, C. (2004). *Becoming a reflective practitioner.* (2nd ed.). Oxford, UK: Blackwell Publishing.

Johns, C. (2006). *Engaging reflection in practice: A narrative approach.* Oxford, UK: Blackwell Publishing.

Jungers, C., & Gregoire, J. (2013). *Counseling ethics: Philosophical and professional foundations.* New York: Springer.

Kitchener, K. S. (1986). The reflective judgment model: Characteristics, evidence, and measurement. In R. A. Mines & K. S. Kitchener (Eds.), *Adult cognitive development: Methods and models* (pp. 76–91). New York: Prager.

Knott, C., & Scragg, T. (2016). *Reflective practice in social work.* Thousand Oaks, CA: Sage.

Kondrat, M. E. (1999). Who is the self in self-aware: Professional self-awareness from a critical theory perspective. *Social Service Review, 73*, 451–477.

Kramer, C. H. (2000). *Therapeutic mastery: Becoming a more creative and effective psychotherapist.* Phoenix, AZ: Zeig Tucker & Theisen, Inc.

Ladany, N., Hill, C. E., Corbett, M. M., & Nutt, E. A. (1996). Nature, extent, and importance of what psychotherapy trainees do not disclose to their supervisors. *Journal of Counseling Psychology, 43*, 10–24.

Lerner, R. M. (1986). *Concepts and theories of human development.* New York: Random House.

Lewis, M., & Brooks-Gunn, J. (1978). Self-knowledge and emotional development. In M. Lewis & L. Rosenblum (Eds.), *The development of affect: The genesis of behavior,* (pp. 205–226). New York: Plenum Press.

Loganbill, C., Hardy, E., & Delworth, U. (1982). Supervision: A conceptual model. *The Counseling Psychologist, 10*, 3–42.

National Association of Social Workers. (2008). *Code of ethics of the National Association of Social Workers.* Retrieved July 6, 2016. https://www.socialworkers.org/pubs/code/code.asp

Mayer, J. D., & Salovey, P. (1997). What is emotional intelligence? In P. Salovey & D. J. Sluyter (Eds.), *Emotional development and emotional intelligence: Educational implications* (pp. 3–34). New York: Harper Collins.

McLean, B., & Whalley, J. (2004). No real tale has a beginning or an end . . . Exploring the relationship between co-supervision, reflective dialogue and psychotherapeutic work with mental health service users, *Reflective Practice, 5,* 225–238. doi: 10.1080/14623940410001690992

Meier, S., & Davis, S. (1997). *The elements of counseling* (3rd ed.). Pacific Grove, CA: Brooks/Cole.

Munby, H. (1989). Reflection-in-action and reflection-on-action. *Education and Culture,* 9. http://docs .lib.purdue.edu/eandc/vol09/iss1/art4

Orchowski, L., Evangelista, N. M., & Probst, D. R. (2010). Enhancing supervisee reflectivity in clinical supervision: A case study illustration. *Psychotherapy: Theory, Research, Practice, Training, 47,* 51–67. http:// dx.doi.org/10.1037/a0018844

Osterman, K. F. (1990) Reflective practice: A new agenda for education. *Education and Urban Society, 22,* 133–152.

Pearlman, L. A., & Saakvitne, K. W. (1995). *Trauma and the therapist: Countertransference and vicarious traumatization in psychotherapy with incest survivors.* New York: W. W. Norton.

Pedro, J. Y. (2005). Reflection in teacher education: Exploring pre-service teachers' meanings of reflective practice. *Reflective Practice, 6,* 49–66.

Ratts, M. J., Singh, A. A., Nassar-McMillan, S., Butler, S. K., & McCullough, J. R. (2015). Multicultural and social justice counseling competencies. Retrieved from http:// www.counseling.org/knowledge-center/ competencies

Reamer, F. G. (2013). *Reflective practice in social work — The ethical dimension.* Retrieved May 18, 2016. http:// www.socialworktoday.com/news/eoe_042513.shtml

Rønnestad, M. H., & Skovholt, T. M. (2013). *The developing practitioner: Growth and stagnation of therapists and counselors.* New York: Routledge.

Rosin, J. (2015). The necessity of counselor individuation for fostering reflective practice. *Journal of Counseling & Development, 93,* 88–95. doi:10.1002/ j.15566676.2015.00184.x

Roysircar, G. (2004). Cultural self-awareness assessment: Practice examples from psychology training. *Professional Psychology: Research and Practice, 35,* 658–666.

Schore, J. R., & Schore, A. N. (2008). Modern attachment theory: The central role of affect regulation in development and treatment. *Clinical Social Work Journal,* 36(1), 9–20. doi:10.1007/s10615-007-0111-7

Schön, D. A. (1983). *The reflective practitioner: How professionals think in action.* New York: Basic Books.

Schön, D. A. (1987). *Educating the reflective practitioner.* San Francisco: Jossey-Bass.

Skovholt, T. M., & Rønnestad, M. H. (1995). *The evolving professional self: Stages and themes in therapist and counselor development.* Toronto, Ontario, Canada: Wiley.

Stern, D. (1985). *The interpersonal world of the infant: A view from psychoanalysis and developmental psychology.* New York: Basic Books.

Sternberg, R. (1990). *Wisdom: Its nature, origins and development.* New York: Cambridge Press.

Stoltenberg, C. D., McNeill, B., & Delworth, U. (1998). IDM *supervision: An integrated developmental model for supervising counselors and therapists.* San Francisco, CA: Jossey-Bass.

Sue, D. W., Capodilupo, C. M., Torino, G. C., Bucceri, J. M, Holder, A M. B., Nadal, K. L., & Esquilin, M. (2007). Racial microaggressions in everyday life: Implications for clinical practice. *American Psychologist, 62,* 271–286. Retrieved July 6, 2016. http://dx .doi.org/10.1037/0003-066X.62.4.271

Tobin, D. J., Willow, R. A., Bastow, E. K., & Ratkowski, E. M. (2009). Reflective learning within a counselor education curriculum. *The Journal of Counselor Preparation and Supervision, 1,* 3–9. Retrieved May 18, 2016. http://repository.wcsu.edu/cgi/viewcontent .cgi? article=1043&context=jcps

U.S. Department of Education (2016). FAQs about accreditation. Retrieved May 16, 2016. http://ope .ed.gov/accreditation/FAQAccr.aspx.

Ward, C. C., & House, R. M. (1998). Counselor supervision: A reflective model. *Counselor Education and Supervision,* 38, 23–33.

Williams, E. N., Judge, A. B., Hill, C. E., & Hoffman, M. (1997). Experiences of novice therapists in prepracticum: Trainees', clients', and supervisors' perceptions of therapists' personal reactions and management strategies. *Journal of Counseling Psychology, 44,* 390–399. http://dx.doi.org/10.1037/0022-0167.44.4.390

Wilson, T. D., & Dunn, E. (2004). Self-knowledge: Its limits, value, and potential for improvement. *Annual Review of Psychology, 55,* 493–518.

Wong-Wiley, G. (2007). Barriers and facilitators of reflective practice in counsellor education: Critical incidents from doctoral graduates. *Canadian Journal of Counselling, 41,* 59–76.

Wong-Wylie, G. (2010). Counsellor 'know thyself': Growing ourselves, shaping our professional practice, and enhancing education through reflection. Saarbrücken, Germany: VDM Verlag Press.

Yeager, K. R., & Roberts, A. R. (2003). Differentiating among stress, acute stress disorder, crisis episodes, trauma, and PTSD: Paradigm and treatment goals. *Brief Treatment and Crisis Intervention, 3,* 3–25.

Chapter 2

Adler, A. (1956). *The Individual Psychology of Alfred Adler.* H. L. Ansbacher and R. R. Ansbacher (Eds.). New York: Harper Torchbooks.

Adolphs, R. (2002). Neural systems for recognizing emotion. *Current Opinion in Neurobiology, 12,* 169–177.

Ainsworth, M. D. (1964). Patterns of attachment behavior shown by the infant in interaction with his mother. *Merrill-Palmer Quarterly of Behavior and Development, 10,* 51–58.

Ainsworth, M. D. S., Blehar, M. C., Waters, E., & Wall, S. (1978). *Patterns of attachment: A psychological study of the strange situation.* Hillsdale, NJ: Erlbaum.

Almedom, A. (2005). Resilience, hardiness, sense of coherence, and posttraumatic growth: All paths leading to "light at the end of the tunnel"? *Journal of Loss and Trauma, 10,* 253–265.

Amato, P. R. (2000). The consequences of divorce for adults and children. *Journal of Marriage and Family, 62,* 1269–1287.

American Academy of Child and Adolescent Psychiatry (2012). When children have children. *Facts for Families, 31.* Retrieved from http://www.aacap.org/App_Themes/AACAP/docs/facts_for_families/31_when_children_have_children.pdf

American Counseling Association. (2010). *20/20 – A vision for the future of counseling.* Retrieved April 4, 2016, http://counseling.org/20-20/definition.aspx

American Psychiatric Association. (1994). *Diagnostic and statistical manual of mental disorders* (4th ed.). Washington, DC: Author.

American Psychiatric Association. (2013). *Diagnostic and statistical manual of mental disorders* (5th ed.). Arlington, VA: American Psychiatric Publishing.

American Psychological Association. (2014). Marriage and divorce. *American Psychological Association.* Retrieved from http://www.apa.org/topics/divorce/

American Psychological Association Dictionary – Crisis Counseling (2018, February 27). Retrieved from https://dictionary.apa.org/crisis-counseling

Andersen, S. L. (2003). Trajectories of brain development: point of vulnerability or window of opportunity? *Neuroscience & Behavioral Reviews, 27,* 3–18.

Anderson, J. A., & Mohr, W. K. (2003). A developmental ecological perspective in systems of care for children with emotional disturbances and their families. *Education and Treatment of Children, 26,* 52–74.

Angelou, M. (1994). *The complete collected poems of Maya Angelou.* New York: Random House.

Attig, T. (1991). The importance of conceiving of grief as an active process, *Death Studies, 15,* 385–393. doi: 10.1080/07481189108252443

Ballantyne, A. O., Spilkin, A. M., Hesselink, J., & Trauner, D. A. (2008). Plasticity in the developing brain: intellectual, language, and academic functions in children with ischemic perinatal stroke. *Brain: A Journal of Neurology, 131,* 2975–2985.

Bard, M., & Ellison, K. (1974). Crisis intervention and investigation of forcible rape. *Police Chief, 41,* 68–74.

Baum, A. (1990). Stress, intrusive imagery, and chronic distress, *Health Psychology, 6,* 653–675.

Blaisure, K. R., & Saposnek, D. T. (2008). Reducing divorce conflicts. In *Clinical updates for family therapists: Research and treatment approaches for issues affecting today's families, Volume 3.* (pp. 209–224). Alexandria, VA: American Association for Marriage and Family Therapy.

Blakemore, S., & Robbins, T. W. (2012). Decision-making in the adolescent brain. *Nature Neuroscience, 15,* 1184–1191.

Boss, P. (2002). *Family stress management: A contextual approach* (2nd ed.). Thousand Oaks, CA: Sage.

Boss, P., & Sheppard, R. (1988). Family victimization and recovery. *Contemporary Family Therapy: An International Journal, 10,* 202–215.

Bowen, M. (1978). *Family therapy in clinical practice.* New York: Aronson.

Bowlby, J. (1980). *Attachment and loss.* London, UK: Hogarth Press & Institute of Psychoanalysis.

Bowlby, J. (1982). Attachment and loss: retrospect and prospect. *American Journal of Orthopsychiatry, 52,* 664–678.

Bowlby, J. (1992). *Charles Darwin: A new life*. New York: Norton.

Brammer, L. M. (1985). *The helping relationship: Process and skill* (3rd ed.). Upper Saddle River, NJ: Prentice Hall.

Bremner, J. D. (2008) Hippocampus. In G. Reyes, J. D. Elhai, & J. D. Ford (Eds.), *Encyclopedia of psychological trauma* (pp. 313–315). Hoboken, NJ: Wiley.

Brown, L. M., Shiang, J., & Bongar, B. (2003). Crisis intervention. In G. Stricker & T. A. Widiger (Eds.), *Handbook of Psychology* (Vol. 8) (pp. 431–451). Hoboken, NJ: Wiley.

Buchanan, M., & Robbins, C. (1990). Early adult psychological consequences for males of adolescent pregnancy and its resolution. *Journal of Youth and Adolescence, 19*, 412–424.

Buonomano, D. V., & Merzenich, M. M. (1998). Cortical plasticity: from synapses to maps. *Annual Review of Neuroscience, 21*, 149–186.

Cagney, K. A., Browning, C. R., Iveniuk, J., & English, N. (2014). The onset of depression during the great recession: foreclosure on adult mental health. *American Journal of Public Health, 104*, 498–505.

Campbell, J. (1970). *Myths, dreams, and religion*. New York: Dutton.

Caplan, G. (1961). *An approach to community mental health*. New York: Grune & Stratton.

Caplan, G. (1964). *Principles of preventative psychiatry*. New York: Basic Books.

Carballo, M., Smajkic, A., Zeric, D., Dzidowska, M., Gebre-Medhin, J., & Van Halem, J. (2004). Mental health and coping in a war situation: The case of Bosnia and Herzegovina. *Journal of Biosocial Science, 36*, 463–477.

Cavaiola, A., & Colford, J. (2006). *A practical guide to crisis intervention*. Boston, MA: Lahaska Press.

Cavaiola, A., & Colford, J. (2011). *Crisis intervention case book*. Belmont, CA: Brooks/Cole.

Centers for Disease Control and Prevention. (2012). 10 leading causes of death by age group, United States. https://www.cdc.gov/injury/wisqars/LeadingCauses.html

Centers for Disease Control and Prevention. (2017). 10 leading causes of death by age group, United States. https://www.cdc.gov/injury/images/lc-charts/leading_causes_of_death_by_age_group_2017_1100w850h.jpg

Charney, D. S., Woods, S. W., Goodman, W. K., & Heninger, G. R. (1987). Serotonin function in anxiety. *Psychopharmacology, 92*, 14–24.

Cheng, W., Ickes, W., & Kenworthy, J. B. (2013). The phenomenon of hate crimes in the United States. *Journal of Applied Social Psychology, 43*, 761–794.

Choudhury, S., Blakemore, S., & Charman, T. (2006). Social cognitive development during adolescence. *Social Cognitive and Affective Neuroscience, 1*, 165–174.

Cicchetti, D., Ackerman, B. P., & Izard, C. E. (1995). Emotions and emotion regulation in developmental psychopathology. *Development and Psychopathology, 7*, 1–10.

Cloninger, C. R., Sigvardsson, S., & Bohman, M. (1988). Childhood personality predicts alcohol abuse in young adults. *Alcoholism: Clinical and experimental research, 12*, 494–505.

Coates, S., & Gaensbauer, T. J. (2009). Event trauma in early childhood: symptoms, assessment, intervention. *Child and Adolescent Psychiatric Clinics of North America, 18*, 611–626.

Cohen, M., & Numa, M. (2011). Post-traumatic growth in breast cancer survivors: a comparison of volunteers and non-volunteers. *Psycho-Oncology, 20*, 69–76.

Cohn, D. A., Silver, D. H., Cowan, C. P., Cowan, P. A., & Pearson, J. (1992). Working models of childhood attachment and couple relationships. *Journal of Family Issues, 13*, 432–449.

Colcombe, S. J., Erickson, K. I., Scalf, P. E., Kim, J. S., Prakash, R., McAuley, E., . . . Kramer, A. F. (2006). Aerobic exercise training increases brain volume in aging humans. *Journals of Gerontology, 6*, 1166–1170.

Collins, B. G., & Collins, T. M. (2005). *Crisis and trauma: Developmental-ecological intervention*. Lahaska, PA: Lahaska Press.

Colt, G. H. (2006). *November of the soul: The enigma of suicide*. New York: Scribner.

Cotman, C. W., & Berchtold, N. C. (2002). Exercise: a behavioral intervention to enhance brain health and plasticity. *Trends in Neurosciences, 25*, 295–301.

Dass-Brailsford, P. (2007). *A political approach to trauma: Empowering interventions*. Thousand Oaks, CA: Sage.

Diedericks, J. C. (2014). The effects of motor vehicle accidents on careers and the work performance of victims. *South Africa Journal of Industrial Psychology, 40*.

Dong, W. K., & Greenough, W. T. (2004). Plasticity of nonneural brain tissue: roles in developmental disorders. *Mental Retardation and Developmental Disabilities Research Reviews, 10,* 85–90.

Dorsey, J. M. (1968). Observations on Hiroshima survivors. In H. Krystal (Ed.), *Massive psychic trauma* (pp. 168–188). New York: International Universities Press.

Doussard-Roosevelt, J. A., Porges, S. W., Scanlon, J. W., Alemi, B., & Scanlon, K. B. (1997). Vagal regulation of heart rate in the prediction of developmental outcome for very low birth weight preterm infants. *Child Development, 68,* 173–186.

Draganski, G., Gaser, C., Kempermann, G., Kuhn, H. G., Winkler, J., Büchel, C., & May, A. (2006). Temporal and spatial dynamics of brain structure changes during extensive learning. *The Journal of Neuroscience, 26,* 6314–6317.

Dyregov, A. (2003). Threat in the life of Iraqi children. In R. D. Macy, S. Barry, & G. G. Noam (Eds.), *New directions for youth development* (pp. 111–118). San Francisco: Jossey-Bass Psychology Series.

Echterling, L. G., Presbury, J. H., & McKee, J. E. (2005). *Crisis intervention: Promoting resilience and resolution in troubled times.* Upper Saddle River, NJ: Pearson Merrill Prentice Hall.

Enander, A., Lajksjö, Ö., & Tedfeldt, E. (2010). A tear in the social fabric: communities dealing with socially generated crises. *Journal of Contingencies and Crisis Management, 18,* 39–48.

Enman, N. M., Sabban, E. L., McGonigle, P., & Van Bockstaele, E. J. (2015). Targeting the neuropeptide y system in stress-related psychiatric disorders. *Neurobiological Stress, 1,* 33–43.

Erikson, E. H. (1997). *The Life Cycle Completed.* Extended Version with New Chapters on the Ninth Stage of Development by Joan M. Erikson. New York: Norton

Erikson, K. T. (1976). *Everything in its path: Destruction of community in the Buffalo Creek flood.* New York: Simon & Schuster.

Everly Jr., G. S., Phillips, S. B., Kane, D., & Feldman, D. (2006). Introduction to and overview of group psychological first aid. *Brief Treatment and Crisis Intervention, 6,* 130–136.

Federal Bureau of Investigation (2014). Hate crime – Overview. *Civil Rights.* Retrieved from http://www.fbi.gov/about-us/investigate/civilrights/hate_crimes/overview

Fine, R. (1973). Psychoanalysis. In R. J. Corsini (Ed.), *Current psychotherapies* (pp. 1–33). Itasca, IL: F. E. Peacock.

Ford, J. D. (2009a). Neurobiological and developmental research. In C. A. Courtois & J. D. Ford, (Eds.), *Treating complex traumatic stress disorders: An evidence-based guide.* New York: Guilford Press.

Ford, J. D. (2009b). *Posttraumatic stress disorder* (1st ed.) Academic Press: Cambridge, Mass.

Ford, J. D. (2014). Complex PTSD: research directions for nosology/assessment, treatment, and public health. *European Journal of Psychotraumatology, 6,* 1–5, Article number 27584.

Ford, J. D., Hartman, J. K., Hawke, J., & Chapman, J. F. (2008). Traumatic victimization, posttraumatic stress disorder, suicidal ideation, and substance abuse risk among juvenile justice-involved youth. *Journal of Child & Adolescent Trauma, 1,* 75–92.

Fraley, R. C., & Waller, N. G. (1998). Adult attachment patters: A test of the typological model. In J. A. Simpson & W. S. Rholes (Eds.), *Attachment theory and close relationships,* (pp. 77–114). New York: Guilford.

Galante, R., & Foa, D. (1986). An epidemiological study of psychic trauma and treatment effectiveness for children after a natural disaster. *Journal of the American Academy of Child and Adolescent Psychiatry, 25,* 536–541.

Gelles, R. J., & Straus, M. A. (1979). Determinants of violence in the family: Towards a theoretical integration. In W. R. Burr, R. Hill, F. I. Nye, & I. L. Reiss (Eds.), *Contemporary theories about the family* (Vol. 1, pp. 550–581, Chapter 21). New York: Free Press.

Giedd, J. N., Blumenthal, J., Jeffries, N. O., Castellanos, F. X., Liu, H., Zijdenbox, A., Paus, T., Evans, A. C., & Rapoport, J. L. (1999). Brain development during childhood and adolescence: A longitudinal MRI study. *Nature Neuroscience, 2,* 861–863.

Glick, R. A., & Meyerson, A. T. (1981). The use of psychoanalytic concepts in crisis intervention. *International Journal of Psychoanalytic Psychotherapy, 8,* 171–188.

Goldsteen, R., & Schorr, J.K. (1982). The long-term impact of a man-made disaster: An examination of a small town in the aftermath of the Three Mile Island nuclear reactor accident. *Disaster, 6,* 50–59. doi: 10.1111/j.1467-7717.1982.tb00744.x. Retrieved April 11, 2018.

Gordon, N. S., Farberow, N. L., & Maida, C. A. (1999). *Children and disaster.* London: Psychology Press.

Green, B. L., Korol, M., Grace, M. C., Vary, M. G., Leonard, A. C., Gleser, G. C., & Smitson-Cohen, S. (1991). Children and disaster: Age, gender, and parental effects on PTSD symptoms. *Journal of American Academy of Child & Adolescent Psychiatry, 30,* 945–951.

Green, C. S., Pouget, A., & Bavelier, D. (2010). Improved probabilistic inference as a general learning mechanism with action video games. *Current Biology, 20,* 1–7.

Guiffrida, D., & Douthit, K. Z. (2007). Book review of Crisis and trauma: Developmental-ecological intervention. *Journal of Counseling & Development, 85,* 378–379. doi:10.1002/j.1556-6678.2007.tb00487.x

Halpern, J., & Tramontin, M. (2007). *Disaster mental health: Theory and practice.* Belmont, CA: Thomson.

Havighurst, R. J. (1949). Developmental tasks and education. Chicago, IL: University of Chicago Press.

Heim, C., & Nemeroff, C. B. (2001). The role of childhood trauma in the neurobiology of mood and anxiety disorders: preclinical and clinical studies. *Biological Psychology, 49,* 1023–1039.

Hein, L. C., & Scharer, K. M. (2012). Who cares if it is a hate crime? Lesbian, gay, bisexual, and transgender hate crimes—mental health implications and interventions. *Perspectives in Psychiatric Care, 49,* 84–93.

Herman, J. L. (1997). *Trauma and recovery* (Rev. ed.). New York: BasicBooks.

Hill, R. (1949). *Families under stress.* New York: Harper and Row.

Hill, R. (1958). Generic features of families under stress. *Social Casework, 49,* 139–150.

Hirsch, J. (2004). Uniqueness, diversity, similarity, repeatability, and heritability. In C. Garcia Coll, E. Bearer, & R. M. Lerner (Eds.), *Nature and nurture: The complex interplay of genetic and environmental influences on human behavior and development* (pp. 127–138). Mahwah, NJ: Erlbaum.

Hoffman, M. A., & Kruczek, T. (2011). A bioecological model of mass trauma: Individual, community, and societal effects Ψ. *The Counseling Psychologist, 39,* 1087–1127. https://doi.org/10.1177/0011000010397932

Hubel, D. H., & Wiesel, T. N. (1970). Stereoscopic vision in macaque monkey: Cells sensitive to binoc-

ular depth in area 18 of the macaque monkey cortex. *Nature, 225*(5227), 41–42.

Jackson-Cherry, L., & Erford, B. T. (2010). *Crisis intervention and prevention.* Upper Saddle River, NJ: Prentice Hall.

Jacob, S. R. (1993). An analysis of the concept of grief. *Journal of Advanced Nursing, 18,* 1787–1794. doi:10.1046/j.1365-2648.1993.18111787.x

James, R. K., & Gilliland, B. E. (2013). *Crisis intervention strategies* (7th ed.). Boston, MA: Cengage Learning.

James, R. K., & Gilliland, B. E. (2017). *Crisis intervention strategies* (8th ed.). Boston, MA: Cengage Learning.

Janosik, E. H. (1986). *Crisis counseling: A contemporary approach.* Boston: Jones and Bartlett.

Kagan, J. (2001). Emotional development and psychiatry. *Biological Psychiatry, 49,* 973–979.

Kalat, J. W. (2013). *Biological psychology* (11th ed.). Belmont, CA: Wadsworth.

Kanel, K. (2012). *A guide to crisis intervention* (5th ed.). Stamford, CT: Cengage Learning.

Karakurt, G., Smith, D., & Whiting, J. (2014). Impact of intimate partner violence on women's mental health. *Journal of Family Violence, 29*(7), 693–702. doi:10.1007/s10896-014-9633-2

Kessler, R. C., Berglund, P., Demler, O., Jin, R., Merikangas, K. R., & Walters, E. E. (2005). Lifetime prevalence and age-of-onset distributions of DSM-IV disorders in the national comorbidity survey replication. *Archives of General Psychiatry, 62,* 593–602.

Kidwell, J. S., Dunham, R. M., Bacho, R. A., Pastorino, E., & Portes, P. R. (1995). Adolescent identity exploration: a test of Erikson's theory of transitional crisis. *Adolescence, 30,* 785–793.

Kinderman, P. (2014). The role of the psychologist in social change. *International Journal of Social Psychiatry, 60,* 403–405.

Kolb, B., Gibb, R., & Robinson, T. E. (2003). Brain plasticity and behavior. *Current Directions in Psychological Science, 12,* 1–5.

Koren, D., Arnon, I., & Klein, E. (1999). Acute stress response and posttraumatic stress disorder in traffic accident victims: A one-year prospective, follow-up study. *American Journal of Psychiatry, 156,* 367–373.

Kübler-Ross, E. (1969). *On death and dying.* New York: Macmillan

Kübler-Ross, E. (1975). *Death: The final stage of growth.* Englewood Cliffs, NJ: Prentice-Hall.

Lau, E. E., & Kosberg, J. I. (1979). Abuse of the elderly by informal caregivers. *Aging,* 10–15.

Lazarus, R. S. (1966). *Psychological stress and the coping process.* New York: McGraw-Hill.

Lazarus, R. S., & Folkman, S. (1984). *Stress, appraisal, and coping.* New York: Springer.

Leaning, J., & Guha-Sapir, D. (2013). Natural disaster, armed conflict, and public health. *New England Journal of Medicine, 369,* 1836–1842.

Lenroot, R. K., & Giedd, J. N. (2006). Brain development in children and adolescents: insights from anatomical magnetic resonance imaging. *Neuroscience & Behavioral Reviews, 30,* 718–729.

Lenroot, R. K., Gogtay, N., Greenstein, D. K., Wells, E. M., Wallace, G. L., Clasen, L. S., . . . Giedd, J. N. (2007). Sexual dimorphism of brain development trajectories during childhood and adolescence. *Neuroimage, 36,* 1065–1073.

Lerner, M. D., & Shelton, R. D. (2001). *Acute traumatic stress management: Addressing emergent psychological needs during traumatic events.* Commack, NY: The American Academy of Experts in Traumatic Stress.

Levendosky, A. A., Huth-Bocks, A. C., Semel, M. A., & Shapiro, D. L. (2002). Trauma symptoms in preschool-age children exposed to domestic violence. *Journal of Interpersonal Violence, 17,* 150–164.

Levers, L. L. (2012). *Trauma counseling: Theories and interventions.* New York: Springer.

Lewis, C. M., Scarborough, M., Rose, C., & Quirkin, K. B. (2007) Fighting stigma: an adolescent mother takes action. *Affilia, 22,* 302–306.

Lieberman, A. F., & Knorr, K. (2007). The impact of trauma: a developmental framework for infancy and early childhood. *Pediatric Annals, 36,* 209–215.

Lifton, R. J. (1968). Observations on Hiroshima survivors. *Massive Psychic Trauma,* 168–189.

Lindemann, E. (1944). Symptomatology and management of acute grief. *American Journal of Psychiatry, 101,* 141.

Loue, S. (2001). *Intimate partner violence: Societal, medical, legal and individual responses.* Berlin: Springer Science & Business Media.

Lowes, L., Gregory, J. W., & Lyne P. (2005). Newly diagnosed childhood diabetes: a psychosocial transition for parents? *Journal of Advanced Nursing, 50,* 253–261.

Main, M., & Solomon, J. (1986). Discovery of an insecure-disorganized/disoriented attachment pattern. In T. B. Brazelton, & M. W. Yogman (Eds.), *Affective development in infancy* (pp. 95–124). Westport, CT: Ablex.

Markese, S. C. (2007). *Rhythms of dialogue in infancy and attachment narratives in childhood.* ProQuest.

Markwell, P., & Ratard, R. (2014). *Deaths directly caused by Hurricane Katrina.* Louisiana Department of Health Report. Accessed March 23, 2018. http://ldh.la.gov/assets/oph/Center-PHCH/Center-CH/stepi/specialstudies/2014PopwellRatard_KatrinaDeath_PostedOnline.pdf

Maslow, A. H. (1943). A theory of human motivation. *Psychological Review, 50,* 370–396.

McCubbin, H. I., & Patterson, J. (1983). The family stress process: The Double ABCX Model of adjustment and adaptation. In H. I. McCubbin, M. Sussman, & J. Patterson (Eds.), *Social stress and the family: Advances and developments in family stress theory and research* (pp. 7–37). New York: Haworth.

Mechanic, D. (1978). Sex, illness, illness behavior, and the use of health services. *Journal of Human Stress,* 2, 29–40.

Meyer, R. E., Salzman, C., Youngstrom, E. A., Clayton, P. J., Frederick, K. G., Mann, J. J., . . . Sheehan, D. V. (2010). Suicidality and risk of suicide—definition, drug safety concerns, and a necessary target for drug development: A consensus statement. *Journal of Clinical Psychiatry, 71,* e1–e21.

Mikulincer, M., & Shaver, P. R. (2012). Adult attachment and caregiving: Individual differences in providing a safe haven and secure base to others. In S. L. Brown, R. M. Brown, & L. A. Penner (Eds.), *Self-interest and beyond: Toward a new understanding of human caregiving* (pp. 39–52). New York: Oxford University Press.

Milad, M. R., Wright, C. I., Orr, S. P., Pitman, R. K., Quirk, G. J., & Rauch, S. L. (2007). Recall of fear extinction in humans activates the ventromedial prefrontal cortex and hippocampus in concert. *Biological Psychiatry, 62,* 446–454.

Miller, D. N., & Gould, K. (2013). Forgotten founder: Harry Marsh Warren and the history and legacy of the Save-A-Life League. *Suicidology Online, 4,* 12–15.

Ming, G. L., & Song, H. (2005). Adult neurogenesis in the mammalian central nervous system. *Annual Review of Neuroscience, 28,* 223–250.

Minuchin, S. (1974). *Families and family therapy.* Cambridge, MA: Harvard University Press

Mitchell, J. T., & Everly, G. S. (1993). *Critical incident stress debriefing: An operation manual for the prevention of trauma among emergency service and disaster workers.* Baltimore, MD: Chevron.

Moos, R. H., & Tsu, V. (1976). *Human adaptation: Coping with life crises.* Lexington, MA: Heath.

Morgan, C. A., Rasmusson, A. M., Wang, S., Hoyt, G., Hauger, R. L., & Hazlett, G. (2002). Neuropeptide-Y, cortisol, and subjective distress in humans exposed to acute stress: replication and extension of previous report. *Biological Psychiatry, 52,* 136–142.

Morgan, C. A., Wang, S., Rasmusson, A., Hazlett, G., Anderson, G., & Charney, D. S. (2001). Relationship among plasma cortisol, catecholamines, neuropeptide y, and human performance during exposure to uncontrollable stress. *Psychosomatic Medicine, 63,* 412–422.

Morgan, C. A., Wang, S., Southwick, S. M., Rasmusson, A., Hazlett, G., Hauger, R. L., & Charney, D. S. (2000). Plasma neuropeptide-y concentrations in humans exposed to military survival training. *Biological Psychiatry, 47,* 902–909.

Murray, J. S., & Hudson-Barr, D. (2006). Understanding the effects of disaster on children: A developmental-ecological approach to scientific inquiry. *Journal for Specialists in Pediatric Nursing, 11,* 199–202. http://dx.doi.org/10.1111/j.1744-6155.2006.00067.x

Myer, R. A., & Moore, H. B. (2006). Crisis in context theory: An ecological model. *Journal of Counseling & Development, 84,* 139–147.

National Center on Domestic and Sexual Violence. (2014). Power and control wheel. Retrieved from http://www.ncdsv.org/publications_wheel.html

National Research Council. (2000). *How people learn: brain, mind, experience, and school.* Washington, DC: National Academy Press.

Neimeyer, R. A. (2001). The language of loss: Grief therapy as a process of meaning reconstruction. In R. A. Neimeyer (Ed.), *Meaning reconstruction and the experience of loss* (pp. 261–292). Washington, DC: American Psychological Association. http://dx.doi.org/10.1037/10397-014

Nelson, C. A., & Bosquet, M. (2000). Neurobiology of fetal and infant development: Implications for infant mental health. In C. H. Zeanah, Jr. (Ed). *Handbook of infant mental health* (2nd ed.) (pp.37–59). New York: Guilford Press.

Palmer, G., & Lee, A. (2008). Clinical update: Adult attachment. *Family Therapy Magazine, 7,* 36–42.

Papadopoulos, L. (1995). The impact of illness on the family and the family's impact on illness. *Counselling Psychology Quarterly, 8,* 27–34.

Parkes, C. M. (1971). Psycho-social transitions: A field study. *Social Science & Medicine, 5,* 101–115.

Parkes, C. M. (1988). Bereavement as a psychosocial transition: Process of adaptation to change. *Journal of Social Issues, 44,* 53–65.

Parkes, C. M. (2006). *Love and loss: The roots of grief and its complications.* London, UK: Routledge.

Parkes, C. M. (2013). Elisabeth Kübler-Ross, on death and dying: A reappraisal. *Mortality, 18,* 94–97.

Patterson, J. M. (1988). Families experiencing stress: I. The Family Adjustment and Adaptation Response Model II. Applying the FAAR Model to health-related issues for intervention and research. *Family Systems Medicine, 6,* 202–237.

Pearlin, L. I., & Schooler, C. (1978). The structure of coping. *Journal of Health and Social Behavior, 19,* 2–21.

Piaget, J. (1952). *The origins of intelligence in children.* New York: International University Press.

Ponti G., Peretto P., & Bonfanti L. (2008) Genesis of neuronal and glial progenitors in the cerebellar cortex of peripuberal and adult rabbits. *PLoS ONE, 3,* e2366. https://doi.org/10.1371/journal.pone.0002366.

Puleo, S., & McGlothlin, J. (2010). Overview of crisis intervention. In L. R. Jackson-Cherry, & B. T. Erford (Eds.), *Crisis assessment, intervention, and prevention* (2nd ed.). London: Pearson.

Raphael, B. (1977). The Granville train disaster: Psychological needs and their management. *Medical Journal of Australia, 1,* 303–305.

Reeves, A., Stuckler, D., McKee, M., Gunnell, D., Chang, S., & Basu, S. (2012). Increase in state suicide rates in the USA during economic recession. *The Lancet, 380*, 1813–1814.

Roberts, A. R. (1996). *Helping battered women: New perspectives and remedies.* New York: Oxford University Press.

Roberts, A. R. (2002). Assessment, crisis intervention, and trauma treatment: the integrative ACT intervention model. *Brief Treatment and Crisis Intervention, 2*, 1–22.

Roberts, A. R. (Ed.). (2005). *Crisis intervention handbook: Assessment, treatment, and research* (3rd ed.). New York: Oxford University Press.

Roberts, A. R., & Ottens, A. J. (2005). The seven-stage crisis intervention model: A road map to goal attainment, problem solving, and crisis resolution. *Brief Treatment and Crisis Intervention, 5*, 329–339. doi:10.1093/brief-treatment/mhi030

Rogeness, G. A., & McClure, E. B. (1996). Development and neurotransmitter-environmental interactions. *Development and Psychopathology, 8*, 183–199.

Rogers, C. (1959). A theory of therapy, personality and interpersonal relationships as developed in the client-centered framework. In S. Koch (ed.), *Psychology: A study of a science. Vol. 3: Formulations of the person and the social context.* New York: McGraw Hill.

Ruzek, J. I., Brymer, M. J., Jacobs, A. K., Layne, C. M., Vernberg, E. M., & Watson, P. J. (2007). Psychological first aid. *Journal of Mental Health Counseling, 29*, 17–49.

Sattler, M., Mohi, M. G., Pride, Y. B., Quinnan, L. R., Malouf, N. A., Podar, K., & Neel, B. G. (2002). Critical role for Gab2 in transformation by BCR/ABL. *Cancer Cell, 1*, 479.

Saul, R. (2014). *ADHD does not exist.* New York: Harper Collins.

Schlossberg, N. K. (1981). A model for analyzing human adaptation to transition. *The Counseling Psychologist, 9*, 2–18. https://doi.org/10.1177/001100008100900202

Selye, H. (1956). *The stress of life.* New York: McGraw-Hill.

Shumaker, S. A., & Brownell, A. (1984). Toward a theory of social support: closing conceptual gaps. *Journal of Social Issues, 40*, 11–36.

Siann, G. (1985). *Accounting for aggression: Perspectives on aggression and violence.* London: Allen Unwin.

Siegel, D. J. (1999). *The developing mind: How relationships and the brain interact to shape who we are.* New York: Guilford Press.

Silver, R. C., & Wortman, C. B. (2007). The stage theory of grief. *The Journal of the American Medical Association, 297*, 2692–2694.

Sluzki, C. E. (1992). Disruption and reconstruction of networks following migration/relocation. *Family Systems Medicine, 10*, 359–363.

Smith, S. R., & Handler, L. (Eds.) (2007). *The clinical assessment of children and adolescents: A practitioner's guide.* Mahwah, NJ: LEA.

Smith-Battle, L., Lorenz, R., & Leander, S. (2013). Listening with care: Using narrative methods to cultivate nurses' responsive relationships in a home visiting intervention with teen mothers. *Nursing Inquiry, 20*, 188–198.

Solomon, Z., Laror, N., & McFarlane, A. (1996). Acute posttraumatic reactions in soldiers and civilians. *Traumatic Stress: The effects of overwhelming experience on mind, body and society.* (pp. 102–114). New York: Guildford Press.

Sowell, E. R., Thompson, P. M., Leonard, C. M., Welcome, S. E., Kan, E., & Toga, A. W. (2004). Longitudinal mapping of cortical thickness and brain growth in children. *Journal of Neuroscience, 24*, 8223–8231.

Spear, L. P. (2013). Adolescent neurodevelopment. *Journal of Adolescent Health, 52*, S7–S13.

Sroufe, L. A. (2000). Early relationships and the development of children. *Infant Mental Health Journal, 21*, 67–74.

Stern, G. M. (1972). *The Buffalo Creek disaster: The story of the survivors' unprecedented lawsuit*, New York: Random House.

Stroebe, M., Schut, H., & Boerner, K. (2017). Cautioning health-care professionals: Bereaved persons are misguided through the stages of grief. *OMEGA - Journal of Death and Dying, 74*, 455–473. https://doi.org/10.1177/0030222817691870

Terr, L. C. (1991). Childhood traumas: an outline and overview. *American Journal of Psychiatry, 148*, 10–20.

Thompson, R. A. (1998). Early sociopersonality development. In N. Eisenberg (Ed.), W. Damon (Series Ed.). *Handbook of child psychology: Vol. 3. Social, emotional, and personality development* (5th ed., pp. 25–104). New York: Wiley.

Tyler, K. A. (2000). The effects of an acute stressor on depressive symptoms among older adults. *Research on Aging, 22*, 143.

Usdansky, M. L. (2009). A weak embrace: popular and scholarly depictions of single-parent families, 1900–1998. *Journal of Marriage and Family, 71,* 209–225.

Voelcker-Rehage, C., & Willimczik, K. (2206). Motor plasticity in a juggling task in older adults – a developmental study. *Age and Ageing, 35,* 422–427.

Volling, B. L. (2005). The transition to siblinghood: a developmental ecological systems perspective and directions for future research. *Journal of Family Psychology, 19,* 542–549.

Wall, J. T., Xu, J., & Wang, X. (2002). Human brain plasticity: an emerging view of the multiple substrates and mechanisms that cause cortical changes and related sensory dysfunctions after injuries of sensory inputs from the body. *Brain Research Reviews, 39,* 181–215.

Walsh, F. (2007). Traumatic loss and major disaster: strengthening family and community resilience. *Family Process, 46,* 207–227.

Wang, W., Chen, D., Yebing, Y., Liu, X., & Miao, D. (2010). A study of psychological crisis intervention with family members of patients who died after emergency admission to hospital. *Social Behavior & Personality: An International Journal, 38,* 469–478.

Ward, J. W., & Butler, R. J. (2008). *The Richard Wright Encyclopedia.* Westport, CT: Greenwood Press.

Willison, C. E., Singer, P. M., Creary, M. S., & Greer, S. L. (2019). Quantifying inequities in US federal response to hurricane disaster in Texas and Florida compared with Puerto Rico. *BMJ Global Health, 4,* e001191.

Wills, T. A., Vaccaro, D., & McNamara, G. (1994). Novelty seeking, risk taking, and related constructs as predictors of adolescent substance use: An application of Cloninger's theory. *Journal of Substance Abuse, 6,* 1–20.

Wolf, R. S., & Pillemer, K. A. (1989). *Helping elderly victims: the reality of elder abuse.* New York: Columbia University Press.

Yan, J. H., Thomas, J. R., Stelmach, G. E., & Thomas, K. T. (2000). Developmental features of rapid aiming arm movements across the lifespan. *Journal of Motor Behavior, 32,* 121–140.

Yeager, K. R., & Roberts, A. R. (2003). Differentiating among stress, acute stress disorder, crisis episodes, trauma, and PTSD: Paradigm and treatment goals. *Brief Treatment and Crisis Intervention, 3,* 3–25.

Yehuda, R. (2002). Post-traumatic stress disorder. *New England Journal of Medicine, 346,* 108–114.

Young, M. A. (1995). Crisis response teams in the aftermath of disaster. In A. R. Roberts (Ed.), *Crisis intervention and time-limited cognitive treatment* (pp. 151–187). Thousand Oaks, CA: Sage.

Zhang J., & Lester D. (2008). Psychological tensions found in suicide notes: A test for the strain theory of suicide. *Archives of Suicide Research, 12,* 67–73.

Ziebland, S., & Kokanovic, R. (2012). Emotions and chronic illness. *Chronic Illness, 8,* 159–162.

Ziemann, U., Iliać, T. V., Pauli, C., Meintzschel, F., & Ruge, D. (2004). Learning modifies subsequent induction of long-term potentiation-like and long-term depression-like plasticity in human motor cortex. *The Journal of Neuroscience, 24,* 1666–1672.

Zubenko, W. N., & Capozzoli, J. (2002). *Children and disaster: A practical guide to healing and recovery.* Oxford: Oxford University Press.

Chapter 3

Agronin, M. E. (2014). From Cicero to Cohen: Developmental theories of aging, from antiquity to the present. *Gerontologist, 54,* 30–39.

Ahmed, A. (2007). Post-traumatic stress disorder, resilience and vulnerability. *Advances in Psychiatric Treatment, 13,* 369–375. doi: 10.1192/apt.bp.106.003236

Alvarez, J., & Hunt, M. (2005). Risk and resilience in canine search and rescue handlers after 9/11. *Journal of Traumatic Stress, 18,* 497–505. doi:10.1002/jts.20058

American Counseling Association. (2014). *2014 ACA code of ethics.* Retrieved July 6, 2016. http://www.counseling.org/docs/ethics/2014-aca-code-of-ethics.pdf? sfvrsn=4

American Educational Research Association, American Psychological Association, National Council on Measurement in Education [AERA/APA/NCME]. (1999). *Standards for educational and psychological testing.* Washington, DC: American Psychological Association.

American Psychological Association. (2010). *Ethical principles of psychologists and code of conduct.* Retrieved July 6, 2016. http://www.apa.org/ethics/code/

Athey, J., & Moddy-Williams, J. (2003). U.S. Department of Health and Human Services. *Developing cultural competence in disaster mental health programs: Guiding principles and recommendations.* DHHS Pub. No. SMA 3828. Rockville, MD: Center for Mental Health Services, Substance Abuse and Mental Health Services Administration.

Benotsch, E. G., Brailey K., Vasterling, J. J., Uddo, M., Constans, J. I., & Sutker, P. B. (2000). War zone stress, personal and environmental resources, and PTSD symptoms in Gulf War veterans: A longitudinal perspective. *Journal of Abnormal Psychology, 109,* 205–213.

Bonanno, G. A. (2004). Loss, trauma, and human resilience: Have we underestimated the human capacity to thrive after extremely aversive events? *American Psychologist, 59,* 20–28.

Bremner, J. D. (2002). *Does stress damage the brain? Understanding trauma-related disorders from a mind-body perspective.* New York: W.W. Norton.

Breslau, N., Kessler, R. C., Chilcoat, H. D., Schultz, L. R., Davis, G. C., & Andreski, P. (1998). Trauma and posttraumatic stress disorder in the community: The 1996 Detroit area survey of trauma. *Archives of General Psychiatry, 55,* 626–632. doi:10.1001/archpsyc.55.7.626

Bychowski, G. (1968). Permanent character change as an aftereffect of persecution. In H. Krystal (Ed.), *Massive psychic trauma* (pp.75–86). New York: International Universities Press.

Carkhuff, R. R. (1969). *Helping and human relations. Volume I. Selection and training.* New York: Holt, Rinehart & Winston.

Carter, S. C. (1998). Neuroendocrine perspectives on social attachment and love. *Psychoneuroendocrinology, 23,* 779–818.

Cavaiola, A., & Colford, J. E. (2011). *Crisis intervention casebook.* Belmont, CA: Brooks/Cole.

Connor, K. M. (2006). Assessment of resilience in the aftermath of trauma. *Clinical Journal of Psychiatry, 67,* 46–49.

Connor, K. M., & Davidson, J. R. T. (2003). Development of a new resilience scale: The Connor-Davidson resilience scale, CD-RISC. *Depression and Anxiety, 18,* 76–82.

Cormier, S. L., Nurius, P., & Osborn, C. J. (2009). *Interviewing and change strategies for helpers: Fundamental skills and cognitive behavioral interventions.* Belmont, CA: Brooks/Cole.

Crandall, C.S., Eshleman, A., & O'Brien L.T. (2002). Social norms and the expression and suppression of prejudice: The struggle for internalization. *Journal of Personal Social Psychology, 82,* 359–78.

Darwin, C. (1859). *On the origin of species by means of natural selection, or, the preservation of favoured races in the struggle for life.* London: J. Murray.

Davidson, J., Swartz, M., Storck, M., Krishnan, R. R., & Hammett, E. (1985). A diagnostic and family study of posttraumatic stress disorder. *American Journal of Psychiatry, 142,* 90–93.

Davis, L. E., King, M. K., & Shultz, J. L. (2005). *Fundamentals of neurologic disease: an introductory text.* New York: Demos Medical Publications

DeHart, D. D. (2008). Pathways to prison: Impact of victimization in the lives of incarcerated women. *Violence Against Women, 14,* 1362–1381. doi: 10.1177/1077801208327018

deWaal, F. B. M. (1996). *Good natured: the origins of right and wrong in humans and other animals.* Cambridge, MA: Harvard University Press.

Drummond, R. J., & Jones, K. D. (2010). *Assessment procedures for counselors and helping professionals* (7th ed.). New York: Pearson.

Echterling, L. G., Presbury, J. H., & McKee, J. E. (2005). *Crisis intervention: Promoting resilience and resolution in troubled times.* Upper Saddle River, NJ: Pearson.

Eriksen, K. P., & McAuliffe, G. J. (2003). The Counseling Skills Scale: A measure of counselor competence. *Counselor Education and Supervision, 43,* 120–133.

Erikson, E. H. (1959) *Identity and the life cycle.* New York: International Universities Press.

Fehr, E., & Henrich, J. (2003). Is strong reciprocity a maladaptation? In P. Hammerstein (Ed.), *Genetic and cultural evolution of cooperation.* Cambridge, MA: MIT Press.

Felitti, V. J., Anda, R. F., Nordenberg, D., Williamson, D. F., Spitz, A. S., Edwards, V., Koss, M. P., & Marks, J. S. (1998). Relationship of childhood abuse and household dysfunction to many of the leading causes of death in adults: The Adverse Childhood Experience (ACE) Study. *American Journal of Preventative Medicine, 14,* 245–258. doi: http://dx.doi.org/10.1016/S0749-3797(98)00017-8

Flynn, S. V., & Black, L. L. (2011). An emergent theory of altruism and self-interest. *Journal of Counseling & Development, 89,* 459–469. doi:10.1002/j.1556-6676.2011.tb02843.x

Flynn, S. V., & Hays, D. G. (2015). The development and validation of the comprehensive counseling skills rubric. *Counseling Outcome Research and Evaluation.* doi: 10.1177/2150137815592216

Folstein, M. F., Folstein, S. E., & McHugh, P. R. (1975). "Mini-mental state": A practical method for grading the cognitive state of patients for the clinician. *Journal of Psychiatric Research, 12,* 189–198. doi:10.1016/0022-3956(75)90026-6

Fowler, J. W. (1995). *Stages of faith: The psychology of human development and the quest for meaning.* New York: Harper Collins.

Fraser, M. W., Kirby, L. D., & Smokowski, P. R. (2004). Risk and resilience in childhood. In M. W. Fraser (Ed.), *Risk and resilience in childhood: An ecological perspective* (2nd ed., pp. 13–66). Washington, DC: NASW.

Friborg, O., Hjemdal, O., Rosenvinge, J. H., & Martinussen, M. (2003). A new rating scale for adult resilience: What are the central protective resources behind healthy adjustment? *International Journal of Methods in Psychiatric Research, 12,* 65–76.

Goodell, J. (2011). Steve Jobs in 1994: The Rolling Stone interview. *Rolling Stone.* Retrieved August 8, 2016. http://www.rollingstone.com/culture/news/steve-jobs-in-1994-the-rolling-stone-interview-20110117

Hamlet, H. S., & Burnes, T. (2013). Professional School Counseling Internship Developmental Assessment of Counseling Skills (CIDACS). *Counseling Outcome Research and Evaluation, 4,* 55–71. doi: 10.1177/2150137812472196

Hardy, C., & Van Vugt, M. (2006). Nice guys finish first: The competitive altruism hypothesis. *Personality and Social Psychology Bulletin, 32,* 1402–1413.

Holmes, J. G., Miller, D. T., & Lerner, M. J. (2002). Committing altruism under the cloak of self-interest: The exchange fiction. *Journal of Experimental Social Psychology, 38,* 144–151. doi: 10.1006/jesp.2001.1494

Hood, A. B., & Johnson, R. W. (2007). *Assessment in counseling: A guide to the use of psychological assessment procedures* (4th ed.). Alexandria, VA: American Counseling Association.

Horvath, A. O., & Greenberg, L. S. (1989). Development and validation of the Working Alliance Inventory. *Journal of Counseling Psychology, 36,* 223–233. http://dx.doi.org/10.1037/0022-0167.36.2.223

International Strategy for Disaster Reduction. (2004). *Living with risk: A global review of disaster reduction initiatives* (Vol. I). Geneva, Switzerland: United Nations.

Ivey, A. E. (1971). *Microcounseling: Innovations in interviewing training.* Springfield, IL: Charles C Thomas.

Ivey, A. E., Ivey, M. B., & Zalaquett, C. P. (2010). *Intentional interviewing and counseling: Facilitating client development in a multicultural society* (7th ed.). Belmont, CA: Brooks/Cole.

Jackson-Cherry, L., & Erford, B. T. (2010). *Crisis intervention and prevention.* Upper Saddle River, NJ: Prentice Hall.

James, R. K., & Gilliland, B. E. (2017). *Crisis intervention strategies* (8th ed.). Boston, MA: Cengage Learning

James, R. K., Myer, R., & Moore, H. (2006). *Triage assessment checklist for law enforcement. (TACKLE) manual and CD.* Pittsburgh, PA: Crisis Intervention and Prevention Solutions.

Kessler, R. C., Sonnega, A., Bromet, E., Hughes, M., & Nelson, C. B. (1995). Posttraumatic stress disorder in the national comorbidity survey. *Archives of General Psychiatry, 52,* 1048–1060. doi:10.1001/archpsyc.1995.03950240066012

Kocarek, C. E., Talbot, D. M., Batka, J. C., & Anderson, M. Z. (2001). Reliability and validity of three measures of multicultural competency, *Journal of Counseling and Development, 79,* 486–496.

Labouuie-Vief, G. (2006). Emerging structures of adult thought. In J. J. Arnett & J. L. Tanner (Eds.), *Emerging adults in America: Coming of age in the 21st century.* Washington, DC: American Psychological Association.

Larson, L., Suzuki, L., Gillespie, K., Potenza, M., Bechtel, M., & Toulouse, A. (1992). Development and validation of the counseling self-estimate inventory. *Journal of Counseling Psychology, 39,* 105–120.

Levinson, D. J. (1978). *Seasons of a man's life.* New York: Ballantine Books.

Levinson, D. J., & Levinson, J. D. (1996). *The seasons of a woman's life.* New York: Ballantine Books.

Marsh, N., Scheele, D., Gerhardt, H., Strang, S., Enax, L., Weber, B., Maier, W., & Hurlemann, R. (2015). The neuropeptide oxytocin induces a social altruism bias. *Journal of Neuroscience, 35,* 15696–15701. doi: 10.1523/JNEUROSCI.3199-15.2015

Maslow, A. H. (1943). A theory of human motivation. *Psychological Review, 50, 370–396. doi:10.1037/h0054346*

Mattessich, P., & Hill, R. (1987). Life cycle and family development. In M. B. Sussman & S. K. Steinmetz (Eds.), *Handbook of marriage and the family* (pp. 437–470). New York: Plenum.

Mitchell, J. K. (Ed.) (1998). *The long road to recovery: Community responses to industrial disaster.* Tokyo: United Nations University Press.

Myer, R. A. (2001). *Assessment for crisis intervention: A triage assessment model.* Belmont, CA: Thompson Brooks/Cole.

Myer, R. A., & James, R. K. (2005). *Crisis intervention workbook and CD rom.* Belmont, CA: Thompson Brooks/Cole.

Myer, R. A., & Moore, H. B. (2006). Crisis in context theory: An ecological model. *Journal of Counseling & Development, 84,* 139–147.

Myer, R. A., Rice, D., Moulton, P. Cogdal, P., Allen, S., & James, R. (2007). *Triage assessment system for student learning environments (TASSLE) manual and CD.* Pittsburgh, PA: Crisis Intervention and Prevention Solutions.

Myer, R. A., Williams, R. C., Ottens, A. J., & Schmidt, A. E. (1992). Triage assessment form: Crisis intervention. Unpublished manuscript.

National Association of Social Workers. (2008). *Code of ethics of the National Association of Social Workers.* Retrieved July 6, 2016.

Olff, M., Langeland, W., Draijer, N., & Gersons, B. P. R. (2007). Gender differences in posttraumatic stress disorder. *Psychological Bulletin, 133,* 183–204. doi:10.1037/0033-2909.133.2.183

Orcutt, H. K., King, L. A., & King, D. W. (2003). Male-perpetrated violence among Vietnam veteran couples: Relationships with veteran's early life characteristics, trauma history, and PTSD symptomatology. *Journal of Traumatic Stress,* 16, 381–390. doi:10.1023/a:1024470103325

Oshio, A., Kaneko, H., Nagamine, S., & Nakaya, M. (2003). Construct validity of the adolescent resilience scale. *Psychological Reports, 93,* 1217–1222.

Piaget, J. (1952). *The origins of intelligence in children.* New York: International University Press.

Pitman, R. K., Orr, S. P., Forgue, D. F., De Jong, J. B., & Claiborn, J. M. (1987). Psychophysiologic assessment of post-traumatic stress disorder imagery in Vietnam combat veterans. *Archives of General Psychiatry, 44,* 970–975.

Ponce-Garcia, E., Madewell, A. N., & Kennison, S. M. (2015). The development of the Scale of Protective Factors: Resilience in a violent trauma sample, *Violence and Victims, 30,* 735–755.

Ponterotto, J. G., & Potere, J. C. (2003). The multicultural knowledge and awareness scale (MCKAS): Validity, reliability and user guidelines. In D. B. Pope-Davis, H. L. K. Coleman, W. M. Liu, & R. Toporek (Eds.), *Handbook of multicultural competencies.* pp.137–153. Thousand Oaks, CA: Sage.

Porter, E. J. (1943). The development and evaluation of a measure of counseling interview procedures, II. The Evaluation. *Educational and Psychological Measurement, 3,* 215–238.

Puleo, S., & McGlothlin, J. (2010). Overview of crisis intervention. In L. R. Jackson-Cherry & B. T. Erford (Eds.), *Crisis assessment, intervention, and prevention* (2nd ed.). New York: Pearson.

Reik, T. (1948). *Listening with the third ear: The inner experience of a psychoanalyst.* Oxford, England: Farrar, Straus & Co.

Rogers, C. R. (1951). *Client-centered therapy: Its current practice, implications and theory.* London: Constable.

Rogers, C. R. (1957). The necessary and sufficient conditions of therapeutic personality change. *Journal of Consulting and Clinical Psychology, 21,* 95–103.

Rutledge, P. (2011, November). Social networks: What Maslow misses. *Psychology Today.* Retrieved August 30, 2016. https://www.psychologytoday.com/blog/positively-media/201111/social-networks-what-maslow-misses-0

Samovar, L. A., & Porter, R. E. (2001). *Communication between cultures* (4th ed.). Belmont, CA: Wadsworth/Thomson Learning.

Smith, W. (2012). Triage in mass casualty situations. *CME: Continuing Medical Education, 30,* 413–415.

Sober, E. (1993). Evolutionary altruism, psychological egoism and morality; disentangling the phenotypes. In M. H. Nitecki et al. (Eds.) *Evolutionary ethics.* Albany, NY: SUNY Press.

Sodowsky, G. R., Taffe, R. C., Gutkin, T. B., & Wise, S. L. (1994). Development of the multicultural counseling inventory (MCI): A self-reported measure of multicultural competencies. *Journal of Counseling Psychology, 41,* 131–148.

Swank, J. M., Lambie, G. W., & Witta, E. L. (2012). An exploratory investigation of the counseling competencies scale: A measure of counseling skills, dispositions, and behaviors. *Counselor Education and Supervision, 51,* 189–206. doi:10.1002/j.1556-6978.2012.00014.x

Taft, C. T., Pless, A. P., Stalans, L. J., Koenen, K. C., King, L. A., & King, D. W. (2005). Risk factors for partner violence among a national sample of combat veterans. *Journal of Consulting and Clinical Psychology, 73,* 151–159.

Teyber, E., & McClure, F. H. (2010). *Interpersonal process in therapy* (6th ed.). Belmont, CA: Brooks/Cole

Truax, C. B., & Carkhuff, R. R. (1967). *Toward effective counseling and psychotherapy.* Chicago: Aldine.

True, W. R., Rice, J., Eisen, S. A., Health, A. C., Goldberg, J., Lyons, M. J., & Nowak, J. (1993). A twin study of genetic and environmental contributions to liability for posttraumatic stress symptoms. *Archives of General Psychiatry, 50,* 257–264.

Vaillant, G. (2002). *Aging well.* Boston: Little, Brown and Co.

van der Kolk, B. A., & McFarlane, A. C. (1996). The black hole of trauma. In B. A. van der Kolk, A. C., McFarlane, & L. Weisaeth (Eds.) *Trauma stress: The effects of overwhelming experience on the mind, body, and society* (pp. 3–23). New York: Guilford.

Walsh, W. B., & Betz, N. E. (1995). *Tests and Assessment* (3rd ed.). Upper Saddle River, NJ: Prentice Hall.

Whyte, D. (2015). *Vulnerability-A poem by David Whyte.* Accessed online May 4, 2019. http://www.passionart.guide/project/vulnerability-a-poem-by-david-whyte/

Wispé, L. G. (1972). Positive forms of social behavior: An overview. *Journal of Social Issues, 28,* 1–19. doi:10.1111/j.1540-4560.1972.tb00029.x

World Health Organization (2011). Psychological first aid: A guide for fieldworkers. Retrieved July 21, 2016. http://apps.who.int/iris/bitstream/10665/44615/1/9789241548205_en

Yalom, I. D. (1995). *The theory and practice of group psychotherapy* (4th ed.). New York: Basic Books.

Yehuda, R., Schmeidler, J., Wainberg, M., Binder-brynes, K., & Duvdevani, T. (1998). Increased vulnerability to posttraumatic stress disorder in adult offspring of Holocaust survivors. *American Journal of Psychiatry, 155,* 1163–1171.

Young, M. E. (2013). *Learning the art of helping: Building blocks and techniques* (5th ed.). New York: Pearson.

Chapter 4

Adams, J. T. (1931). *The epic of America.* Boston: Little, Brown, and Company.

Adler, A. (1938). *Social interest: A challenge to mankind, Alfred Adler,* translated by Linton John, Richard Vaughan, pp. 275–276.

Adler-Nevo, G., & Manassis, K. (2005). Psychosocial treatment of pediatric posttraumatic stress disorder: The neglected field of single-incident trauma. *Depress Anxiety, 22,* 177–189.

Alford, C. F. (2016). *Trauma, culture and PTSD.* New York: Palgrave McMillian.

American Psychiatric Association. (1952). *Diagnostic and statistical manual of mental disorders I.* Washington DC: American Psychiatric Association Mental Hospital Service.

American Psychiatric Association. (1968). *Diagnostic and statistical manual of mental disorders II* (2nd ed.). Washington DC: American Psychiatric Association.

American Psychiatric Association. (1980). *Diagnostic and statistical manual of mental disorders III* (3rd ed.). Arlington, VA: American Psychiatric Publishing.

American Psychiatric Association. (1987). *Diagnostic and statistical manual of mental disorders III-R.* Arlington, VA: American Psychiatric Publishing.

American Psychiatric Association. (2013). *Diagnostic and statistical manual of mental disorders* (5th ed.). Arlington, VA: American Psychiatric Publishing.

Andreasen, N. C. (2004). Acute and delayed posttraumatic stress disorders: A history and some issues. *American Journal of Psychiatry, 161,* 1321–1323.

Antze, P., & Lambek, M. (1996). *Tense past: Cultural essays in trauma and memory.* New York: Routledge.

Bartlett, F. (1958). *Thinking: An experimental and social study.* New York: Basic Books.

Beck, A. T. (1985). Cognitive approaches to anxiety disorders. In B. F. Shaw, Z. V. Segal, T. M. Vallis, & F. E. Cashman (Eds.*), Anxiety disorders: Psychological and biological perspectives* (pp. 115–135). New York: Plenum.

Beck, A. T., Emery, G., & Greenberg, R. L. (1985). *Anxiety disorders and phobias: A cognitive perspective.* New York: Basic Books.

Becker, C., Zayfert, C., & Anderson, E. (2004). A survey of psychologists' attitudes towards and utilization of exposure therapy for PTSD. *Behaviour Research and Therapy, 42,* 277–292.

Benjet, C., Bromet, E., Karam, E. G., Kessler, R. C., McLaughlin, K. A., Ruscio, A. M., . . . Koenen, K. C. (2015). The epidemiology of traumatic event exposure worldwide: Results from the World Mental Health Survey Consortium. *Psychological Medicine, 46,* 327–343. doi:10.1017/S0033291715001981

Bennett, J. (2017). *Passions of the soul: Rene Descartes.* Accessed online April 2019. https://www.earlymoderntexts.com/assets/pdfs/descartes1649.pdf

Bisson, J. I., McFarlane, A. C., Rose, S., Ruzek, J. I., & Watson, P. J., (2009). Psychological debriefing for adults. In E. B. Foa, T. M. Keane, M. J. Friedman, J. A. Cohen (Eds.) *Effective treatments for PTSD, second edition: Practice guidelines from the international society for traumatic stress studies* (pp. 83–105). New York: Guilford Press.

Blatner, A. (1985). The dynamics of catharsis. *Journal of Group Psychotherapy, Psychodrama & Sociometry, 37,* 157–166.

Brave Heart, M. Y. H. (2000). Wakiksuyapi: Carrying the historical trauma of the Lakota. *Tulane Studies in Social Welfare, 21–22,* 245–266.

Brave Heart, M. Y. H., & DeBruyn, L. M. (1998). The American Indian holocaust: Healing historical unresolved grief. *American Indian and Alaska Native Mental Health Research, 8,* 60–82.

Bremner, J. D. (2006). Traumatic stress: Effects on the brain. *Dialogues in clinical neuroscience, 8,* 445–461.

Breuer, J., & Freud, S. (1955). On the psychical mechanisms of hysterical phenomena: Preliminary communication. In J. Strachey (Ed. & Trans.). *The standard edition of the complete psychological works of Sigmund Freud* (Vol. 2, pp. 1–181). London: Hogarth Press. (Original work published 1893).

Bronfenbrenner, U. (1979). *The ecology of human development.* Cambridge, MA: Harvard University Press.

Bronfenbrenner, U., & Ceci, S. J. (1994). Nature-nurture reconceptualized in developmental perspectives: A bioecological model. *Psychological Review, 101,* 568–586. http://dx.doi.org/10.1037/0033-295X.101.4.568

Brouardel, P. (1909). *Les attentats aux moeurs* (Attack on morals). London: Librairie J.–B. Baillère Et Fils. University of Leeds Library. Retrieved January 2018.

Browning, E. B. (1843). The cry of the children. *Blackwood's Edinburgh Magazine, 54,* 260–262. British Library. Retrieved January 2018.

Bruner, J. S., Goodnow, J. J., & Austin, G. A. (1956). *A study of thinking.* New York: Wiley.

Burgess, A., & Holmstrom, L. (1974). Rape trauma syndrome. *American Journal of Psychiatry, 131,* 981–986.

Cahill, S. P., & Foa, E. B. (2007). Psychological theories of PTSD. In M. J. Friedman, T. M. Keane, & P. A. Resick (Eds.) *Handbook of PTSD: Science and practice* (pp. 55–77). New York: Guilford.

Calhoun, J. T. (1864). Nostalgia as a disease of field service. *The Medical and Surgical Reporter, 11,* 130–132.

Caplan, E. M. (1995). Trains, brains, and sprains: Railway spine and the origins of psychoneuroses. *Bulletin of the History of Medicine, 69,* 387–419.

Caruth, C. (1996). *Unclaimed experience: Trauma, narrative, and history.* Baltimore, MD: Johns Hopkins University Press.

CATS Consortium (2007). Implementing CBT for traumatized children and adolescents after September 11: Lessons learned from the Child and Adolescent Trauma Treatments and Services (CATS) Project. *Journal of Clinical Child & Adolescent Psychology, 36,* 581–592.

Chaffin, M., Funderburk, B., Bard, D., Valle, L. A., & Gurwitch, R. (2011). A motivation-PCIT package reduces child welfare recidivism in a randomized dismantling field trial. *Journal of Consulting and Clinical Psychology, 79,* 84–95.

Chaffin, M., Silovsky, J., Funderburk, B., Valle, L. A., Brestan, E. V., Balachova, T., . . . Bonner, B. L. (2004). Parent–child interaction therapy with physically abusive parents: Efficacy for reducing future abuse reports. *Journal of Consulting and Clinical Psychology, 72,* 500 –510. doi:10.1037/0022-006X.72.3.500

Chambless, D. L., Baker, M. J., Baucom, D. H., Beutler, L. E., Calhoun, K. S., Crits-Cristoph, P., . . . Woody, S. R. (1998). Update on empirically validated therapies, II. *The Clinical Psychologist, 51,* 3–16.

Chambless, D. L., Sanderson, W. C., Shoham, V., Bennett Johnson, S., Pope, K. S., Crits-Cristoph, P., . . . McCurry, S. (1996). An update on empirically validated therapies. *The Clinical Psychologist, 49,* 5–18.

Choi, S. E., Oh, M. Y., Kim, N. R., Jung, Y. J., Ro, Y. S., & Shin, S. D. (2017). Comparison of trauma care systems in Asian countries: A systematic literature review. *Emergency Medicine Australasia, 29,* 697–711.

Chomsky, A. N. (1967). A review of B. F. Skinner's *verbal behavior.* In L. A. Jakobovits & M. S. Miron (Eds.), *Readings in the psychology of language.* Englewood Cliffs, NJ: Prentice-Hall. Accessed online February 2018. https://chomsky.info/1967

Cicchetti, D., Rogosch, F. A., & Toth, S. L. (2006). Fostering secure attachment in infants in maltreating families through preventive interventions. *Development and Psychopathology, 18,* 623–650.

Cohen, J. A., Mannarino, A. P., Berliner, L., & Deblinger, E. (2000). Trauma-focused cognitive behavioral treatment for children and adolescents: An empirical update. *Journal of Interpersonal Violence, 15,* 1202–1223.

Cohen, J. A., Mannarino, A. P., & Iyengar, S. (2011). Community treatment of posttraumatic stress disorder for children exposed to intimate partner violence: A randomized controlled trial. *Archives of Pediatrics and Adolescent Medicine, 165,* 16–21.

Conching, A. K. S., & Thayer, Z. (2019). Biological pathways for historical trauma to affect health: A conceptual model focusing on epigenetic modifications. *Social Science & Medicine, 230,* 74–82. https://doi.org/10.1016/j.socscimed.2019.04.001

Corrigan, F. M., & Hull, A. M. (2015). Recognition of the neurobiological insults imposed by complex trauma and the implications for psychotherapeutic interventions. *BJ Psychiatric Bulletin, 39,* 79–86. doi:10.1192/pb.bp.114.047134

Crocq, M.-A., & Crocq, L. (2000). From shell shock and war neurosis to posttraumatic stress disorder: A history of psychotraumatology. *Dialogues in Clinical Neuroscience, 2,* 47–55.

Dalgleish, T. (1999). Cognitive theories of posttraumatic stress disorder. In W. Yule (Ed.), *Wiley series in clinical psychology. Post-traumatic stress disorders: Concepts and therapy* (pp. 193–220). New York: Wiley.

Dalgleish, T. (2004). Cognitive approaches to Posttraumatic Stress Disorder: The evolution of multirepresentational theorizing. *Psychological Bulletin, 130,* 228–260. http://dx.doi.org/10.1037/0033-2909.130.2.228

Descartes, R. (1649/1989). *The Passions of the soul.* Translated by S. H. Voss (1989). Indianapolis, IN: Hackett Publishing Company.

De Styrap, J. (1890). *The young practitioner: With practical hints and instructive suggestions.* London: H. K. Lewis. https://archive.org/details/youngpractitione00destuoft

Devine, S. (2014). *Learning from the Wounded: The Civil War and the Rise of American Medical Science.* Chapel Hill: University of North Carolina Press.

Dickens, C. (1854). *Hard Times.* London: Bradbury & Evans.

Droz̆dek, B., Kamperman, A. M., Bolwerk, N., Tol, W. A., & Kleber, R. J. (2012). Group therapy with male asylum seekers and refugees with posttraumatic stress disorder: A controlled comparison cohort study of three day-treatment programs. *The Journal of Nervous and Mental Disease, 200,* 758–765.

Ebert, L., Amaya-Jackson, L., Markiewicz, J. M., & Fairbank, J. A. (2012). Development and application of the NCCTS Leaning Collaborative Model for the implementation of evidence-based child trauma treatment. In R. K. McHugh & D. Barlow (Eds.), *Dissemination of evidence-based psychological interventions* (pp. 97–123). New York: Oxford University Press.

Ebert, L., Amaya-Jackson, L., Markiewicz, J. M., Kisiel, C., & Fairbank, J. A. (2012a). Use of the breakthrough series collaborative to support broad and sustained use of evidence-based trauma treatment for children in community practice settings. *Administration and Policy in Mental Health and Mental Health Services Research, 39,* 187–199.

Ecker, B., Ticic, R., & Hulley, L. (2013). Unlocking the emotional brain: Is memory reconsolidation the key to transformation? *Psychotherapy Networker, 37,* 18–25, 46–47.

Ehlers, A., & Clark, D. M. (2008). Post-traumatic stress disorder: The development of effective psychological treatments, *Nordic Journal of Psychiatry, 62,* 11–18. doi:10.1080/08039480802315608

Eitinger, L. (1964). *Concentration camp survivors in Norway and Israel.* Oslo: Universitetsforlaget.

Ellenberger, H. F. (1969). *The discovery of the unconscious: The history and evolution of dynamic psychiatry.* New York: Basic Books.

Erichsen, J. E. (1866). *On railway and other injuries of the nervous system.* London: Walton & Moberly.

Erichsen, J. E. (1886). *On concussion of the spine, nervous shock and other obscure injuries to the nervous system in the clinical and medico-legal aspects.* New York: William Wood.

Erikson, E. (1950). *Childhood and society* (1st ed.). New York: Norton

Eriksson, P. S., Perfilieva, E., Bjork-Eriksson, T., Alborn, A. M., Nordborg, C., Peterson, D. A., & Gage, T. (1998). Neurogenesis in the adult human hippocampus. *Nature Medicine, 4,* 1313–1317. doi: 10.1038/330

Eulenburg, A. (1878). Lehrbuch der Nervenkrankheiten, [Textbook of Nervous Diseases]. Berlin: August Hirschwald.

Everly, G. S., Lating, J. M., & Mitchell, J. T. (2000). Innovations in-group crisis intervention: Critical incident stress debriefing (CISD) and critical incident stress management (CISM). In A. R. Roberts (Ed.), *Crisis intervention handbook,* (2nd ed., pp. 78–92). New York: Oxford University Press.

Eyberg, S. (1988). Parent-child interaction therapy. *Child & Family Behavior Therapy, 1,* 33–46. doi:10.1300/J019v10n01_04.

Feldman, E. (2007). Implementation of the Cognitive Behavioral Intervention for Trauma in Schools (CBITS) with Spanish-speaking, immigrant middle-school students: Is effective, culturally competent treatment possible within a public school setting? (Doctoral dissertation, University of Wisconsin-Madison, 2007). *Dissertation Abstracts International, 68*(A), 1325.

Ferenczi, S. (1949). Confusion of tongues between adults and the child. *The International Journal of Psychoanalysis, 30,* 225–230. In M. Balint, (Ed.), Final Contributions to Psychoanalysis (1955/1994). London: Hogarth Press.

Figley, C. (Ed.). (1978). *Stress disorder among Vietnam veterans: Theory, research, and treatment implications.* New York: Brunner/ Mazel.

Fitzgerald, M. (2017). Why did Sigmund Freud refuse to see Pierre Janet? Origins of psychoanalysis, Janet, Freud or both? *History of Psychiatry, 28,* 358–364. doi:10.1177/0957154X17709747

Foa, E. B. (2011). Prolonged exposure therapy: past, present, and future. *Depression and Anxiety, 28,* 1043–1047. doi: 10.1002/da.20907

Foa, E. B., Hembree, E. A., & Rothbaum, B. O. (2007). *Treatments that work. Prolonged exposure therapy for PTSD: Emotional processing of traumatic experiences: Therapist guide.* New York: Oxford University Press. http://dx.doi.org/10.1093/med:psych/9780195308501.001.0001

Foa, E. B., Huppert, J. D., & Cahill, S. P. (2006). Emotional processing theory: An update. In B. O. Rothbaum (Ed.), *Pathological anxiety: Emotional processing in etiology and treatment* (pp. 3–24). New York: The Guilford Press.

Foa, E., Keane, T. M., Friedman, M. J., & Cohen, J. A. (2009). *Effective treatments for PTSD: Practice guidelines from the international society for traumatic stress studies* (2nd ed.). New York: Guilford Press.

Foa, E. B., & Kozak, M. J. (1986). Emotional processing of fear: Exposure to corrective information. *Psychological Bulletin, 99,* 20–35. http://dx.doi.org/10.1037/0033-2909.99.1.20

Foa, E. B., & McNally, R. J. (1996) Mechanisms of change in exposure therapy. In M. Rapee (Ed.), *Current controversies in the anxiety disorders* (pp. 329–343). New York: The Guilford Press.

Foa, E. B., & Meadows, E. A. (1997). Psychosocial treatments for posttraumatic stress disorder: A critical review. *Annual Review of Psychology, 48,* 449–480. http://dx.doi.org/10.1146/annurev.psych.48.1.449

Foa, E. B., & Riggs, D. S. (1993) Post-traumatic stress disorder in rape victims. In J. Oldham, M. B. Riba, & A. Tasman, (Eds.), *American psychiatric press review of psychiatry,* Vol. 12, (pp. 273–303). Washington, DC: American Psychiatric Press.

Foa, E., Riggs, D. S., Dancu, C. V., & Rothbaum, B. O. (1993). Reliability and validity of a brief instrument for assessing post-traumatic stress disorder. *Journal of Traumatic Stress, 6,* 459–473.

Foa, E. B., & Rothbaum, B. O. (1998). *Treatment manuals for practitioners. Treating the trauma of rape: Cognitive-behavioral therapy for PTSD.* New York: Guilford Press.

Foa, E. B., Steketee, G. S., & Rothbaum, B. O. (1989). Behavioral/cognitive conceptualizations of posttraumatic stress disorder. *Behavior Therapy, 20,* 155–176.

Freud, S. (1886). Report of my studies in Paris and Berlin. In J. Strachey (Ed. & Trans.), *The standard edition of the complete psychological works of Sigmund Freud* (Vol. 1, pg. 8). London: Hogarth Press.

Freud, S. (1896). *The aetiology of hysteria. Standard edition* (Vol. 3, pp. 163–168) London: The Hogarth Press.

Gailiene, D. (2011). Viennese professor in Vilnius: The earliest case descriptions of traumatology? Paper presented at the 12th European Conference on Traumatic Stress, Vienna, Austria.

Galton, F. (1874). *English men of science: Their nature and nurture* (2nd ed.). Reprint. London: Frank Cass, 1970.

Gantt, L., & Tinnin, L. (2009). Support for a neurobiological view of trauma with implications for art therapy. *The Arts in Psychotherapy, 36,* 148–153.

Grand, D. (2013). *Brainspotting: The revolutionary new therapy for rapid and effective change.* Boulder, CO: Sounds True.

Green, B. L., Grace, M. C., Lindy, J. D., Gleser, G. C, & Leonard, A. (1990). Risk factors for PTSD and other diagnoses in a general sample of Vietnam veterans. *American Journal of Psychiatry, 147,* 729–733.

Green, B. L., Grace, M. C., Vary, M. G., Kramer, T. L., Gleser, G. C., & Leonard, A. C. (1994). Children of disaster in the second decade: a 17-year follow-up of Buffalo Creek survivors. *Journal of American Academy of Child and Adolescent Psychiatry, 33*, 71–79.

Green, B. L., Lindy, J. D., Grace, M. C., Gleser, G. C., Leonard, A. C., Korol, M., & Winget, C. (1990). Buffalo Creek survivors in the second decade: stability of stress symptoms. *American Journal of Orthopsychiatry, 60,* 43–54.

Green, J. G., McLaughlin, K. A., Berglund, P. A., Gruber, M. J., Sampson, N. A., Kessler, R. C., & Zaslavsky, A. M. (2010). Childhood adversities and adult psychopathology in the National Comorbidity Survey Replication (NCS-R) I: Associations with first onset of DSM-IV disorders. *Archives of General Psychiatry, 67,* 113–123.

Heider, F. (1958). *The psychology of interpersonal relations.* New York: Wiley.

Herman, J. L. (1981). *Father-daughter incest.* Cambridge, MA: Harvard University Press.

Herman, J. L. (1992). *Trauma and recovery: The aftermath of violence—From domestic abuse to political terror.* New York: Basic Books.

Herman, J. L. (1997). *Trauma and recovery* (Rev. ed.). New York: BasicBooks.

Hildebrand, A., Grand, D., & Stemmler, M. (2017). Brainspotting – the efficacy of a new therapy approach for the treatment of posttraumatic stress disorder in comparison to eye movement desensitization and reprocessing. *Mediterranean Journal of Clinical Psychology, 5.* Retrieved from http://cab.unime.it/journals/index.php/MJCP/article/viewFile/1376/pdf_2

Hinton, D. E., & Lewis-Fernandéz, R. M. (2011). The cross-cultural validity of posttraumatic stress disorder. *Depression and Anxiety, 28,* 783–801.

Hoffman, M. A., & Kruczek, T. (2011). A bioecological model of mass trauma: Individual, community, and societal effects Ψ. *The Counseling Psychologist, 39,* 1087–1127. https://doi.org/10.1177/0011000010397932

Hood, K. K., & Eyberg, S. M. (2003). Outcomes of Parent-Child Interaction Therapy: Mothers' reports of maintenance three to six years after treatment. *Journal of Clinical Child and Adolescent Psychology, 32,* 419–429.

Isaacs, A. R. (1997). *Vietnam shadows: The war, its ghosts, and its legacy.* Baltimore, MD: Johns Hopkins University Press.

Jackson, L. A. (2000). *Child sexual abuse in Victorian England.* London, New York: Routledge.

Jackson, S. W. (1994). Catharsis and abreaction in the history of psychological healing. *Psychiatric Clinics of North America, 17*(3), 471–491.

James, W. (1907/1981). *Pragmatism: A new name for some old ways of thinking.* Indianapolis, IN: Hackett Publishing Company.

Janet, P. (1904). *Les nervoses.* Paris: Flammarion.

Janet P. (1919/1925). *Psychological healing,* Vols. 1–2. New York: Macmillan (originally published 1919).

Janoff-Bulman, R. (1992). *Shattered assumptions: Towards a new psychology of trauma.* New York: Free Press.

Jaspers, J. K. (1997). *General psychopathology.* Originally published 1913. Translated by J. Hoenig, &

M. W. Hamilton. Baltimore, MD: Johns Hopkins University Press.

Jaycox, L. H., Langley, A. K., & Hoover, S. A. (2018). *Cognitive behavioral intervention for trauma in schools (CBITS)* (2nd ed.). Santa Monica, CA: RAND Corporation, TL-272, 2018. Accessed 16, 2019, https://www.rand.org/pubs/tools/TL272.html

Jaycox, L. H., Stein, B., Kataoka, S., Wong, M., Fink, A., Escudera, P., & Zaragoza, C. (2002). Violence exposure, PTSD, and depressive symptoms among recent immigrant school children. *Journal of the American Academy of Child and Adolescent Psychiatry, 41*, 1104–1110.

Jones, E., & Wessely, S. (2005). A paradigm shift in the conceptualization of psychological trauma in the 20th century. *Journal of Anxiety Disorders, 21,* 164–175. https://doi.org/10.1016/j.janxdis.2006.09.009

Jones, E., & Wessely, S. (2006). Psychological trauma: a historical perspective. *Psychiatry, 5*(7), 217–220. doi:10.1053/j.mppsy.2006.04.011

Kardiner, A. (1941). *The traumatic neuroses of war.* New York: Hoeber.

Karlin, B. E., Ruzek, J. I., Chard, K. M., Eftekhari A., Monson, C. M., Hembree, E. A., Resick, P. A., & Foa, E. B. (2010). Dissemination of evidence-based psychological treatments for posttraumatic stress disorder in the Veterans Health Administration. *Journal of Traumatic Stress, 23*, 663–673. doi:10.1002/jts.20588

Kendall-Tackett, K. (2009). Psychological trauma and physical health: A psychoneuroimmunology approach to etiology of negative health effects and possible interventions. *Psychological Trauma: Theory, Research, Practice, and Policy, 1*, 35–48. http://dx.doi.org/10.1037/a0015128

Kilpatrick, D. G., Veronen, L. J., & Resick, P. A. (1979). The aftermath of rape: Recent empirical findings. *American Journal of Orthopsychiatry, 49*, 658–669.

Kitzinger, C. (1996). "The Freudian coverup": A reappraisal. *Feminism and Psychology, 6,* 251–259. https://doi-org.unco.idm.oclc.org/10.1177/0959353596062014

Klengel, T. (2016). PTSD: Can genetics affect your risk? Blogpost accessed May 2019 https://www.huffpost.com/entry/ptsd-how-does-genetics af_b_13411350?guccounter=1&guce_referrer=aHR0cHM6Ly93d3cuZ29vZ2xlLmNvbS8&guce_referrer_sig=AQAAACpGIg8E_Zn5gobfLzIoMNlA0DZDimz

8To6Aqt5smfaCmdzCvoItsOK10lbb4MVEPGQE1B9BpPqVjnulGvCXXjHjbdedCPw6qjFRwHkimGFbK3xJz-VyH9Q4d6mgstYj9dctOvpqj6mdMj7LjzmECvhMNS1zf9K_G5I-uFVV0QQK

Kolb, L. C. (1987). A neuropsychological hypothesis explaining posttraumatic stress disorders. *American Journal of Psychiatry, 144*, 989–995.

Kottman, T. (2010). *Play therapy: Basics and beyond.* (2nd ed.). Alexandria, VA: American Counseling Association.

Krystal, H. (Ed.). (1968). *Massive psychic trauma: Wayne State University, Workshops on the Late Sequelae of Massive Psychic Trauma, Detroit (1962–1965).* New York: International Universities Press.

Kurtz, J. R. (2014). Literature, trauma and the African moral imagination. *Journal of Contemporary African Studies, 32*(4), 421–435, doi: 10.1080/02589001.2014.979607

Lang, P. J. (1977). Imagery in therapy: An information processing analysis of fear. *Behavior Therapy, 8,* 862–886.

Lazarus, R. S. (1966). *Psychological stress and the coping process.* New York: McGraw-Hill.

Lazarus, R. S., & Folkman, S. (1984). *Stress, appraisal, and coping.* New York: Springer.

La Greca, A. M., & Silverman, W. K. (2009). Treatment and prevention of posttraumatic stress reactions in children and adolescents exposed to disaster and terrorism: What is the evidence? *Child Development Perspectives, 3*, 4–10. doi:10.1111/j.1750-8606.2008.00069.x

Lieberman, A. F., Ippen, C. G., & Van Horn, P. (2006). Child-parent psychotherapy: 6-month follow-up of a randomized controlled trial. *Journal of the American Academy of Child & Adolescent Psychiatry, 45*(8), 913–918.

Lenze, S. N., Pautsch, J., & Luby, J. (2011). Parent-child interaction therapy emotion development: A novel treatment for depression in preschool children. *Depression and Anxiety, 28*, 153–159. http://doi.org/10.1002/da.20770

Lieberman, A. F., Van Horn, P., & Ghosh-Ippen, C. (2005). Toward evidence-based treatment: Child-parent psychotherapy with preschoolers exposed to martial violence. *Journal of the American Academy of Child and Adolescent Psychiatry, 44*, 1241–1248.

Lifton, R. J. (2005). *Home from the war: Learning from Vietnam veterans.* New York: Other Press.

Lilienfeld, S. O., & Arkowitz, H. (2008). EMDR: Taking a closer look. *Scientific American Special Edition, 17,* 1–2.

Main, T. (1989). *"The aliment" and other psychoanalytic essays.* London: Free Association Press.

Management of Post-Traumatic Stress Working Group (2010). *VA/DoD clinical practice guideline for management of post-traumatic stress.* Washington, DC: Department of Veterans Affairs, Department of Defense. Available from: http://www.healthquality.va.gov/ptsd/ptsd_full.pdf 11.

Marinova, Z., & Maercker, A. (2015). Biological correlates of complex posttraumatic stress disorder-state of research and future directions. *European Journal of Psychotraumatology, 6,* 25913. doi:10.3402/ejpt.v6.25913

Masson, J. M. (1984). *Assault on the truth.* New York: Farrar Straus & Giroux.

McNeil, C. B., & Hembree-Kigin, T. L. (2010). *Parent–child interaction therapy,* 2nd Ed. New York: Springer.

McSweeney, F. K., & Murphy, E. S. (2014). *The Wiley Blackwell handbook of operant and classical conditioning.* Hoboken, NJ: Wiley-Blackwell.

Mitchell, J. T. (2003). Major misconceptions in crisis intervention. *International Journal of Emergency Mental Health, 5,* 185–197.

Mitchell, J. T., & Everly, G. S. (1996). *Critical incident stress debriefing: An operations manual.* Ellicott City, MD: Chevron.

Monson, C. M., Friedman, M. J., & La Bash H. (2014). A psychological history of PTSD. In M. J. Friedman, T. M. Keane, & P. A. Resick (Eds.), *Handbook of PTSD: Science and practice,* 2nd ed. (pp. 60–78). New York: Guilford.

Mowrer, O. H. (1951). Two-factor learning theory: summary and comment. *Psychological Review, 58*(5), 350–354. http://dx.doi.org/10.1037/h0058956

Mowrer, O. H. (1960). *Learning theory and behavior.* Hoboken, NJ: Wiley.

Nardo, D., Hogberg, G., Looi, J. C. L., Larsson, S., & Hallstrom, T. (2010). Gray matter density in limbic and paralimbic cortices is associated with trauma load and EMDR outcome in PTSD patients. *Journal of Psychiatric Research, 44,* 477–485.

North, C. S., Pfefferbaum, B., Narayanan, P., Thielman, S., McCoy. G., Dumont, C., . . . Spitznagel, E. L. (2005). Comparison of post-disaster psychiatric disorder after terrorist bombings in Nairobi and Oklahoma City. *British Journal of Psychiatry, 186,* 487–493.

O'Brien, L. S. (1998). *Psychiatry and medicine. Traumatic events and mental health.* New York: Cambridge University Press. http://dx.doi.org/10.1017/CBO9780511570124

Oppenheim, H. (1889). *Die traumatische neurosen.* Berlin: Hirschwald.

Pavlov, I. P. (1927). *Conditioned reflexes: An investigation of the physiological activity of the cerebral cortex.* London: Routledge and Kegan Paul.

Paynter, R. A. (2009). Evidence-based research in the social sciences. *Reference Service Review, 37,* 435–450.

Perry, B. D. (1993). Neurodevelopment and the neurophysiology of trauma II: Clinical work along the alarm-fear-terror continuum. *The APSAC Advisor, 6,* 14–20.

Perry, B. D. (1996). Childhood trauma. The neurobiology of trauma and adaptation: Clinical innovations with maltreated children. Presented at the Rosenberry Conference Arvada, Colorado, April 5, 1996.

Perry, B. D. (2000). Traumatized children: How childhood trauma influences brain development. *Journal of the California Alliance for the Mentally Ill, 11,* 48–51.

Perry, B. D. (2001). The neuroarcheology of childhood maltreatment: The neurodevelopmental costs of adverse childhood events. In K. Franey, R. Geffner, & R. Falconer (Eds.), *The cost of maltreatment: Who pays? We all do* (pp. 15–37). San Diego, CA: Family Violence and Sexual Assault Institute.

Perry, B. D. (2006). *Applying principles of neurodevelopment to clinical work with maltreated and traumatized children: The neurosequential model of therapeutics.* New York: Guilford Press.

Perry, B. D., & Hambrick, E. P. (2008). The neurosequential model of therapeutics. *Reclaiming Children and Youth, 17,* 38–43.

Perry, B. D., Pollard, T. L., Blakley, T. L., Baker, W. L., & Vigilante, D. (1995). Childhood trauma, the neurobiology of adaptation, and "use-dependent" development of the brain: How "states" become "traits". *Infant Mental Health Journal, 16,* 271–291.

Perry, B., & Szalavitz, M. (2006). *The boy who was raised as a dog: And other stories from a child psychiatrist's notebook—What traumatized children can teach us about loss, love, and healing.* New York: BasicBooks.

Phillips, R. D. (2010). How firm is our foundation? Current play therapy research. *International Journal of Play Therapy, 19*(1), 13. doi:10.1037/a0017340

Rachman, S. (1980). Emotional processing. *Behaviour Research and Therapy, 18*, 51–60. http://dx.doi.org/10.1016/0005-7967(80)90069-8

Radstone, S. (2007). Trauma theory: Contexts, politics, ethics. *Paragraph, 30*, 9–29 http://www.jstor.org/stable/43152697

Ray, D. C, & McCullough, R. (2015; revised 2016). *Evidence-based practice statement: Play therapy* (Research report). Retrieved from Association for Play Therapy website: http://www.a4pt.org/?page=EvidenceBased

Resick, P. A., Galovski, T. E., Uhlmansiek, M. O., Scher, C. D., Clum, G. A., & Young-Xu, Y. (2008). A randomized clinical trial to dismantle components of cognitive processing therapy for posttraumatic stress disorder in female victims of interpersonal violence. *Journal of consulting and clinical psychology, 76*, 243–258. doi:10.1037/0022-006X.76.2.243

Resick, P. A., Monson, C. M., & Chard, K. M. (2008). *Cognitive processing therapy: Veteran/military version.* Washington, DC: Department of Veterans' Affairs.

Resick, P. A., & Schnicke, M. K. (1993). *Interpersonal violence: The practice series, Vol. 4. Cognitive processing therapy for rape victims: A treatment manual.* Thousand Oaks, CA: Sage.

Roberts, J. L. (2018). *Trauma and the ontology of the modern subject: Historical studies in philosophy, psychology, and psychoanalysis.* London, New York: Routledge.

Rush, F. (1996). The Freudian coverup. *Feminism and Psychology, 6*, 260–276. https://doi-org.unco.idm.oclc.org/10.1177/0959353596062015

Ryan, J., Chaudieu, I., Ancelin, M-L., & Saffery, R. (2016). Biological underpinnings of trauma and post-traumatic stress disorder: Focusing on genetics and epigenetics. *Epigenomics, 11*, 1553–1569

Saakvitne, K. W., Gamble, S., Pearlman, L. A., & Lev, B. T. (2000). *Risking connection: A training curriculum for working with survivors of childhood abuse.* Baltimore, MD: The Sidran Press.

Sacco, L. (2009). *Unspeakable: Father-daughter incest in American history.* Baltimore, MD: Johns Hopkins University Press.

Scheeringa, M. S., Salloum, A., Arnberger, R. A., Weems, C. F., Amaya-Jackson, L., & Cohen, J. A. (2007). Feasibility and effectiveness of Cognitive-Behavioral Therapy for posttraumatic stress disorder in preschool children: Two case reports. *Journal of Traumatic Stress. 20*, 631–636.

Schimek, J. G. (1987). Fact and fantasy in the seduction theory: A historical review: *Journal of the American Psychoanalytic Association, 35*, 937–965. https://doi-org.unco.idm.oclc.org/10.1177/000306518703500407

Schivelbusch, W. (2014). *The railway journey.* Oakland: University of California Press.

Schubert, S., Lee, C., & Drummond, P. D. (2011). The efficacy and psychophysiological correlates of dual-attention tasks in eye movement desensitization and reprocessing (EMDR). *Journal of Anxiety Disorders, 25*, 1–11. doi:10.1016/j.janxdis.2010.06.024

Shalev, A. Y. (1991). Historical group debriefing following combat exposure lecture to the Royal Army Medical College. Military Psychiatry Seminar (October, 1991). Accessed online February 2018. http://www.dtic.mil/dtic/tr/fulltext/u2/a247839.pdf

Shapiro, F. (1989). Efficacy of the eye movement desensitization procedure in the treatment of traumatic memories. *Journal of Traumatic Stress, 2*, 199–223.

Shapiro, F. (1995). *Eye movement desensitization and reprocessing: Basic principles, protocols, and procedures.* New York: Guilford Press.

Shapiro, F. (2001). *Eye movement desensitization and reprocessing: Basic principles, protocols and procedures* (2nd ed.). New York: Guilford Press.

Shapiro, F., & Maxfield, L. (2002). Eye movement desensitization and reprocessing (EMDR): Information processing in the treatment of trauma. *Journal of Clinical Psychology, 58*, 933–946. http://dx.doi.org/10.1002/jclp.10068

Shatan, C. F. (1972). *Post-Vietnam syndrome.* New York Times, May 6, 1972.

Shatan, C. F. (1973). The grief of soldiers in mourning: Vietnam combat veterans' self help movement. *American Journal of Orthopsychiatry, 43,* 640–653.

Silverman, W. K., Ortiz, C. D., Viswesvaran, C., Burns, B. J., Kolko, D. J., Putnam, F. W., & Amaya-Jackson, L. (2008). Evidence-based psychosocial treatments for children and adolescents exposed to traumatic events. *Journal of Clinical Child and Adolescent Psychology, 37,*156–183.

Solomon, E. P., & Heide, K. M. (2005). The biology of trauma: Implications for treatment. *Journal of Interpersonal Violence, 20,* 51–60.

Sotero, M. M. (2006). A conceptual model of historical trauma: implications for public health practice and research. *Journal of Health Disparities Research and Practice, 1,* 93–108.

Spates, C. R., Koch, E., Pagoto, S., Cusack, K., & Waller, S. (2008) Eye movement desensitization and reprocessing for adults, children, and adolescents. In E. Foa, T. Keane, M. Friedman, and J. Cohen, *Effective treatments for PTSD* (pp. 279–305). New York: Guilford Press,

Stallard, P. (2006). Psychological interventions for post-traumatic reactions in children and young people: A review of randomized controlled trials. *Clinical Psychology, 26,* 895–911.

Stein, B. D., Jaycox, L. H., Kataoka, S. H., Wong, M., Tu, W., Elliott, M. N., & Fink, A. (2003). A mental health intervention for schoolchildren exposed to violence: A randomized controlled trial. *Jama, 290*(5), 603–611.

Stierlin, E. (1911). Nervöse und psychische störungen nach katastrophen [Nervous and psychological disturbances after catastrophes]. *Deutches Medizinische Wochenschrift, 37,* 2028–2035. Accessed online January 2018. https://www.thieme-connect.com/products/ejournals/issue/10.1055/s-002-17690

Summerfield, D. (2004). Cross-cultural perspectives on the medicalization of human suffering. *Posttraumatic Stress Disorder,* 233–245. doi:10.1002/9780470713570.ch12. ISBN 9780470713570.

Tardieu, A. A. (1862). Étude médico-légale sur les attentats aux moeurs. (Forensic study on sexual offenses). Paris: J. B. Baillere et Fils. Accessed online January 2018. https://archive.org/details/tudemdicol186/tard

Toth, S. L., Maughan, A., Manly, J. T., Spagnola, M. & Cicchetti, D. (2002). The relative efficacy of two interventions in altering maltreated preschool children's representational models: Implications for attachment theory. *Developmental Psychopathology, 14,* 877–908.

van der Hart, O., & Brown, P. (1990). The concept of psychic trauma. *American Journal of Psychiatry, 147*(12), 1691.

van der Hart, O., & Horst, R. (1989). The dissociation theory of Pierre Janet, *Journal of Traumatic Stress 2,* 397–412. doi:10.1007/BF00974598

van der Kolk, B. A. (1996). The complexity of adaptation to trauma: Self-regulation, stimulus discrimination, and characterological development. In B. A. van der Kolk, A. C. McFarlane, and L. Weisaeth (Eds.), *Traumatic stress* (pp. 182–213). New York: Guilford Press,

van der Kolk, B. A. (2005). Developmental trauma disorder. A new, rational diagnosis for children with complex trauma histories. *Psychiatric Annals, 35,* 401–408.

van der Kolk, B. A. (2007). The history of trauma in psychiatry. In M. J. Friedman, T. M. Keane, & P. A. Resick (Eds.), *Handbook of PTSD: Science and practice* (pp.19–36). New York: Guilford.

van der Kolk, B. A. (2014). *The body keeps the score: Brain, mind, and body in the healing of trauma.* New York: Penguin Group, LLC.

van der Kolk, B. A., Hart, van der Hart, O., & Marmar, C. R. (1996). Disassociation and Information Processing in Posttraumatic Stress Disorder. In B. A. van der Kolk, A. C. McFarlane, & L. Weisaeth, (Eds), *Traumatic stress: The effects of overwhelming experience on mind, body and society.* New York: Guilford.

van der Kolk, B. A., Herron, N., & Hostetler, A. (1994). The history of trauma in psychiatry. *Psychiatric Clinics of North America, 17,* 583–600.

van der Kolk, B. A., McFarlane, A. C., & Weisaeth, L. (Eds). (1996). *Traumatic stress: The effects of overwhelming experience on mind, body and society.* New York: Guilford.

van der Kolk, B. A., Roth, S., Pelcovitz, D., Sunday, S., & Spinazzola, J. (2005). Disorders of extreme stress: The empirical foundation of a complex adaptation to trauma. *Journal of Traumatic Stress, 18,* 389–399.

van Minnen, A., Harned, M. S., Zoellner, L., & Mills, K. (2012). Examining potential contraindications for prolonged exposure therapy for PTSD. *European Journal of Psychotraumatology, 3,* 10.3402/ejpt .v3i0.18805. doi:10.3402/ejpt.v3i0.18805

van Minnen, A., Hendriks, L., & Olff, M. (2010). When do trauma professionals choose exposure therapy for PTSD-patients? A controlled study about the influence of therapist and patient factors. *Behaviour Research and Therapy, 48,* 312–320.

Webster, D. C., & Dunn, E. C. (2005). Feminist perspectives on trauma. *Women & Therapy, 28,* 111–142. doi: 10.1300/J015v28n03_06

Weisaeth, L. (2014). *The history of psychic trauma.* In M. J. Friedman, T. M. Keane, & P. A. Resick (Eds.), *Handbook of PTSD: Science and practice* (2nd ed.) (pp. 38–59). New York: Guilford.

Wessely, S., Rose, S., & Bisson, J. (1998). A systematic review of brief psychological interventions ("debriefing") for the treatment of immediate trauma related symptoms and the prevention of post traumatic stress disorder. *Cochrane Review.* Accessed online March 2019. https://www.ncbi.nlm.nih.gov/ pubmed/10796724

Wilson, G. T. (1982). Psychotherapy process and procedure: The behavioral mandate. *Behavior Therapy, 13,* 291–312.

Wolpe, J. (1954). Reciprocal inhibition as the main basis of psychotherapeutic effects. *Archives of Neurology and Psychiatry, 72,* 205–226.

Wundt, W. (1909). Logic: An examination of the principles of knowledge and the methods of scientific research, *Philosophical Review, 18,* 84–85.

Chapter 5

American Psychiatric Association. (1994). *Diagnostic and statistical manual of mental disorders* (3rd ed.). Washington, DC: Author.

American Psychiatric Association. (2013). *Diagnostic and statistical manual of mental disorders* (5th ed.). Arlington, VA: American Psychiatric Publishing.

Axline, V. (1969). *Play therapy.* (1st ed.). New York: Ballantine Books.

Beck, J. G., Grant, D. M., Read, J. P., Clapp, J. D., Coffey, S. F., Miller, L. M., & Palyo, S. A. (2008). The Impact of Event Scale–Revised: Psychometric properties in a sample of motor vehicle accident survivors. *Journal of Anxiety Disorders, 22,* 187–198.

Ben-Ezra, M. (2011). Traumatic reactions from antiquity to the 16th century: Was there a common denominator? *Stress and Health, 27,* 223–240. https://doi.org/10.1002/smi.1338

Berg, R. C., & Landreth, G. (2017). *Group counseling concepts and procedures* (6th ed.). New York: Routledge.

Blevins, C. A., Weathers, F. W., Davis, M. T., Witte, T. K., & Domino, J. L. (2015). The Posttraumatic Stress Disorder Checklist for DSM-5 (PCL-5): Development and initial psychometric evaluation. *Journal of Traumatic Stress, 28,* 489–498.

Bovin, M. J., Marx, B. P., Weathers, F. W., Gallagher, M. W., Rodriguez, P., Schnurr, P. P., & Keane, T. M. (2015). Psychometric properties of the PTSD Checklist for Diagnostic and Statistical Manual of Mental Disorders-Fifth Edition (PCL-5) in veterans. *Psychological Assessment, 28,* 1379–1391. doi: 10.1037/pas0000254

Brock, S., Sandoval, J., & Lewis, S. (2001). *Preparing for crises in the school: A manual for building school crisis response teams* (2nd ed.). Hoboken, NJ: Wiley.

Capstick, C., & Fraenkel, P. (2004). Child abuse and neglect. In R.H. Coombs (Ed.), *Family therapy review: Preparing for comprehensive and licensing exams* (pp. 393–411). Boston: Lahaska Press.

Center for Substance Abuse Treatment (US). (2014). Trauma-informed care in behavioral health services. Rockville (MD): Substance Abuse and Mental Health Services Administration (US) (Treatment Improvement Protocol (TIP) Series, No. 57.) Chapter 3, Understanding the Impact of Trauma. Available from: https://www.ncbi.nlm.nih.gov/books/NBK207191/

Chadwick Center for Children and Families. (2009). *Assessment-based treatment for traumatized children: A trauma assessment pathway (TAP).* San Diego, CA: Author.

Cognitive Neuroscience Society. (2018, March 26). Prenatal stress changes brain connectivity in-utero. New findings from developmental cognitive neuroscience. *ScienceDaily.* Retrieved November 22, 2019 from www .sciencedaily.com/releases/2018/03/180326110123.htm

Corey, G. (2011). *Theory and practice of group counseling.* (8th ed.). Belmont, CA: Brooks/Cole.

Cormier, L. S., Nurius, P., & Osborn, C. J. (2009). *Interviewing and changes strategies for helpers: Fundamental skills and cognitive behavioral interventions.* Pacific Grove, CA: Brooks-Cole Publishing.

Courtois, C. A. (1988). *Healing the incest wound: Adult survivors in therapy.* New York: Norton.

Courtois, C. (2008). Complex trauma, complex reactions: Assessment and treatment. *Psychological Trauma Theory Research Practice and Policy, 1,* 86–100. doi: 10.1037/1942-9681.S.1.86

Courtois, C., & Ford, J. (2009). *Treating complex traumatic stress disorders: An evidence-based guide.* New York: Guilford Press.

Creamer, M., Bell, R., & Failla, S. (2003). Psychometric properties of the Impact of Event Scale-Revised. *Behaviour Research and Therapy, 41*(12), 1489–1496.

Davidson, J. R. T., Kudler, H. S., & Smith, R. D. (1990). Assessment and pharmacotherapy of posttraumatic stress disorder. In J. E. L. Giller (Ed.) *Biological assessment and treatment of post-traumatic stress disorder* (pp. 205–221). Washington, DC: American Psychiatric Press.

Davidson, J. R., Malik, M.A., & Travers, J. (1997). Structured interview for PTSD (SIP): psychometric validation for DSM-IV criteria. *Depression and Anxiety, 5,* 127–129.

Demetriou, C., Ozer, B. U., & Essau, C. A. (2015). The self-report questionnaires. *Encyclopedia of Clinical Psychology* (pp. 1–6). Edited by R. L. Cautin & S. O. Lilienfeld. Hoboken, NJ: Wiley. doi: 10.1002/9781118625392.wbecp507

Dubowitz, H., Black, M., Starr, R., & Zuravin, S. (1993). A conceptual definition of child neglect. *Criminal Justice and Behavior, 20,* 8–26.

Epstein, N. E. (2014). Multidisciplinary in-hospital teams improve patient outcomes: A review. *Surgical Neurology International, 5* (Suppl 7), S295–303. doi:10.4103/2152-

Finkelhor, D. (1979). *Sexually victimized children.* New York: Free Press.

Flynn, S. V., & Hays, D. G. (2015). The development and validation of the comprehensive counseling skills rubric. *Counseling Outcome Research and Evaluation, 6,* 87–99.

Foa, E. B., McLean, C. P., Zang, Y., Zhong, J., Rauch, S., Porter, K., . . . Kauffman, B. Y. (2016). Psychometric properties of the Posttraumatic Stress Disorder Symptom Scale Interview for DSM–5 (PSSI-5). *Psychological Assessment, 28,* 1159–1165. http://dx.doi .org/10.1037/pas0000259

Foa, E., Riggs, D. S., Dancu, C. V., & Rothbaum, B. O. (1993). Reliability and validity of a brief instrument for assessing post-traumatic stress disorder. *Journal of Traumatic Stress, 6,* 459–473.

Ford, J. D., Connor, D. F. & Hawke, J. (2009). Complex trauma among psychiatrically impaired children: A cross-sectional, chart-review study. *Journal of Clinical Psychiatry, 70,* 1155–1163.

Ford, J. D., & Courtois, C. A. (2009). Defining and understanding complex trauma and complex traumatic stress disorders. In C. A. Courtois & J. D. Ford, (Eds.), *Treating complex stress disorders: An evidence based guide* (pp. 13–30). New York: Guilford Press.

Ford, J. D., & Courtois, C. A. (2014). Defining and understanding complex trauma and complex traumatic stress disorders. In C. A. Courtois & J. D. Ford (Eds.), *Treating complex traumatic stress disorders: Scientific Foundations and Therapeutic Models* (pp. 13–30). London, UK: Guilford Press.

Ford, J. D., Fallot, R. D., & Harris, M. (2009). Group therapy. In C. A. Courtois & J. D. Ford, (Eds.), *Treating complex traumatic stress disorders: An evidence-based guide* (pp. 415–440). London, UK: Guilford Press.

Fraser, B. (1986). A glance at the past, a gaze at present, a glimpse at the future: A critical analysis of the development of child abuse reporting statutes. *Journal of Juvenile Law, 10,* 641–686.

Frazier, P., Tennen, H., Gavian, M., Park, C., Tomich, P., & Tashiro, T. (2009). Does self-reported posttraumatic growth reflect genuine positive change? *Psychological Science, 20,* 912–919.

Green, J. G., McLaughlin, K. A., Berglund, P. A., Gruber, M.J., Sampson, N. A., Kessler, R. C., & Zaslavsky, A. M. (2010). Childhood adversities and adult psychopathology in the National Comorbidity Survey Replication (NCS-R) I: Associations with first onset of DSM-IV disorders. *Archives of General Psychiatry, 67,* 113–123.

Harris, M., & Fallot, R. D. (Eds.). (2001). *New directions for mental health services. Using trauma theory to design service systems.* San Francisco, CA: Jossey-Bass.

Herman, J. L. (1992). Complex PTSD: A syndrome in survivors of prolonged and repeated trauma. *Journal of Traumatic Stress, 5,* 377–391. http://dx.doi .org/10.1002/jts.2490050305

Herman, J. L. (1997). *Trauma and recovery* (Rev. ed.). New York: BasicBooks.

Horowitz, M., Wilner, N., & Alvarez, W. (1979) Impact of Event Scale: a measure of subjective stress. *Psychosomatic Medicine, 41,* 209–218.

Ivey, A. E., Ivey, M. B., & Zalaquett, C. P. (2010). *Intentional interviewing and counseling: Facilitating client development in a multicultural society.* Pacific Grove, CA: Brook-Cole Publishing.

Jenkins, M. A., Langlais, P. J., Delis, D. A., & Cohen, R. A. (2010). Attentional dysfunction associated with posttraumatic stress disorder among rape survivors. *Clinical Neuropsychologist, 14,* 7–12.

Kempe, C. (1987). *Current pediatric diagnosis & treatment* (9th ed.). Norwalk, CT: Appleton & Lange.

Kendall C., Wilkins, B. A., Lang, A. J., & Norman, S. B. (2011). Synthesis of the psychometric properties of the PTSD checklist (PCL) military, civilian, and specific versions *Depression and Anxiety, 28,* 596–606. https://doi.org/10.1002/da.20837

Kim, W., Kim, D., Seo, H. J., Lee, S. Y., Ryu, S. H., Kim, J. B., . . . Chae, J. H. (2009). Psychometric validation of the Korean version of structured interview for Post-Traumatic Stress Disorder (K-SIP). *Journal of Korean Medical Science, 24,* 26–31. doi:10.3346/jkms.2009.24.1.26

Kinsella, M. T., & Monk, C. (2013). Impact of maternal stress, depression & anxiety on fetal neurobehavioral development. *Clinical Obstetrics and Gynecology, 3,* 425–440.

Kisiel, C., Fehrenbach, T., Small, L., & Lyons, J. S. (2009). Assessment of complex trauma exposure, responses, and service needs among children and adolescents in child welfare. *Journal of Child & Adolescent Trauma, 2,* 143–160. http://dx.doi.org/10.1080/19361520903120467

Kisiel, C., Patterson, N., Torgersen, E., den Dunnen, W., Villa, C., & Fehrenbach, T. (2018). Assessment of the complex effects of trauma across child serving settings: Measurement properties of the CANS-Trauma Comprehensive. *Children and Youth Services Review, 86,* 64–75.

Kitchener, K. S. (1984). Intuition, critical evaluation and ethical principles: The foundation for ethical decisions in counseling psychology. *Counseling Psychologist, 12,* 43–55.

Klein, R., & Schermer, V. (2000) Introduction and overview: Creating a healing matrix. In R. Klein & V. Schermer (Eds.) *Group psychotherapy for psychological trauma* (pp. 3–46). New York: Guilford Press.

Kottman, T. (2010). *Play therapy: Basics and beyond* (2nd ed.). Alexandria, VA: American Counseling Association.

Larsson, G. (2000). Dimensional analysis of the Impact of Event Scale using Structural Equation Modeling. *Journal of Traumatic Stress, 13,* 192–204.

Levers, L. L., & Buck, R. P. (2012). Contextual issues of community-based violence, violence-specific crisis, and disaster, and institutional response. In. L. L. Levers, (Ed.), *Trauma counseling: Theories and interventions* (1st ed.), (pp. 317–334). New York: Springer.

Lewis, M. D. (2005). Self-organizing individual differences in brain development. *Developmental Review, 25,* 252–277.

Markese, S. (2007). Taping together broken bones: Treatment of the trauma of infant abuse. *Journal of Infant, Child and Adolescent Psychotherapy, 6,* 309–326.

Maslow, A. H. (1943). A theory of human motivation. *Psychological Review, 50,* 370–396.

McFarland, C., & Alvaro, C. (2000). The impact of motivation on temporal comparisons: Coping with traumatic events by perceiving personal growth. *Journal of Personality and Social Psychology, 79,* 327–343. http://dx.doi.org/10.1037/0022-3514.79.3.327

McFarlane, A. C., & de Girolamo, G. (1996). The nature of traumatic stressors and the epidemiology of posttraumatic reactions. In B. A. van der Kolk, A. C. McFarlane, & L. Weisaeth (Eds.), *Traumatic stress: The effects of overwhelming experience on mind, body, and society* (pp. 129–154). New York: Guilford Press.

National Institute of Mental Health. (2002). Mental health and mass violence: Evidence-based early psychological intervention for victims/survivors of mass violence. A workshop to reach consensus on best practice. [NIH Pub. No. 02-5138]. Washington, DC: U.S. Government Printing Office. Retrieved July 25, 2019. www.nimh.nih.gov/research/massviolence.pdf

Peck, B. (2012). Treating adult trauma survivor. In. L. L. Levers, editor. *Trauma counseling: Theories and interventions* (1st ed.) (pp. 161–177). New York: Springer.

Perlman, S., & Doyle, A. (2012). Trauma experienced in early childhood. In. L. L. Levers, (Ed.), *Trauma counseling: Theories and interventions* (1st ed.) (pp. 132–145). New York: Springer.

Phillips, J. (2015). PTSD in DSM-5: Understanding the changes, *Psychiatric Times, 32,* Accessed June 2019. https://www.psychiatrictimes.com/ptsd/ptsd-dsm-5-understanding-changes.

Powers, M. B., Gillihan, S. J., Rosenfield, D. Jerud, A. B., & Foa, E. B. (2012). Reliability and validity of the PDS and PSS-I among participants with PTSD and alcohol dependence. *Journal of Anxiety Disorders* Jun; 26(5):617–23. doi: 10.1016/j.janxdis.2012.02.013.

Ray, D. (2004). Supervision of basic and advanced skills in play therapy. *Journal of Professional Counseling: Practice, Theory, & Research, 32*, 28–41.

Ray, D. (2011). *Advanced play therapy: Essential conditions, knowledge, and skills for child practice.* New York: Routledge.

Riggs, D., & Keane, T. M. (2006). Assessment strategies in the anxiety disorders. In B.O. Rothbaum (Ed.), *Pathological anxiety: Emotional processing in etiology and treatment of anxiety* (pp. 91–114). New York: Guilford.

Rosenfeld, L. B., Caye, J. S., Lahad, M., & Gurwitch, R. H. (2010). *When their world falls apart: Helping families and children manage the effects of disaster* (2nd ed.). Washington, DC: NASW Press.

Sar, V. (2011). Developmental trauma, complex PTSD, and the current proposal of DSM-5. *European Journal of Psychotraumatology, 2,* 10.3402/ejpt .v2i0.5622. doi:10.3402/ejpt.v2i0.5622

Scheeringa, M. S., & Zeanah, C. H. (1994). *PTSD semi-structured interview and observation record for infants and young children.* Department of Psychiatry and Neurology, Tulane University Health Sciences Center, New Orleans.

Shevlin, M., Hunt, N., & Robbins, I. (2000). A confirmatory factor analysis of the Impact of Event Scale using a sample of World War Two and Korean War veterans. *Psychological Assessment, 12,* 414–417.

Siegel, D. (1999). *The developing mind: Toward a neurobiology of interpersonal experience.* New York: Guilford Press.

Spaccarelli, S. (1994). Stress, appraisal, and coping in child sexual abuse: A theoretical and empirical review. *Psychological Bulletin, 116,* 340–362.

Spaccarelli, S., & Kim, S. (1995). Resilience criteria and factors associated with resilience in sexually abused girls. *Child Abuse & Neglect, 19,* 1171–1182.

Tedeschi, R. G. & Calhoun, L. G. (2004). *Posttraumatic growth: Conceptual foundation and empirical evidence.* Philadelphia, PA: Lawrence Erlbaum Associates.

United States Department of Health & Human Services, Administration for Children and Families,

Administration on Children, Youth and Families, Children's Bureau. (2017). The Child Abuse Prevention and Treatment Act. Retrieved from https://www .acf.hhs.gov/cb/resource/capta2016

van der Kolk, B. (1989). The compulsion to repeat the trauma: Re-enactment, revictimization, and masochism. *Psychiatric Clinics of North America, 12,* 389–411.

van der Kolk, B. (1994). *The body keeps the score: Memory and the evolving psychobiology of posttraumatic stress.* Etats-Unis: Harvard Medical School, Department of Psychiatry.

van der Kolk, B. A. (1996). The complexity of adaptation to trauma: Self-regulation, stimulus discrimination, and characterological development. In B. A. van der Kolk, A. McFarlane, L. Weisaeth (Eds.), *Traumatic Stress* (pp. 182–213). New York: Guilford Press.

van der Kolk, B., McFarlane, A., & Weisaeth, L. (1996). *Traumatic stress: The effects of overwhelming experience on mind, body, and society.* New York: Guilford Press.

van der Kolk, B. A., Roth, S., Pelcovitz, D., Sunday, S., & Spinazzola, J. (2005). Disorders of extreme stress: The empirical foundation of a complex adaptation to trauma. *Journal of. Traumatic Stress, 18,* 389–399. doi:10.1002/jts.20047

Vasterling, J. J., & Brewin, C. R. (2005). *Neuropsychology of PTSD: Biological, cognitive, and clinical perspectives.* New York: The Guilford Press.

Vernon, A. (2009). *Counseling children & adolescents.* (4th ed.). Denver, CO: Love Publishing.

Weathers, F. W., Bovin, M. J., Lee, D. J., Sloan, D. M., Schnurr, P. P., Kaloupek, D. G., Keane, T. M., & Marx, B. P. (2017). The Clinician-Administered PTSD Scale for DSM-5 (CAPS-5): Development and Initial Evaluation in Military Veterans. *Psychological Assessment, 30,* 383–395.

Weiss, D. S., & Marmar, C. R. (1997). The Impact of Event Scale—Revised. In J. P. Wilson & T. M. Keane (Eds.), *Assessing psychological trauma and PTSD* (pp. 399–411). New York: Guilford Press.

Wiggall, S., & Boccellari, A. (2017). The UC San Francisco trauma recovery center manual: A model for removing barriers to care and transforming services for survivors of violent crime. Retrieved from: http://traumarecoverycenter.org/wp-content/uploads/2017/05/TRC-Manual-v1-5-10-17.pdf

Wolfe, D. A. (1999). *Developmental clinical psychology and psychiatry series, Vol. 10. Child abuse: Implications for children development and psychopathology* (2nd ed.). Thousand Oaks, CA: Sage.

Yalom, I. (1995). *The theory and practice of group psychotherapy* (4th ed.). New York: Basic Books, A Division of HarperCollins.

Young, M. E. (2013). *Learning the art of helping: Building blocks and techniques* (5th ed.). New York: Pearson.

Ziguras, S. J., & Stuart, G. W. (2000). A meta-analysis of the effectiveness of mental health case management over 20 years. *Psychiatric Services, 51*, 1410–1421.

Zillmer, E. A., Spiers, M. V., & Culbertson, W. C. (2008). *Principles of neuropsychology* (2nd ed.). Belmont, CA: Thomson Higher Education.

Chapter 6

American Psychiatric Association. (1980). *Diagnostic and statistical manual of mental disorders III* (3rd ed.). Arlington, VA: American Psychiatric Publishing.

Bonanno, G. A. (2004). Loss, trauma, and human resilience: Have we underestimated the human capacity to thrive after extremely aversive events? *American Psychologist, 59*, 20–28.

Bronfenbrenner, U. (1995). Developmental ecology through space and time: A future perspective. In P. Moen, G. H. Elder Jr., & K. Luscher (Eds.), *Examining lives in context: Perspectives on the ecology of human development* (pp. 619–647). Washington, DC: American Psychological Association.

Bronfenbrenner, U. (2008). Ecological models of human development. In M. Gauvain & M. Cole (Eds.), *Readings on the development of children*. New York: Worth Publishers.

Burgess, A., & Holmstrom, L. (1974). Rape trauma syndrome. *American Journal of Psychiatry, 131*, 981–986.

Byrne, J. P. (2004). *The black death*. London: Greenwood Publishing Group.

Centers for Disease Control and Prevention, Emergency Preparedness and Response. (2012). Disaster mental health primer: Key principles, issues and questions. Retrieved March 12, 2019 from https://stacks.cdc.gov/view/cdc/29151

Dunant, H. (1862). *A memory of Solferino*. Accessed online April 4, 2018. https://shop.icrc.org/un-souvenir-de-solferino-2539.html

Federal Emergency Management Agency. (2008, March). National Response Framework, Washington.

Galea, S., Ahern, J., Resnick, H., Kilpatrick, D., Bucuvalas, M., Gold, J., & Vlahov, D. (2002). Psychological sequelae of the September 11 terrorist attacks in New York City. *New England Journal of Medicine, 346*, 982–987. doi: 10.1056/NEJMsa013404

Goldsteen, R., & Schorr, J.K. (1982). The long-term impact of a man-made disaster: An examination of a small town in the aftermath of the Three Mile Island nuclear reactor accident. *Disaster, 6*, 50–59. doi: 10.1111/j.1467-7717.1982.tb00744.x. Retrieved April 11, 2018.

Grattan, L. M., Brumback, B., Roberts, S., Buckingham-Howes, S., Toben, A. C., & Morris, G. (2017). Bouncing back after the Deepwater Horizon oil spill. *Disaster Prevention and Management: An International Journal, 26*, 122–133.

Green, B. L., Grace, M. C., Vary, M. G., Kramer, T. L., Gleser, G. C., & Leonard, A. C. (1994). Children of disaster in the second decade: a 17-year follow-up of Buffalo Creek survivors. *Journal of the American Academy of Child and Adolescent Psychiatry 33*, 71–79.

Green, B. L., Lindy, J. D., Grace, M. C., Gleser, G. C., Leonard, A. C., Korol, M., & Winget, C. (1990). Buffalo Creek survivors in the second decade: stability of stress symptoms. *American Journal of Orthopsychiatry, 60*, 43–54.

Halpern, J., & Tramontin, M. (2007). *Disaster mental health: Theory and practice*. Boston: Cengage.

International Critical Incident Stress Foundation (Website, 2018). *Mission statement*. Accessed June 2018. https://icisf.org/about-us/mission-statement/

James, R. K., & Gilliland, B. E. (2017). *Crisis intervention strategies* (8th ed.). Boston: Cengage.

Joseph, S., Yule, W., Williams, R., & Hodgkinson, P. (1994). Correlates of post-traumatic stress at 30 months: The Herald of Free Enterprise disaster. *Behaviour Research and Therapy 32*, 521–524.

Lazarus, R. S., & Folkman, S. (1984). *Stress, appraisal, and coping*. New York: Springer.

Lewin, K. (1935). *A dynamic theory of personality*. McGraw Hill: New York.

Lewis, S. J., & Roberts, A. R. (2001). Crisis assessment tools: The good, the bad, the available. *Brief Treatment and Crisis Intervention, 1*, 17–28.

Linley, P. A., & Joseph, S. (2004). Positive change following trauma and adversity: A review. *Journal of Traumatic Stress, 17*, 11–21.

Morris, A. J. F. (2011). Psychic aftershocks: Crisis counseling and disaster relief policy. *History of Psychology, 14*(3), 264–286. http://dx.doi.org/10.1037/a0024169

Morris, J. G., Grattan, L. M., Mayer, B. M., & Blackburn, J. K. (2013). Psychological responses and resilience of people can communities impacted by the Deepwater Horizon oil spill. *Transactions of the American Clinical and Climatological Association, 124,* 199–201.

Myer, R., & Moore, H. B. (2006). Crisis in context theory: An ecological model. *Journal of Counseling and Development,* 139–147.

National Organization for Victim Assistance (Website, 2018). Crisis Response Program page. Accessed June 3, 2018. https://www.trynova.org/crisis-response-program/

Neria, Y., Gross, R., Marshall, R. D., & Susser, E. S. (Eds.). (2006). *9/11: Mental health in the wake of terrorist attacks.* New York: Cambridge University Press. http://dx.doi.org/10.1017/CBO9780511544132

Neria, Y., Nandi, A., & Galea, S. (2008). Post-traumatic stress disorder following disaster: a systematic review. *Psychological Medicine, 38,* 467–480. doi.org/10.1017/S0033291707001353

Norris, F. H., Friedman, M. J., & Watson, P. J. (2002). 60,000 disaster victims speak: Part 2. Summary and implications of the disaster mental health research. *Psychiatry: Interpersonal and Biological Processes, 65*(3), 240–260. http://dx.doi.org/10.1521/psyc.65.3.240.20169

Pat-Horenczyk, R. (2005). Post-traumatic distress in adolescents exposed to ongoing terror: Findings from a school-based screening project in the Jerusalem area. In Y. Daniely & D. Brom (Eds.), *The trauma of terrorism: Sharing knowledge and shared care,* (pp. 335–348). New York: Haworth.

Picou, S., Marshall, B., & Gill, D. (2004). Disaster, litigation, and the corrosive community. *Social Forces, 82,* 1497–1526.

START Center. (2018). Global Terrorism Database Codebook. https://www.start.umd.edu/gtd/downloads/Codebook.pdf

Sungur, M., & Kaya, B. (2001). The onset and longitudinal course of a man-made post-traumatic morbidity: Survivors of the Sivas disaster. *International Journal of Psychiatry in Clinical Practice, 5,* 195–202, doi: 10.1080/136515001317021662

U. S. Department of Health and Human Services, Substance Abuse and Mental Health Services Administration. (2000). Training manual for mental health and human services workers in major disaster, (2nd ed.). Washington, DC. Retrieved April 11, 2018. ftp://ftp.snoco.org/Human_Services/HCS-OCHS/SR530-MULTI-AGENCYTASKFORCE/Handouts/Emotional%20Phases%20of%20a%20Disaster.pdf

U.S. Government Accountability Office. (1991, March). *Disaster assistance: Federal, state and local responses to natural disaster need improvement.* (Publication No. GAO-RCED-91-43). Retrieved June 2, 2018. https://www.gao.gov/assets/160/150281.pdf

U.S. Department of Justice. (2000). *Responding to terrorism victims: Oklahoma City and beyond.* Retrieved April 2018. https://www.ovc.gov/pdftxt/NCJ183949.pdf

Walker, K. L., & Chestnut, D. (2003). The role of ethnocultural variables in response to terrorism. *Culture and Diverse Ethnic Minority Psychology, 9,* 251–262.

Zirulnick, A. (2015). Kenya university attack puts security capabilities under fresh scrutiny (+video). *Christian Science Monitor.* Retrieved April 11, 2018. https://www.csmonitor.com/World/Africa/2015/0402/Kenya-university-attack-puts-security-capabilities-under-fresh-scrutiny

Chapter 7

Allen, B., Brymer, M. J., Steinberg, A. M., Vernberg, E. M., Jacobs, A., Speier, A. H., & Pynoos, R. S. (2010). Perceptions of psychological first aid among providers responding to Hurricanes Gustav and Ike. *Journal of Traumatic Stress, 23,* 509–513.

American Psychiatric Association. (2013). *Diagnostic and statistical manual of mental disorders* (5th ed.). Arlington, VA: American Psychiatric Publishing.

Balaban, V. F., Steinberg, A. M., Brymer, M. J., Layne, C. M., Jones, R. T., & Fairbank, J. A. (2005). Screening and assessment for children's psychosocial needs following war and terrorism. In M. J. Friedman & A. Mikus-Kos (Eds.), *Promoting the psychosocial well-being of children following war and terrorism* (pp. 121–161). Amsterdam, NL: IOS Press.

Bandura, A. (1997). *Self-efficacy: The exercise of control.* New York: Freeman.

Benight, C. C., & Bandura, A. (2004). Social cognitive theory of posttraumatic recovery: The role of perceived self-efficacy. *Behavior Research and Therapy, 42,* 1129–1148.

Benight, C. C., & Harper, M. (2002). Coping self-efficacy perceptions as a mediator between acute stress response and long-term distress following natural disaster. *Journal of Traumatic Stress, 15,* 177–186. doi:10.1023/A:1015295025950

Bernstein, D. A., & Borkovec, T. D. (1973). *Progressive relaxation training: A Manual for the helping professions.* Champaign, IL: Research Press.

Birch, W. G., & Martin, M. (1985). Emergency mental health triage: A multidisciplinary approach. *Social Work, 30,* 364–366.

Birkhead, G. S., & Vermeulen, K. (2018). Sustainability of psychological first aid training for the disaster response workforce. *American Journal of Public Health, 108,* S381–S382. doi:10.2105/AJPH.2018.304643

Bonanno, G. A., Westphal, M., & Mancini, A. D. (2011). Resilience to loss and potential trauma. *Annual Review of Clinical Psychology, 7,* 511–535.

Bosmans, M. W., Benight, C. C., Knaap, L. M., Winkel, F. W., & Velden, P. G. (2013). The associations between coping self-efficacy and posttraumatic stress symptoms 10 years postdisaster: Differences between men and women. *Journal of Traumatic Stress, 26,* 184–191. doi:10.1002/jts.21789

Bosmans, M. W., & Van der Velden, P. G. (2015). Longitudinal interplay between posttraumatic stress symptoms and coping self-efficacy: A four-wave prospective study. *Social Science & Medicine, 134,* 23–29. doi:10.1016/j.socscimed.2015.04.007

Bowman, S., & Roysircar, G. (2011). Training and practice in trauma, catastrophes, and disaster counseling. *The Counseling Psychologist, 39,* 1160–1181.

Bromet, E., Atwoli, L., Kawakami, N., Navarro-Mateu, F., Piotrowski, P., King, A., . . . Kessler, R. (2016). Post-traumatic stress disorder associated with natural and human-made disaster in the World Mental Health Surveys. *Psychological Medicine, 47,* 227–241. doi:10.1017/S0033291716002026

Bryant, R. A., Moulds, M., Guthrie, R., & Nixon, R. D. (2003). Treating acute stress disorder following mild traumatic brain injury. *The American Journal of Psychiatry, 160,* 585–587.

Brymer, M., Layne, C., Jacobs, A., Pynoos, R., Ruzek, J., Steinberg, A., . . . Watson, P. (2006). *Psychological first aid: Field operations guide.* (2nd ed.). Los Angeles, CA, Durham, NC: National Child Traumatic Stress Network and National Center for PTSD.

Bureau of Justice Statistics (2016). *What is the difference between jails and prisons?* Retrieved May 18, 2018. http://www.bjs.gov/index.cfm?ty=qa&iid=322

Carlson, L. E., Speca, M., Patel, K. D., & Goodey, E. (2004). Mindfulness-based stress reduction in relation to quality of life, mood, symptoms of stress and levels of cortisol, dehydroepiandrosterone sulfate (DHEAS) and melatonin in breast and prostate cancer outpatients. *Psychoneuroendocrinology, 29,* 448–74.

Center for Behavioral Health Statistics and Quality. (2015). *Behavioral health trends in the United States: Results from the 2014 National Survey on Drug Use and Health* (HHS Publication No. SMA 15-4927, NSDUH Series H-50). Retrieved from http://www.samhsa.gov/ data/

Center for Research on the Epidemiology of Disaster (2015). *The human cost of natural disaster 2015: A global perspective.* UN Office for Disaster Risk Reduction.

Cherry, K. E., Sampson, L., Nezat, P. F., Cacamo, A., Marks, L. D., & Galea, S. (2015). Long-term psychological outcomes in older adults after disaster: Relationships to religiosity and social support. *Aging & Mental Health, 19,* 430–443. doi:10.1080/13607863.2014.941325

Connor, K. M., & Butterfield, M. I. (2003). Posttraumatic stress disorder. *Focus 1,* 247–262.

Creamer, M., Bell, R., & Failla, S. (2003). Psychometric properties of the impact of event scale—Revised. *Behaviour Research and Therapy, 41,* 1489–1496. http://dx.doi.org/10.1016/j.brat.2003.07.010

Dingfelder, S. F. (2006). New needs in New Orleans schools. *Monitor on Psychology, 37.* Retrieved June 11, 2018. http://www.apa.org

Doughty, E. (2009). Investigating adaptive grieving styles: A delphi study. *Death studies, 33,* 462–480.

Elal, G., & Slade, P. (2005). Traumatic Exposure Severity Scale (TESS): A measure of exposure to major disaster. *Journal of Traumatic Stress, 18,* 213–220.

Fisher, J. E., Mauro, C., Cozza, S. J., Wall, M., Simon, N. M., Ortiz, C. D., . . . Katherine Shear, M. (2017). Examination of factor structure of the inventory of complicated grief (ICG) in a sample of bereaved military family members with persistent and elevated grief. *International Journal of Methods in Psychiatric Research, 26.* doi:10.1002/mpr.1571

Foa, E. B., & Rothbaum B. A. (1998) *Treating the trauma of rape: Cognitive behavioral therapy for PTSD.* New York: Guilford Press

Hembree, E. A., & Foa, E. B. (2000). Posttraumatic stress disorder: psychological factors and psychosocial interventions. *Journal of Clinical Psychiatry, 61,* Suppl 7:33–39.

Henslee, A. M., Coffey, S. F., Schumacher, J. A., Tracy, M., Norris, F. H., & Galea, S. (2015). Religious coping and psychological and behavioral adjustment after Hurricane Katrina. *The Journal of Psychology, 149,* 630–642. doi:10.1080/00223980.2014.953441

Hobfoll, S. E., Watson, P., Bell, C. C., Bryant, R. A., Brymer, M. J., Friedman, M. J., . . . Ursano, R. J. (2007). Five essential elements of immediate and mid-term mass trauma intervention: Empirical evidence. *Psychiatry: Interpersonal and Biological Processes, 70*(4), 283–315. doi:10.1521/psyc.2007.70.4.283

Horowitz, M., Wilner, N., & Alvarez, W. (1979). Impact of event scale: a measure of psychological stress. *Psychosomatic Medicine, 41,* 209–218.

James, R. K., & Gilliland, B. E. (2017). *Crisis intervention strategies* (8th ed.) Belmont, CA: Brooks/Cole.

Kaltman, S., & Bonanno, G. A. (2003). Trauma and bereavement: Examining the impact of sudden and violent deaths. *Journal of Anxiety Disorders, 17,* 131–147.

Kanel, K. (2012). *A guide to crisis intervention* (5th ed.). Stamford, CT: Cengage Learning.

Kubler-Ross, E. (1969). *On death and dying.* New York: The Macmillan Company.

La Greca, A. M., Silverman, W. K., & Lochman, J. E. (2009). Moving beyond efficacy and effectiveness in child and adolescent intervention research. *Journal of Consulting and Clinical Psychology, 77*(3), 373–382. doi:10.1037/a0015954

Linzer, N., Sweifach, J., & Heft-LaPorte, H. (2008). Triage and ethics: Social workers on the front line. *Journal of Human Behavior in the Social Environment, 18*(2), 184–203.

Matthews, L., & Marwit, S. (2004). Examining the assumptive world views of parents bereaved by accident, murder, and illness. *Omega - Journal of Death and Dying, 48*(2), 115–136. doi:10.2190/KCB0-NN-VB-UGY6-NPYR

McFarlane, A. C., & Norris, F. H. (2006). Definitions and concepts in disaster research. In F. H. Norris, S. Galea, M. J. Friedman, & P. J. Watson (Eds.), *Methods for disaster mental health research* (pp. 3–19). New York: Guilford Press.

Meichenbaum, D. (1974). Toward a cognitive theory of self-control. In G. E. Schwartz & D. Shapiro (Eds.), *Consciousness and self-regulation.* Boston, MA: Springer.

Milojev, P., Osborne, D., & Sibley, C. (2014). Personality resilience following a natural disaster. *Social Psychological and Personality Science, 5,* 760–768, 10.1177/1948550614528545

Mitchell, T., Griffin, K., Stewart, S., & Loba, P. (2004). 'We Will Never Ever Forget. . .': The Swissair Flight 111 disaster and its impact on volunteers and communities. *Journal of Health Psychology, 9,* 245–262. doi: 10.1177/1359105304040890

National Institute of Mental Health. (2001). Helping children and adolescents cope with violence and disaster. (NIH publication, no. 01-3519). Retrieved September 14, 2018. http://purl.access.gpo.gov/GPO/LPS35195

Neimeyer, R. A., Prigerson, H., & Davies, B. (2002). Mourning and meaning. *American Behavioral Scientist, 46,* 235–251

Neria, Y., & Litz, B. T. (2004). Bereavement by traumatic means: The complex synergy of trauma and grief. *Journal of Loss and Trauma, 9,* 73–88.

North, C. S., & Pfefferbaum, B. (2013). Mental health response to community disaster: A systematic review. *Journal of the American Medical Association (JAMA), 310,* 507–518. doi:10.1001/jama.2013.107799

Prigerson, H. G., Mac'lejewskib, P. K., Reynolds, V. F., Bierhals, A. J., Newsomc, J. T., Fasiczkaa, A., . . . Milleral, M. (1995) Inventory of Complicated Grief: A scale to measure maladaptive symptoms of loss. *Psychiatry Research, 59,* 65–79.

Rose, S., Bisson, J., Churchill, R., & Wessely, S. (2002). Psychological debriefing for preventing post traumatic stress disorder (PTSD). *Cochrane Database Systematic Reviews, 2,* CD000560.

Rosenfeld, L. B., Caye, J., Lahad, M., & Gurwitch, R. H. (2010). *When their world falls apart: Helping families and children manage the effects of disaster* (2nd ed.). Washington, DC: NASW Press.

Ruzek, J. I., Brymer, M. J., Jacobs, A. K., Layne, C. M., Vernberg, E. M., & Watson, P. J. (2007). Psychological first aid. *Journal of Mental Health Counseling, 29,* 17–49.

Sastry, N., & Van Landingham, M. (2009). One year later: mental illness prevalence and disparities among New Orleans residents displaced by Hurricane Katrina. *American Journal of Public Health, 99,* S725–S731. doi:10.2105/AJPH.2009.174854

Saunders, T., Driskell, J., Johnston, J., & Salas, E. (1996). The effect of stress inoculation training on anxiety and performance. *Journal of Occupational Health Psychology, 1,* 170–186. doi:10.1037//1076-8998.1.2.170

Saul, J. (2013). *Collective trauma, collective healing: Promoting community resilience in the aftermath of disaster,* Routledge psychosocial stress series. New York: Taylor & Francis.

Servaty-Seib, H. (2004). Introduction: Perspectives on counseling the bereaved. *AMHCA Journal, 26,* 95–97.

Shing, E. Z., Jayawickreme, E., & Waugh, C. E. (2016). Contextual positive coping as a factor contributing to resilience after disaster. *Journal of Clinical Psychology, 72,* 1287–1306. doi:10.1002/jclp.22327

Solomon, Z., Mikulincer, M., & Hobfoll, S. E. (1986). Effects of social support and battle intensity on loneliness and breakdown during combat. *Journal of Personality and Social Psychology, 51,* 1269–1276.

Stebnicki, M. (2017). *Disaster mental health counseling: Responding to trauma in a multicultural context.* New York: Springer.

Stroebe, M. S. (2002). Paving the way: From early attachment theory to contemporary bereavement research. *Mortality, 7*(2), 127–138.

United States Department of Health and Human Services. Substance Abuse and Mental Health Services Administration. Center for Behavioral Health Statistics and Quality. National Survey on Drug Use and Health. (2014). Ann Arbor, MI: Inter-university Consortium for Political and Social Research [distributor], 2016-03-22. https://doi.org/10.3886/ICPSR36361.v1

Veronen, L. J., & Kilpatrick, D. G. (1983). Stress management for rape victims. In D. Meichenbaum & M. E. Jaremko (Eds.), *Stress reduction and prevention* (pp. 341–374). New York: Plenum.

Watson, P. J., Brymer, M. J., & Bonanno, G. A. (2011). Postdisaster psychological intervention since 9/11. *The American Psychologist, 66*(6), 482–494. doi:10.1037/a0024806

Weiss, D., & Marmar, C. (1997). The Impact of Event Scale-Revised. In J. Wilson & T. Keane (Eds.), *Assessing psychological trauma and PTSD.* New York: Guilford.

Wittouck, C., Van Autreve, S., De Jaegere, E., Portzky, G., & van Heeringen, K. (2011). The prevention and treatment of complicated grief: a meta-analysis. *Clinical Psychology Review, 31*(1), 69–78. doi: 10.1016/j.cpr.2010.09.005

Zoellner, L. A., Feeny, N. C., Bittinger, J. N., Bedard-Gilligan, M. A., Slagle, D. A., Post, L. M., & Chen, J. A. (2011). Teaching trauma-focused exposure therapy for PTSD: Critical clinical lessons for novice exposure therapists. *Psychological Trauma: Theory, Research, Practice and Policy, 3*(3), 300–308.

Chapter 8

American Counseling Association. (2014). *2014 ACA Code of Ethics.* Retrieved July 6, 2018. http://www.counseling.org/docs/ethics/2014-aca-code-of-ethics.pdf? sfvrsn=4

American Psychological Association. (2011). *Road to resilience.* Retrieved from http://www.apa.org/helpcenter/road-resilience.aspx

Baranowsky, A. B., Gentry, J. E., & Schultz, D. F. (2005). *Trauma practice: Tools for stabilization and recovery.* New York: Huber & Hogrefe.

Bemak, F., & Chung, R. C-Y. (2008). New professional roles and advocacy strategies for school counselors: A multicultural/social justice perspective to move beyond the Nice Counselor Syndrome. *Journal of Counseling and Development, 86,* 372–381. doi: 10.1002/j.1556-6678.2008.tb00522.x

Buckwalter, G. (2011). *My definition of resilience.* Access July 11, 2019 https://www.headington-institute.org/files/resiliencedefinition_edited-copy_74370.pdf

Ceschi, A., Demerouti, E., Sartori, R., & Weller, J. (2017). Decision-making processes in the workplace: How exhaustion, lack of resources and job demands impair them and affect performance. *Frontiers in Psychology, 8,* 313. doi:10.3389/fpsyg.2017.00313

Craig, C. D., & Sprang, G. (2010). Compassion satisfaction, compassion fatigue, and burnout in a national sample of trauma treatment therapists. *Anxiety, Stress, and Coping, 23*, 319–339.

Daniels, N. (2010). Self-care for EMDR practitioners. In M. Luber (Ed.), *Eye movement desentization and reprocessing (EMDR) scripted protocols: Special populations.* (pp. 615–616). New York: Springer.

Dass-Brailsford, P. (2010). Secondary trauma among disaster responders: The need for self-care. In P. Dass-Brailsford (Ed.), *Crisis and disaster counseling: Lessons learned from Hurricane Katrina and other disaster.* (pp. 213–228). Thousand Oaks, CA: Sage.

Disease Control and Prevention. (2018). *Youth Risk Behavior Survey Questionnaire.* Accessed on August 4, 2018. www.cdc.gov/yrbs.

Dworkin, E. R., Sorell, N. R., & Allen, N. E. (2016). Individual-and setting-level correlates of secondary traumatic stress in rape crisis center staff. *Journal of Interpersonal Violence, 31*, 743–752. https://doi-org.libproxy.plymouth.edu/10.1177/0886260514556111

Farber, B. A., & Heifetz, L. J. (1982). The process and dimensions of burnout in psychotherapists. *Professional Psychology, 13*(2), 293–301.

Figley, C. R. (1995). Compassion fatigue as a secondary traumatic stress disorder: An overview. In C. R. Figley (Ed.), *Compassion fatigue: Coping with Secondary Traumatic Stress Disorder in those who treat the traumatized* (pp.1–20). New York: Brunner/Mazel. doi:10.1080/10615800903085818

Figley, C. R. (Ed.) (1997). *Burnout in families: The systemic costs of caring.* New York: CRC Press.

Flynn, S. V. (2009). *A grounded theory of the altruism and self-interest phenomenon within the counseling profession.* (Doctoral Dissertation). Retrieved from ProQuest Dissertations and Theses Database (AAT 3378221).

Flynn, S. V., & Black, L. L. (2011). An emergent theory of altruism and self-interest. *Journal of Counseling & Development, 89*, 459–469. doi:10.1002/j.1556-6676.2011.tb02843.x

Flynn, S. V., & Black, L. L. (2013). Altruism-self-interest archetypes: A paradigmatic narrative of counseling professionals. (3). http://tpcjournal.nbcc.org/altruism-self-interest-archetypes-a-paradigmatic-narrative-of-counseling-professionals/

Foreman, T. (2018). Wellness, exposure to trauma, and vicarious traumatization: A pilot study. *Journal of Mental Health Counseling, 40*(2), 142–155. doi: 10.17744/mehc.40.2.04

Golkar, A. J., Johansson, E., Kasahara, M., Osika, W., Perski, A., & Savic, I. (2014). The influence of work-related chronic stress on the regulation of emotion and on functional connectivity in the brain. *PLOS ONE, 9*: e104550. doi:10.1371/journal.prone.014550.

Heaton, K. J., & Black, L. L. (2009). I knew you when: A case study of managing preexisting nonamorous relationships in counseling. *The Family Journal, 17,* 134–138. https://doi.org/10.1177/1066480709332854

Herman, J. (1997). *Trauma and recovery* (Rev. ed.). New York: BasicBooks.

Hobfoll, S. E., Watson, P., Bell, C. C., Bryant, R. A., Brymer, M. J., Friedman, M. J., . . . Ursano, R. J. (2007). Five essential elements of immediate and mid-term mass trauma intervention: Empirical evidence. *Psychiatry: Interpersonal and Biological Processes, 70*, 283–315. doi:10.1521/psyc.2007.70.4.283

Jacobson, D. (1989). Context and the sociological study of stress. *Journal of Health & Social Behavior, 30*, 257–260.

James, R. K., & Gilliland, B. E. (2013) *Crisis intervention strategies* (7th ed.) Belmont, CA: Brooks/Cole.

Jung, C. G. (1966). The psychology of the transference (R. F. C. Hull, Trans.). In H. Read et al. (Eds.), *The collected works of C. G. Jung* (Vol. 16, 2nd ed., pp. 163–323). Princeton, NJ: Princeton University Press. (Original work published 1946).

Lanham, M. E., Rye, M. S., Rimsky, L. S., & Weill, S. R. (2012). How gratitude relates to burnout and job satisfaction in mental health professionals. *Journal of Mental Health Counseling, 34*, 341–354.

Lawson, G., & Myers, J. E. (2011). Wellness, professional quality of life, and career sustaining behaviors: What keeps us well? *Journal of Counseling & Development, 89*, 163–171.

Lawson, G., & Venart, B. (2005). Preventing counselor impairment: Vulnerability, wellness, and resilience. Retrieved from http://www.counseling.org/wellness_taskforce/index.htm

Lee, S. M., Cho, S. H., Kissinger, D., & Ogle, N. T. (2010). A typology of burnout in professional counselors. *Journal of Counseling & Development, 88*(2), 131–138.

Lonergan, B. A., O'Halloran, M. S., & Crane, S. C. (2004). The development of the trauma therapist: A qualitative study of the child therapist's perspectives and experiences. *Brief Treatment and Crisis Intervention, 4,* 353–366.

Mathad, M. D., Pradhan, B., & Rajesh, S. K. (2017, February). Correlates and predictors of resilience among baccalaureate nursing students. *Journal of Clinical and Diagnostic Research, 11,* 5–8. http://dx.doi.org/10.7860/JCDR/2017/24442.9352

Meier, S. T., & Davis, S. R. (1997). *The elements of counseling.* Pacific Grove, CA: Brooks/Cole.

Meyers, J. E., Luecht, R. M., & Sweeney, T. J. (2004). The factor structure of wellness: Re-examining theoretical and empirical modules underlying the Wellness Evaluation of Lifestyle (WEL) and the Five-Factor WEL. *Measurement and Evaluation in Counseling and Development, 36,* 194–208.

Murphy, S. N. (2013, September 1). Attending to Countertransference. Retrieved from http://ct.counseling.org/2013/09/attending-to-countertransference/.

Myers, J. E., & Sweeney, T. J. (2005). *Counseling for-wellness: Theory, research, and practice.* Alexandria, VA: American Counseling Association.

Nelson-Gardell, D., & Harris, D. (2003). Childhood abuse history, secondary traumatic stress, and child welfare workers. *Child Welfare, 82,* 5–26.

Niessen, C., Sonnentag, S., & Sach, F. (2012). Thriving at work – A diary study. *Journal of Organizational Behavior, 33,* 468–487. doi:10.1002/job.763

Ogresta, J., Rusac, S., & Zorec, L. (2008). Relation between burnout syndrome and job satisfaction among mental health workers. *Croatian Medical Journal, 49,* 364–374. http://doi.org/10.3325/cmj.2008.3.364

Osborn, C. J. (2004). Seven salutary suggestions for counselor stamina. *Journal of Counseling & Development, 82,* 354–364.

Paige, M. (2015). Competencies in trauma counseling: A qualitative investigation of the knowledge, skills and attitudes required of trauma-competent counselors. *Dissertation,* Georgia State University, https://scholarworks.gsu.edu/cps_diss/109

Paterson, T., Luthans, F., & Jeung, W. (2014). Thriving at work: Impact of psychological capital and supervisor support. *Journal of Organizational Behavior, 35,* 434–446. doi:10.1002/job.1907

Pearlman, L. A., & Mac Ian, P. S. (1995). Vicarious traumatization: An empirical study of the effects of trauma work on trauma therapists. *Professional Psychology: Research and Practice, 26,* 558–565. http://dx.doi.org.unco.idm.oclc.org/10.1037/0735-7028.26.6.558

Pearlman, L. A., & Saakvitne, K. W. (1995). *Trauma and the therapist: Countertransference and vicarious traumatization in psychotherapy with incest survivors.* New York: W. W. Norton & Co.

Perry, W. G., Jr. (1970). *Forms of intellectual and ethical development in the college years: A scheme.* New York: Holt, Rinehart, and Winston.

Pines, A., & Aronson, E. (1988). *Career burnout: Causes and cures.* New York: Free Press

Roscoe, L. J. (2009). Wellness: A review of theory and measurement for counselors. *Journal of Counseling & Development, 87,* 216–226. doi: http://dx.doi.org/10.1002/j.1556-6678.2009.tb00570.x

Rupert, P. A., & Kent, J. S. (2007). Gender and work setting differences in career-sustaining behaviors and burnout among professional psychologists. *Professional Psychology: Research and Practice, 38,* 88–96. doi:10.1037/0735-7028.38.1.88

Sim, W., Zanardelli, G., Loughran, M., Mannarino, M., & Hill, C. (2016). Thriving, burnout, and coping strategies of early and later career counseling center psychologists in the United States. *Counselling Psychology Quarterly, 29*(4), 382–404. doi:10.1080/09515070.2015.1121135

Skovholt, T. M. (2017). *The resilient practitioner: Burnout prevention and self-care strategies for counselors, therapists, teachers, and health professionals.* Boston: Allyn & Bacon.

Smith, G. D., & Yang, F. (2017). Stress, resilience and psychological well-being in Chinese undergraduate nursing students. *Nurse Education Today, 5,* 49–90.

Turkus, J. (2013). The shaping and integration of the trauma therapist. *Journal of Trauma and Dissociation, 14,* 1–10.

Turner, K., & McCarthy, V. L. (2017). Stress and anxiety among nursing students: A review of intervention strategies in literature between 2009–2015. *Nurse Education in Practice, 22,* 21–29. http://dx.doi.org/10.1016/j.nepr.2016.11.002

Williams, E. N., Judge, A. B., Hill, C. E., & Hoffman, M. (1997). Experiences of novice therapists in prepracticum: Trainees', clients', and supervisors' perceptions of therapists' personal reactions and management strategies. *Journal of Counseling Psychology, 44,* 390–399. http://dx.doi.org/10.1037/0022-0167.44.4.390

Chapter 9

American Psychiatric Association. (1980). *Diagnostic and statistical manual of mental disorders III* (3rd ed.). Arlington, VA: American Psychiatric Publishing.

American Psychiatric Association. (1987). *Diagnostic and statistical manual of mental disorders III-R.* Arlington, VA: American Psychiatric Publishing.

American Psychiatric Association. (2000). *Diagnostic and statistical manual of mental disorders IV-TR.* Arlington, VA: American Psychiatric Publishing.

American Psychiatric Association. (2013). *Diagnostic and statistical manual of mental disorders* (5th ed.). Arlington, VA: American Psychiatric Publishing.

Benjet, C., Bromet, E., Karam, E. G., Kessler, R. C., McLaughlin, K. A., Ruscio, A. M., . . . Koenen, K. C. (2016). The epidemiology of traumatic event exposure worldwide: results from the World Mental Health Survey Consortium. *Psychological Medicine, 46*(2), 327–43.

Berntsen, D., Rubin, D. C., & Johansen, M. K. (2008). Contrasting models of posttraumatic stress disorder: Reply to Monroe and Mineka (2008). *Psychological Review, 115,* 1099–1106.

Besterman, T. (1969). *Voltaire.* London: Longman.

Bowman, M. L. (1999). Individual differences in posttraumatic distress: problems with the DSM-IV model. *Canadian Journal of Psychiatry, 44,* 21–33.

Breslau, N., Chase, G. A., & Anthony, J. C. (2002). The uniqueness of the DSM definition of posttraumatic stress disorder: Implications for research. *Psychological Medicine, 32*(4), 573–576.

Breslau, N., Davis, G. C., Peterson, E. L., & Schultz, L. R. (2000). A second look at comorbidity in victims of trauma: the posttraumatic stress disorder-major depression connection. *Biological Psychiatry, 48,* 902–909.

Brewin, C. R., & Andrews, B. (2016) Creating memories for false autobiographical events in childhood: A systematic review. *Applied Cognitive Psychology, 31,* 2–23. doi: 10.1002/acp.3220

Britton, J. C., Lissek, S., Grillon, C., Norcross, M. A., & Pine, D. S. (2011). Development of anxiety: The role of threat appraisal and fear learning. *Depression and Anxiety, 28,* 5–17. doi:10.1002/da.20733. Accessed September 2018.

Clark, D. M. (2012). The English improving access to psychological therapies (IAPT) program: History and progress. In R. K. McHugh & D. H. Barlow (Eds.). *Dissemination and implementation of evidence-based psychological interventions* (pp. 61–77). New York: Oxford University Press.

Cook, J. M., & Newman, E. (2014). A consensus statement on trauma mental health: The new haven competency conference process and major findings. *Psychological Trauma: Theory, Research, Practice and Policy, 6,* 300–307.

Council for Accreditation of Counseling and Related Educational Programs (CACREP). (2009). Accreditation Standards. Retrieved July 6, 2016. http://www.cacrep.org/wp-content/uploads/2013/12/2009-Standards.pdf

Dalgleish. T., Meiser-Stedman, R., & Smith, P. (2005). Cognitive aspects of posttraumatic stress reactions and their treatment in children and adolescents: An empirical review and some recommendations. *Behavioural and Cognitive Psychotherapy, 33,* 459–486. doi: 10.1017/S1352465805002389

Ehlers, A., & Clark, D. M. (2000). A cognitive model of posttraumatic stress disorder. *Behaviour Research and Therapy, 38,* 319–345.

Erickson, D. J., Wolfe, J., King, D. W., King, L. A., & Sharkansky, E. J. (2001). Posttraumatic stress disorder and depression symptomatology in a sample of Gulf War veterans: A prospective analysis. *Journal of Consulting and Clinical Psychology, 69,* 41–49. doi:10.1037/0022-006X.69.1.41

Fairburn, C. G., & Wilson, G. T. (2013). The dissemination and implementation of psychological treatments: Problems and solutions. *International Journal of Eating Disorders, 46*(5), 516–521.

Foa, E. B., & Kozak, M. J. (1986). Emotional processing of fear: Exposure to corrective information. *Psychological Bulletin, 99,* 20–35. http://dx.doi.org/10.1037/0033-2909.99.1.20

Folkman, S., & Lazarus, R. (1985). If it changes it must be a process: Study of emotion and coping during three stages of a college examination. *Journal of Personality and Social Psychology, 48,* 150–170. doi: 10.1037/0022-3514.48.1.150

Freeman, D., Antley, A., Ehlers, A., Dunn, G., Thompson, C., Vorontsova, N., . . . Slater, M. (2014). The use of immersive virtual reality (VR) to predict the occurrence 6 months later of paranoid thinking and posttraumatic stress symptoms assessed by self-report and interviewer methods: A study of individuals who have been physically assaulted. *Psychological Assessment, 26,* 841–847.

Friedman, M. J. (2013). Finalizing PTSD in *DSM-5:* Getting here from there and where to go next. *Journal of Traumatic Stress, 26,* 548–556.

Friedman, M. J., Keane, T. M., & Resick, P. A. (2014). A psychological history of PTSD. In M. J. Friedman, T. M. Keane, & P. A. Resick (Eds.), *Handbook of PTSD: Science and practice* (2nd ed.) (pp. 3–37). New York: Guilford.

Grinage, B. D. (2003). Diagnosis and management of post-traumatic stress disorder. *American Family Physician, 15,* 2401–2409. Accessed August 2018. aafp.org/afp/2003/1215/p2401.html

Hoge, C. W., Riviere, L. A., Wilk, J. E., Herrell, R.K., & Weathers, F.W. (2014). The prevalence of post-traumatic stress disorder (PTSD) in US combat soldiers: a head-to-head comparison of DSM-5 versus DSM-IV-TR symptom criteria with the PTSD checklist. *Lancet Psychiatry, 1,* 269–277.

Hoge, C. W., Yehuda, R., Castro, C. A., McFarlane, C. A., Vermetten, E., Jetly, R., . . . Rothbaum, B. O. (2016). Unintended consequences of changing the definition of posttraumatic stress disorder in DSM-5 Critique and call for action. *JAMA Psychiatry, 73,* 750–752.

Holmes, T., & Rahe, R. (1967). The Social Readjustment Rating Scale. *Journal of Psychosomatic Research, 12,* 213–233.

Jaycox, L. H., Foa, E. B., & Morral, A. R. (1998). Influence of emotional engagement and habituation on exposure therapy for PTSD. *Journal of Consulting and Clinical Psychology, 66,* 185–192.

Karlin, B. E., & Cross, G. (2014). Enhancing access, fidelity, and outcomes in the national dissemination of evidence-based psychotherapies. *The American Psychologist, 69,* 709–711. http://dx.doi.org/10.1037/a0037384

Karstoft, K.-I., Galatzer-Levy, I. R., Statnikov, A., Li, Z., & Shalev, A. Y. (2015, March). Bridging a translational gap: Using machine learning to improve the prediction of PTSD. *BMC Psychiatry, 16,* 30.

Karstoft, K. I., Statnikov, A., Andersen, S. B., Madsen, T., & Galatzer-Levy, I. R. (2015, September). Early identification of posttraumatic stress following military deployment: Application of machine learning methods to a prospective study of Danish soldiers. *Journal of Affective Disorders, 15,* 170–175.

Keane, T. M. (1995). The role of exposure therapy in the psychological treatment of PTSD. *National Center for PTSD Clinical Quarterly, 56,* 15.

Kessler, R.C., Chiu, W.T., Demler, O., Merikangas, K.R., & Walters, E. E. (2005). Prevalence, severity and comorbidity of 12-month DSM-IV disorders in the National Comorbidity Survey Replication. *Archives of General Psychiatry, 62,* 617–627.

Kessler, R. C., Rose, S., Koenen, K. C., Karam, E. G., Stang, P. E., Stein, D. J., . . . Viana, M. C. (2014). How well can post-traumatic stress disorder be predicted from pre-trauma risk factors? An exploratory study in the WHO World Mental Health Surveys, *World Psychiatry, 3,* 265–274.

Kessler, R. C., Sonnega, A. Bromet, E., Hughes, M., & Nelson, C. B. (1995).Posttraumatic stress disorder in the National Comorbidity Survey. *Archives of General Psychiatry, 52,* 1048–1060. doi:10.1001/archpsyc.1995.03950240066012

Kilpatrick, D. G., Ruggiero, K. J., Acierno, R., Saunders, B. E., Resnick, H. S., & Best, C. L. (2003). Violence and risk of PTSD, major depression, substance abuse/dependence, and comorbidity: Results from the National Survey of Adolescents. *Journal of Consulting and Clinical Psychology, 71,* 692–700. http://dx.doi.org/10.1037/0022-006X.71.4.692

Lazarus, R. S. (1966). *Psychological stress and the coping process.* New York: McGraw-Hill.

Lazarus R. (1991). *Emotion and adaptation.* New York: Oxford University Press.

Lazarus, R. S., & Folkman, S. (1984). *Stress, appraisal, and coping.* New York: Springer.

Markowitsch, H. J., Kessler, J. K., Weber-Luxenburger, G., Van der Ven, C, Albers, M., & Heiss, W. D. (2000). Neuroimaging and behavioral correlates of recovery from mnestic block syndrome and other cognitive deteriorations. *Neuropsychiatry, Neuropsychology and Behavioral Neurology, 13,* 60–66.

McLay, R. N., Wood, D. P., Webb-Murphy, J. A., Spira, J. L., Wiederhold, M. D., Pyne, J. M., & Wiederhold,

B. K. (2011). A randomized, controlled trial of virtual reality-graded exposure therapy for post-traumatic stress disorder in active duty service members with combat-related post-traumatic stress disorder. *Cyberpsychology, Behavior and Social Networking, 14*, 223–229.

Meiser-Stedman R. (2002). Towards a cognitive-behavioral model of PTSD in children and adolescents. *Clinical Child and Family Psychology, 5*, 217–232. doi: 10.1023/a:1020982122107

Monroe, S. M., & Mineka, S. (2008). Putting the mnemonic model in context: Diagnostic, theoretical, and clinical considerations. *Psychological Review, 115*, 1084–1098.

North, C. S., Suris, A. M., Smith, R. P., & King, R. V. (2016). The evolution of the PTSD criteria across editions of the DSM. *Annals of Clinical Psychiatry, 28*, 197–208.

O'Donnell, M. L., Alkemade, N., Nickerson, A. Creamer, M., McFarlane, A. C., Silove, D., . . . Forbes, D. (2014). Impact of the diagnostic changes to post-traumatic stress disorder for DSM-5 and the proposed changes to ICD-11. *The British Journal of Psychiatry, 205*, 230–235. doi: 10.1192.bip/bp.113.135285 Accessed September 2018.

O'Donnell, M. L., Creamer, M., & Patterson, P. (2004). Posttraumatic stress disorder and depression following trauma: Understanding comorbidity. *American Journal of Psychiatry, 161*, 1390–1396.

O'Donnell, M. L., Elliott, P., Wolfgang, B. J., & Creamer, M. (2007). Posttraumatic appraisals in the development and persistence of posttraumatic stress symptoms. *Journal of Traumatic Stress, 20*, 173–182. doi: 10.1002/jts.20198

Ozer, E. J., Best, S. R., Lipsey, T. L., & Weiss, D. S. (2003). Predictors of posttraumatic stress disorder and symptoms in adults: A meta-analysis. *Psychological Bulletin, 129*, 52–73. doi: 10.1037/0033-2909.129.1.52

Pai, A., Suris, A. M., & North, C. S. (2017). Posttraumatic stress disorder in the DSM-5: Controversy, change and conceptual considerations. doi:10.3390/bs.7010007. Accessed September 2018.

Paris, J. F. (2001). *Personality factors in susceptibility to PTSD*. Program and abstracts of the 154th Annual Meeting of the American Psychiatric Association; May 5–10, 2001; New Orleans, Louisiana. Symposium 4E.

Perlman, S.E., Friedman, S., Galea, S., Nari, N. P., Eros-Sarnyai, M., Stellman, D., Hon, J., & Greene, M. (2011). Short and medium term health effects of 9/11. *Lancet, 378*, 925–934.

Reger, G. M., Smolenski, D., Norr, A., Katz, A., Buck, B., & Rothbaum, B. O. (in press). Does virtual reality increase emotional engagement during exposure for PTSD? Subjective distress during prolonged and virtual reality exposure therapy. *Journal of Anxiety Disorders*. Accessed online September 2018. https://doi.org/10.1016/j.janxdis.2018.06.001

Rigoli, M. M., Silva, G. R., de Oliveira, F. R., Pergher, G. K., & Kirstensen, C. H. (2016). The role of memory in posttraumatic stress disorder: implications for clinical practice. *Trends Psychiatry Psychotherapy, 38*, 119–127. doi: 10.1590/2237-6089-2014-0063

Rogers, S., & Silver, S. M. (2002). Is EMDR an exposure therapy? A review of trauma protocols. *Journal of Clinical Psychology, 58*, 43–59.

Rosen, R. C., Ruzek, J. I., & Karlin, B.E. (2017). Evidence-based training in the era of evidence-based practice: Challenges and opportunities for training of PTSD providers. *Behaviour Research and Therapy, 88*, 37–48.

Rubin, D. C., Berntsen, D., Ogle, C. M., Deffler, S. A., & Beckham, J. C. (2016). Scientific evidence versus outdated beliefs: A response to Brewin (2016). *Journal of Abnormal Psychology, 125*(7), 1018–1021. http://dx.doi.org/10.1037/abn0000211

Salmon, K., & Bryant, R. A. (2002). Posttraumatic stress disorder in children. The influence of developmental factors. *Clinical Psychology Review, 22*, 163–188.

Schlund, M. W., Brewer, A. T., Richman, D. M., Magee, S. K., & Dymond, S. (2015). Not so bad: avoidance and aversive discounting modulate threat appraisal in anterior cingulate and medial prefrontal cortex. *Frontiers in Behavioral Neuroscience, 9*, 142. Published online. doi:10.3389/fnbeh.2015.00142

Selye, H. (1956). *The stress of life*. New York: McGraw-Hill.

Shin, L. M., Whalen, P. J., Pitman, R. K., Bush, G., Macklin, M. L., Lasko, N. B., . . . Rauch, S. L. (2001). An MRI study of anterior cingulated function in posttraumatic stress disorder. *Biological Psychiatry, 50,* 932–942.

Stewart, M. O., Karlin, B. E., Murphy, J. L., Raffa, S. D., Miller, S. A., McKellar, J., & Kerns, R. D. (2015). National dissemination of cognitive-behavioral therapy for chronic pain in veterans: Therapist and patient-level outcomes. *The Clinical Journal of Pain, 31,* 722–729. http://dx.doi .org/10.1097/AJP.0000000000000151

Torous, J., Onnela, J. P., & Keshavan, M. (2017, March). New dimensions and new tools to realize the potential of RDoC: Digital phenotyping via smart-phones and connected devices. *Translational Psychiatry, 7*(3), e1053.

van der Kolk, B. A. (2006). Clinical implication of neuroscience research in PTSD. *Annals of the New York Academy of Sciences, 1071,* 277–293. doi: 10.1196/annals.1364.022

• Index •

Note: Page references with (fig.) or (table) refer to figures and tables, respectively.